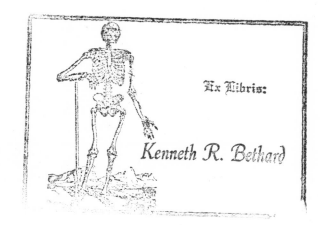

HORN AND CRESCENT

AFRICAN STUDIES SERIES   53

OTHER BOOKS IN THE SERIES

HORN AND CRESCENT

Cultural change and traditional
Islam on the East African coast, 800–1900

RANDALL L. POUWELS

Department of History, University of Central Arkansas

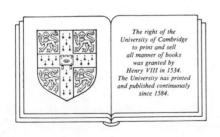

The right of the
University of Cambridge
to print and sell
all manner of books
was granted by
Henry VIII in 1534.
The University has printed
and published continuously
since 1584.

CAMBRIDGE UNIVERSITY PRESS

CAMBRIDGE
LONDON   NEW YORK   NEW ROCHELLE
MELBOURNE   SYDNEY

Published by the Press Syndicate of the University of Cambridge
The Pitt Building, Trumpington Street, Cambridge CB2 1RP
32 East 57th Street, New York, NY 10022, USA
10 Stamford Road, Oakleigh, Melbourne 3166, Australia

First published 1987.

Printed in Malta at Interprint Limited

British Library cataloguing in publication data
Pouwels, Randall L.
Horn and crescent: cultural change and
traditional Islam on the East African coast,
800–1900. – (African studies series; 53)
1. Civilization, Islamic   2. Africa, East –
Civilization
I. Title   II. Series
967′.004927   DT379.5

Library of Congress cataloguing in publication data
Pouwels, Randall L.
Horn and crescent.
(African studies series; 53)
Bibliography
Includes index.
1. Islam – Africa, East – History.   2. Africa, East –
Civilization. I. Title. II. Series.
BP64.A4E26 1986   297′.089963   86–17115

ISBN 0 521 32308 8

IP

Contents

Illustrations

Maps

Preface

Much has been written about the East African coast, probably more than about any other part of Eastern Africa if not about Africa as a whole. Why then am I adding to this already long list? What skills, expertise or insights might I hope to add to those of my venerable predecessors like Burton, Coupland, Freeman-Grenville, Gray, Kirkman, and Chittick among others? In short, what does this new work represent considering all that already has been said about the coast?

As a personal contribution, *Horn and Crescent* represents a major component in a broader continuum of about fifteen years of study, plus ten years of writing about Swahili history. In one sense, then, it might be understood within this context of on-going personal intellectual growth and change. More specifically, as a research project it is the product of several rethinkings and two periods of field research: fifteen months during 1974–5 spent in Kenya and the United Kingdom where field interviews and archival research were conducted, and another ten weeks during 1984 when additional fieldwork was done in Zanzibar.

As a contribution to coastal history, I have no illusions that what I have written is 'definitive'. Nor does it represent any major breakthroughs from the standpoint of the sources used. Yet new material has been presented based upon my fieldwork (and to a lesser degree that of others), and it is the synthesis of past research along with the presentation of this new material that I feel merits publication in book form. To my knowledge, too, this is the first attempt to publish a synoptic history of traditional Islam (though not of the wider cultural history) for the East African coast. Various shorter works have dealt with this topic more briefly or within a narrower framework – for example, the first chapter of Trimingham's *Islam in East Africa* or el-Zein's structuralist study of Islam in Lamu. Surely, too, considering the amount of ink spilled on the history of Islam in North and West Africa, a major study of the equally venerable East African Islamic tradition is, if anything, overdue. I am sure that this will not be the last such worthy effort.

One fact that is certain to elicit such future undertakings (and perhaps even controversy) is that this work is slanted in several significant ways. These biases first reflect the area where I conducted my fieldwork, my sources and my interpretation of the data thus obtained. For instance, the title of this book conveys the impression that it covers the cultural and religious history of the entire coast from Mogadishu to Mozambique. It is, I confess, primarily a study of the Kenya coast and Zanzibar since these are the areas where fieldwork was done and on which I obtained most of my information.

Perhaps more importantly this is meant to be a historical study of the culture and religion which are specific to the East African coast. This imposes quite a selectiveness in the people I consider and in the sources I regard as the most useful and important for interpreting this history. It does not concern, for example, the cultures and religions of the Asian minorities. Nor is it a history of immigrant Arabs, despite the fact that their religious and cultural impact on the coast has been a considerable one. Rather, it concerns the Islam which is peculiar to the wider cultural environment of the East African coast. This means it especially involves the indigenous people of the coast, since culture has a strongly homologous relationship to human society. It thus focuses on the Swahili; their culture generally, their religion more narrowly.

But who are the Swahili? First, they are the Afro-Asiatic people who inhabit the East African coastal fringe roughly from Mogadishu in the north to Kilwa in the south, along with the offshore Bajun Islands, the Lamu archipelago, Pemba, Zanzibar, Mafia, and – some argue – the Comoro Islands. They are Muslims who speak Kiswahili, a Bantu language with an Arabic vocabulary reaching up to 30 per cent of its total lexicon in places. Their culture represents a unique adaptation to the coastal environmental niche, and, while most are townspeople, they frequently maintain second residences in the neighbouring rural hinter-lands of the coast proper. Most live by a combination of farming, fishing, and trading.

Yet to understand who these people are requires the adducement of more than this 'bundle of traits'. Who a people are in the present can be meaningfully comprehended if we know who they were in the past. Certainly, African societies like the Swahili are fully conversant with such an interpretation of their identity, for local historical tradition is both a constant source of entertainment and a chart to the present and future. It is preserved and disseminated among the Swahili principally as oral narratives and poetry, much like other African societies. As such, these traditions can serve as excellent indices of what present-day Swahili consider to be important in their culture and how that culture developed. In addition, they serve as very useful sources of 'history' as it is understood in a Western academic sense, provided that any historical reconstruction that utilizes them is supported by ancillary sources. Such traditions represent, as Thomas Spear says, both *their* history and ours.[1]

My fieldwork in East Africa thus was directed first at obtaining the local perspective on their past, then at reconstructing this history on the basis of internal evidence contained within the accounts and the additional relevant evidence revealed in ancillary sources. The emphasis of my work was, consequently, on obtaining Swahili memories and views of their past.

On the other hand, very little use has been made of sources in Arabic. A number of reasons account for this. First of all, there have been relatively few sources discovered in Arabic which are of historical interest – at least since Sir John Kirk's great luck in obtaining the so-called Kilwa chronicle from Sultan Barghash, as well as the several versions of the *Book of Zenj*. There are, of course, quite a few manuscripts in collections at Dar es Salaam and Zanzibar, but these are principally religious tracts (that is, *Qurans* and standard Shafi'i or Ibadi works in the religious sciences) which would be of greater value in a phenomenological study of Islam than in a historical one. Also, I am aware that there are valuable privately owned materials, such as diaries, in the possession of various individuals and families in Mombasa, Lamu, and Zanzibar. Few such individuals are willing to allow researchers to examine these treasures. My own experience has been that they prefer relating information from such sources through an oral interview (following consultation of these written sources, or even reading from them in my presence). Unlike the case in West African Islamic studies,[2] then, the East African researcher presently has relatively few useful sources available to him in Arabic.

This is not to say that there might be external sources in Arabia or India which might throw new light some day on coastal history. However, such sources are yet to be discovered. Therefore, postponing publication of this history until such a time might come would be a disservice to the subjects at hand. In addition, any study which relies primarily on external materials would skew the resulting account in some very critical ways. I believe it would, for instance, assist yet again in perpetuating the old fallacy that non-Africans have been the most important actors on the stage of coastal history. Such a presentation would be yet another 'colonialist' view of African history, just as surely as if I relied principally on European sources. Again, it is local traditions, supplemented by other such information where available, which provide the richest sources of local history in Africa. My choice of oral traditions as my primary sources of information represents a conscious decision which was made early in my research programme.

The arrangement of this book is divided informally into four parts. The first of these includes Chapters 1 and 2. These constitute an interpretive introduction to the origins and early development of Swahili culture. They are not intended to introduce new data, but as a reasonably intelligent rendering of the information known to date on the subject. Potentially, they are the most controversial chapters for scholars who interpret coastal culture principally in terms either of African or 'Arab' inspiration. Here and elsewhere I have endeavoured to explain Swahili as the result of a rough (though swinging) equilibrium which has been maintained between both cultural extremes.[3] Arguments have been made for both sides of this problem.[4] One thing seems certain, however: presently, there is precious little in the way of a 'range of received ideas' on coastal cultural and religious history, as one critic once suggested somewhat inaccurately.

Chapter 3 stands alone in several ways. Chronologically, it represents a progression beyond the phase covered in the first 'part'. It presents and analyses new oral data from the Lamu region where 'modern' Islamic culture on the coast first flourished. Traditions in connection with this chapter have been presented elsewhere as examples of the general types of oral tradition found along the coast and how they might be utilized for historical purposes.[5] In this instance, a related collection (Chapter 3 appendix) has been applied more narrowly to illustrate the effects which the second of three major 'Arabizing' phases had on culture and religion in the Lamu archipelago specifically.

Part three, consisting of Chapters 4 and 5, is a general discussion of the overall intellectual, social, and political *arrondissement* in which coastal Islam was embedded in the eighteenth and nineteenth centuries. Essentially, it is a backdrop for the final section of the book.

The entire second half of the book comprises part four. Chronologically, it covers the nineteenth and early twentieth centuries, the period of the so-called Zanzibar Sultanate. The period represents the last of the three major Arabizing phases on the coast, a period of extensive Arab immigration. The dominance of a Zanzibar-based *ᶜulama* and growing literacy among local peoples distinguished the period. These chapters (6 through 10) outline the nature of Zanzibar cultural influences on the coast, with additional attention given to the actions and reactions of Swahili Muslims to these influences.

Finally, I must acknowledge the intellectual debts owed to so many people. First, of course, come those scholars who either have come before me or who are my contemporaries whose works have affected my own thinking. Sir Reginald Coupland's work, though it is outdated in so many ways, still has an interpretive validity which has influenced my own views on the nature of the Zanzibar Sultanate. Abdu'l-Hamid el-Zein's work, too, provided an invaluable basis for a lot of the work I carried out in Lamu (though I doubt the historical accuracy of some of his material). Professor B. G. Martin's recent work on sources external to the coast and the evidence they contain concerning Arab settlement of the coast has been most important for coastal historiography. The debt owed to the two pioneers of coastal archaeology, James Kirkman and the late H. Neville Chittick, is simply incalculable. Important new work in this field has been done by Mark Horton, Hamo Sassoon, Paul Sinclair, and Thomas H. Wilson, all of which has been consulted for the following work. Other crucial influences on my thinking have come from Norman R. Bennett, G. S. P. Freeman-Grenville, Jan Knappert, A. H. J. Prins, and J. Spencer Trimingham. Among my younger contemporaries whose influences deserve mention are A. I. Salim, F. J. Berg, A. P. Caplan, Margaret Strobel, James deV. Allen, William McKay, and Marguerite Ylvisaker, all of whom have done recent work which has added significantly to our knowledge.

Special thanks go to my mentors from my UCLA days, Professors Edward Alpers and Christopher Ehret whose inspiration, intelligence, and critical support have sustained me over the years. Also, I owe special thanks to Professor Peter von Sivers, now of the University of Utah, for his criticisms and the many hours of (for me) fruitful intellectual exchange we enjoyed together in the past. Finally, I must acknowledge the initial support of Dr D. J. M. Muffett in whose class at Duquesne University I first was drawn to coastal history.

Besides the above-mentioned individuals, others who read and commented on various portions of this text were Neville Chittick, Thomas Spear, John Graham, and Derek Nurse. I owe them my gratitude. For sponsoring my field research, I thank the Fulbright-Hayes programme and the Social Science Research Council, as well as the archivists and Governments of Great Britain, Kenya, and Zanzibar for allowing me to carry out the research required to complete my work. Special thanks go to my research assistants, Athman Lalli Omar in Lamu and Ramadhani Talib Juma in Zanzibar. In Mombasa, Yahya Ali Omar was both a research assistant and an informant whose name, therefore, appears frequently in my notes. Words hardly can express my gratitude to the late Shaykh Abdallah Salih Farsy, ex-Chief Qadi of Kenya, who sat through many interviews and corresponded freely to provide me with very crucial information. Shaykh Abdallah's reputation as an Islamic scholar and expert on the history of East African Islam is well remembered. Finally, I must thank Professor Micheal Lofchie and the UCLA African Studies Center for allowing me Research Associate status to carry out my fieldwork in Zanzibar, as well as the University of Central Arkansas Research Council for Funding final manuscript revisions.

As a final word, I should like to point out that, in many instances, the names of informants have been deleted from the notes. This was done where I felt that the confidentiality of the informants in question needed protection. However, the names of these informants and, where helpful, transcripts of the actual interviews themselves will be made available to applicants who require such data for their own research. It should also be mentioned that typescripts of my field interviews and notes have been deposited with the Kenya National Archives and with the East African Centre for Research in Oral Traditions and African National Languages (EACROTANAL) in Zanzibar.

With love for Eric, Ethan, and
Lauren Jane Pouwels

Abbreviations

AARP	*Art and Archaeology Research Papers*
AHS	*African Historical Studies*
BPP	*British Parliamentary Papers*
BSOAS	*Bulletin of the School of Oriental and African Studies*
CRME	*Correspondence Respecting Sir Bartle Frere's Mission to the East Coast of Africa, 1872–73*
CUP	Cambridge University Press
EACROTANAL	East African Centre for Research in Oral Traditions and African National Languages
EALB	East African Literature Bureau
EAPH	East African Publishing House
HA	*History in Africa*
IJAHS	*International Journal of African Historical Studies*
JAH	*Journal of African History*
JEASC	*Journal of the East African Swahili Committee*
JRAI	*Journal of the Royal Anthropological Institute*
JRAS	*Journal of the Royal Anthropological Society*
KNA	Kenya National Archives
OUP	Oxford University Press
TNR	*Tanganyika* (now *Tanzania*) *Notes and Records*

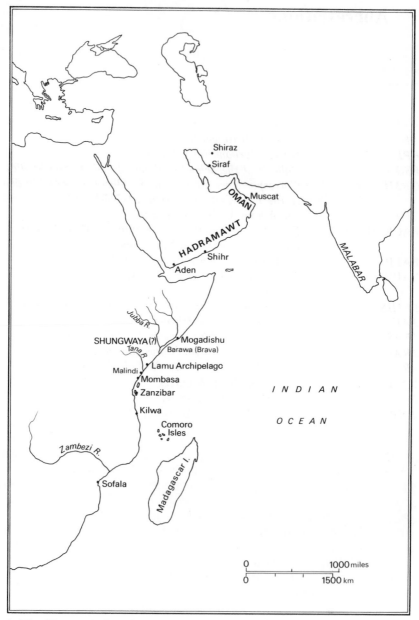

1. The Western Indian Ocean.

Introduction

The history of coastal culture outlined in this work differs significantly from past interpretations. Prior to the nineteenth century, at least, coastal urban culture and religion were uniquely local phenomena essentially dominated by their African physical and intellectual ambience, while remaining open and responsive to transoceanic intellectual stimuli. This, of course, implies certain things about coastal Africans and Islam. It means, for one thing, that their intellectual and cultural traditions were substantial enough to continue having 'meaning' for them even when and where pressures for change were greatest. It means that these people and their traditions were sufficiently strong and supple to respond positively to new opportunities while maintaining control over potentially destabilizing changes they brought with them. It means that monotheism (in the form of Islam) presented supplementary doctrines and symbols to which local traditions could be adapted and which were suitably representative of this changing intellectual environment to an extent that cannot be ignored. In the end, it also implies that 'Arabs' were rarely, if ever, in a position to *impose* change so much that local peoples more frequently *adapted* to it.

Exactly what were the 'origins' of coastal culture and when they emerged are contentious issues among scholars. It is admittedly a matter of definition, for example, to say just when coastal towns were 'founded'.[1] One obvious approach is to note when and under what conditions various features usually associated with this culture can be said to have manifested themselves. Done this way, then, the 'origins' of coastal culture began when humans first occupied and adapted themselves to the coastal environmental niche – as is outlined in Chapter 1. The 'cultural history' of the coast, at this level of analysis, simply involved the successive introductions of increasingly complex and varied modes (and therefore relations) of production, each of which somewhat more efficiently exploited this environment than the previously dominant mode(s). Each successive socio-economic configuration was introduced into areas physically capable of supporting it and the larger populations that went along with it. 'Older', simpler forms were increasingly confined to areas less amenable to more complex modes of production. The coast proper presented a rich variety of marine, agronomic, topographic, and hydrographic settings. A mode which initially emphasized cultivation, with limited secondary skills in herding, hunting, and fishing, accompanied the introduction of Sabaki Bantu speech. Evidence presently on hand indicates that by the end of the first millennium AD, a distinctly

1

Swahili language and economy based on cultivation of specifically coastal products, a sophisticated maritime technology, potting, and iron-making had emerged which was fully adapted to this complex physical environment. Given this information, a substantial case can be made that a (recognizably) coastal culture already was in place by that time.

Yet to leave an interpretation of the emergence of coastal civilization at that point would be inadequate from several perspectives. First, such a position denies that imported, non-African ideas influenced the nature and direction of change in coastal societies – as extreme a position as the old one which viewed coastal culture essentially as 'Arab'. It ignores the historical predicament of the seaside towns as heavily immigrant communities which stood on the frontiers of continental African and transoceanic cultures. As such, cultural change was an inescapable fact of life which imparted its own stamp on the fundamental character and traditions of these communities. The towns were geared for change; if nothing else at least so that they could control it. Their physical arrangements, institutions like the *ngoma* 'parties', even local small-scale street battles, combined to help maintain a rough equilibrium between local peoples and strangers ('Arab' or African), old and new, status quo and change. Yet this was a swinging equilibrium which tilted in one direction or the other according to the extent of immigration towns were experiencing. Thus, the thirteenth through fourteenth centuries, covered in Chapter 2, saw extensive southern Arab immigration and Islamization. A sixteenth-century migration led to the further spread of Islam among the yet unconverted (for example, WaTikuu), while it temporarily (at least) re-established the prestige of a more literate Islam identified with Arab immigrants, as shown in Chapter 3. In between times, many such immigrants – even *shurafa*ʾ – became partially 'Africanized' through intermarriage and cultural fusion with local peoples. In these interstices between the great periods of large-scale Arab immigration, literacy in Arabic waned, intellectual contacts with the great southern Arabian centres of scholarship abated, and a semi-literate religious leadership and orally based religious traditions, like those described in Chapters 4 and 5, predominated.

In retrospect, too, Islamization of the coast and the 'origins' of coastal culture were related phenomena. This is readily apparent if one starts with Clifford Geertz's definition of culture as a 'locally perceived system of significance', representing the sum total of all locally meaningful symbols. Although, as argued by the Rationalists, conversion to Islam/monotheism did not require that local Africans totally repudiate their intellectual past and the symbols into which it was distilled, their conversion and profession of faith (*shahada*) would have amounted to a wilful act by which they rededicated their lives to an altered concept of the divine (one God without partners), new rituals to worship that divinity, new symbols embodying what is sacred and holy (the Quran, religious texts, etc.), and new sources of guidance for righteous living (Muhammad and the *ʿulamaʾ*).[2] Conversion to Islam was a psychologically overt act taken by coastal Africans which made them distinct from their neighbours, if not from their ancestors. With this wilful act, or series of acts which probably spanned generations, coastal culture became reoriented not away from Africa so much as towards many new symbols, images, and outward trappings of what local peoples perceived to be genuinely Islamic. The Islamic civilization which emerged obviously was greatly influenced by its African setting. Yet the fact that at least some elements of this civilization (for example, mosque features, house design) were taken from Asian models indicates that there was an openness to imported ideas and symbols, so long as coastal Africans could be convinced that these represented a greater (or more useful) truth than that known to their neighbours.

This truth and the symbolic system which encapsulated it separated coastal Muslims from their neighbours in the most crucial way. If indeed the appearance of a distinct coastal economy and language were important beginnings in the evolution of coastal culture, it appears certain that to whatever extent coastal peoples had begun to experience a psychological separation from neighbouring cultures with these developments, their conversion to Islam consummated this process. This position is supported by coastal traditions, even where a pre-Islamic past is remembered vaguely (and grudgingly). In most of these, the fundamental importance of Islam to local identity is evident from the frequent equation made between the 'founding' of coastal communities and the legendary arrival of Muslim immigrants. And, as Thomas Spear has argued most cogently, no serious history can ignore local peoples' own perceptions of their past.[3]

In various ways, the nineteenth century represented a major departure from the past equilibrium that had existed between local and imported influences on coastal life. For the first time the ideal of a civilized lifestyle became associated explicitly with foreign, especially Arab, cultural traits. A number of factors accounted for this. The first, of course, was the rapid acceleration in trade which started in the eighteenth century and reached its zenith in the nineteenth. It was this, along with growing European involvement in the Indian Ocean, which led to the assertion of Omani claims in East Africa and, finally, to the founding of the Zanzibar Sultanate. Under this Sultanate, and its success in making Zanzibar the most important entrepôt in the western Indian Ocean, East Africa experienced an unprecedented expansion of scale and, consequently, unparalleled celerity of change which were swept along mostly on Indian- and European-generated commercial revenues.

As demonstrated in Chapters 6 and 7, the direct beneficiaries of this new wealth were the Arabs, particularly the Omani clans of Zanzibar and the ruling Busaidi house. It was they who (initially anyway) were the middlemen between coastal exporters and the Zanzibar market, who benefited from additional tax revenues, who controlled the western Indian Ocean carrying trade, and whose plantations produced the valuable cloves for export. Outside Zanzibar, these Arabs and their Sultans were not welcomed along the coast at first. They were viewed as threats to local sovereignty, as an alien presence only to be tolerated (as in the past) so long as they did not interfere with local customs and as long as they could benefit local trade.

3

The commercial prosperity that came with their arrival, however, benefited many townspeople who found Zanzibar a place with a growing demand for coastal and mainland African products. Thus, a new leisured class was created, led by the Arab planters of Zanzibar but including also many Swahili traders and planters of coastal towns from Lamu to Kilwa. Many people saw the Arabs as the most successful in this new age of plenty and not surprisingly came to emulate the Arab 'gentleman planter' as representing the model of how a civilized person should live.

In addition to Omanis, many southern Arabs were attracted to Zanzibar and East Africa as a result of the region's growing prosperity. Hadramis from all socio-economic backgrounds came to the coast, as they had in previous centuries, without their women and seeking employment. Among these were some from the Hadhramawt's clans of *ʿulamaʾ* and *shurafaʾ* whose arrival helped establish coastal links with southern Arabia's scholarly traditions. As in the sixteenth century, Arabic literacy once again was available to those who had the right social background and the leisure time necessary for serious study. Learning in the religious sciences, especially Ibadi, but Shafii too, received some succour from the Busaidi Sultans who employed *ʿulamaʾ* as counsellors and *muftis*. Sultan Barghash, particularly, appointed Ibadi and Shafii *qadis* and subsidized learning.

While coastal people often were willing to accept new fashions in such things as clothing, furniture, and house styles from wealthy Arabs, such acceptance did not extend to Arab attempts at intellectual browbeating. This is not to say that *waungwana* were not willing to learn from the more literate Arab *ʿulamaʾ*. The two greatest obstacles to this, however, were the unwillingness of the Arabs to open their *darasa* to 'blacks' and the continued Swahili confidence in the merits of their own cultural and religious traditions (even where they were subtly being Arabized). A few Swahili did manage to obtain training in the sciences under Arab masters, especially those who were scions of the established religious leadership of the towns. Among these were people with clan names like Husayni, Mahdali, Maawi, Mandhry, or Mazrui – people who claimed, in short, to be from the 'old' Arab families of the coast – or the occasional person with a name like Mungwana, or Mkilindini, or Mshirazi. The latter situation, however, was rare.

Even where the occasional local person managed to obtain such training, this did little to bridge the gap of intellectual tolerance between literate Islam and Islam as it was locally understood and practised. The fact that the established social system did not itself provide such opportunities to all comers drove many Swahili with the leisure and the desire for learning to look elsewhere. Some, of course, already had some training in the local 'little' Islamic tradition as *walimu*. With nineteenth-century extensions of commercial involvement into the African interior and greater opportunities for contact with the Arab 'little' tradition, for many such people new knowledge simply meant adoption of Arab pseudo-sciences like geomancy (*raml*) and astrology (*falak*). Others, women in particular, found their opportunities through involvement in one or another of the new *Mawlidis* or recently introduced religious brotherhoods (*tariqas*).

The age, as shown in Chapters 9 and 10, with its money economy, cash-dropping, and wage labour, also fostered rejection of values and ideas associated with the old order, *uungwana*. For those traditionally excluded from access to wealth and status, the new order represented a welcome change towards individualism and the chance to 'get ahead' (*kuinuka juu*). If anything, this trend accelerated during the early years of colonial rule. European capital investment, new educational opportunities, the mushroom-like growth of the cities, and finally the freeing of slaves encouraged the appearance of a new socio-economic order and an alternative system of values.

While the Busaidi and colonial administrations embraced the 'orthodox' (literate) Islam of the ᶜ*ulama*ᵓ, the real future of Islam in East Africa lay with the *tariqas*. The brotherhoods, of course, provided an alternative system of instruction in the Islamic sciences and Arabic literacy where the usual channels were closed to most. They, along with the *Mawlidis*, served as useful vehicles for anti-Government and anti-establishment (usually Arab *qadis*, *liwalis*, etc.) propaganda among low status and upwardly mobile Muslims. It was the Islamic *tariqas*, therefore, which proved to be the most popular instrument for the conversion of the African victims of colonial abuses.

As the twentieth century began, Islam was on the rise among many East Africans, and Muslims of all backgrounds were facing the new era in different ways. Some, both Arabs and Swahili, were withdrawing into a shell of conservatism and orthodoxy, as they respectively understood it. Others, new converts mostly, sought conversion and membership in the Islamic community as an alternative to the more oppressive aspects of colonialism. Many of the younger generation began to question the values and beliefs of their elders. They sought their answers in the ways and beliefs of their colonial masters, sometimes being seduced by the worst features of Western civilization. A few individuals, too, felt that if Islam was going to survive the onslaught of technological superiority of the Imperialist Powers, it had to discard the ethical edifice created between the eighth and tenth centuries and be totally reconceptualized, retaining only the basic, core message of their Prophet. The consequences of these different roads taken are still being experienced in contemporary East Africa.

1

The roots of a tradition, 800–1500

North of Mombasa the coast stands out as a separate ecological zone from the interior. Rendering it especially dramatic definition is the *nyika*, a parched and jejune wilderness behind the coastal fringe which served throughout history as a natural barrier to all who contemplated travel inland. The *nyika* usually remains about 15 kilometres from the sea, but as one moves north of the Lamu archipelago it begins approaching the seaside itself. Around the present Kenya–Somalia border, this 'coastal fringe' effectively disappears. Thus, the so-called Benadir coast of southern Somalia consists largely of coral outcrops and a sandy shore covered by gigantic dunes of up to 150 metres in height. North of the Jubba River there are few natural harbours and even the best of them, Mogadishu, is of mediocre quality.

As one moves southwards, however, soils and topography improve. The barren dunes gradually yield to a flatter terrain covered with grasses, bush, doum palm, and some savannah vegetation in the region of the Lamu archipelago itself, while the appearance of mangrove swamps grows more and more common. In this region north of the Tana River, soils generally are unsuitable for intensive cultivation and, being essentially sandy, shifting cultivation techniques with long fallow periods of up to fifteen years are required. Such land is suitable for herding activities and for cultivation of dryland cereals (for example, sorghums and millets) and some fruits. Some forests still exist, though it is likely that more extensive forests and, perhaps, somewhat better soils existed before the nineteenth century.[1]

Beginning just south of the Jubba River stands a long series of coral outcroppings called variously the 'coast of isles', the Bajun islands, or the Dundas islands.[2] Positioned as they are between 100 and 300 metres offshore and stretching clear down to the Lamu archipelago, this string of islands historically has served a dual role. The first has been as a narrow shipping lane for small vessels engaged in the coastal trade from the Lamu region northwards. During the period of the long rains, when seas have been rough and storms frequent, these islands have served as naturally protective breakwaters sheltering both the mainland shores and the small coastal craft from damaging winds and tumultuous seas. The islands themselves mostly are covered with sand dunes, topped with low bush and scrub, and suffer from the same lack of water as the opposite mainland. These drawbacks notwithstanding, it is apparent from the surface fragments of pottery, tombs, and ruins frequently encountered on many of these small islands that they have served as safe harbours and settlement sites over the centuries for small groups of people wishing to avoid the mainland upheavals occasioned by desultory population shifts.[3]

The Lamu archipelago forms the southernmost end of this string of offshore coral formations and consists of three islands. Of these, both Manda and Lamu are sandy, covered with dunes, and, especially Lamu, ringed on the eastern side by broad sandy beaches bordering the warm azure waters of the Indian Ocean. The northernmost island, Pate, is by far the largest. It is blessed with a variety of topsoils, including fertile loams that make many areas of the interior suitable for intensive cultivation. The sandy soils of Lamu, however, have given that island a reputation for having the sweetest water on the northern coast – a fact which probably attracted settlers at an early date – while they have been rich enough to support deeper rooted mango trees and coconut palms, the traditionally 'noble' trees of the coast.[4] Finally, the harbours of the archipelago are far better than those of any other region north of Mombasa. Those afforded by the northern side of Manda island (near ancient Manda town) and the narrow channel separating Lamu from Manda island are among the best on the northern coast, second only to Kilindini (Twaka) harbour at Mombasa. From Malindi southwards the coastal belt attains its greatest level of development and contrasts with the *nyika* and the huge white sand dunes which line the coastline north of Mambrui. Here mainland vegetation is more luxuriant. Green grasses and bush are interspersed with dense forests, and soils are capable of yielding a somewhat greater array of crops than the dryland cereals of the north. As early as the fourteenth century, these mainland areas were producing millet, rice, and vegetables for consumption or trade at Mombasa, while Portuguese eyewitnesses reported similarly plentiful yields from Malindi. Mombasa itself historically was noted for producing an abundance of lemons, oranges, bananas, pomegranates, and figs.[5] Standing on an island barely separated from its mainland, Mombasa possesses the best port facilities on the coast in Kilindini harbour to the south of the island, while the inlet to the north of the island (and Mombasa town) can accommodate all but modern deep draught vessels.

Between Mogadishu and Mombasa three major rivers and a series of creeks break up the coastline and have served as channels of communication with the interior. The northernmost of these rivers, the Jubba, seems to have been a route used by interior Somali peoples who have followed it on migrations to the coast. In addition, it and its tributary, the Webi Shebeelle, flood semi-annually, leaving a rich black topsoil (*arro madow*), which makes the region the 'breadbasket' of southern Somalia.[6] Similarly, the Tana River is blessed with fertile alluvial soils, and a large area north of the river benefits from generally favourable watering from the semi-annual floodings as well as from the relatively high level of rainfall enjoyed by the region.[7] The Tana, then, has been notable primarily for rice production. The last of these rivers is the Sabaki, which debouches just north of Malindi. Permanent and tidal creeks (*mto*, pl. *mito*) also break up the shoreline and allow boat traffic up to 15 kilometres inland. Such creeks are most numerous around the Lamu archipelago and historically have proven valuable both for their bordering thickets and of mangrove, the wood of which has been a major Lamu export, and as highways of direct communication and transport between the grain-producing farms of the mainland and the island commercial centres. Between Malindi and Mombasa the *mito* have served as the sites for the only significant Swahili settlements along that strip of the coast, Takaungu, Kilifi, and Mtwapa.

The entire coast is subject to two major monsoon seasons, each of which is divided into a major and a minor season. The first of these, the season of the southeasterly monsoon (called *Kusi*), lasts roughly from May through September. It is divided into the *Mwaka*, the major wet season of the year, which is followed by a season of cool, dry days that begins about July and ends in September. These months constitute the planting season. Sometime in October, the monsoon (now called *Kaskazi*) begins shifting to the north-northeast. This period between October and November is that of the lesser rains (*Vuli*) and ushers in the major season of the *Kaskazi* monsoon, the dry season. The dry season is usually the longest of the year, lasting from December to May, and is a period of hot, cloudless days when the ground bakes and topsoils are subject to erosion by dry winds. While obviously this season is unfruitful for cultivating, it is suited for marine activities. This is the time of year when cultivators turn to fishing to supplement their diet of fruits, cereals, and vegetables. For the major towns it was also the business season which saw the arrival of dhows from the Red Sea, southern Arabia, the Persian Gulf, and India.

From the previous description, it is apparent that the coastal physical environment of the north is varied and complex, and in all its facets it potentially can support a wide array of economic activities. Thus, this section has two purposes. The first of these is to give a brief account of the peoples who have inhabited the northern coast over the past eight millennia, some of whom are ancestral to the Swahili. The second purpose is to make manifest the relationships which these peoples had with this environment, and particularly the evolution, in range and complexity, of subsistence 'uses' to which they put this environment. These are crucial points, as it will be demonstrated later how northern coastal Bantu culture, particularly Swahili culture, largely can be comprehended in terms of its relationship with the human and physical environment.

Coastal demography between about 6000 and 2000 BC was apparently dominated by people who used a variety of stone blades, bone chips, and stone microliths, some of which they compounded into larger weapons. Archaeologists consider such tools as constituting a 'Wilton' stone culture. Living as they did in what probably were larger forests than are found near the coast today (because today's forests have been reduced by centuries of destruction by cultivators and iron workers), these people were hunter-gatherers. Though they still lived passively off their environment, the use of missiles such as arrows improved the productive efficiency of these Neolithic men and women and permitted them to live in rather more successful and specialized hunting societies than their predecessors. Perhaps most significant of all, the use of barbed stone and bone points possibly made these people the first to exploit the coastal waters as fishermen and consumers of small shellfish, a pattern of life more recently followed by Dahalo hunter-gatherers in the Lamu region.[8]

Both linguistic and archaeological evidence indicates that the first food producers to arrive in East Africa were Southern Cushites.[9] Coming from the southern Ethiopian highlands sometime before 2000 BC,[10] the Southern Cushites were Late Stone Age peoples who herded sheep, cattle, and goats, and who cultivated grain crops such as millet and sorghum. Apparently, they both bled and milked their cattle. They might also have been responsible for introducing irrigation and manuring to East Africa.[11] While most of the Southern Cushites appear to have settled central Kenya, the coastal Dahalo still speak a Southern Cushitic language and there is additional loan-word evidence of Southern Cushitic influence on coastal Bantu languages such as Swahili, Pokomo, and Miji Kenda. Most interesting, though, is evidence that, unlike upcountry Bantu, the coastal Bantu borrowed few herding terms from Southern Cushites, while at the same time they did borrow items related to cultivation.[12] Having had a taboo against fish, it is unlikely that the coastal Southern Cushites exploited their marine environment in the manner of their hunter-gatherer neighbours. (Dahalo, however, were an apparent exception since they descended in part from Khoisan food gatherers who adopted the language of dominant Southern Cushitic neighbours sometime in the last millennium BC.)[13]

Other Cushitic-speaking peoples who are more familiar and who have played a more recent part in coastal history are the Somali and the Oromo. The first of these to enter the coastal scene were the Somali. Certainly in the period 1000–1500 they were playing a determinant role in the history of the Benadir towns and there is evidence which suggests strongly that Garre and Tunni groups were already settled on the mainland opposite the Lamu archipelago in the tenth century, perhaps even earlier.[14] It appears very likely, as will be demonstrated in material presented below, that these Somali probably played a role in Shungwaya. Their place, however, as the dominant force in the northern coastal hinterland was taken by their cousins, the Oromo, in the sixteenth and seventeenth centuries. Like the Southern Cushites, Eastern Cushites such as the Oromo and Somali have a fish taboo and are camel and cattle pastoralists for the most part, although sedentarized groups live by cultivating cereals, eleusine, sesame, beans, bananas, and other fruits.[15]

Without doubt, the most important and complex groups to settle the coastal region were Bantu-speakers. Originally coming from a natal area northwest of the equatorial rain forest, it appears from archaeological and linguistic attestations that Bantu were living around the East African lakes by 400 BC, and by the end of the first millennium of the Christian era almost all of sub-equatorial Africa was Bantu-speaking.[16] Some Bantu-speaking communities had settled the coast before AD 300. There, their presence has been associated with a particular variety of unglazed ceramic called Kwale ware, which archaeologists have determined is related to the pre-Christian era Urewe ware found throughout the Lakes region.[17] Kwale ware turns up in a roughly triangular zone extending from the Ngulu mountains in the south, northwards to the Mombasa hinterland, and west to the central highlands of Kenya. Some sherds which are possibly Kwale have also been found farther north in the Barawa area.[18]

Complementing archaeological documentation of the spread of the Bantu to the coastal region is the linguistic data afforded by Ehret, Nurse, and Hinnebusch.[19] According to this information, a northern coastal branch of Eastern Bantu-speakers, called the proto-Sabaki by linguists, appeared in the interior of the northeastern Tanganyika coast sometime aroung AD 500 and advanced northwards as far as the Jubba River. As is the usual pattern across so long an expanse of territory, dialects began to emerge in different areas of their spread. By the end of the first millennium, these had evolved into increasingly distinct dialects, well on their way to becoming the separate Swahili, Pokomo, Elwana, Miji Kenda, and Comorian languages of recent centuries.[20]

From the work of Guthrie and Nurse,[21] it is clear that the early coastal Sabaki-speakers primarily were agriculturalists with knowledge of pottery. They cultivated a variety of yams, vegetables, beans, and bananas, along with cereals, while they kept goats, sheep, chickens, and a few cattle. A considerable array of game was hunted to supplement their vegetable diet. Equally significant as their knowledge of agriculture were their activities as fishermen who used lines, nets, and baskets to snare their prey, while they also had knowledge of canoe-making and iron-working. Of social importance is the inference that they tended to live in compact villages wherever they settled among scattered groups of non-Bantu. Because of their generally more complex manufacturing activities (woodworking, potting, iron-making, basketry), 'the village [acted] as a center for a region and in time set standards of value'.[22] Of all the groups described herein, then, it would appear that the Bantu who settled the northern coastal region in the first millennium probably were the best equipped to exploit the full range of economic possibilities presented by the coastal environment and to play a commanding role in the formation of later coastal culture.

SHUNGWAYA?

One set of questions which seems to fit into considerations of early coastal culture involves the Shungwaya traditions. The controversies surrounding Shungwaya, of course, are longstanding and numerous. Where, for example, was Shungwaya? What exactly was it? How should the claims made by certain peoples of their migration from Shungwaya be interpreted and their accuracy gauged? These are important questions whose answers bear directly on the history of the entire coastal region and the peoples who have inhabited that region. They are of particular interest in the context of Swahili history not only because the northern Swahili are linguistically Bantu-speakers, related to other 'Sabaki' Bantu, but also because Shungwaya represents what was the pre-'Shirazi', pre-Islamic cultural, social, and economic milieu from which northern coastal civilization emerged as a distinct cultural and religious entity. Indeed, like the Miji Kenda and others, in an important sense the earliest Swahili ('Shirazi') were 'from' Shungwaya.

But, briefly, what is the Shungwaya myth? Basically, it consists of a number of traditions which tell the story of a series of migrations which took place (probably) in the sixteenth and seventeenth centuries from a central region north of the Tana River by various Somali groups, Sabaki Bantu-speakers, and possibly smaller numbers of people from other ethnic groups. They tell how Katwa (Garre or Tunni Somali) came to settle the coast from Shungwaya, as well as how the Miji Kenda and the Kilindini came to their present homelands.[23] And, likewise, they relate how some Bajun, who previously had inhabited a string of villages on the mainland littoral opposite Pate island and northwards, came to settle the islands from Pate to Koyama.[24] The usual reasons given for these population shifts centre on the hostility of pastoralists – either Somali or Oromo – to the Bantu groups mentioned.

For two reasons the historicity of Shungwaya seems beyond doubt. First, as shown above, it appears in the traditions of such a large number of disparate, though related, peoples. And, second, Shungwaya was known to the Portuguese already by the sixteenth century.[25] The precise location of Shungwaya, however, is a mystery which even the Portuguese appear not to have solved, and to this day it remains a puzzle.[26] The *Book of Zenj* places it at Bur Gao on the southern Somalia coast; Burton, on the other hand, places it near the Tana River;[27] while most sources locate it on the mainland littoral just north of Lamu.[28] Equally debatable is what Shungwaya was or represented. The *Book of Zenj* identifies it as a city, Bur Gao, but Chittick's archaeological survey of that site indicated that it was too late (post-1500) to qualify for the traditional Shungwaya.[29]

Spear's view of a basically Bantu-only Shungwaya, too, rather oversimplifies matters, while at same time the extensive population shift it envisions as having had to occur is too uneconomical.[30] Nurse's linguistic work on Sabaki Bantu, accurate and important as far as it goes, does not satisfactorily account for linguistic evidence of possible non-Bantu influences in early coastal history.[31] While Nurse's recent work largely is supportive of Spear's views, ironically the linguists Hinnebusch and Ehret point out the strains which the theory of a proto-Sabaki homeland north of the Tana River (associated with Shungwaya by Spear) imposes on the overall linguistic evidence. Ehret, for example, indicates the Miji Kenda probably was spoken in its present locale at least five hundred years before the Shungwaya emigrations supposedly took place (that is, 1000, rather than AD 1500). More important still is that both linguists indicate that the proto-Sabaki language was brought by people coming from the Ruvu River area of northeastern Tanzania.[32] Spear also hypothesizes (what would have to have been) an improbably rapid migration of Sabaki-speakers from this natal area northwards to Shungwaya. It was at Shungwaya, he says, that Sabaki Bantu split into its constituent languages and from whence the famous exodus southwards took place in the sixteenth century.[33] While one cannot rule out Spear's hypothesis completely, it would seem that a simpler explanation of the Shungwaya traditions might be found if one reconsiders the possible nature of Shungwaya itself.

According to Ehret, the migrants who brought the Shungwaya traditions southwards, besides some of Spear's Sabaki Bantu, could have included some sedentarized ex-pastoralists.[34] Their identity is uncertain, but there are two possible candidates. The first are the Southern Cushites, mentioned already, whose former presence on the coast is betrayed by the Southern Cushitic dialect spoken by the Dahalo, as well as by evidence of Southern Cushitic influences in all five of the Sabaki-derived languages themselves (Swahili, Elwana, Pokomo, Miji Kenda, and Comorian).

Another group at least equally likely to have played a role at Shungwaya were Eastern Cushites who spoke dialects of the greater Somali language ancestral to present day Somali, Rendille, Tunni, and Garre (Aweera or 'Boni' being a dialect of Garre).[35] Evidence indicates that this language group evolved in or near the Jubba watershed. Sometime early in the first millennium AD, Somali cattle herders, who appear to have included groups presently called Garre and Tunni, migrated down the river to the Benadir coast and southwards as far as the Tana River. Some of them, being cattle herders, were not economically self-sufficient. According to Cassanelli, such cattle pastoralists tended to live symbiotically alongside cultivators, and when camel pastoralists appeared on the scene many cattle herders were forced to make territorial claims to pasture lands and water holes. Eventually, some even settled in villages themselves and took up dryland agriculture.[36] By the tenth century, some had settled at Kismayu and around Lamu.[37] On evidence given by Idrisi and Ibn Said, by the twelfth century other groups of these semi-sedentarized cattle pastoralists were living in the hinterland of Merka and, most likely, along river banks and the coast itself.[38] Even after the Oromo had become the most powerful force on the mainland in the seventeenth century, pockets of Garre Somali still could be found in the coastal hinterland from the Jubba region to Malindi. They appear, for example, in the contemporary Portuguese documents as the 'Maracatos', an apparent distortion of 'Katwa', a name given them by Swahili-speakers.[39] This Somali legacy in coastal history is still apparent in the large number of Aweera/Somali lexical items in northern coastal Bantu, especially among the Bajun.[40] In conclusion, then, oral traditions of a Katwa Somali migration from Shungwaya and settlement among the Bajun also logically raise the possibility that there could have been a corresponding movement of some sedentarized ex-pastoralists (Bantuized?) southwards into Miji Kenda areas or Mombasa.[41] It would have been this mixed lot of Bantu cultivators and sedentarized ex-pastoralists who were responsible for Shungwaya traditions told by Miji Kenda, Bajun, Kilindini, and Jomvu oral historians.

What then was Shungwaya? It appears not to have been a specific place or town, first of all, but a region itself or a region in which several 'Shungwayas' might have existed. This region, judging by the various locations given for Shungwaya in the traditions, might have stretched from the Jubba/Webbi Shebeelle River system southwards to the Tana River. It included the coast and offshore islands and reached inland for an indefinite distance.[43] The date of its origin is open to argument since the region described apparently always has been inhabited. Yet traditionally Shungwaya was destroyed in the sixteenth and seventeenth centuries when the Oromo forced its inhabitants to emigrate to the south and to the coastal islands.[44] While traditions exist which say that Shungwaya was 'ruled' by a mysterious group called the Kilio, the meaning of 'ruling' (as is the meaning of 'migration')[45] is probably symbolic of something less formal than suzerainty. Indeed, just as it appears unlikely that Shungwaya was one specific place or town, it seems equally improbable that it was under any single form of government.

If one considers this region as it probably was between about 800 and 1600, particularly if one considers its ecological diversity and the varieties of peoples inhabiting Shungwaya at that time, something slightly different is suggested. In what was basically a dry region bordered by green areas and forests in the river regions and along the coast, a wide range of human types were living often in fairly close proximity to each other and were exploiting this environment in a variety of ways. Each of these groups would have been settled in its own ecological niche, carrying on a mode of production best suited to that environment. One can imagine pastoralists, for example, occupying drier regions between the green areas, regions more suitable for hunting and herding activities. In among them moved the hunters who lived off the game and traded some ivory, horn, and skins. These were the ancestors of the Aweera and Dahalo. Around the rivers and on the coast small communities of Bantu were settled in among semi-sedentarized cattle pastoralists.[46] These Bantu probably cultivated a variety of cereal crops, including rice. In addition, archaeological evidence recently uncovered at a Tana River site indicates that they were iron-workers who made a characteristic type of pottery called either Kilwa Kitchen or Wenje ware. Besides engaging in cultivating, the association of fish bones and shells with Kilwa/Wenje ware strongly suggests that these early coastal and riverain Bantu were fishermen.[47]

In this social and physical environment something of a community of shared economic interests evolved, much as is found in other parts of East Africa among hunters, herders, and cultivators. The fact that the region is environmentally unstable no doubt contributed to alliances, exchange, and even cohabitation among these various peoples as hedges against environmental disaster.[48] Sedentary cultivators perhaps kept a little stock, for example, and tended that of their pastoralist neighbours in exchange for manure, much as the Pokomo in the Tana region and the Gosha/Habash of the Webi Shebeelle have been observed to do in more recent centuries.[49] At the same time, the partial dependence of some pastoralists, especially cattle nomads, on sedentary cultivators ensured that there was some identity of interests between groups involved in one productive mode or another. Out of these shared interests units of economic self-sufficiency evolved which

13

included both herding and cultivating components. Agreements were worked out where critical watering holes lay in territory held by cultivators. In exchange, the pastoralists guaranteed protection of the farmers' croplands from interlopers, and sometimes these agreements appear to have developed into defensive alliances (*diyya*). 'From there,' Cassanelli says, 'it was a short step to the exercise of hegemony by one group over another, most commonly by the mobile and militant nomads.' However, if this was what Shungwaya was like, this does not mean that it was 'ruled' outright by pastoralists. For again Cassanelli observes, 'the two sides of any relationship depended . . . on the particular needs of a herding or farming unit'; and, 'To characterize the period of Somali migrations as a time when warlike pastoralists overran societies of peaceful cultivators is to misrepresent the situation'.[50]

From available traditions and recent archaeological evidence, it appears that relations between the cultivators and pastoralists in the Shungwaya region varied a great deal. By way of illustration, a Jomvu tradition recalls that town dwellers/cultivators ('Shirazi') and the pastoralists (identified as Tunni), while not the same people, were closely related through intermarriage (*walivyalikana*, 'they bore children together').[51] This is hardly surprising in view of historical evidence from the coast that pastoralists actually settled in the towns from time to time. Stigand and LeRoy, for instance, collected traditions that the first inhabitants of Siyu included Somali and Bajun whom hostile Oromo had driven from (mainland) Dondo.[52] Cohabitation in 'mixed villages,' Lewis has observed, sometimes also was the end point in the socio-economic fusion which often took place.[53] Recent archaeological discoveries of camel and cattle bones in some of the earliest strata (ninth and tenth centuries) at Manda and Shanga suggest, indeed, that these earliest known coastal towns were just such 'mixed villages' in origin.[54]

The Bajun have an interesting tradition that, over the centuries, formal pacts were concluded between Bantu cultivators and Katwa Somali which bound them together 'by condition and fortune' (*waka-ahidiyana kwa hali na mali*).[55] Likewise, in the seventeenth century, when Pate was becoming a paramount power on the northern coast, traditions from Faza and Siyu say that it was alliances of this sort which allowed them to resist Pate's aggressions. In Siyu's case, however, the price of this assistance was the agreement by the ruling Famao clan to share power with their Somali allies.[56] Twice in the seventeenth century also, Pate, Siyu, Faza, Manda, and Lamu drew upon alliances with Oromo and Somali to rebuff Portuguese interference in their affairs.[57] Thus, where pastoralists and cultivators did not cohabit, client relations (*shegaad*) and alliances (*diyya*) seem to have been common.

Where client relations existed, of course, one group was recognized as subordinate to the other. In regions like the Webi Shebeelle where pastoralists clearly had the advantage, cultivators like the Habash were in a dependent position. Along the coast, however, Bantu-speaking agriculturalists were numerically stronger. Thus, the villages and towns of the Bantu (or early Swahili), especially when they were on offshore islands, had the advantage, and it was the pastoralists like the Garre who came to the coastal fringe and islands as clients (*shegat*).[58]

Whatever the arrangements, occasional attempts by erstwhile client groups to refute them or the arrival of new groups claiming hegemony caused friction and broken ties. One example, provided by recent work on southern Benadir history, of a successful assertion of authority by one ruling clan over a wide area involved the Ajuran confederation. The Garen, the ruling clan, extended its hegemony over various herding and cultivating groups of the Webi Shebeelle region with a skilful combination of *jihad*, trade linkages, and alliances.[59] One political device they employed is especially noteworthy. The Garen sultans (*boqor*) claimed the right of *ius primae noctis*, the right to initiate intercourse with brides-to-be without payment of compensation (*meher*), a right they appear to have exploited in creating marriage ties and reinforcing their political grasp over all the important clans of the sultanate.[60] The fact that there are traditions of similar customs having been practised in the coastal region of Kenya makes this information striking, indeed. Thus, the Bajun, the Famao clan of Siyu, and the Miji Kenda all tell versions of a tradition of how a pastoralist chief, called Pununu or Ruruna, was killed, usually by a youth or jealous bridegroom posing as a woman or by a woman herself, for demanding the right of *ius primae noctis*.[61] Now, just who the chief Pununu or Ruruna represents is uncertain. Does he, for example, specifically represent an Ajuran sultan? Or, in fact, was the practice of *ius primae noctis* a political device commonly connected with *diyya* alliances throughout Shungwaya? (It is equally significant that all versions of the tradition collected so far come from various scattered peoples who claim to have come 'from' Shungwaya.) In any event, the meaning of the tradition is clear. All of these groups, Bajun, Famao, and Kashur/Miji Kenda, broke with Shungwaya when pastoralists, like the Oromo in the case of the Kashur, attempted to involve them too closely in an alliance or confederation of the Ajuran type which they found to be culturally unacceptable. Thus, these cultivators (including some previously settled pastoralists) 'left' Shungwaya.

ORIGINS OF SWAHILI CIVILIZATION

A growing body of evidence indicates, then, that coastal civilization had its origins in Shungwaya. Oral traditions certainly suggest this.[62] And, despite the presence of pastoralists at Shungwaya, ethnolinguistic analysis previously mentioned establishes the fact that the Swahili language evolved out of Sabaki Bantu (and less so from Cushitic influences).[63] Wenje ware, too, has been found at or near the lowest strata of a number of coastal sites such as Kiunga, Manda, Shanga, Kilwa, Lamu, and Bagamoyo, where it appears to have been in use between about AD 800 at Shanga and Manda and about 1150 at Kilwa.[64] The archaeological work which has established this connection between a pre-Islamic Shungwaya settlement (indicated by the presence of Kilwa/Wenje ware) and a later town more recognizably coastal is that which has been done at Shanga by Horton. There, the 'intensive conservatism in morphology of the site through time, from pre-Islamic to Islamic or from wood to stone' firmly establishes this connection.[65] At Shanga, house construction appears to have evolved from the round, mud-and-timber huts commonly found among coastal Bantu into the rectangular coral rag and mud or limestone usually associated with the coast. Also, a timber wall gave way by the tenth century to one made out of porites coral.[66]

From other evidence found at Shanga, it is clear that it remained non-Islamic until at least the late eleventh century. No mosques or Islamic burials were found until those strata were reached.[67] Village economy involved both cultivating and herding activities. In addition, evidence of fishing activities was found in the earliest levels, and there were indications that by the tenth century this had evolved into a fairly complex maritime society possessing a significant oceanic technology.[68]

Finally, as at the Tana River site, iron-working had a prominent part in the technological repertoire of early, pre-Islamic coastal towns associated with Shungwaya. It appears that wherever Kilwa/Wenje ware is found, iron-working occurred. A great deal of evidence of iron-working has been found by Chittick and Horton at Kilwa, Manda, and Shanga, with several furnaces, in addition, having been found at both Manda and Shanga.[69] The proximity of Manda and Shanga, along with the remarkable concentration of later iron-working sites around the Mtangawanda in Manda Bay, suggest that the Lamu archipelago might have been at the centre of an early trade network extending to neighbouring (pastoralist) peoples and the Middle East based on superior Bantu iron technology. A number of other factors support this contention. First, there is a Meru tradition that the Mtangawanda was an area where 'blacksmiths gathered', while at Lamu it is said of the autochthonous Wamea 'clan' that, 'Les forgerons se recrutent en grande parti parmi eux.'[70] As far as the trade goes, Elliott mentions a tradition of Bajun trade in iron to the Somalis who 'were unacquainted with its use'.[71] Lombard, obtaining his information out of Biruni, also mentions the East African coast as having been a major source of iron to India and the Persian Gulf region in the eleventh century, while Idrisi and Abu'l-Fida tell how Malindi (Manda?) had become the leading producer of Middle Eastern iron by the twelfth century.[72]

Shungwaya, then, probably was a region between the Jubba and Tana Rivers which included the coast, the offshore islands, and the immediate hinterland. Hunters, pastoralists, and cultivators inhabited this region, much as they do today, in the centuries when coastal civilization began to take shape. Throughout this region various local ties, based on common interests in the land, developed between peoples and villages involved in different economies. In some instances, common interests, closer social relations, and sedentarization of pastoralists even resulted in settlement of Bantu and Cushitic-speakers together in what Lewis has called 'mixed villages'. Thus, the earliest levels of coastal settlements like Shanga and Manda indicate that they probably were part of the social and economic region called Shungwaya. It was out of this environment, 'from Shungwaya', that coastal civilization emerged.

16

2

The emergence of a tradition, 900–1500

Analysis of the cultural history of the northern coast in the 'medieval' period encounters two major difficulties, the information available for assessment and the terminology. (Thus, any resolution of the earlier part of this period, especially, has to be very speculative and stated in the broadest terms possible.) Coastal historians are not faced with the usual problem of paucity of sources. Indeed, they are, if anything, especially fortunate among Africanists for having a comparatively large number of written documents and recorded oral traditions at their disposal, all of which have been augmented in the past twenty-odd years by the published results of various crucial archaeological and ethnolinguistic studies.[1] Each type of source used, be it oral tradition(s), written eyewitness accounts, archaeological reports, or linguistic studies, presents its own peculiar set of strengths and pitfalls of which the historian must be aware if he is going to use it effectively. Fortunately, these various sources of historical data often complement each other in terms of their relative strengths and in the nature of the information they provide. The historian, then, draws upon as wide a range of information as possible, if he is wise, in his historical interpretations. While this usually is quite rewarding, problems inevitably appear in efforts to reconcile different types of data and the terminology applied to these data, which are often at some variance with each other.

The classic example of such problems in coastal historiography concerns the applicability of the epithet 'Shirazi' to this period or any portion of it. The name comes from oral traditions which purport that groups of immigrants from Shiraz or Persia 'founded' many coastal towns in the early Middle Ages (c. tenth to fourteenth centuries). According to the 'Kilwa Chronicle', most notable among these early 'Shirazi' sites were M-n-d-k-h (Manda?), sh-w-gh (Shanga?), Y-n-b-ᶜ (Yanbu or Yumbe?), M-n-f-s-t (Mombasa or Mafia), the 'Green Isle' (Pemba), Kilwa, and Anjouan. Shirazi traditions exist for many other coastal sites as well.[2] The first problem one encounters concerning these traditions is that of ascertaining just who the Shirazi were or what they represent. Should one accept the traditions literally, for example, and assume that Persian migrants 'founded' Kilwa or Manda sometime in the tenth century as it is alleged? Or do they stand for something else? A dynasty, perhaps? A family of nobles? Or even an epoch (no doubt pre- or non-'Arab') in coastal history?[3] To complicate matters even further, some scholars have tried to associate the term with certain phases in the medieval history of the coast or occasionally with certain features of coastal culture which emerged in the medieval period. Sometimes this has occurred where these scholars have tried to associate the Shirazi of the oral traditions with data obtained from non-traditional sources. Chittick's archaeological work, for instance, has led him to identify the earliest recognizably Islamic period at Kilwa (Period II) with a phase of Shirazi rule in that city's history.[4] Still more ambiguous has been Allen's association of a specific 'mode of dominance' among coastal political institutions with the Shirazi.[5] The main obstacle to associating the Shirazi of the traditions with cultural features which appeared in the early medieval period is that there is little mention of these Shirazi in oral or written forms before the early sixteenth century (the so-called 'Kilwa Chronicle'). None of the Arab or Chinese travellers' accounts dating from the ninth to the fourteenth centuries mentions actual Persian settlers in East Africa, nor is there linguistic evidence of any significant Persian part in coastal history.[6] Obviously then, this indicates a need for historians to exercise great care in combining data from differing sources and, especially, in associating 'Shirazi' with such tenuous notions as a 'mode of dominance', for example, without some qualifications. The above criticisms aside, historians have not been entirely remiss in how they have employed the Shirazi epithet. Using Chittick and Allen as examples, again, it is clear that they often have intended to associate the term with cultural traits they have encountered in their work which they have recognized as having been distinctly and uniquely coastal (as opposed to something distinctly 'Arab', for example), yet in a pristine form. Indeed, however much one might query who or what the Shirazi represent in local accounts, associations such as those Chittick and Allen have made are very much in keeping with the traditions that the Shirazi 'founded' most coastal societies. Thus, one can identify the Shirazi traditions specifically as origin myths. As in most African origin myths, their creators identify certain fundamental symbols and institutions as uniquely their own, all of which set them apart from other peoples. As other origin myths, too, they relate the appearance/creation of these symbols/institutions to a single significant episode.[7] In reality, of course, such episodes usually conceal what were complex social and cultural transformations which took place over many decades and even centuries, while the traditions, like the civilization whose history they relate, are themselves the end-products of this historical process.[8] Cultures emerge, they do not spring into existence full-blown. History is an on-going process, so the coastal civilization of the eighteenth century differed notably from that of the tenth and even the fifteenth centuries. Yet certain features recognizable in the eighteenth century already existed in the tenth century, while more and more such features accrued throughout the medieval period and coastal townsmen became increasingly conscious of themselves, their culture, and their history as uniquely different from other peoples with whom they had former cultural and historical links. At this point, then, it is important that the story of this cultural emergence be told.

THE FIRST PHASE, 800–1100

As indicated in the first chapter, coastal culture had its origins in the cultures and demographic shifts of various peoples residing at Shungwaya. Traditional 'memory' of this exists in two forms. First, there are the oral traditions of a number of Swahili (and non-Swahili) communities which concern the alleged migrations from Shungwaya, all of which have been cited already. This particular 'form' of tradition does seem, in fact, to refer to the well-documented exodus of many northern coastal and riverain peoples out of the region called Shungwaya in the sixteenth and seventeenth centuries.[9] Considering the long-standing ties which the coastal towns had with neighbouring Bantu and Cushitic peoples, this migration and the Pununu/Rurunu traditions associated with it probably represent the climax of a historical process which, over about eight hundred to a thousand years, had seen the slow evolution of the coast as a cultural and linguistic zone distinct from the so-called *nyika*. The emphasis in these traditions clearly is on ruptures which initiated independent lines of development for many. The second form of tradition is visible in what Miller and Sigwalt would call a 'seam' in the Shirazi traditions.[10] While most of these traditions attempt to establish claims to Persian descent for older Swahili houses (see Chapter 3), and assert that migrants from Shiraz 'founded' coastal towns, some versions collected in the past actually associate the mythical Shirazi not with Persia directly, but with Shungwaya.[11] Thus, while such versions seek to explain the origins of Swahili culture and language in terms of a series of identifiable episodes, the fact that they also assign a significant part to Shungwaya in this drama is noteworthy. Such traditions pay honour to the uniqueness of coastal civilization; explain its creation (by their 'coming from' Shiraz/Shungwaya) in mythical time; and, somewhat more rarely, repay a historical debt coastal culture owes to its African roots.

To achieve a better understanding of how coastal culture was 'born' in Shungwaya, a useful beginning can be made with Feierman's hypothesis of the 'indigenous' definition of ethnicity. According to this formulation, Africans perceive the ethnic group to which they belong partly in terms of the natural environment in which they live and by the language they speak as a unique instrument for understanding this environment.[12] Local culture represents a people who live in a particular natural setting. Furthermore, they possess an empirical understanding of this setting's identifiable flora, fauna, and climate which they turn to advantage in exploiting that environment for the purposes of their physical survival and comfort. Stated another way, culture partly is the end-product of a distinct interaction between a physical setting and its human inhabitants.[13] This interaction and the culture that results, of course, extend beyond the simple matters of subsistence and survival described by Feierman. Many elements in the physical composition of simple cultures, for instance, are used as building materials for housing and tools, clothing, cosmetics, and furniture. Furthermore, in cultures where people live so close to what nature provides, they tend to adopt naive naturalist views of reality. From such close relationships with their physical environment, they often believe that basic epistemological and ethical categories are directly observable in the workings of the natural world in which they live. Perceived experiential criteria such as colours, shapes, sounds, tastes, pressures, and pains are taken as universal and suitable for the basic organization not only of their own, but all human socio-economic institutions.[14] The final identification between human society and the world of nature is observable in peoples' use of nature in their religious beliefs and practices. As they observe their natural environment, experience it, adapt their language to describe it, and live with its rhythms and laws, they begin to identify with it personally. It becomes a meaningful and organic part of their culture and language. Natural objects on one hand become religious symbols, while on the other hand the actions of nature become more personalized and subject to controls accessible through contractual relationships which exist between living beings and the spirits (ancestral and territorial) whose field of action includes natural events.[15] Through such alleged covenants, human society and nature become consorts from which culture is born.

By the end of the first millennium AD, the first instalments in the steady emergence of a distinct coastal ethnicity were appearing. First, and probably most important, a basic core of Sabaki Bantu speakers, possibly along with some ancestral Somali and Southern Cushitic cattle keepers and cultivators, were settled in small mixed villages at various places in the coastal environment. There they had adjusted their cultures to maximize the terms of the dialogue they were establishing with this unique natural ambience. Bantu groups, although they already were experienced farmers, learned much about the cultivation of local cereals from long-established Southern Cushites.[16] No doubt, too, at a very early date they domesticated the coconut, mango, citruses, and groundfruits which characterize the coastal ecozone. Fishing was as important as cultivating activities in the economies of the earliest coastal settlements. The earliest Bantu groups to inhabit the coast seem to have introduced some knowledge of fishing techniques into coastal life. By the tenth century, this had developed into a fairly sophisticated maritime technology involving deep sea diving for porities coral and reef shells and deep sea fishing for shark, turtle, and parrot fish. Shellfish, however, were consumed at some sites.[17] Finally, some cattle keeping was evident, though only as a secondary feature of coastal economies.

The truly remarkable feature about this mixed economy is, again, its peculiar suitability for the coastal setting. The complementarity of farming and livestock husbandry already has been discussed in terms of the respective activities they represent, but also it is crucial to note that the products they generate, along with fish, balance each other from a nutritional standpoint.[18] Marine and farming operations, too, are performed in and out of seasons which complement each other. The farmer of one season is the fisherman of the next. Thus, life can go on for the coastal villager wishing to broaden his subsistence base very much by the special rhythms of the coastal climate and in conformity with the singular opportunities and restrictions offered by the varied elements of sea, island, shore, and mainland interior found in such close proximity only on the coast.

Besides the unexampled way in which this environment was developed for economic purposes, the natural products of the coast themselves were put to distinctive uses. Evidence of this exists at the earliest sites excavated so far on the coast. At Manda, Shanga, and Kilwa, settlements of timber and daub structures gradually gave way, from the ninth through the eleventh centuries, to stone walls, massively cut and laid sea barriers, foundations, and finally to rectangular dwellings built of mud mortar and coral rag.[19] In addition to porites coral quarried from nearby reefs, coastal palms yielded fronds for roofing purposes (*makuti*), and mangrove was utilized for adding strength to walls and for roofing. Taken altogether, then, the evidence suggests that by about 1100, coastal culture was emerging specifically as a culture of the coastal environment.

Development in language, of course, paralleled this cultural emergence. As coastal dwellers observed this coastal environment, learned to understand it, and mastered it, their language also evolved to comprehend all aspects of the unexampled sort of dialogues between man and nature that unfolded. The basic language core from which Kiswahili emerged was Sabaki Bantu. From presently available linguistic studies, Sabaki Bantu first appeared somewhere around the Ruvu River in northern Tanzania and spread northwards, possibly as far as the Jubba River.[20] Eventually, several dialects (then societies) developed. Kiswahili appears to have been the first to evolve as a separate dialect and language, probably, according to Ehret, around AD 1000 or earlier – that is, roughly corresponding to the cultural developments described above.[21] Slightly later, four other languages emerged also: Miji Kenda, Elwana, Comorian, and Pokomo. Like Kiswahili each evolved in its own unique ecozone.[22]

A final component in the early stages of coastal cultural history was trade. Iron, as previously discussed, was found in the lowest strata at Kilwa, Shanga, and Manda, and at Shungwaya it was a major commodity in local or regional trade.[23] By the eleventh century it appears that overseas trade had advanced considerably on the northern coast. Iron, again, seems to have been an important trade item, but it is likely that other coastal products such as rhino horn, ivory, ambergris, and animal skins were also exported.[24] To their mainland neighbours coastal dwellers exported shells, shell beads, iron, and overseas imports, while they themselves imported Persian Gulf ceramics, Chinese porcelains, and Indian glass beads. What is most significant about this external trade is that it suggests that a common culture might already have been developing up and down the coast even in this earliest phase. Detection of Persian Gulf Sassanian-Islamic and Islamic glazed wares from Manda to Chibuene, Mozambique, testifies to the extent which commercial ties already were in place by the tenth century.[25] At most of these sites, too, Kilwa/Wenje wares have been found.[26] This, of course, is an even more telling disclosure since it firmly indicates that this growing commercial network involved a local coasting trade as well as an overseas one.

THE SECOND PHASE, 1100–1300

In three ways, the second phase of the medieval history of the coast was simply a further development of the first. Yet these elaborations, increased trade, growing wealth, and expanding urbanization (and cosmopolitanism), were directly responsible for the one major shift which set off the second phase from the first, namely Islamization. Once again, it is archaeological evidence which provides the most valuable clues to the waxing in the commercial fortunes and wealth of coastal sites. For the pre-twelfth century phase, for example, eleven settlement sites so far have been identified: Munghia, Gezira, Shanga, Manda, Pate, Unguja Ukuu, Mkokotoni, Anjouan, Kisimani Mafia, Kilwa, and Chibuene. Of these, only Manda has shown any signs of having enjoyed extensive overseas commercial contact and opulence.[27] In the twelfth and thirteenth centuries at least eighteen more major settlements were added to this list: Mogadishu, Merka, Barawa, Faza, Lamu, Ungwana (Ozi), Malindi, Gedi, Kilepwa, Mombasa, Kizimkazi, Zanzibar town; Jongowe, Mtambwe Mkuu, Ras Mkumbuu, Mkia wa Ngombe, Mduuni, and Sanje ya Kati. Almost all locations present ceramic evidence of having undergone a noticeable increase in trade and commercial wealth. Whereas Sassanian-Islamic and imported white-glazed wares were fairly rare (except, again, at Manda) at most sites previously, in this second phase there was a marked increase in imported sgraffiato wares (so-called hatched and Champleve varieties), Chinese celadons and porcelains, black-on-yellow ceramics, and glass beads (which largely replaced locally made shell varieties).[28]

The greater wealth of this phase is noticeable, too, in the augmented use of 'stone' for building purposes. At Shanga, for example, the well was lined in stone, while the enclosure wall was rebuilt of porities coral, continuing a trend which seems to have begun in the first phase.[29] Kilwa, too, exhibited an increase in stone structures 'on a substantial scale', as noted by Chittick. Coral lime was burned for the first time and applied as a floor covering and as a particularly hard, water-resistant binding material in wall construction.[30]

The most important by-product of this expanded contact with Middle Eastern and Indian merchants was the spread of Islam. In the preceding phase, there is some evidence of the presence of Muslims on the coast. However, their identity and significance are unknown.[31] In the twelfth century Idrisi and Yaqut mention the presence of Muslims at Zanzibar and Pemba, a fact which is supported by the 1106/7 date on the famous reconstructed *mihrab* at Kizimkazi.[32] In that same century and in the following one, migrations of Arab clans from Yemen to Mogadishu were responsible for establishing the first of a series of Arab dynasties and that city's prominence in coastal commerce throughout the thirteenth century.[33] Along with this went Mogadishu's fame as an important centre of Islamic learning, a reputation supported by the renowned Qahtani al-Wa'il clan of ᶜ*ulamā*᾿.[34] Thus, it is not surprising that Mogadishu possesses three of the earliest mosques built on the coast, and the fact that these structures are all built of stone testifies to the wealth and Islamization of that city in its thirteenth-century heyday.[35]

Elsewhere on the coast the story of the twelfth and thirteenth centuries seems to have been very much the same. Trade brought wealth and Islam, and surviving evidence of that wealth is in the tombs and mosques built during those centuries. Suddenly, towns started erecting mosques out of coral rag and either mud or lime mortar, while graves were aligned along the *qibla* line (facing Mecca). At Manda and Kilwa, for example, distinctively styled tombs were fashioned out of stone and located outside town precincts.[36] Early in the twelfth century, Shanga had its first Friday mosque constructed out of mud mortar and coral, and later in the same century it was rebuilt out of stone.[37] At about the same time, the first stage of Kilwa's Great Mosque was constructed out of dressed coral blocks and lime mortar.[38] Other locations where stone mosques or funerary evidence betoken the likely presence of significant Muslim populations at this period are Merka, Barawa, Ungwana, Kisimani Mafia, and Sanje ya Kati.[39]

Having related physical evidence of the connections between trade in this period and conversion to Islam, it would be useful at this point to query the nature of this connection. Given the material presented so far, then, how might one explain coastal Africans' conversion to Islam starting in the twelfth and thirteenth centuries? A good beginning might be made by extending what has been said already about a developing sense of ethnicity among coastal dwellers. Ethnicity and culture, it will be remembered, arise out of the dialogue established between man and his environment. This implies that people's self-consciousness, their awareness of themselves as a distinct cultural group, is profoundly affected by their collective experiences of the world in which they live both in time and space. Thus, a culture evolves as a

> historically transmitted pattern of meanings embodied in symbols, a system of inherited conceptions expressed in symbolic forms by means of which men communicate, perpetuate and develop their knowledge about the attitudes towards life.[40]

As man experiences the world in which he lives, many symbols of his existence are drawn from this world. These are arranged into what Geertz calls a 'locally perceived system of significance' which provides 'a model *of* and a model *for* reality'.[41] 'Religion', of course, is closely related to culture. It articulates man's perceived relationships with his world. Like culture, it is comprised of bundles of symbols which unite the physical, organic world and man's experience of it with the sociomoral order.[42] To paraphrase Geertz, what religion expresses in symbolic form is what men actually experience in the world, and to what men encounter in actual experience it imparts a broader form and deeper meaning. 'It draws its persuasiveness out of a reality it itself defines.'[43] This 'magic circle' which exists between 'religion' and 'reality', however, is highly vulnerable to the extent that as man's experiences of his world alter, 'concepts and symbols lose their air of simple realism [and] perplexities ensue'.[44] Thus, in the end, world-view, culture, and religion prove to be highly susceptible to the exigencies of history.

In the case of the coast, its Islamization in the 'second phase' can be interpreted as having been one part of a more pervasive historical process. From about the ninth century onwards, coastal societies and cultures had been undergoing a metamorphosis from simpler, parochial forms to more complex versions of themselves. This process unfolded in two ways. On one hand, groups of people living within the coastal fringe were becoming identifiably 'local' as a result of having adapted to peculiarly coastal environmental exigencies, while on the other hand these same conditions presented new opportunities for a broadened world-view through the contacts with non-African cultures which also were a part of the coastal world. Bantu groups particularly had a fairly sophisticated technological and intellectual tradition which could be adapted to exploit the full range of coastal resources. But the sea presented additional opportunities. Adapting their skills at husbandry and hunting to this setting probably presented little challenge to them. The marine technology they developed out of the (apparently) rudimentary fishing and canoe-making skills they had inherited from their continental ancestors, however, represented a true innovation meant to take advantage of a part of this environment which their forefathers and cousins did not have. Coastal Africans actively and consciously, it appears, innovated and adjusted to pursue new possibilities. When further opportunities and experiences were presented in the form of foreign merchants seeking African products, coastal peoples were ready for them culturally as well as materially. Growing cosmopolitanism in some burgeoning towns produced shifts in local centres of political and economic power. This, in turn, engendered parallel adjustments in local world-views.[45] Certainly, coastal Africans were not unprepared for this, since change, even conscious innovation, always had been as much a part of their experience as that which was occurring in the twelfth and thirteenth centuries. A new culture was emerging, albeit at an accelerating pace; and Islam simply was engulfed in this wider historical process which had started well before the twelfth century. So when people began constructing Islamic tombs and mosques, it is not at all surprising that they applied their own architectural styles to them and built them out of mangrove, sea shells, and corals.

THE THIRD PHASE, 1300–1600

The phase from the fourteenth through the sixteenth centuries often has been called the 'golden age' of coastal history. Indeed, there are many compelling reasons for this. In these centuries, it appears that much of what had been occurring in the previous two phases to set the coast off as a clearly defined cultural zone advanced to the most refined level of development. Though the northern coast would see another peak period in the eighteenth century, never again would so many fortuitous circumstances converge to rival life as it was on the coast in the late 'Middle Ages'. Trade and wealth reached a climax, an unprecedented number of locations were 'founded' (built in stone?), a palpably distinct style in architecture was established, and Islam became the accepted coastal cult. On one hand, city-states kept one foot in Shungwaya, retaining many institutions from their African past. On the other, as the period came to a close northern coastal centres clearly manifested signs of becoming more insulated culturally and even physically from neighbouring Somali, Oromo, Miji Kenda, and Pokomo societies.

Historians and archaeologists generally agree that the coast was at the acme of its prosperity at this time. This view is reinforced by the fact that between 1300 and 1700, as observed by Wilson and Allen, fully 50 per cent of all known coastal settlements were 'founded'.[46] The origins of this prosperity can be associated with major shifts in Indian Ocean trading networks by the fourteenth century. Formerly, coastal contacts with the world of the Indian Ocean largely had been with the Persian Gulf, as indicated by the Persian and Iraqi wares found at earlier sites. A developing carrying trade between the East and Europe in the thirteenth century, however, attracted the attention of Egypt's *Karimi* merchant community and that of their Mamluk overlords who extended formal control over the Red Sea trade as far as Suakin and exerted themselves in every way to promote this expanding source of revenue.[47] This provided a stimulus which drew the entire Red Sea and western Indian Ocean commercial nexus into active participation. In the Red Sea itself, a trade network was created which, besides Egypt, included Zeila, Berbera, Jidda, and Aden.[48] The extension of this network into the western Indian Ocean principally involved trade between Aden and Cambay and, as such, commercial groups from Yemen and Indian *vanya* merchants from Gujerat were its most active participants. The Cambay dealers provided two crucial components of this system. The first was dyed cloth and glass beads which they themselves manufactured for trade. The second was the commercial link to eastern ports of call at Malacca and China which were the sources of the spices, jewels, silks, brocades, celadons, and porcelains which were in heavy demand in East African ports as well as in Europe at that time. As described by Tome Pires in 1511, 'And this trade is carried out by ships from Aden and ships from Cambay, many of one and many of the other.'[49]

As it developed from the thirteenth century onwards, the trade involving East Africa was merely a secondary, though important, extension of this network. Mogadishu, it will be recalled, was the first coastal entrepôt which benefited from this new commercial link-up. It was the first location to establish close ties with southwestern Arabia, as shown by literary evidence of extensive migrations there from Yemen, which began in the twelfth century, and by the presence of early forms (twelfth and thirteenth centuries) of black-on-yellow pottery, a ceramic known to have been made in southwestern Arabia.[50] Where Indian merchants were concerned, as early (at least) as the eleventh century, iron and animal products seem to have been the key trade items which attracted their attention. The emergence of Mogadishu as a commercial power in the thirteenth century, however, besides the role of its Arab merchant, is explained by its apparent 'monopoly' of the gold and ivory trade from Sofala. This control was snapped near the end of the thirteenth century when Kilwa got its own ruling house of Yemeni *sharifs*, the Mahdali, and assumed primacy in the gold trade.[51] Two other entrepôts emerged in the second half of the fourteenth century to challenge Kilwa's pre-eminence, namely, Mombasa and Malindi. Most other coastal settlements which appeared at this time developed as 'feeder' centres to the major entrepôts. The fact that Kilwa maintained such a strong control over the southern coast, coupled with the fact that the trade of the northern entrepôts was more broadly based, explains why these 'feeder' ports preponderated on the Kenyan coast rather than on the littorals of Tanzania and Mozambique. Their function, apparently, was to supply large ports like Mombasa and Malindi with ancillary products for trade, such as ivory, skins, agricultural products, ambergris, and cowries.[52] In all cases, the link between their prosperity and the Cambay–Aden–Red Sea network is registered by the large amounts of Chinese porcelains and celadons and Yemeni black-on-yellow ceramics (the more familiar fourteenth-century varieties), of which India and Aden were the principal suppliers.[53]

The relative wealth of the era likewise is betokened by the rather extensive use of stone at some sites, while the techniques and substances used resulted in the period's unique style of architecture. As in the preceding era, essential building materials were obtained locally. Mud and rough coral rag applied within a mangrove pole latticework constituted the walls of single story, free-standing houses, while palm fronds were bound together to make *makuti* roofs left open and gabled at both ends to catch refreshing sea breezes. In many towns, houses were abutted or backed onto each other and remained single-storied and rectangular, though usually there was more use of dressed coral blocks and limestone mortar.[54] Roofs in towns and cities often were flat, being fabricated out of coral slabs laid atop lateral mangrove supports. Plaster made from coral lime was used frequently to cover walls and pave floors. City houses were laid out in similar ways, with a door opening onto a sunken courtyard, followed in succession by a verandah, a reception room, and two or three more private rooms. Latrines commonly were placed somewhere near the 'public' areas.[55] Larger 'feeder' towns and entrepôts like Kilwa and Mombasa contained many two- and three-story houses which were constructed much like their more modest single-story neighbours, but contained cut and squared roof supports and more internal decoration such as early forms of wall niching, wall carpets, and the usual porcelains and ceramics proudly displayed.

The most elaborate work, naturally, went into religious architecture. Mosques especially were the most lavish and distinctive buildings of the era. Almost every town had at least its Friday mosque (and tombs) built out of 'stone', even though all other structures might be of the wattle-and-daub varieties. Also, mosques were larger and more elaborate, testifying both to the rapid growth of some towns overall and to the growing ranks of Muslims found in most coastal centres during this period.[56] Varieties of coral were used in their construction, with rougher species used for foot rubbers and the finer porities corals cut into blocks for arched doorways and trefoliated *mihrabs.* Their surfaces were carved into the telltale cable and herring-bone motifs. Finally, unlike houses, mosque roofs sometimes were vaulted and domed. The prototypes for these features remain a mystery, so it is quite likely that, taken altogether, they represent a local stylistic innovation.[57]

Almost as lavish as mosque architecture was tomb design. Two types basically have been identified, the smaller 'tombstone' sort, and the generally larger and more elaborate pillar tomb. The latter type, as the name reveals, often was quite large, being several metres in length and width and having a pillar at its head which reached heights of 3 to 9 metres. The pillar itself could be of almost any configuration, but almost invariably it displayed at least one example of an imported ceramic or porcelain bowl.[58] As Revoil noted, they could be found almost everywhere. Some surrounded mosques, others were far removed from any sign of habitation.[59] Called *ziara,* their obvious extravagance and the fact that they were (and still are) objects of religious patronage indicate that this type of tomb was reserved for the wealthiest and most charismatic members of coastal societies, people who remained powerful ancestral figures despite the fact that official Islam frowned on such veneration as *kufr,* unbelief.[60] Kirkman and Wilson claim to have identified distinct architectural typologies on the coast based largely on pillar tomb styles. Both, for instance, have recognized a 'northern' style found along the southern Somali and northern Kenyan coast. A related though independent style also exists between Lamu and Kilifi which Kirkman calls the 'Malindi' group.[61]

The precise origins of the pillar tomb are uncertain, though it seems likely that they developed from African rather than Asian prototypes. Allen has suggested one tempting hypothesis. Noting that the Miji Kenda *kayas,* like their Swahili counterparts, were 'quite sizeable towns' in which burials were made, much as occurred in many cases of Swahili burials with which pillar tombs are associated, he likens the pillar tomb to the Miji Kenda gravepost (*kigango*) both in form and in function. There are a number of serious historiographic difficulties which stand in the way of admission of this theory, however.[62] Another possibility is that they were influenced by Cushitic models. Megaliths dating from the ninth through fourteenth centuries found by Azais, Chambard, and Joussaume around Harar and Sidamo bear a striking resemblance to coastal pillar tombs. The fact that Islamic inscriptions have been found on them and that there were trade routes from Zeila and Berbera through that region in the fourteenth century give additional weight to the argument.[63] It must be said, however, that though pillar tombs and mosque styles of this period might have taken features from African or Middle Eastern archetypes, essentially they were unique facets of coastal material culture in this phase. They were unique specimens of local innovation, built of coastal materials to serve local purposes.

By this last phase, some coastal towns appear to have possessed certain distinctive regalia. Among these, the most frequently found were royal drums, spears, turbans, and a side-blown horn (*siwa*) usually carved from wood or ivory. Additional symbols of power which sometimes would have been encountered were royal palanquins (*kiti cha enzi*), an umbrella or canopy, a medicine kit, a cloak, a brass or wooden plate, and the privilege of being allowed to wear sandals. Such paraphernalia are known to have been fairly common in the nineteenth and twentieth centuries, but their existence at some locations already in the late Middle Ages appears equally certain. Ibn Battuta found a cloak, a palanquin, sandals, a turban, drums, and the ubiquitous *siwa* at Mogadishu in 1331, while two Portuguese witnesses report seeing a chair, a canopy, a turban, and two *siwas* at Malindi in the late fifteenth and early seventeenth centuries.[64] Oral traditions recall the existence of similar symbols of authority by the seventeenth (and earlier?) century at Vumba Kuu, Ozi, Pate, and Manda or Uziwa.[65] The African (Shungwaya) origins of the spears, the medicine bag, and drums can easily be guessed, and the side-blown horn, too, is found extensively throughout both East and West Africa.[66] The turban, sandals, and palanquin, on the other hand, are difficult to identify, although Hrbek points out that Ibn Battuta's canopied throne surmounted by gold birds appears to have been taken from Fatimid models.[67]

One further aspect of African social life continued to prevail in late medieval coastal life. There is strong evidence that women in northern 'Shirazi' (pre-1600) towns enjoyed much higher status than what increasingly became their lot in later centuries.[68] Coastal traditions, dating from as far back as the sixteenth century, and Portuguese sources are awash with stories of influential women and queens who played prominent parts in the public affairs of late medieval and early modern towns.[69] They helped oversee important events concerning their kin groups, participated in public celebrations like the 'New Year' ceremonies, attended mosques with their men, and were encouraged to become literate and to study the formal Islamic sciences (*elimu*). They wielded greater social and economic power than was possible later, apparently having rights of inheritance and the enjoyment of property equal to those enjoyed by men.[70] There also are some scraps of evidence that governing authority in some 'Shirazi' locations was inherited through female members of ruling lineages. The epic quarrel of Fumo Liongo and his half-brother, Mringwari, for example, centred on the opposition between Islamic patrilineage and an older Bantu tradition of matrilineal inheritance.[71]

Despite the continued attachment of medieval coastal towns to certain facets of their African past, there is physical and oral historical evidence that by the sixteenth century most towns were becoming self-consciously insulated from the world beyond the coastal fringe. Indeed, there were good reasons for this. Besides the obvious fact that coastal culture, religion, economy, and language had evolved in their own special ways, the towns were under increasing danger from external threats from 'northern' Arabs and Portuguese raiders who appeared without warning from the ocean to pillage or to kidnap victims to be sold into slavery.[72] Moreover, relations between the towns and their African neighbours had not always been amicable. There are a few hints in pre-sixteenth-century sources which indicate, for example, that there had been occasional hostilities with neighbouring peoples.[73] In the sixteenth century itself, many Shungwayan and mainland Swahili communities were endangered by population shifts in the coastal hinterland. This was the case especially north of the Sabaki River where movements of Oromo and other mysterious peoples like the Mozungullos and the Zimba terrorized communities of agriculturalists, including Swahili, at various times and forced their occupants to seek refuge in island towns or Swahili communities and Miji Kenda *kayas* farther south.[74] Where walls do not appear to have been a feature of Swahili towns previously, then, their deteriorating relations with the outside world in the late medieval period forced many of them to erect barriers. Besides Kilwa and Mombasa to the south, most of the (known) major towns of the northern coast had defensive barriers by 1505. Thus, one early Portuguese commentator observed how Swahili towns were, 'oft-times at war but seldom at peace with those of the mainland', while another summed up his remarks concerning town–rural relations by remarking that,

> there are quarrels between all of them [that is the towns], and none of them owns a yard of land in the hinterland because the Kafirs do not allow them to have it, and they are in fact afraid of them. For this reason their towns are surrounded by walls ...[75]

Given these dangers to coastal peoples, townsmen came to imagine all evil as lurking just beyond the walls they constructed. All cultures, of course, in their positive expressions imply a certain exclusivity about them. For instance, Muslims traditionally have split the world between believers, members of a charismatic community (*umma*) who will receive God's dispensation on Judgement Day through the Prophet's intercession, and unbelievers who inhabit a world with which Muslims must strive and who are destined for eternal torment in Satan's grip. African cultures have been no different in this respect. Evidence of this was noted by a seventeenth-century Italian who commented that Angolan societies 'with nauseating presumption think themselves the foremost in the world...They think... they have not only the biggest country in the world, but also the happiest and the most beautiful.'[76]

Middleton found similar evidence of moral exclusiveness among the Lugbara:

> But the farther away people live, the worse they become. Near neighbours may be witches and sorcerers: far strangers are altogether horrible. Of the most distant strangers who live beyond the bounds of Lugbara society, 'beyond the magicians and sorcerers', the Lugbara say desperately hard things. They hold that these creatures are barely human in appearance, habitually walk on their heads, eat each other, and generally live in ways which men – that is, Lugbara – cannot hope to understand, much less approve.[77]

Swahili townsmen, by similarly positioning evil outside the precincts of their communities, divided the world and their imaginary nemeses into two categories. On one hand were the spirits of the sea and abandoned settlements, the *jinnis*. Like the sea and the Arabs who came from it, they were viewed as not totally incomprehensible. Rather, they were thought of as human-like and even as Muslims. They were associated with phenomena which might be described best as unusual, weird, or characteristic of a world gone sour. Their actions were not so much monstrous as mischievous, bringing chaos, splitting families, or causing madness.[78] Considerably more fear-inspiring, however, was the mainland *nyika* (bush) and the malevolence associated with it. Much like Middleton's Lugbara, the Swahili townsmen imagined all sorts of monsters and demons (*shaitan*) as haunting their hinterlands: creatures in the form of chickens or owls, Kibwegu spirits with their white faces and red beards, the cleft-footed Ngoloko who lingered in mangrove swamps and lured men to their deaths on their iron pointed fingernail. The farther one moved into the African interior, the more fearsome the prospects. Stigand, for example, relates Swahili beliefs in the great snake, Nondo, and even an entire hill, both of which were capable of swallowing whole caravans.[79] Thus, Swahili townsmen traditionally have divided their universe in true structuralist fashion between their town – representing order, civilization (*uungwana*), and predictability – and the world outside it – representing chaos, barbarity (*ushenzi*) and the fear-inspiring unknown.

Not surprisingly, this arrangement of the moral universe is featured prominently in oral traditions. Due to the fact that this order (as was the building of town walls) was conditioned greatly by late medieval historical developments, it is quite likely that such traditions date from this era. Certainly the various stories of migration out of Shungwaya do. More interesting are traditions which tell of definite 'breaks' made with the mainland. Examples include the various Pununu/Rurunu stories previously mentioned, as well as Bajun tales of their conversion to Islam after which, it is claimed, they were forced to destroy all traces of their African identity.[80] Included in this category, also, are the stories of the ritual separation of the coastal town from the outside world. In all three versions of the 'Kilwa Chronicle', including the sixteenth-century Arabic and Portuguese renderings, the town is separated from the 'Kafir' mainland through a purchase and a ritual reading of the Quran over the island.[81] Similar traditions exist for Pate, Mogadishu, and Takwa (though they might date from a later time). The Pate and Mogadishu versions tell again how Islamic magic, formulated by charismatic *shurafa* or *°ulama°* detach the town in question from the mainland or protect it from the attacks of Oromo or Portuguese insurgents.[82] Takwa, a small town which existed from the fifteenth to the late seventeenth centuries, appears to have been settled largely by migrants from the mainland towns (for example, Uziwa) of the Lamu hinterland which were under siege at that time by the Oromo, the Portuguese, or soldiers of Pate. It also appears to have been selected and built primarily for its defensive potential. As Wilson observes, its location made it fairly inaccessible from the sea; it was surrounded by a wall and a mangrove swamp, and its single-storied construction effectively cut it off from the vision of mainland and ocean-borne marauders. In the traditions, rather than having been separated from the mainland, it was said to have been made invisible by its ritual experts, the *wanavyuoni*.[83]

By the end of the Middle Ages, then, many northern coastal towns were becoming what they since have been remembered as being, namely, refuges for those fleeing from danger, shelters to those who sought a 'civilized' existence.[84] Where some started as mixed villages of Bantu and Cushitic farmers, herders, and fishermen, by the sixteenth century some had expanded into cosmopolitan centres of mixed African and Middle Eastern peoples which had evolved their own distinct forms of language, economy, culture, and religion. In evolving this new civilization, coastal peoples started simply by filling an ecological niche based on an accumulated storehouse of African experience and wisdom. Yet special opportunities were presented by the niche along with its special conditions. Adaptation to these conditions presented coastal Africans with opportunities to accumulate new and more forms of wealth and to assume new cultural and religious forms not available to their African ancestors and neighbours. Theirs was a new world at the edge of a cultural frontier. As this world expanded through widening cultural contacts, new experiences engendered cultural and religious experimentation. Yet the culture that developed remained still a child of its human and physical environment, being neither wholly African nor 'Arab', but distinctly 'coastal', the whole being greater than the sum of its parts. Thus, if they became Muslims, they did not become 'Arabs'; if they built mosques, their styles were neither recognizably African nor Middle Eastern; if their houses were stone, the 'stone' in fact was coral; and if they took Cushitic megaliths for their tomb markers, the tombs faced Mecca and again were constructed from locally available materials. And finally, if they still were Shungwayans in the fourteenth century, by the sixteenth century changing populations in the northern hinterland certainly destroyed this psychological association. More easily defended towns of the islands became safe areas for the inhabitants of mainland Shungwayan and Swahili settlements which did not survive the onslaughts of new immigrant peoples from the interior. Safety and the preservation of a civilization were found in stone fortifications and ritualized casting out of evil from the town, such as the *kuzunguo mji* rites.[85] While coastal peoples started out as 'Shungwayans', then, by the sixteenth century many had become Islamized 'Shirazi'. While a golden age was just ending, another era was about to begin.

3

A northern metamorphosis, 1500–1800

The purpose of this chapter is to examine the oral traditions of the northern coast dating from the sixteenth to the eighteenth centuries to see what they reveal about the evolution of northern coastal culture and religion in the early 'modern' period. Since much of this history centred on changes introduced when high-status immigrants settled among a local social core of 'Shirazi', it is important, first, to briefly review who or what these Shirazi represent in coastal traditions. Next, some attention will be given to information available from external (Arabic and Portuguese) sources concerning the nature of these immigrants and the impact they made on East African societies. Finally, a particular effort will be made to elucidate the meanings of the northern (especially Lamu) traditions themselves in light of the previous two sections.

THE SHIRAZI

The history and character of coastal towns, of course, developed not only from the relationships obtained with their natural environments, but also from those established among the various groups of people who settled the towns. A primary social ingredient of each town was a core of relatively ancient descent groups who were in fact often spread throughout several villages and towns of an entire region. These autochthonous clans underpinned larger economic, social, and political communities which might be characterized as confederations, alliances, or city-states. The ultimate unity of such communities of settlements depended on the type and degree of cooperation and coordination there was among these locally acknowledged indigenous 'families'. To cite one obvious example, there usually existed marriage or kinship bonds which transcended a particular town's precincts. Somewhat more formally, some descent groups seem to have observed critical rites of passage together, such as births, circumcisions, weddings, and funerals. Tacit recognition of common social, economic, and ethnic affinities and interests existed where descent groups, scattered throughout several neighbouring settlements, shared a monopoly of crucial regalia for political as well as social purposes. A Manda 'Shirazi' federation, based on a sharing of *siwa* and drums, for example, seems to have existed for Manda, Uziwa, Kitau, Kinarani, and possibly pre-'Arab' Lamu.[1] A similar alliance founded on the sharing of regalia and common military action existed for Ozi, another 'Shirazi' network which included some clans from 'Quitau',

Mwana, Shaka, Ungwana, Malindi, and possibly Uziwa and the Hidabu Hill settlement at Lamu. Farther south, other towns like Mombasa, Vumba Kuu, and Kilwa were at the heads of their own alliances (and probably trade networks).[2]

Another feature of Swahili towns was that they were heavily populated by people who had, at one time or another, immigrated to them from other locations. As towns grew and developed, groups of immigrants from neighbouring peoples and nearby city-states undergoing various stages of decay were added onto the local social 'underlayer'. Both Lamu and Pate, for instance, played host to people who had abandoned the old Manda confederation, as well as to WaTikuu (later called Bajun, from the coast north of Lamu) and Somali who sought refuge from the social upheavals of mainland Shungwaya in the sixteenth and seventeenth centuries. As has been indicated, too, coastal towns had been experiencing overseas immigration since at least the thirteenth century. Continued arrivals, primarily from the Hadhramawt, were to remain an especially important facet of northern coastal history during the period under consideration here.

A crucial aspect of the development of many coastal settlements was the persistent, frequent necessity of integrating groups of such newcomers (*wageni*) with the established social order within them. One thing, then, which characterized the coastal town was that it institutionalized change introduced by such immigrants and, furthermore, the internal structures created to institutionalize such change reflected the fundamental ambivalence townspeople felt towards the outside world. The basic problem for the Swahili town was that of maintaining order and continuity in town life while creating unity out of diversity, one society out of many. Not surprisingly, in the larger towns where several or many ethnic groups of diverse ethnic origins were found, there was a tendency towards social fragmentation.[3] Extended kinship units (initially at least) usually settled individually in their own residential areas or wards (*mitaa*). Social and economic rivalry among all the wards, therefore, was a normal feature of town life. Yet there were countervailing institutions which helped make the town a unit. The first was Islam itself, a monotheistic religion for all people regardless of their genealogies, antiquity of settlement, wealth, ethnicity, or origins. Associated with this were the Friday mosque, which 'belonged' to all townspeople, and the various religious functionaries and notables who kept local Muslims in a state of righteousness and grace. Then there were also the community-wide rituals, often associated with the solar new year (*siku ya mwaka*), such as the *kuzunguo* rites and annual visits to tombs of local saints and heroes.

Paradoxically, though, the most integrating aspect of town life was its dual structure, its organization into paired opposites, as observed by Lienhardt and Prins.[4] The moieties, called *mikao*, served as institutions by which networks of relationships basically found in the ward could be recast into larger communities of commitment or alliances more capable of representing the interests of whole collections of descent groups on a community-wide basis.[5] The organizational principle should be most familiar to structuralists, centred as it was on the human tendency to impose overlaying symmetrical patterns of organization on diverse phenomena. In such an arrangement, the world is cast into positives and negatives, of 'we' versus 'them', of 'yeas' and 'nays', where community issues are concerned.

In the Swahili town such structuring reflected the ambivalence which townspeople felt towards the world outside the town inasmuch as the town binaries were organized around principles of inclusiveness versus exclusiveness, usually expressed in terms of putative seniority of arrival and settlement in the town.[6] Diversity, ethnic multiplicity, and the striving of forces and ideas representing older social descent groups pitted against (relative) newcomers, of haves against have-nots, came to focus on the actions of these matched but opposed pairs of alliances. Standing as they did between the anarchy represented by allegiance to the kin group and the conservatism of local aristocracy, between new arrivals and old 'families', the moieties functioned as socio-political instruments of controlled change. Indeed, it was from contesting binaries within towns that change took place at all, while it was through the functional complementarity of the moieties that it was controlled.

Yet to conclude discussion of town societies and of the moieties specifically, it was through this institutionalization of social tensions that ultimately made town unity possible. As Turner expresses it,

> The unity of such a pair is that of a tensed unity or *Gestalt*, whose tension is constituted by ineradicable forces or realities, implacably opposed, and whose nature as a unit is constituted and bounded by the very forces that contend within it. If these mutually involved irrepressibles belong together in a human being or social group, they can also constitute strong unities, the more so if both principles or protagonists in the conflict are consciously recognized and accepted.[7]

This understanding of the problems of accommodating immigrants and the specific institutions which many urban societies evolved for handling these problems constitutes an important key for unlocking the meanings of many oral narrative traditions from the coast.[8] Of particular interest among these are the so-called Shirazi traditions. As indicated in the last chapter, these stories of the alleged Persian or Shirazi origins of many coastal clans should not be taken at face value. Rather, most oral narrative histories like the Shirazi accounts are recited by oral historians as highly personalized interpretations of the past based upon their own understanding of present social arrangements.[9] Thus, the structures and functions of such accounts relate more to very recent history or to the present itself than to the more remote happenings which they purport to elucidate.

This does not mean that traditions like the Shirazi accounts are useless as sources of history as it is understood by the Westerner. Quite the contrary is true. Recent studies of various East and Central African peoples have shown that, while oral histories cannot be accepted in literal form as history, they are structured, highly interpretive *secondary* renderings of history which frequently do preserve some useful historical information (called clichés) from the past.[10] Presumably, then, one can hope to obtain such historically useful information from oral traditions by taking into consideration their relationships with present social arrangements. Yet it is important to add here that even structuring, as a reflection of social institutions, people's cosmologies, and their self-perceptions – in short, as a reflection of culture itself – is an end result of historical evolution. Accordingly, the way in which traditions are structured can be historically instructive. Thus, where humans tend to interpret the past in terms of the present, the precise terms in which these tendencies are articulated are revealing to the historian.[11]

The so-called Shirazi traditions are very widespread and there are far more extant versions than the few which have been published so far. Certainly, nowhere near all of them have been collected and of those which have, only a few will be considered here. This brief study obviously cannot claim to be exhaustive since it is not within the scope of this work to attempt such an undertaking. (However, the approach taken herein has been dealt with in greater detail in another publication, and the interested reader is referred to it.[12]) Rather, only a couple of relevant points will be made as a suitable introduction to a more detailed analysis of some northern coastal traditions. What is desired at this point is to suggest a new method of understanding the Shirazi genre of traditions through examining a few published versions, to which attention must now be drawn.

Two points immediately emerge from such an examination.[13] The first is that extravagant claims of Middle Eastern origins usually are made. As pointed out above, such claims are rarely to be taken literally since they primarily represent the tendency of many Swahili to invent conspicuous genealogies for themselves. That they usually purport Middle Eastern origins for the coastal townsman is easily understandable in view of their Islamic religion in which Persians and Arabs have been its most prestigious representatives as well as its greatest rivals. Such genealogies and claims, like Arabic *nisbas*, are easily assumed and mirror the coastal Muslim's personal identification with his faith. Since he understands that Islam came from the Middle East, and since his ancestors were Muslims, then, unless he is prepared to acknowledge openly the non-Muslim status of his more remote (African) forefathers, he reasons that they must have immigrated from the Middle East at some time.

A revealing feature of these traditions, though, is how the ambivalence of the Swahili townsman's relationships with the outside world is expressed in the dualisms built into their structures. Again, it is important to note that, while the tendency of people to think, to organize, and to act in pairs is universal, the nature of these pairings in Swahili society, the terms in which such oppositions were perceived and expressed, were historically conditioned by the frequent arrival of strangers. The conditions they describe were genuine. And the fact that such ambivalence existed expressed the 'historical' connections between Swahili society and African and Middle Eastern societies alike.

Two varieties of dualisms can be observed in the traditions. The first concerns the opposition of the town to its African environment. The three versions of the Kilwa tradition (nos. 1–3: again, see note 13) illustrate this well, as was discussed already in the last chapter. In the last four traditions (nos. 13–16 in note 13), too, something of the traditional Swahili attitude towards the bush (*nyika*) is present. In these, it is clear that being savage, lost, uncouth, astray, or without religion is associated with being on the mainland, outside coastal society.

More striking is that, with the exception of no. 3, all these stories through no. 12 present the essential opposition of Shirazi (or African locals) to 'Arab' strangers. Simple opposition of Arabs sent by an Umayyad Caliph and Shirazi/Persians sent by an Abbasid is stated explicitly in nos. 7 and 8. Such opposition is implied in two versions (nos. 1 and 2) of the Kilwa Chronicle. In the Arabic rendition (no. 1), the author appears to be defending the nobility of the pre-Arab inhabitants against later Yemeni (Mahdali) settlers by relating a story of the Shirazi origins of the town's previous rulers, then stating, 'and this is firm evidence that they were kings in their own land'. Likewise, in the Barros account (no. 2), Ali b. Hocen, the Shirazi, avoids Arab Mogadishu and Brava (Barawa), significantly enough, because he is both black and Persian. Explicit pairing or opposition appears in the remaining samples, but they go somewhat further in equating 'Arabs' with intrusive late-comers who displace more ancient and indigenous African or Shirazi regimes through intermarriage (nos. 5, 11, and 12), chicanery (nos. 4 and 6), conquest (no. 9), or murder (no. 10). Taken altogether, then, these samples betray an essential meaning of the Shirazi genre of traditions. In all these, the Shirazi exist as one half of a pair of which earlier indigenous Africans or Arab interlopers are the other (and opposing) half. Such pairs exist by virtue of each other as 'ineradicable forces implacably opposed', in Turner's words, contending within Swahili societies through time as 'mutually involved irrepressibles'. In part, their origins lie in the Swahili penchant for inventing genealogies which put them squarely in the mainstream drama of Islamic history, noble genealogies which gave them impeccable credentials as Muslims. It is easy to see how local Muslims, with their, if anything, frequently 'unorthodox' (neither African nor Arab) religious practices, might have been subjected to the censure of immigrant *sharif* and *shaykh* clans, as did occur from time to time. In defending themselves and their religious heritage, a counter-myth was assumed which accounted for their cultural differences from Arabs in terms of the cultural rivalry which historically has existed between Persian and Arab Muslims. By this interpretation, then, the notion of a Shirazi 'period' in coastal history, spoken of by some historians, requires modification. One set of traditions could not exist without the other. Given this, rather than speaking of a Shirazi tradition, perhaps it would be more accurate to speak of a Shirazi/Arab tradition in coastal history – or even in other circumstances, of an African/Shirazi pairing.

The 'Shirazi' then were the Swahili *par excellence*, those original 'people of the coast' mentioned above. Though they were first cousins to Bantu-speaking neighbours and assumed some cultural traits of Middle Eastern peoples, they had evolved as a distinct people and culture in the Middle Ages. Traditions of the sort discussed above show an awareness of these distinctions through the pairings and dualities they portray. Their origins are difficult to ascertain. However, their historicity lies in the conditions which gave rise to them. These, of course, would logically have emerged in periods and places where change and the influx of 'Arab' strangers were at a peak. Such peaks did occur on the northern coast in the thirteenth century and centred on Mogadishu. In the late thirteenth and fourteenth centuries, again there was widespread settlement of immigrant Arabs on the southern coast, a fact which was connected with the rise of Kilwa's commercial fortunes. The tradition, then, probably originated sometime after the twelfth century and thereafter spread along the coast to the many coastal centres which experienced the social and cultural tensions that accompanied expansion of scale, noticeably heightened levels of immigration, and intensified contact with imported ideas.[14]

The term 'Shirazi' originally also might have been used as a distinctive designation of the people of the coast in place of the more recent 'Swahili'.[15] The culture implications of how the term is used in the traditions, however, seem clear. The 'Shirazi' were the original social core of recognized local kin groups, referred to above, whose claims to residence in their coastal environs were putatively the most ancient. North of the Tana River, they were those Islamized, urban Africans who had experienced a cultural 'migration' from Shungwaya to become 'Shirazi'; hence, they were the 'Shirazi' who 'came from' Shungwaya, as some nineteenth-century visitors to the coast were told.[16] They lived as palm tappers, farmers, fishermen, and small-scale traders who practised a few crafts such as canoe-making and shipbuilding, as well as iron-working, carpentry, and stone work. They dwelt in single-storied, rectangular mud and wattle houses, though as Muslims they built lavish mosques and tombs out of more durable coralline materials.[17] Also, in his fairly easy relations with the African hinterland and peoples, the legendary Fumo Liongo probably represents, as much as any model, an idealized Shirazi.[18] Like Fumo Liongo, too, Shirazi possessed such regalia as the *siwa*, drums, spears, and medicine bag which they inherited as part of their African patrimony from Shungwaya. Their Islam, like their literature, was primarily unlettered, their religious outlooks and 'laws' less 'orthodox' because they included practices inherited from their African past and transmitted orally.[19] In short, they were those predominantly rural and village Swahili who, in the cosmopolitan environment of growing commercial centres where they encountered their African neighbours and more sophisticated, lettered immigrants from the Middle East and India, felt compelled as Muslims themselves to establish a distinctive identity and to defend their ways of life, culture, and religious ideals by inventing counter-myths and genealogies of their own offset to the pretensions of their new neighbours. Despite their efforts to preserve their identity however, change was inevitalbe in their lives and towns.

THE RISE OF PATE AND THE LAMU 'ARABS'

The Lamu archipelago in the sixteenth and seventeenth centuries served as the setting for an important groundswell in modern coastal history. Where the older centres of commercial wealth and refinement at Kilwa and Mombasa[20] had entered a declining phase in the sixteenth century, a new impetus was imparted to coastal trade and cultural advancement by events in Pate and Lamu. Immigration once again was a prominent feature of these occurrences. The arrival of newcomers from the Benadir ports and from southern Arabia led to increased conversions to Islam, along with the partial displacement of the older 'Shirazi' groups and cultural traits by new ideals which were more urban and, from a religious standpoint, more lettered and more 'orthodox'.[21] While new cultural vistas were opened up and more people converted to Islam, most people pulled together in the face of Portuguese missionary activity and, in an important sense, old religious principles were simply reaffirmed despite the fact that it was the presence of Arab strangers who did the strengthening. In the meantime, it is essential that the causes and nature of this cultural and religious rebirth be explored from available external sources.

First, what began in the sixteenth century as a cultural revival on the northern coast, in fact, was a continuation of the commercial and cultural developments which had begun in the thirteenth century. Contact and trade primarily had been with southern, southwestern, and western Arabia, often through Indian merchants. Eastern Africa, from Zeila and Berbera north of the Horn to Kilwa and the Comoros in the south, had experienced fairly extensive migrations from those regions. North of the Horn, Muslims had been infiltrating areas east and southeast of the Ethiopian plateau, putting pressure on the Solomonic dynasts of Abyssinia. By the fifteenth century, holy wars had been declared on Christian Ethiopia and, under the capable generalship of Ahmad Grañ, by the 1520s these *jihads* were close to eliminating Christianity from northeast Africa altogether.[22] South of the Horn, Yemeni ruling houses had been ensconced at Kilwa and Mogadishu. Under their rule, these towns had played host to leading *shurafaᵓ* and Hadrami intellectuals and had become important centres for the Islamization of coastal Africans.[23] By the fifteenth century the northern part of this coastline, especially Mombasa, Malindi, and probably Mogadishu, had overshadowed Kilwa as the focus of overseas trade routed principally through the Red Sea nexus.

The fortunes of Islam, however, were thrown into temporary abeyance in the sixteenth century when the Portuguese, led by Affonso d'Albuquerque, seized effective control of the western Indian Ocean. The hardest blow to coastal fortunes was the severance of the gold and ivory trade through Sofala, which followed the assaults on Kilwa in 1505 and their seizure of the Zambezi route.[24] Mombasa, likewise, suffered three devastating attacks in the sixteenth century, while Portuguese attempts at imposing monopolies and customs stations at Mombasa, Dondo, Siyu, and Pate had a dampening effect on northern trade for a while.[25] In Ethiopia, they allied themselves with the *Negus* and finally defeated Ahmad Grañ's *jihad* in 1543.

Islam south of the Horn also suffered reversals under Portuguese hegemony. For their part, the Portuguese partially considered their activities on the coast and elsewhere as a crusade against infidel Muslims. Hence, they could hardly have been expected to give quarter where the interests of Muslims were at stake. Violent assaults against civilian populations were launched under the eyes, and with the apparent approval, of Catholic clergymen who sailed with the fleets.[26] Once a town had been occupied by force, often these same clergy were introduced with or without the consent of local peoples.[27] Active proselytization began in the 1560s when the Jesuits started work on the southern coast, to be followed soon afterwards by the Dominicans and Augustinians at Mombasa, Zanzibar, Faza, and Pate.[28] Though these missions do not appear to have achieved great overall success, some concern must have been felt among local Muslims by their ability to make inroads among the lower classes and non-Muslim Africans. There are a number of reports, too, of a few triumphs among ruling families at Pemba, Zanzibar, and Faza.[29] More serious damage was done, though, by direct interference in the administration of local religious law and practice. At Kilwa in 1506, for instance, they appointed *qadis*,[30] and in 1596 the Sultan of Malindi was compelled to report all civil and criminal cases against local Muslims to the Portuguese captain.[31] Beyond this, too, there was the notorious Inquisition which was introduced in the 1560s, and produced, no doubt, a general atmosphere of fear and demoralization among some Muslims.[32] Consequently, Muslim merchants began avoiding the larger towns, fearing denunciations of their faith and blatant disrespect for their religious laws.[33]

Ironically, it was this commercial and religious aggressiveness of the Portuguese which was a major factor in stirring cultural and religious revival on the coast. This revival was rooted, in the first instance, in resistance to Portuguese oppression in ports which had maintained strong commercial links with the north and Red Sea region. The fact that the Portuguese never conquered Mogadishu, let alone imposed any control over her trade, meant, for one thing, that the old coastal connections with Arabia and the Red Sea remained unbroken.[34] Once Mombasa had been effectively destroyed as the key entrepôt on the Kenyan coast, Pate was in a position to assume a leading part in coastal trade. After taking advantage of Aweera willingness to trade, and having established a *modus vivendi* with the powerful Oromo, Pate secured a standing as the most important supplier of ivory on the coast. Other valuable mainland products also were obtainable for overseas trade. Among these were cowries, beeswax, tortoise shell, civet, and ambergris.[35] The real key to Pate's fortunes, though, was its ability to maintain the old 'northern connection' as a means of sidestepping the meddlesome Portuguese. In 1569, Monclaro noted that Pate already enjoyed 'a large commerce' with Mecca and the Red Sea. Another seventeenth-century source mentioned the extent of Indian Ocean trade passing through Pate by then, much of it 'illegally', while on the other hand, Patean skippers plied their seagoing trade northwards to Barawa, Merka, and Mogadishu, none of which was paying customs due to the Portuguese.[36]

As had happened in previous centuries, this 'northern connection' was a source of much more than trade goods. It appears that a combination of opportunism and an extension of the religious (and commercial) war that had been lost in Ethiopia brought a number of Benadir, Hadrami, and Yemeni clans to Pate and Lamu after the 1520s. Many of these new arrivals were clans of *shurafaʾ* and *mashayikh* who had fought beside Ahmad Grañ. While initial successes had attracted them to the *jihad*, heavy casualties suffered after 1500, floods in 1532–3, famine in 1538–9, and finally their bitter defeat drove many of them to look elsewhere for places to settle.[37] The northern East African coast was a logical choice for those with a crusading zeal and a desire to trade.

How and why these immigrants chose Pate seems likely to have stemmed both from a desire on their part to rid the Indian Ocean of the Christians and Pate's need to cope with the Oromo and the Portuguese to develop its trade. For the purposes of dealing with the Portuguese, some of these clans were particularly well qualified. Among them were various *sharif* clans like the famed Abu Bakr bin Salim, the Jamal al-Layl, and the Shatiri, as well as families of *mashayikh* like the Ba Barayk. All of these clans were famous for their piety and erudition in Islamic law (*fiqh*) and Quranic exegesis (*tafsir*) and had produced many *qadis*, *khatibs*, and *faqihs*. Most noteworthy was their affiliation with the Alawi *tariqa*, an especially austere brotherhood devoted to learning and the veneration of saints.[38] Its principal shrine at Inat was founded and maintained by the Abu Bakr b. Salim.[39] This clan was the most charismatic of southern Arabia's famous clans of *manasib* notable for their piety, militancy, and sterling qualities as mediators of disputes among the warring bedouins.[40] In short, they possessed many qualities which were needed on the coast in the sixteenth and seventeenth centuries.

Another clan, the Ba Barayk of Shihr, also was famous for its learning, as well as for its commercial acumen in a city which had become the most important commercial centre in southern Arabia by the sixteenth century. They were divided into two sub-clans, one of which, the Nabhan, became the famous ruling dynasty in Pate during the course of the sixteenth century.[41] Another branch settled in Lamu where they became locally known as the Bereki.

The Benadir port of Barawa made its contribution to the changing situation on the northern coast through the resettlement of the Amarani, particularly the Hatami clan, which probably arrived in the area sometime between 1540 and 1650.[42] Again, trade seems to have been an important motive which brought the Barawans to the Lamu archipelago, though they too played a crucial role in its cultural revival.

A number of sources are most explicit and in general agreement over what brought the 'Arabs' to the Lamu region and how they were perceived locally. The Swahili were aware, particularly, of the reputation for militancy and religious purity among these families of southern and Yemeni Arabs who had fought and proselytized in Ethiopia.[43] The Portuguese and Oromo had been oppressing them and splitting their loyalties.[44] Above all, then, they needed leadership to unite them, to reaffirm their religious values, and to help them advance their budding commercial fortunes. Thus, they 'sent for' assistance from the most charismatic of the Hadhramawt's saintly *mansab* clans, the Abu Bakr b. Salim of Inat.

According to tradition, two scions of this house, brothers named Ali and Husayn, came to renew the people's faith and to made supplications so that the land might be delivered from the infidels.[45] Traditions differ as to which enemy the *shurafa°* overcame, the Oromo or the Portuguese.[46] However, the outcome is the same in all versions. Bringing with them the favour of God that comes with piety and righteousness, their enemies were bound to fail. The *shurafa°* thereafter resided in Inati and Shindoni *mitaa* at Pate. Though they never shared formal power with the Nabahani, they were heavily involved with its commercial fortunes and they maintained their religious influence. Thus, in 1569–71, a Catholic priest was led to say of Pate and its newly found religious leadership, 'Its Moorish priest was the chief of all on the coast.'[47]

The Barawans, too, had an important part in the renewal of the coast. They are remembered in Pate tradition, as well as from those collected on the Mrima coast, for having been instrumental in bringing commercial wealth and for building stone houses and wells – presumably all related phenomena.[48] More importantly, though, is that some traditions remember them as 'Arabs' (that is, Muslim immigrants from the north?) who taught 'religion' and the Quran to local non-Muslims or lapsed Muslims (see note 13, nos. 8 and 15). Again, the question is how to interpret such traditions. Did these 'Arabs', be they Amarani or Abu Bakr bin Salim or Barayk, actually convert coastal people to Islam? Undoubtedly they did in many cases. While it is true that many coastal peoples, particularly those associated with the major commercial centres in the late medieval period, were already Muslims, it is likely that large numbers in the more remote rural areas still were non-Muslims. It is equally likely that coastal Islam, often as a local indigenized form, was not recognized as 'true' Islam by militant purists and proselytizers like the Abu Bakr bin Salim or the more urbanized Amarani of Barawa. In short, these local Muslims again were the 'Shirazi', and these traditions relate the sort of Shirazi/Arab stand-off discussed above.[49]

Once this movement for religious renewal caught on in the Lamu archipelago, it spread. Various Arab houses moved on to other coastal locations and produced important changes wherever they settled. Besides Pate, the Barayk also went to Lamu along with various *sharif* houses. Among the *shurafa°*, the Husaynid branch of the Abu Bakr bin Salim spread to Siyu (where they are called Saqqaf) and to Lamu, while members of both the Husaynid and Alid branches migrated to the Comoro Islands.[50] Other Alawi *shurafa°* houses moved to the Comoros, Zanzibar, Ozi, and Vumba Kuu. Especially prominent were the Al-Masila Ba Alawi.[51] Some of this clan apparently settled within the old Shirazi federation of Ozi, while others went to Lamu and Moheli in the Comoro Islands.[52] Sometime between about 1650 and 1705, a number of them resettled in Zanzibar, where, it is related, they were invited to help avert a plague.[53] From there, some migrated to Kilwa and to the Vumba Kuu area where, in conjunction with the Ba Amiri *shurafaʾ* and other Al-Masila and Bauri from Ozi, sultanates were established. The most notable of these was that of the Diwan Ruga at Vumba Kuu.[54]

Before concluding this section, brief attention must be paid to the impression these newcomers made on coastal peoples. First of all, it is very clear from the lone Portuguese reference to them (Monclaro), as well as from the traditions, that the *shurafaʾ* and the Barayk had enormous charisma everywhere they settled. As noted by Professor Martin, often they were viewed as healers and mediators. Traditions recall that they were invited to Pate, Zanzibar, and Vumba Kuu to mediate in local squabbles, to ward off internal discord and external enemies alike. They were viewed as God's special people, capable of interceding in relief of the unfortunate, of guaranteeing peace and prosperity (*imani*), of acting in defence of a town against its assailants both seen and unseen.

In some places they capitalized on this prestige by establishing a political base. Thus, Ba Alawi sultanates were secured in the Comoros, Kilwa, Zanzibar, Tumbatu, and at Vumba Kuu. The methods varied according to the situation. Peaceful intermarriage with local dynasts appears to have been the means followed in the Comoros and at Vumba Kuu. At the same time, violent opposition to their pretensions seems to have been fairly common. For instance, oral tradition suggests that opposition was met from older 'Shirazi' houses at Ozi, Vumba Kuu, and Tumbatu.[55] The nature of this conflict in the Lamu region is the subject of the following section.

ORAL TRADITION AND LAMU'S 'TIME OF TROUBLES'

It will be noted that previous discussions of the pre-sixteenth-century history have been based almost entirely on linguistic, archaeological, and written accounts. Why not oral traditions? Of course, there are some traditions available that actually were recorded in the sixteenth century, most notably the various versions of the 'Kilwa Chronicle' which have been used appropriately in discussions of the late medieval period. Where the northern coast is concerned, however, there are no traditions at hand which were recorded before the middle of the nineteenth century. Therefore, it seems extremely unlikely that, out of the collection presently available for historical analysis, there is anything much which refers to events which occurred, at the outside, earlier than the sixteenth century. It is more likely, in fact, that most recorded oral traditions from the northern coast are post-seventeenth century.

And why should one reach this conclusion? First, because as a general rule, it is now believed that oral traditions, especially narratives, rarely refer to events which occurred more than about three hundred years before the time of their collection.[56] Secondly, while these traditions seem to contain some vague, stylized references to the late medieval period, for the most part they refer to conditions which are known to have originated only in the period of the northern coast's 'time of troubles' which started in the

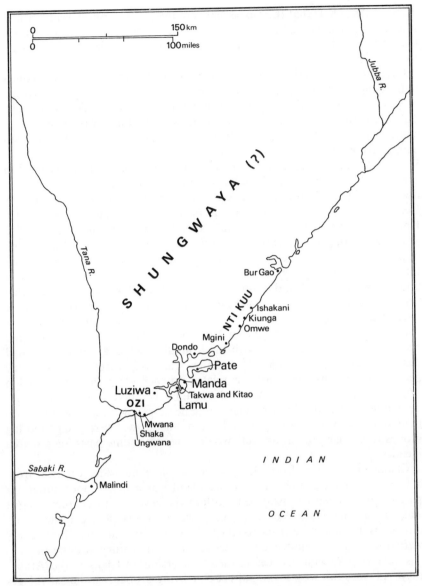

2 The Northern coast

sixteenth century and which reached a climax in the seventeenth. Thus, a fairly detailed historical analysis, which uses the traditions employed herein, is possible only for this period.

An important point is immediately apparent from a review of some of the traditions from the coast north of the Tana River. There was a pre-seventeenth-century population in this region whose modes of living were broadly alike and who shared vaguely similar sources of identity. Most

43

decisive, though, is that their experiences of the period from the sixteenth to seventeenth centuries made it a 'time of troubles' for many of them, which thus reinforced and gave additional meaning to their erstwhile more vaguely shared identity.

One clue to this is the claim commonly made by northern coastal peoples to have migrated from Shungwaya. Such traditions exist among the Pokomo and the Bajun, particularly those of Somali descent, which Wakefield, Talbot-Smith and Elliott recorded (and which Nurse has managed to collect more recently).[57] By the fifteenth century (earlier in some cases), an entire string of proto-Bajuni settlements existed along the shoreline of Shungwaya, stretching from Bur Gao to the region of the Tana River.[58] In oral traditions, these small, ocean-hugging fishing and farming villages north of Lamu comprised a region called Nti Kuu ('the great country'). Hence, coastal Shungwayans living in places like Yumbo, Kisimayu, Ishakani, Omwe, Kiunga, Uwani, Dondo, and Mgine were called WaTikuu.[59] In the sixteenth and seventeenth centuries, when the Oromo began making their presence felt, many of the WaTikuu and Somali immigrants from the Shungwaya hinterland fled to the nearby islands and became known as the Bajun and Famao.[60] Among the Pokomo, the Buu clan generally maintain that they migrated from a land to their northeast, while their legendary ancestor, Songo Vere, more specifically is reputed to have come from Munghia or Mgine in Nti Kuu.[61] The Dzundza and Kalindi clans have similar traditions, with the Kalindi alleging, again, to have had past associations with Mgine.[62] A Bajun tradition relates that almost all peoples of the northern coast are 'related' to each other through common origins and intermarriage.[63] While this is unlikely if taken literally, it should be pointed out that migration tales do indicate people's identification with their putative places of origin, and claims made by several neighbouring groups to similar origins, as such, would constitute some basis for a shared identity.[64]

Claims of migration from Shungwaya and Nti Kuu aside, it is clear from a variety of other sources that the mainland was a much more important part of the northern coastal scene before the seventeenth century than it was to be afterwards. For one thing, the archaeological evidence from numerous mainland settlements (like those of Nti Kuu) which suddenly were abandoned or destroyed in the seventeenth century is quite plain.[65] Also, the Bajun recall that before their 'conversion' to Islam by the 'Arabs', they had close ties with mainland peoples, living probably in mixed villages of the sort described in Chapter 1.[66] In one version of the classic stand-off between local 'Shirazi' and Arab interlopers, that model Shirazi, Fumo Liongo, is fabled to have ruled a kingdom which included the entire mainland littoral.[67] In the sixteenth century, Portuguese interrogators were told that the people of Uziwa and 'Quitau' once were 'lords' of most of the coast between Lamu and Malindi. The Bauri sultan of Malindi thus asserted that the rulers of these two mainland towns were his royal ancestors.[68]

With its own ties to various places and peoples of the mainland, Lamu

44

was undeniably an integral part of this northern coastal society before the seventeenth century. Uziwa, referred to in Lamu traditions as Ndeo, Mudiwo, or Miro.[69] seems to have been a conspicuous source of mainland influences in Lamu just as it was for Malindi. Its importance in the late medieval social history of Lamu is intimated, first, by Barros's disclosure that Lamu was one of Uziwa's 'subject' towns, and, secondly, by traditions from Lamu that Uziwa/Mrio was the original home of its *siwa* and drums. In several other stories, too, it is even claimed that the original name for Lamu itself was Mrio or Kiwa-Ndeo.[70] Other evidence, however, suggests that Uziwa was not sovereign to Lamu, but a sister city with which it shared a common social base and regalia.[71] Portuguese sources on at least one occasion even confused the respective identities of the two towns, and on another they implied that these towns shared the same ruler when they mentioned 'the king of Lamu or Luziva'.[72]

Lamu society consists of four major 'ethnic' groupings, as shown below:

Wayumbili ('not recognized')
Kinamti or *Kinanti*
   Bwana Maalim
   Bwana Mbakea (Mahdali)
   Bwana Mwinyi Mui (Makhzumy)
   Waungwana Ithnaashara ('abolished')
Famao
   Bwana Gogo
   Maawi (from Bwana Gogo)
   Bwana Hamisi wa Mwinyi Mui
   Bwana Tumani Ali
Waungwana wa Yumbe
   Bakari
   Bwana Mshuti Waziri
   Muhammad bin Yusuf
   Bwana Mbakea wa Mwinyi Mui (Jahadhmy)[73]

Tradition has it that originally Lamu consisted of two villages, one at Hidabu Hill, another at Weyoni. Of the above social groupings, the one thought to have been the earliest inhabitants of Hidabu Hill were the Kinamti. Some traditions claim that they came from Mrio/Uziwa, suggesting again that they were an autochthonous social element which tied the two communities together.[74] The Kinamti of Hidabu Hill, according to other traditions (see this chapter's Appendix, nos. 1 and 4), also had clear associations with some Pokomo clans. For example, where traditions associate Hidabu Hill with the Kinamti, others say its original inhabitants were Pokomo.[75] Likewise, some Pokomo traditions suggest such links. The Kalindi clan claim that they migrated from Shungwaya/Nti Kuu via Lamu and, under a chief named 'Hidabo', they eventually settled at Shaka. The Karara moiety of the Buu clan, at the same time, aver that they came originally from Hidabu Hill and, led by Songo Vere, they trekked to Moa and Mpekatoni 'near Kapini' in the company of the 'Kinamwiti'.[76]

Traditions of the Meru collected by Fadiman, who claim a Manda Island origin, also recall that the Buu lived on an adjacent island (that is, Pate or Lamu).[77] The tradition, however, which clinches the Kinamti–Pokomo link is the assertion made by the sultan of Malindi (a Bauri and a Pokomo) that his ancestors were 'kings' of Uziwa.[78]

All of Lamu's other three ethnic groups have traditions which tie them to Nti Kuu. When asked, informants were almost unanimous in their belief, for example, that Yanbu[c] or Yumbe or Yumbwa was the homeland of the Wayumbili, as shown in the traditions published in this chapter's Appendix.[79] Most said that this was the Yanbu[c] found in the Hijaz since they claim to be Arabs. However, there are several Yumbes and Yumbos, one of which was a village on the lower Jubba, while another was on the Nti Kuu coast near Ngumi and Koyama. A third existed on the mainland opposite Pate Island.[80] Some Waungwana wa Yumbe also claim to be from Yumbe in Nti Kuu, where it is said they were shipwrecked on a 'voyage' from the Hijaz.[81] The Famao, of course, are related to the Famao of Siyu, Dondo, and other Nti Kuu villages. While it is said they were of mixed overseas ancestry, it is more likely they are of WaTikuu and Somali blood, having ancient connections with Shungwaya.[82] Of these, the Bwana Gogo (and the Maawi clan of Lamu) are particularly interesting since they are noted in both Siyu and Lamu as the towns' ritual and religious specialists.[83]

Whatever 'original' identity some of these people north of the Tana River might have shared before the sixteenth century was reinforced by similar experiences most of them underwent between about 1500 and 1700. Most faced the multiple traumas of assaults from mainland pastoralists and the Portuguese, as well as social stresses arising from the arrivals of high status Arab immigrants in their midst. One result of these pressures was the creation of a newly styled coastal society by 1700 (see Chapters 4 and 5). While this mostly was a further elaboration of late medieval society on the northern coast, this society was a decidedly wealthier one. It incorporated new ideas and new norms, and the lifestyle it represented for some was altered from that of the old society it replaced.[84] External sources, of the sort used in the preceding section, and evidence from the remains of material culture of the period go far in supporting such views. The oral traditions of the period, however, tell rather more of the social, economic, and even cultural gaps which were opened between the new and old orders at that time.

For coastal mainland centres especially, it was an era of violence. Entire societies were forced to evacuate Shungwaya and flee southwards and to offshore islands, while social disruption caused by large-scale immigrations marked town life on the islands. The old social order which had existed before 1500 came under direct attacks, a common predicament remembered in a number of northern coastal traditions in remarkably similar ways. An examination of Table 1 and the traditions encapsulated in this chapter's Appendix reveals this. All of them employ similar clichés and recall congruent events. Stated in their most common and general terms, each tells how a charismatic community, under the special grace of God,[85] prevailed

Table 1: *Cultural breaks*

Location/subject	Action	Object	Reason
Set 1 – Reference:			
Chapter 1, pp. 15			
a. *Miji Kenda*			
Bridegroom	kills	a chief	*ius primae noctis*
b. *Bajun*			
Youth disguised as	kills	Ruruna	*ius primae*
a woman			*noctis*
b1. Variation: chief and	kill	chief of	*ius primae*
woman ruler		Pununu	*noctis*
c. *Famao*			
Famao	emigrate from	Pununu	*ius primae noctis*
Set 2 – Reference:			
Appendix			
d. *Lamu – no. 12*			
Woman and 40 youths	kill	Persian king of Manda	political and social?
d1. Variation: people	kill	many of 40	revenge
of Manda			
e. *Lamu – no. 9*			
40 youths	steal	Mudio/Mrio regalia	political and social?
Set 3 – Reference:			
note 13			
f. *Pate – no. 6*			
Nabahani	kill	40 African elders	cultural and social?
g. *Ozi – no. 10*			
Nabahani	kill	40 Shirazi elders	cultural and social?
Set 4 – Reference:			
Appendix			
h. *Lamu – no. 4*			
Pokomo and Suudi	kill	40 Tundani	cultural and social?
Arabs of Hidabu		Wayumbili	
i. *Lamu – no. 5*			
Kinamti and	kill	40 Wayumbili	cultural and social?
Makhzumy 'Arabs'			
j. *Lamu – nos. 1–3, 6, 10*			
Hidabu Arabs	kill/ defeat	Weyuni elders	cultural and social?

against another which was not so blessed. In Sets 1 and 2, the subjects of the drama depicted, a woman and some youths, specifically represent the wisdom and strength of the communities in question. Together with women, youths sometimes are used to represent the elders (*wazee*) of a community, a collective group who, through God's wisdom and the strength of its youthful warriors, assure the town's future.[86] *Wazee* is a term which refers to older people or elders in general, but specifically connotes *female* wisdom.[87] Wisdom, particularly the sagacity of the elderly, seems to be associated with femininity, a fact which is supported by the customary persona of wisdom, Mwana Mizee. A fine illustration of this interpretation is a poem which was composed in Lamu about 1812, at the time of its celebrated war with Pate and Mombasa which ended in a resounding victory for Lamu at Shela. In this poem, victory for the *waungwana* is sought through the blowing of the *siwa* 'of Mrio' and calling upon Mwana Mizee for wisdom. Thus, it is hoped that by these measures,

> God will judge between us and save us.
> By the help of the Blessed One who is highest and richest,
> By following this, [indeed] by following we shall triumph.[88]

In Sets 3 and 4, the situation is much the same, but the subject is precisely identified as 'Arabs' – the Nabahani of Pate and those of Lamu's Hidabu Hill/Suudi faction.

Two basic formulas are employed to describe what happened. Both indicate, again, the presence of internal discord due to social and economic distinctions. Several northern traditions explain the disappearance of entire communities by employing a simple cliché that wealth gives way to greed, which in turn leads to destruction. Elliott recorded two from Ngumi and 'Lukuva', whose annihilation is brought about when excessively affluent and greedy townspeople invite God's displeasure with attempts to cheat Portuguese or Arab merchants. The Arabs and Portuguese in turn destroy the towns.[89] Something quite similar happens at Hidabu Hill where God wreaks vengeance on the people for their intemperate use of milk for bathing.[90] At Kitau (Kitao or the unidentified 'Quitau'), the town is abandoned after a chicken (that is, witchcraft) enters the Friday mosque (town unity), causing bickering among the townspeople.[91] Finally, the traditional story of Manda's ultimate destruction relates how the wealth and overbearing pride of its ruling clan led to their downfall. The sultan abuses the little people, personified by the lowly fisherman Bakiumbe who betrays the town to Pate after complaining that the common people and fishermen have been treated 'as lowly folk unto slaves'. The social and economic disharmony at the root of Bakiumbe's grievance is revealed further when he laments that, 'we are all as well bred as they, save that everyone follows his own calling. This one hoes, another is a smith and another a palm-tapper.'[92]

Most traditions from this period, though, are of the classic Shirazi variety. Once more, they are structured around a break or stand-off between new principles standing for change (for example, immigrants) and an older regime. The breaks commonly employ similar action clichés. Thus, they are stories of murder, conquest, theft, or emigration, perhaps echoing graphically the violence of that age, but ultimately also the crucial and lasting cultural changes that ensued from it. When viewed in the latter way, however, they differ profoundly from the type of cliché exemplified in the previous paragraph. Where above, the destruction of defunct communities is explained in terms of the social splits brought on by their very prosperity, in surviving societies like Pate and Lamu, such divisions, as in Turner's *Gestalt* theory on social variance, constitute creative forces for synthesizing a new order.

Where these traditions thus present a 'Shirazi-like' predicament, in fact there are some versions which represent explicitly the old effete order as Shirazi or Persians. Fumo Liongo and the Bauri clan, *shahs* of Ozi and 'lords' of the coastal mainland from Lamu to Malindi, are reputed to have been descendants of Persians sent to the coast by Harun ar-Rashid.[93] At Ozi, as illustrated in Table 1, it was forty Shirazi elders who were assassinated by the Nabahani 'Arabs'. Likewise, Arabs at Lamu and Vumba Kuu are alleged to have 'conquered' Persians of the Manda federation and the eight Shirazi towns of ancient Vanga.[94]

In other traditions, it will be noted that they tell the same type of story but do not actually identify the vanquished order as Shirazi. For instance, while traditions collected in the nineteenth and early twentieth centuries equate ancient (coastal) Shungwaya with Shiraz, such traditions no longer are in circulation.[95] In one Pate tradition (Table 1, tradition 'f'), forty Africans are 'killed' rather than forty Shirazi. The Famao, seventeenth-century rivals of the Nabahani (clearly 'Arabs'), claim alternatively to be of Portuguese and Chinese, as well as Persian, descent.[96] In the various Lamu traditions recorded in Table 1 and this chapter's Appendix, it is said that the Wayumbili of Weyoni/Tundani were from Yanbuᶜ, Hijaz, rather than from Shiraz or Persia. Informants at Lamu, however, were very clear that these Wayumbili were the true autochthones of Lamu and the northern coast, the 'oldest' people of the town, its original owners (Appendix, no. 3). It is they, of course, who are 'conquered' in these traditions through a ruse employed by the 'Arabs' of Hidabu Hill – their implied stolidity thus justifying their low social status. The claims of their 'Arab' origins are, of course, fictitious and probably date from the (later) nineteenth century when they began assuming the Arab-like *nisba* of al-Lami.[97] There is little surviving information as to what previous form of identity they might have had.

Unquestionably, the 'conquests' of Hidabu Hill's 'Arabs' were closely tied to the rise of Pate's Arabs (Nabahani and *shurafaᵓ*) to a position of pre-eminence. Both towns experienced immigrations of the Barayk clan and various *sharif* houses, it will be recalled, and both claim to have 'conquered' older autochthonous groups at places like Uziwa and neighbouring Manda federation communities like Takwa.[98] Moreover, close social ties between the Arab elite in both towns also are indicated. Evidence of the noticeable rise in the material culture which both communities exhibit for the post-sixteenth-century period, and indications from the so-called Pate chronicle

49

that their commercial fortunes were linked, support this view.[99] While both towns maintain that they subdued (killed, conquered, stole from, etc.) an older social order, both claimed, and apparently shared and fought over, the symbols of that older regime's legitimacy, its regalia.[100] Several Pate sultans, too, had Lamu mothers and actually resided at Lamu rather than at Pate.[101]

Lamu was not alone in feeling Pate's preponderating influence since, as recounted in the preceding section, new ruling dynasties of *shurafaʾ* who arrived via Pate were founded at Ozi, Vumba Kuu, Tumbatu, Kilwa, and in the Comoros. Except possibly for Lamu, though, Pate's assertion of formal suzerainty over these other towns appears exaggerated. Rather, more informal influences from the wealth and trade routed through Pate[102] and the cultural lead taken by its *shurafaʾ* ('Its Moorish priest was chief of all on the coast') established the Arabs of Pate in a different role. Quite likely, what many places experienced were major changes funnelled through Pate. They recognized its growing lead in cultural and religious affairs, especially in the face of Portuguese opposition, and the cultural metamorphosis which was emerging from this confrontation.[103]

The subversion of the old order linked the 'defeated' Wayumbili and elements of the old Manda federation through their shared predicament. Traditions indicate clearly that after their own 'defeat', Shirazi from Uziwa, Manda, Takwa, and Kitao resettled in Lamu and became (at least attached to) the Waungwana wa Yumbe. It is said these 'newcomers' (*wageni*) settled 'north of Mrio', where at least some of them merged with the Wayumbili to form the Zena faction and succoured the Wayumbili in their 'struggle' with the 'Arab' Suudi faction.[104] These subverted people, Wayumbili and Waungwana wa Yumbe, nevertheless managed to hold on to some measure of status as the indigenous people of the coast, the 'children of the soil'. It is said, for example, that after Manda was vanquished, Pate and Lamu divided the regalia (Appendix, no. 12), while in another story the two towns actually quarrelled over which one the Manda 'Persians' were going to inhabit.[105] Some, like the Bakari and the Bwana Mshuti, actually did live in both towns and managed to intermarry with some of the leading 'Arab' families of both places.[106]

However, the Bwana Mshuti clan presents the most intriguing study. With reputed pre-seventeenth-century ties with Shungwaya and connections with Takwa, they must have been one of the original 'Shirazi' people of the coast.[107] They were among the 'Persians' of Takwa said to have resettled in Lamu following their 'conquest' by Pate of Lamu (see Table 1, Set 2; Appendix, nos. 13–15). At Lamu, they were given the title of Waziri and stewardship of the bronze *siwa*. This, of course, made perfect sense in view of the fact that they came from the federation from which the *siwa* reportedly was 'stolen', while, as one informant put it, their *shaykh* was the 'oldest person' around ('age' or alleged priority of habitation representing entitlement).[108]

Other traditions (Appendix, nos. 13 and 15), however, say that not all the old Shirazi order were content with their lot under the new 'Arabs' in towns

Table 2: *Terms of settlement*

Oral traditions	Terms
Lamu	
Appendix, no. 1	not to build defences, not to wear shoes; to wash the dead
Appendix, no. 2	not to intermarry with 'Arabs', not to wear shoes; gravediggers and washers of the dead
Appendix, no. 3	not to wear turbans; blacksmiths, to slaughter ritual ox, *kuzunguo, khatibs* of the Friday mosque
Appendix, no. 5	not to wear turbans or shoes; washers of the dead, 'insulting duties'
Appendix, no. 7	'Wayumbe' were fishermen and blacksmiths
alternative (Clive, 'Short History', 10)	Wayumbili represented the artisan class of the town
Manda and Shela	
Appendix, nos. 9–12	Manda confederation towns 'defeated', regalia 'stolen'
Appendix, no. 13	'defeated', not to wear turbans or sandals, not to build in stone
Appendix, no. 14	not to wear shoes or come to Lamu with (pack?) animals
Appendix, no. 15	'defeated', not to build in stone, could not live in Lamu as they wished
Vumba Kuu	
A.C. Hollis, 'Vumba', 282; W.F. McKay, 'Precolonial History', 71–5	*siwa*, drums, cymbals and throne 'stolen'; sandals, turbans, veils on women, umbrellas, wooden doors on houses not 'permitted'

like Lamu. Why not? The answer perhaps is summed up best in the tradition (no. 15) where it is said that in the new order of things they 'were not able to live altogether as they would wish [*sic*]'. Some chose to move to Shela where, however, terms by Lamu's Suudi Arabs were imposed on them in exchange for permission to settle. These conditions bear a striking resemblance to similar ones borne by other communities of 'conquered' Shirazi along the coast, including those of Vumba Kuu and the Wayumbili of Lamu. A comparison of these various terms, as shown in Table 2, goes farther than anything to support the case that all these versions of wars of conquest, emigration, murder, and theft related herein actually are relating similar phenomena. They also reveal the real nature of the notorious 'Arab' victories over the old regimes in that 'time of troubles'.

First, it is important to note that these 'terms' of agreement can be divided into positive and negative 'sanctions' which supposedly were imposed on the old order. Those they were enjoined to perform at Lamu were related to critical local rituals: guarding sacred regalia (Mshuti Waziri),

Table 3: *Cultural associations*

		Shungwayans	Shirazi	'Arabs'
Economy	Farmers	+	+	+/−
	Craftsmen	+	+	−
	Herders	+	+/−	−
	Fishermen	+/−	+	−
	Seamen	−	+	+
	Merchants	−	+/−	+
Education	Crafts	+	+	−
	Husbandry	+	+	−
	'Informal'[a]	+	+	+/−
	Quran	−	+	+
	Literary[b]	−	−	+
Literary	Oral	+	+	+
	Written	−	+/−	+
Houses	'Beehive'	+	−	−
	Nyumba[c]	−	+	−
	Majumba[d]	−	−	+

Notes:
+ = a likely activity or cultural association of the type indicated
− = an unlikely activity or association
+/− = only slight activity or an ambiguous cultural association
[a] Informal education = mores, norms, values, skills transmitted through oral traditions, narratives, tales, proverbs, saws, poems, songs, and dances
[b] Literary education = advanced Islamic sciences learned at a *madrasa* or in the house of a *mwanachuoni/shaykh*
[c] Nyumba = single-storied dwellings, rectangular in shape, built out of mud, coral rag, and thatch
[d] Majumba = multi-storied mansions built typically out of cut coral, coral lime plaster, and *makuti*

acting as *khatibs* in the Friday mosque (Bwana Gogo-Maawi), performance of *kuzunguo* rites, and funerary duties. In many ways, as in the instance of the Mshuti Waziri clan, such continuing functions would be expected of the old 'children of the soil', since African history is replete with similar situations where subverted old regimes continued as cult and ritual experts.

The rest of the terms of settlement establish, in a functionalist sense, these stories as elegant charter myths, related 'on the ground' to reflect the state of affairs as they existed after about 1700. By relating the socio-economic activities that people of the old order could *not* do, as well as what their avocations were, some of the structural features which separated 'Arabs' from 'Shirazi' are discernible. Thus, the fact that the 'conquered' peoples could be blacksmiths, palm-tappers (craftsmen in Table 3), farmers, and fishermen, while they could not live in multi-storied mansions with wooden doors (*majumba*) and veil their women, tells a great deal about the nature of the 'Arab' conquests in question. While the utilization of actual violence by Pate and Lamu Arabs cannot be dismissed, it would seem that the real conquests were less dramatic. As illustrated in Table 3, the time of troubles in the sixteenth and seventeenth centuries culminated in a socio-economic and cultural evolution which had started in 'Shungwaya', passed to an indigenous coastal ('Shirazi', people of the coast) phase, and ended in the emergence of some wealthy societies dominated cuturally by a *nouveau riche*, leisured class of 'Arabs'.

What (actual) Arab immigrants brought to Pate and Lamu was, first, a new lease of life. The old regimes were spiritually exhausted in the face of highly damaging assaults from mainland pastoralists and from the succession of Portuguese attacks, occupations, and reprisals.[109] The Arabs, bringing spiritual unction from the Islamic heartlands, plus reputations for aggressiveness and charisma, acted as a badly needed counterpoise to all this. Besides, they gave a fillip to the growing commercial importance of Lamu and Pate. The social and commercial contacts of clans like the Ba Barayk and the Jamal al-Layl which reached from the Comoro Islands to Indonesia made Pate and Lamu the hubs of a new coastal trade network from the seventeenth to the nineteenth centuries.[110] The wealth thus generated only further added to the charisma of the 'Arabs', drawing even some older coastal clans to identify with them – the so-called *waungwana* ('civilized', free Swahili).

It is these terms of settlement which reinforce this view. Only the wealthy 'Arabs' (Arabs and *waungwana* 'Arabs') could afford the luxuries of secluding ('veiling') their women who, in poorer times or less affluent rural ('Shungwayan') settings, were needed on the farm. Only the wealthy 'Arabs' could afford to build in stone; to erect magnificent, multi-storied mansions of the seventeenth and eighteenth centuries; to embellish them with carved wooden doors, plaster wall carvings, and niches.[111] Indeed, it seems that it was the stone mansion more than anything else which stood for the victory of the Arab 'haves' over the old order, the 'little people' who were the town craftsmen and menials, as well as their Portuguese enemies whom they defied and ultimately defeated.[112]

The fact that the Lamu 'Arabs' usually are associated with the Suudi faction (*Suudi* means 'successful' in Swahili), and the Pate Arabs with Shindoni ('place of conquest') quarter, suggests that these 'wars' in Lamu (and Pate?) might have taken the form of dance and poetry competitions (or *ngoma*) between moieties. This certainly has been one institutional means by which stresses for change have been handled. The fact that such competitions are called 'rivalries' (*mashindano*, from *kushinda* which means to conquer, overcome), reinforces this perspective. Professor Ranger identifies such competitions clearly as integrative mechanisms, built into Swahili urban societies as institutional channels for controlling change introduced from the outside. As Lienhardt observed of the *ngoma*, 'If one or other rival side embraces an innovation which proves to attract more people, the other

Table 4: *Recognition of mainland ties*

	Social	Cultural	Religious	Historical
Shungwayans	+	+	+	+
Shirazi	+	+	−	−
Arabs	+/−	−	−	−

Historical flow: Shungwayans → Shirazi → Arabs ⋯→ Shirazi

Note: + =recognized; − =not recognized

has to copy it.'[113] If this interpretation is correct, the 'wars' and 'conquests' actually refer to what was a fairly protracted process of social integration and cultural change from the sixteenth through the eighteenth centuries. The 'terms of settlement' tell us that the distinctions between Suudi and Zena (not places of residence, but factions composed of residents of binaries competing for prestige) grew to be mostly cultural. The fact that such growing disparities were reinforced by vocational differences and restrictions on intermarriage among *shurafa*', 'Arabs', and Wayumbili (in addition to the Swahili preference for cross-cousin marriage), means that a hypergamous class system developed in Lamu, a system of 'haves' and 'have-nots'.

What had started culturally in Shungwaya ended in 'Arabia', then, after having passed through an intermediate 'Shirazi' phase. The entire process was underscored and propelled forward by three factors: a growing cultural self-consciousness among coastal peoples, growing wealth, and immigration. Religious change came primarily in the form of greater numbers of converts to Islam, but also by a renewal, if only temporarily, of contact with the literate Islamic tradition of southern Arabia. The Husayni and Abu Bakr bin Salim clans, especially, seem partially to have avoided total integration in this period, and managed to retain at least some of their literate tradition. The process of changing cultural associations for most, however, did not proceed in one direction only. Before the nineteenth century at least, Africa, like Persia, usually conquered its conquerors. Within two or three generations, even the 'Arabs' were strongly integrated into Swahili society and culture.[114] The last and most intensive period of Arabization of the coast was yet to come.

Appendix

1. Arabs from Damascus were sent by Caliph Abdu'l-Malik ibn Marwan and settled at Hidabu Hill. More came and they grew ever more powerful, but they learned that another town was nearby named Weyoni whose people came from Yunbuᶜ. The people of Weyoni were called Wayumbili. The people of Hidabu wanted to conquer Weyoni, so they fought until both sides were exhausted. Each side then sent a messenger seeking peace. The messengers met between the two towns. The man from Hidabu asked the Weyoni messenger what his message was and the Weyoni man told him he had a letter asking for peace. When the Hidabu messenger heard this, he said, 'As for me, I have been given a letter demanding war to the finish!' They returned together to Hidabu and a message was sent to Weyoni saying, 'We want war to the end.' But the men of Weyoni wanted peace. So they were told to send unarmed representatives to Hidabu to conclude a peace agreement. An elder warned them not to go unarmed, but they went nonetheless and were killed by the Hidabu people who secretly were carrying daggers. No men of Weyoni were left alive. Thus, the people of Weyoni were tricked and forced to submit. The terms of surrender were that they were not to build defences, they were not to wear shoes, and they were to wash the dead.[115]

2. 'What I know I got from my mother and from people who got it from their ancestors. The Weyoni area is where the Wayumbili settled. At Hidabu there were other people. The people at Weyoni were not aware that there were people settling at Hidabu area. Then later they came to know that there were people settling at the Hidabu area. Maybe they came by dhow or something else, I do not know. So they became aware of the settlement at Hidabu and they decided to go and fight to get possession of the land at Hidabu as well as their own. So they fought until both of them were exhausted. So both sides decided to send messengers to ask for peace. So the two messengers met on the way. So then the man from Weyoni started, giving the information first, saying, "I have been sent to ask you for peace." The man from Weyoni said this, and the Hidabu man said, "No, I am told to come and tell your people to get ready, for we are coming to fight you" – that is, he did not give actual information; he cheated the man. So when the Hidabu man returned to his area, he told them that the Weyoni people had become weak and told them to fight and take them as prisoners. So when these

people defeated the Weyoni, that is how the Wayumbili became weak after that. So they became very weak, almost like slaves. They were not allowed to wear shoes. Those were the Wayumbili. They were not allowed to mix with other people. They also were not allowed to marry with other people except when they found a very weak family. They were not allowed to perform some [types of] work, and the only work they could do was to wash the dead and to dig graves. Some of them were tailors making *kanzus*. Their names changed and they became known later as Washa. However, this name also has disappeared.'

Question: 'Who were the Kinamti?'

Answer: 'The Weyoni area was just full of Wayumbili. The Kinamti were the people who settled in the Hidabu area. What I heard is that the Wayumbili were Arabs; those who came from Yumba. The Wayumbili were those who settled at Weyoni, and the Kinamti were the people who settled at Hidabu. The reason why they were called Kinamti is because they brought coconut seedlings. Therefore, they were known as Kinamti.'[116]

3. *Question*: 'Who were the first to settle at Lamu?'

    Answer: 'Wayumbili.'

    Question: 'Where did they come from?'

    Answer: 'In Weyoni ... half of them, and half at Hidabu. Half were staying in Hidabu and half in Weyoni. The owners (*wenyewe*) were Wayumbili. In the centre was just a forest, all was a forest except Weyoni and Hidabu. In the middle is where they used to build *shambas* [farms].'

    Question: 'What about the war between Hidabu and Weyoni?'

    Answer: 'They fought because everyone wanted to be the king – both sides wanted it. But they were tired of fighting, and at the centre there were these *shambas*. The people at Hidabu wrote a letter asking for peace and the Weyoni people also sent a letter. So the messengers were sent and they met in the centre, at the place of the *shambas*. And the other said, "We are seeking peace. We do not want to fight anymore. We want to be one." So the other lied and said, "But oh! We [too] want peace. We want to be under one flag." So one said, "Let us go to my *boma*." The Hidabu man said to the Weyoni man, "Come and we shall make peace. But do not take any weapons with you – swords or knives – just come yourself." But there was one man who told them, "No, take weapons with you. Where there is peace, there is also fighting." But they did not agree with that man and thought he was a nuisance who didn't know anything because he was so [very] old.

    'When they came to Hidabu then, they were beaten. Hidabu beat the Weyoni people. They defeated them. When they defeated them, there was this forest in the centre. So they came where the forest was and started building houses and told the Weyoni people, "Do not come here anymore. You are not to marry our people." So when they defeated them, they made them do so many things. One was that they were not to wear turbans and that they were to smelt iron (*kuponda chuma*). And the Kirumes were the rulers at that time. They were the rulers of Weyoni. The work they were given was to slaughter cattle, to accompany the *khatib* to the Friday mosque (*kupandisha khatibu*). Any tribe which was not valuable was given lowly work to do. Also, if someone wanted to build a house, the Wayumbili gave them the plot on which to build.'

Question: 'Who settled here first, those at Hidabu or those at Weyoni?'

Answer: 'There was a forest in between. Then they started cutting it down and building there. The people of Weyoni and the people of Hidabu started cutting at the opposite ends and started coming closer together. Before, there weren't houses there, only forest. There were houses at Hidabu and Weyoni only.'

Question: 'Were the people of Hidabu and Weyoni related?'

Answer: 'Yes, some relation. Originally, there were Africans here. Then they came: they were Arabs, and they beat them [the Africans] and converted them to Islam. Afterwards, they settled at Hidabu and Weyoni. Originally, they were Arabs and some wanted to settle at Hidabu and some at Weyoni, each in his own place.'[117]

4. 'Before the Portuguese, Lamu was called Mrio. At that time the people who were there were the Suudi and the Zena. The Zena were at Tundani [*mtaa* just south of Weyoni]. Pokomo were living at Hidabu, and they thought they were stronger than the people at Tundani. So they wanted to put the Tundani people under their authority. Before they took any steps in what they intended [though], Arabs came. These Arabs were called Suudi and were few in number. So these Suudi invaded Hidabu from the direction of Shela in dhows.

'Because these Pokomo of Hidabu were not strong enough, these Arabs invaded them. Afterwards, these Suudi had the same intentions as the Pokomo [that is invading Tundani]. They fought only a little with the Pokomo. Then they intended to invade Tundani, but the Tundani people resisted them. Therefore, they had to fight.'

Question: 'Who were the people of Tundani?'

Answer: 'The Wayumbili.

'So they asked the people of Tundani to leave, but they refused. Therefore, it was necessary to send an army against them and they fought. They fought for two or three weeks. After almost a month, the fighting ceased.'

Comment: At this point in the narrative, the informant repeats the story of the two messengers. His narrative, however, took the following twist:

'And they went [to Hidabu, following the exchange of messages]. When they got there, the Hidabu man went in alone, leaving the Tundani man outside. The king asked, "What is all this?" And he [the messenger] explained the whole story of the trick and that the Tundani man was waiting outside. The king told him to bring the man inside.

He greeted him and asked, "What is the news?" And he said, "I have been given a letter which requires an answer." The king was also the commander-in-chief. He read the letter and told him, "No, stopping the fight is impossible. I gave my messenger a letter to take to Tundani saying that the fighting must go on, and he made a very big mistake coming back. This letter of yours is a trick. You really do not want peace. So, to prove you really desire peace, bring forty unarmed people with whom we shall discuss matters and see if we can restore peace."

'The Hidabu messenger was profoundly thanked for the ruse he had used. So the ruler (*mkubwa wa mui*) sent a letter to Tundani and said, "We will have peace only if you send us forty men." The ruler of Tundani got the letter and read it and was happy because he thought the people of Tundani wanted peace. He informed the people of the condition of sending forty unarmed men and they all accepted. But there was one elder who disapproved.'

Question: 'What was the elder's name?'

Answer: 'Sh. Zahidi Ngumi. He said, "Don't send those forty people unarmed, though the people want it." He said, "Although these people should carry arms, they should leave them outside the *boma* in case any quarrel arises." But they refused and sent forty unarmed people. They went and were welcomed, then thirty-nine out of the forty were killed. And one man had the chance to escape from Hidabu, and he went to Tundani to give them the news.'[118]

5. Questioning elicited the following information: The people who settled at Weyoni were called Wayumbili who came from Yunbo. Those at Hidabu Hill were Makhzumy (Kinamti) and came to Lamu after the Wayumbili.

'The Hidabu people came after the people of Weyoni, but they did not mix with these Weyoni people. So the people of Hidabu wanted to rule over the Weyoni people, and Weyoni people were against this idea. So the people who came to settle at Hidabu found Swahili there who accepted their rule. Since these Swahili at Hidabu accepted the rule of these strangers, these newcomers also thought that the Weyoni people should come under their authority. But the Weyoni people did not agree since they were the first ones to settle here. And the Hidabu people looked down on the Weyoni people, not thinking they were clever. Actually, the Weyoni were strong and had about 2,000 brave men-at-arms. The Hidabu people were not aware of this. Some people say the Hidabu people were not aware of people settled at Weyoni. That is not true. The people who came to settle at Hidabu knew that there were people at Weyoni, but [thought] that they were not clever like the Swahili who were at Hidabu when they arrived. The Weyoni people refused, so the Hidabu people sent poems to them to start war.

'They met here near the fort and had a big battle. Some people say it lasted for six months, but actually it was only for a few days. The war went on until all of them were exhausted. So these people at Hidabu wrote a letter requesting peace, and the same thing happened at Weyoni. The messenger from Weyoni gave the information first. Other people say that it was the Hidabu people who gave the information first. So the one from Weyoni said, "We want peace", but the one from Hidabu said, "I have a letter saying we want the war to continue. So we must fight tomorrow. It's better that we go to our *boma* to look into this matter further."

'So the Hidabu man took the Weyoni man to the *boma*, but did not take him inside. Instead, he went inside and told all that he heard. Then the Weyoni man came in and read his letter. So they said, "No, it is impossible for us to make peace. You must agree to be our subjects, or if not you must bring forty strong and clever people to us. If they agree, then we can make peace. Also, the forty people are not to bring any weapons – not even a dagger or a spear. They should come just like women." So they sent a letter to Weyoni and all the conditions were accepted. There was one old man who told them not to agree to go without arms, and told them, "The day you make peace is the day you start war. You had better take arms. Even if you do not take them inside, at least they will be nearby."

'But they left their arms and went. But when they arrived they were beaten and killed. In other words, they were defeated. So they were not to wear shoes or turbans. They were given the work of washing the dead and all those duties which were considered an insult at Lamu.'[119]

6. Summary of information obtained through questioning: Originally, there were two settlements with a forest between them. The Kinamti (or Makhzumy) were from the Hijaz and settled at Hidabu Hill. Weyoni had been settled earlier by Wayumbili from Yumbwa, also in the Hijaz. The Banu Umayya came and defeated the Hidabu Hill people, and afterwards they were referred to as the Banu Lami. They then fought Weyoni and defeated them, taking their women for wives. Thereafter, the progeny of this union on the Weyoni side were called al-Lami.[120]

7. Summary of information obtained through questioning: The first to settle were the Wayumbe in Arabia, who settled at Kitapemba, followed by the Kinamti at Hidabu Hill. The Wayumbe were blacksmiths and fishermen, and they were called Lami, Maawi, and Bakari. Afterwards came the Arabs, the Jahadhmy and the Washiri from the Hadhramawt. The 'fight' that occurred between the two settlements was a dispute, like a *ngoma*. The two sides united in the end in a war against Pate.[121]

8. Summary of information obtained through questioning: The first to settle were the Wayumbili, who came from Yambu near Mecca. They settled both at Kiwandeo and at Tundani, in addition to other locations. The Wayumbili of Kiwandeo were called Wayumbili Pembe because they were of noble birth. Those at Tundani were slower witted (*dufu*) and came to be called Wayumbili Ngombe. Soon afterwards, the Arabs of the Twelve Tribes arrived in the time of Abdu'l-Malik ibn Marwan because of the religious wars in Mecca. The Wayumbili of Tundani were given the name of Ngombe because they sold their land to the Twelve Tribes for a strip of cowhide (*ukanda wa ngozi wa ngombe*) which was stretched out for them from their location to the

mainland shore. The Wayumbili Pembe demurred in this sale. Afterwards, a war was fought between Kiwandeo and Tundani. Even though the soldiers of Kiwandeo were braver, the Friday mosque fell in on them, killing all of them. The story of the messengers is repeated, briefly, but the outcome was reversed: the Kiwandeons (Hidabuans) were tricked into a surrender and had to intermarry with the Wayumbili of Tundani.[122]

9. *Question*: 'What do you know about the (Lamu) *siwa*?'

Answer: 'The dates have been lost because there was a misunderstanding among the people of Lamu, so they threw it away. It wasn't made by the people of Lamu, but I know where it came from. There was a fight between the people of Lamu and the people of Mudio.' (Salim Heri)

Question: 'Who brought it here?'

Answer: 'The Twelve Tribes. The *siwa* was made at Mudio. During weddings they used to blow this *siwa*, so the Twelve Tribes wanted it. So they went to fight Mudio and forty youths were the ones who went. The dhow in which they went was burnt. There was a *siwa* and a *totomo* [small drum], but when they were swimming [back with them from Mudio], some of them died. The one who was carrying the *totomo* was drowned, so it was lost. But the *siwa* was not lost. It was the Twelve Tribes who brought it to Lamu. It was blown only for the Twelve Tribes, anyone from the Twelve Tribes was entitled to its use. It was not for newcomers – only the Busaidi. Even *shurafaʾ* could not use it. Even if a person paid 100,000–shillings they would not blow it for him. Of the forty youths who went to Mudio from the Twelve Tribes, only three remained.' (Salim Heri)

'When they were coming with the *siwa* and *totomo*, the one with the *totomo* died. But the one with the *siwa* was carrying it [over the shoulder demonstrated] like a gun. But when the youth reached the beach and they took the *siwa* from him, he also died. When they went to fight at Mudio, they won, but they burnt the dhow. So they didn't have another one to come down here.' (Aisha binti Salim)

Question: 'Before the British came, who looked after it?'

Answer: 'The owners were the people of Lamu. There was a special house called Nana bin Waziri. They were Jahadhmy.' (Salim Heri)

Question: 'How did they become the custodians?'

Answer: 'Because he [referring to Nana, but meaning the Waziri] was the oldest person, so they agreed that he should take it. He was a neighbour of mine. It was a tribe of the Jahadhmy, the Waziri. The Twelve Tribes gave it to him because he was old.' (Salim Heri)[123]

10. 'Then, on the mainland there was a town called Mudiwo and the men of Lamu went and fought with the folk of Mudiwo and defeated them. Thus, the brass *siwa*-trumpet which is now there ... came from Mudiwo. And it came about that they fought with Kitao and subdued it.'[124]

11. 'Formerly, there was something which was given to some people. Do

you know the *siwa*? That *siwa* formerly stayed with the Waziri tribe. And anyone who wants to have a wedding or something like that they should go to Waziri and take that *siwa* and something is given, say like a present, to the Waziri. And [they] give that *siwa* [for] use at their wedding and return it back.' (interview in English).

Question: 'Could you tell me why that particular family – the Waziri – were made caretakers of the *siwa*?'

Answer: 'Because formerly when these people came from Arabia, or something like that, they used to come to Lamu. Then, they went to fight with the people at Kinarani – there's a place near Kitao called Kinarani. They went there to fight with the people there. Then they got the *siwa* of Kinarani and brought it here. Then those Waziris, so many of them were killed that the people of Lamu gave that *siwa* to be a title to them – and called them Waziri.'[125]

12. Persian colonists settled at Wangwana Washah (Ozi), close to Kipini. Others settled at Manda, which was at loggerheads with Lamu over certain ceremonial accessories held by the Manda ruler – a brass trumpet, a chair, a drum, and a wooden dish reserved for the ruler's food and brought from Persia. Lamu wanted it. First they tried force, but failing, they selected a woman to ingratiate herself with the Manda ruler. Forty men were picked and the woman led three of them into the town disguised as women. They went to the ruler's house and killed him, taking the regalia. On the way back to Lamu, they were pursued by the Manda people and almost all the Lamu group were drowned. The *siwa* and drum reached Lamu safely, while the chair was saved by Pate.[126]

13. There is no record or tradition of the capture of the towns of Takwa or Kitao on Manda Island by Pate, but it is alleged that the refugees from Manda, Takwa, and Kitao got permission from Lamu to settle at Shela. The people of Lamu granted permission on the understanding that the refugees would not wear sandals or turbans and they should never build in stone nor fortify their settlement.[127]

14. 'One thing I heard is about a war between Manda and Lamu. Manda was a big town; just like Lamu it had everything. She had her own king. The town was walled up against enemies. One time the Manda people were beaten. And when they were exhausted, they asked for help from the Lamu people. So when they came to Lamu, they were given the land at Shela to settle. When they came to settle at Shela, they were given special conditions. As you know, old people used to quarrel even among their own relatives ... just like Omar at Pate. Because of a quarrel between him and a relative, he went to settle at Witu. So they kept special conditions for the people who settled at Shela. This was just to show them their power. They gave such conditions like not to put on shoes when they came to Lamu and not to come to Lamu with an animal.'[128]

15. After Manda was defeated, the inhabitants of Takwa and Kitao fled to Lamu for safety. There they remained as strangers for about two

hundred years, not mixing with the people of Lamu, nor able to live 'as they would have wished'. So some began building Shela. The Lamu people, however, looked upon this new settlement with great distrust. So the Sultan of Lamu issued an order that no stone building could be erected at Shela.[129]

16. 'And as to Manda, they entered it by a war of cunning, and destroyed it utterly and carried off some of the people to Pate, and part (of them) ran away and went to every place: they came to Shela and Malindi and other towns. Those who came to Shela put themselves under the protection of the man of Lamu. The king [of Pate] demanded them of the men of Lamu, they refused, as regards those words ... The king died in the year 732.

'He left one son, Sultan Omar bin Muhammed bin Ahmad bin Muhammed bin Seleman. He reigned after his father and returned his father's words to the men of Lamu, demanding from them the men of Manda; the men of Lamu refused to surrender them, and he made war on them.'[130]

4

Town Islam and the *umma* ideal

La *ᶜilmu ridda illaᵓllah* (Any knowledge save that of God is apostasy).[1] Such is the view of a *mwanachuoni mkubwa* ('big' *ᶜalim*) concerning the inclusion of ancestral spirits, territorial spirits, or saint worship in Islam. Such views might be encountered anywhere in the Islamic world, for everywhere within it, 'high' Islam, reflective of an absolute view of transcendence, and 'popular' Islam, which often treats transcendence merely as being relative, are to be found coexisting in single communities. The implicit antagonism between these two cosmic dispositions has produced widely divergent opinions within Islamic communiti s concerning what sins one can commit and still be accepted as a Muslim. In the century or so after the Prophet Muhammad's death, opinions on these questions varied greatly from the relative tolerance of early Shiᶜites to the highly exclusive views of some Khariji groups. In spite of these differences, all Muslims shared one common notion: the idea that certain enlightened personalities or societies enjoy God's special favour, and that for one to expect eternal salvation he must attach himself to these individuals or communities. Muslim theologians, however, learned to deal with such religious differences among the Faithful by 'leaving' the final judgement in such matters to God (that is, constituting the thesis of 'suspended judgement'). Out of this developed the conviction that, through a condign and enlightened leadership, God extends his special dispensation to *all* members of the Islamic community (*umma*). Thus, in theory, anyone professing Islam deserves to be counted among an exclusive 'charismatic community' of believers who can expect salvation simply by accepting God's laws as they were enunciated by Muhammad in their final and perfect form.

Traditionally, much the same idea has existed on the East African coast, and almost all the ideas associated with the Islamic *umma* as a sacred community have been applied to the Islamic coastal towns and to their associated mainland areas. Evidence of this exists in various forms. One form has existed implicitly in the positive expresssions of local culture which made each town an exclusive entity even in relation to other coastal communities. This centred on the common opinion among coastal townspeople that their particular community, above all others, enjoyed God's special favour and could be expected to prevail over all others in war and politics.[2] Even more revealing is the fact that the town was taken as the basic ritual and ideological unit among coastal townspeople. Newly trained youths, for example, had to win recognition from town elders (*wazee*) and locally established *walimu* (scholars), on locally determined criteria, if they hoped to gain acceptance as scholars in their own right. Even after explicit recognition was extended, community opinion continued to have a decisive sway over a *mwalimu*'s mastery and administration of socially sensitive sciences like law (*fiqh*) and Quranic interpretation (*tafsir*). If a particular *mwalimu* exceeded the bounds of local etiquette or sense of propriety in religious matters, he risked losing community sanction of his work.[3] Ritual unity of the town was maintained through the celebration of annual holidays, such as the *siku ya mwaka* (New Year), or in special situations when the welfare of the town called for community-wide action through ritual and prayer. In all of these cases the community was underscored as the sacral unit through the performance of the *kuzunguo mji* (circumambulation of the town), whereby a sacred ox was led around the town's perimeter, after which it was taken to the community (Friday) mosque, slaughtered, and eaten either communally or by the town's poor.[4] Though details of this particular ceremony differed from town to town, interestingly enough in all cases it appears to have functioned as a traditional means of ridding the zone so circumscribed and defined (that is, the town) of evil and of restoring it to God's protection.[5] Finally, though the evidence for the period before 1860 admittedly is scarce, it appears likely that local elders or rulers were mentioned in the *khutba* (Friday sermon).[6] Normally, this distinction has been reserved among Muslims for those recognized as leaders of all the Muslims of the world. That this occurred in some instances would suggest that Muslims considered their own local leaders as heads of a 'charismatic' Islamic society which was, of course, their own community.

To understand the notion of the town as *umma*, both the Islamic legal tradition and various elements of African religious practices which contributed to the Swahili concept of the *umma* have to be explored. Particularly, it is important to understand how the concept of the *umma* has existed on the East African coast as a universal Islamic institution which has been adapted locally to accommodate diverse perceptions of transcendence among groups having assorted ethnic backgrounds and legal traditions which commonly coexisted in the same town.

Above all, religious belief and practice in Africa have centred on ritual. Beliefs, and the rituals associated with them, have developed as the means of understanding the universe and influencing its operation. Together, they guarantee the spiritual, social, and physical well-being (*imani*) of the community. Naturally, belief and ritual can take many forms, depending on the problems to be dealt with and the type of medicine required for their solution.[7] Bohannon and Curtin observe that,

> Perhaps the most characteristic quality of African religion is that there are many strings to the bow ... African religion does not in most places have undeniable orthodoxy. It must be understood rather as a set of goals, a dogma on the nature of man and God, and a more or less experimental (and therefore constantly and rapidly changing) set of rituals for achieving those goals within the conceptual framework of dogma.[8]

A specific example of these observations in action can be found in a study of religion among the Balozi. In her work, Mainga has demonstrated how one African people can manipulate a particular set of circumstances by choosing to employ one or more among three distinct rituals, 'each with a character and order of its own'.[9] If faced with drought, then, the Balozi can choose to address prayers for rain to the sky god Nyambe at planting time, to pray to the ancestral spirits of their ruling household, or to employ magic and medicine which involves local clan and nature spirits.[10] This same flexibility, found among African societies, also explains partly religious tolerance within coastal communities which, after all, evolved and have existed in an African ambience.

Where 'high' Islamic principles have existed in coastal centres, therefore, so have elements of local traditional belief systems. Rarely have they existed side by side and independently of each other, but rather more commonly as parallel systems. Whichever view of transcendence has prevailed in particular moments has been circumstantial – depending on situations encountered, 'historical' pressures (for example, cycles of large-scale population movements, more intensive inter-ethnic contact, trade), and class origins of the personalities involved.

This seeming 'split personality' of town Islam is not unique to the coast, of course. Christianity, for example, has evolved an elaborate hierarchy of saints, each of whom exhibits a distinct personality and who represents a particular aspect of reality. It is this particularity of reality as represented by a saint which makes him the one through whom prayers are addressed to God in certain circumstances calling for certain types of solutions. Hindus, likewise, view reality in three principal manifestations – as Brahma, Vishnu, or Shiva. Islam, as discussed already, subsumes both absolute and relative views of transcendence where mystical brotherhoods and saint worship coexist with the ᶜ*ulama*ᵓ and their legalistic and intellectualist views. Thus, ultimate reality is not perceived only in one form among coastal Muslims, but as taking many forms. Whichever view of reality is entertained at a particular moment is situational and usually is dependent on the particular problem faced at that moment which calls for an explanation or solution.

Perhaps the best way to understand the townsperson's view of the community in which he lives is to compare the coastal town to what usually is called (imprecisely for other African peoples) the tribe. To the *mungwana* (townsman), his community is his 'tribe'. If asked what his ethnic background is, the townsman might give several answers which, as is the case with all Africans, reflects the complex matrix of the socio-economic referents in which he lives. As often as not, what one person might call himself, another might deny. A man might say he is a *sharif* or an Arab which another man might deny; or a poor man (for example, a Myumbili in Lamu) might claim to be a *mungwana*, which another might question on putative ethnic or 'religious' grounds. However, one referent which all coastal dwellers would fall back upon, whatever their social origins, is that they 'belong' to a town. Thus, if all else fails, a townsperson might say, 'I am a Lamuan' or 'I am a Mombasan', or something very similar.

Thus, in coastal communities all problems of a religious nature (as opposed, say, to clan problems for, even if an appeal is made to ancestral spirits, they are not to be thought of as religious, nor are the solutions to such problems thought of as being 'religious' since, properly speaking, to the townsman only Islam is thought to be 'religion') are solvable through the status of the town as a sacred community. In other words, solutions to community problems exist only inasmuch as the community is a sacred entity whose welfare (*imani*) is safeguarded by the grace of God. Problems can be averted or solved through preserving the sacredness of the town. Two general types of problems exist for townspeople: the 'preventive' problem of preserving the sacredness of the community by keeping it free of evil, apostasy (*shirk*), and unbelief (*kufr*); and the 'corrective' problem of restoring the sacredness of the town after it has offended God. The *imani* of a town is maintained or restored by virtue of God's grace which, in turn, is maintained or restored through rituals appropriate to both situations. Thus, there is an essential link between ritual and *imani*.

The link between ritual and community welfare is both African and Islamic in its origins. Both Islamic and non-Islamic African traditions view the community as having a special status in the 'order of things' be it in the Islamic *umma*, or, for example, in a Somali-like belief that, 'The best people are ourselves, of that I have always been sure.' Also, both rely on ritual to preserve this status. The only difference would seem to lie in the fact that the potential threat of retribution from the supernatural is seen as immediate in African traditions, but put off until Judgement Day for Muslims. Thus, neither wholly absolute nor wholly relative views of transcendence exist in reality in so far as ritual, be it in the form of prayer or sacrifice or simply in righteous living, attempts to control cosmic forces to some extent. Man is perceived as an active agent in the universe whose task is to contribute to its motive power, be it through 'acquisition' of God's will[11] or through divination and sacrifice.[12]

The idea of the *umma* implies a 'communalistic' view of individual shortcomings which has its origins in pre-Islamic, desert, 'tribal' life. As mentioned already, it is quite compatible with African notions of social and ethnolinguistic identity in which dealings with the supernatural are on a community-wide basis. It emphasizes the corporate unity of the 'People of Paradise' at the expense of certain points of individual morality and goes against the more individualistic outlook of the Quran and Islamic law.[13] However, the sacred community is defined as 'knowledge of God and public acknowledgement of him together with knowledge of the Messenger (Muhammad) and acknowledgement of what was revealed through him.'[14] Knowledge of God's will, as revealed through Muhammad, along with living by his commandments, is required in addition to mere profession of faith if the sacredness of the *umma* is to be preserved. Worship and supplication to God must be done in specific, prescribed ways if the goal of preserving or restoring the sanctity of the community is to be effective. Man must search out God's will at all times and in all situations so that he might carry out his will. This, of course, can be stated as seeking out (through 'effort' – *ijtihad*) the nature of reality and living in conformity to its requirements. Thus, the notion of the 'right path' exists, that is as reality having a specific form to which men must conform in their daily lives and rituals.

A community, be it Islamic or non-Islamic, in Africa or in the Middle East, owes its sanctity to its conformity to the revealed will of God, by sticking to the 'right path'. In African societies there are always those who are thought to know what is the 'right path' and who know how to live in conformity with this revealed way more than others do. Others in society are obliged to follow those who possess this superior wisdom, those who are especially blessed in God's (or the spirits') eyes. These people often are said, in fact, to possess God's 'blessing' (*baraka*), and adherence to them and imitation of their life styles are thought to benefit those who do so. Through those who possess this 'blessing', channels are kept open to the supernatural, to ultimate reality, and a community exists in a state of *imani* because of them and their actions. Such people enjoy this special status with the supernatural for any one of a number of reasons: birth in a family of reputed experts, 'charismatic' leadership qualities, or personal intelligence. Whatever the reason, though, they are the people who understand best the societies in which they live and who have the greatest facility in grasping and manipulating the local forms of symbolism and social arrangements to their advantage and to the advantages of the 'network of dependence' created among those who adhere to them. These people might be called many things: diviners, elders, priests, or medicine men. As summarized by Bohannon and Curtin (who labelled such people as diviners), 'Divination is one of the specialties most likely to attract the person with the intellectual bent. Diviners must have an intuitive knowledge of the societies in which they live – and often that knowledge is not merely intuitive, but can be made explicit'.[15]

In Islamic societies, the *ᶜulama*ᵓ play a similar role. 'Comprehension' (*fiqh*) of God's will, as revealed in the Quran and in the *Sunna* ('way') of the Prophet, can be obtained through legitimate 'effort' (*ijtihad*). The 'right path' is not open to all, but only to those who make the required 'effort'. Yet, 'effort' itself must follow certain guidelines and rules if it is to lead to 'comprehension'.[16] For one thing, it must follow not only the commandments laid down in the Quran, but also the 'way' (*Sunna*) of the Messenger of God. But even more important than the *Sunna* is the interpretation (*tafsir*) of the Quran and 'traditions' (*hadith*) of the Prophet by the consensus of opinion (*ijmaᶜ*) among legal scholars who qualify as the sole experts in such matters by virtue of their erudition (*ᶜilm*) concerning God's will and of the means by which it can be ascertained most reliably. But even more significant, in the classical exposition of Islamic law, the community (*umma*) and its welfare became equated with the consensus (*ijmaᶜ*) of the *ᶜulama*ᵓ. In fact, the *ijmaᶜ* of the legal scholars came to be deemed infallible, just as the *umma* itself was infallible.[17] The infallibility of the *umma*, its very sanctity, derived from the infallible judgement of the *ᶜulama*ᵓ in ascertaining the will of God, the 'right path'. The *ᶜulama*ᵓ came to represent the opinion, theoretically, of the entire *umma*, and the consensus of these scholars operated, 'as a material source of law [and doctrine] in itself.'[18]

The power of the *ʿulamaʾ* and their consensus (*ijmaʿ*) is demonstrable in situations where written law and local customary practices have conflicted. To begin with, as noted by Coulson.

> Perhaps the degree of rigidity which the doctrine attained has been unduly exaggerated, particularly in spheres other than that of family law; and the notion of a uniform Shariʿa is seriously qualified by wide variations in opinion among different schools and individual jurists.

Furthermore,

> and where the Shariʿa was unable to make the necessary accommodations, local customary law continued to prevail in practice, and the jurisdiction of non-Shariʿa tribunal was extended.[19]

Even within the same sect, differences of opinion were common in classical theory, and, 'Doctrine graded the relative authority of conflicting views on the basis of the support they commanded among its representative scholars.'[20] Thus, opinions on points of doctrine rarely were labelled extremely as mandatory or forbidden, but more broadly as 'dominant' (*mashhur*), 'preferable' (*rajih*), or 'weak' (*daʿif*). Also, in the Shariʿa, provision was made for customary practices (*ʿada* or *ʿurf*) as subsidiary sources of law.[21] Faced with this situation, *ʿulamaʾ*, especially if they themselves were of local origin, in the interests of locally accepted notions of justice, sometimes admitted a 'preferable' or even a 'weak' opinion which favoured local usages.[22] But what was most conducive to the establishment of local 'schools' of religious thought in Islam is that once a *qadi* gave sanction to some local usage, even if classified legally as 'weak', such a decision tended to find favour with other and succeeding *qadis* and *ʿulamaʾ*, and the usage, once admitted, could become established practice. Often such changes were legitimized further by written opinions (*fatwa*) issued by qualified *muftis* and compiled into collections which came to have an authority complementary to other standard Shariʿa manuals.[23] Thus, schools of law took on a largely local character, especially where the *ʿulamaʾ* were of local origins and where they were relatively isolated from other bodies of scholars. Local *ijmaʿ* came into being which admitted large areas of local religious practice.

RELIGIOUS LEADERSHIP IN THE TOWNS

In coastal towns, then, a locally born learned elite evolved which, through their learning and knowledge of legal tradition which contained elements both of the written Islamic legal tradition and of local customary practices, guaranteed the infallibility of the coastal town as the sacred community. Something of a 'parish' situation developed in which an elite group of officials, connected both with neighbourhood mosques and community Friday mosques, guaranteed the efficacy of community-related rituals.[24] Among the duties of these mosque officials was the supervision of 'life-cycle' rituals, leading prayers, teaching the basics of the faith to the uninitiated, marriage and inheritance matters, and delivery of the *khutba* on Fridays.[25] The importance of these individuals and their function in guaranteeing the ritual purity of the town in which they lived is evident in some of the terminology found on the coast which applied to them. Among these terms are *waongozi* ('rightly guided'), *wacha Mungu* ('God's pious ones'), *watukufu* ('exalted ones'), and *wenyenyekevu* ('those who are humble before God'). Their connection with specific communities is indicated with the use of phrases like, 'Bwana huyu ni mmoja katika wacha Mungu/waongozi wakubwa [name of town] (This gentleman is one of the pious/rightly guided ones of [name of town]).'[26]

The concept of the *umma* and the place of the learned elites in East African towns have been influenced by several prevailing social and historical conditions. Historically, as discussed above, notions of a local elite of 'blessed' ones who enjoy the favours of God and special relationships with other aspects of the supernatural are indigenous to Africa as well as a feature of Islam. The persistent importance of the non- or pre-Islamic religious tradition enters into town Islam through the continued reverence for departed ancestors as founding figures of the clan and community. Where Lord Clark says that one attribute of civilization is a 'sense of permanence', in Africa this 'permanence' (and sacredness)[27] is thought of in terms of lineages and groups of lineages which last and endure through time.[28] Frequently, ancestors are the ones who are thought to have engendered the civilization of the town/community as it exists in the (hypothetical) present. These ancestors, therefore, are believed to have been superior in wisdom, nearer to God, and deserving to be revered as the ones to dispense advice (through living 'mediums', diviners, or *walimu*) and through whom one must approach God. In this, African religions 'also tend to have a precise one-to-one association with a particular form of social group', since, 'God and the spirits are ... members of the same society which enfolds living human beings.'[29] Therefore, once a tradition – a way of perceiving and acting upon the world – is established, it is difficult to change matters when pressures are exerted for change. Familiar symbols and social usages linger even where the vision of reality behind them changes. Generation after generation of Africans grow up and are taught to emulate their ancestors in their thoughts and ways of living. The argument is employed that, because a community is Islamic in tradition, so then its customs must be Islamic even when many of the customs are of local origin and clearly are not derived from the mainstream of Islamic legal thought.[30] Because customs are handed down from the great men and women of the past they must be valid today, for 'were not the people of olden times more pious and more learned than the backsliders and opportunists of nowadays?'[31] Whether or not, in fact, the ancestors actually were Muslims is irrelevant. The important point is that the community is Islamic and the ancestors, as founding figures, had to have been Muslims in townspeople's eyes. And what better proof of the propriety of current usages than the piety and righteousness and sanctity of the community itself?

A local town elite of those learned in Islamic tradition and law is one which is knowledgeable not only of the mainstream of written legal thought, but one which also is steeped in local Islamic life. In fact, the two are perceived by local leadership as being indistinct. Islam is town civilization, and town Islam is exemplary Islam. This local variety of Islam is heavily influenced by local tradition as it has been handed down generation after generation, and belief in the ancestors' ways is characteristic of the Islamic leadership of the town as much as it is characteristic of other segments of town society, if not more so in fact (since it is the learned elite, as guardians of the *umma*, who actually manipulate and control local religious symbolism). Thus, Islamic tradition and learning in the coastal town is both oral and written, with the written one containing the elements not only of the mainstream legal tradition (that is, strictly adhering to acts labelled mandatory or dominant), but also of local customary practices which have been sanctioned at some time by an ᶜ*alim* and promulgated in written form as a *fatwa* or orally as aphorisms, proverbs, or adages. Even written tradition, then, takes on a local flavour. The 'African' way of using tradition to reflect accepted usage is visible in coastal towns where the locally evolved tradition is sanctioned by religious consensus which is, again, local and which protects the sanctity of the town. Traditional ways of doing things are translated as being *taqlid* (imitation), the classical injunction for jurists to 'imitate' their forbears.[32] The legal forbears in coastal towns, of course, include dead ancestors and previous generations of scholars who pronounced on local Islam. The coincidence of *taqlid* and African conservatism in matters concerning religious symbolism and social usage is evident in Coulson's remark that, 'An exaggerated respect for the personalities of former jurists [or ancestors] induced the belief that the work of interpretation has been exclusively accomplished by scholars of peerless ability whose efforts had fashioned the Shariᶜa into its final and perfect form.'[33]

Just how African views on the place of learned or 'blessed' individuals in the community have affected views on the Islamic learned elite in coastal towns is evident in the concept of intercession (*uombezi*) in town Islam.[34] While God is the only deity in Islam, it is understood by all Muslims that the only path to salvation is through Muhammad, God's Messenger and the bringer of his word. Thus, while other sacred books exist, only the Quran and the Shariᶜa represent the truth in unadulterated form, and acceptance of the truth as represented by Muhammad is what characterizes the *umma* from other communities and guarantees its sanctity. So at least in this sense Islam might be thought of as Muhammadanism – that is, submission (*islam*) to God as prescribed through Muhammad. Salvation will come for the Muslims through Muhammad. At least on the coast, one further step has been taken in that not only is Muhammad the Messenger, but actually the Intercessor. For Swahili townsmen, salvation comes not only through living by the word of God as it was brought by Muhammad, but also through Muhammad's prayers for the 'unhindered admission of all his faithful followers. The prayer will be granted and behind Muhammad's banner (*liwa*), all the devout Muslims will march into Paradise.'[35] Islam on the coast, as it centres on Muhammad, can be characterized as a personality cult.[36] A more relative view of transcendence prevails where, 'Muhammad is much more alive and more powerful in popular Islam than one would assume on the basis of rationally influenced religious doctrine. The believer has a living relationship to Muhammad' and he is 'very close to being an object of worship ... Allah is often mentioned, but Muhammad lives.'[37] Muhammad is not merely human, but a bringer of miracles.[38] As pointed out by a former Anglican bishop of Zanzibar,[39] 'there have existed many books and traditions on the coast, relating the principal events in the life of the Prophet, which represent him as a worker of miracles, as being without sin, superhuman, and the bringer of the Holy Quran.'[40]

According to the Swahili, Muhammad was all these things because he possessed the 'divine light' (*nur*) or 'blessedness' (*baraka*).[41] This was a gift of God which stamped him as a prophet from the very moment of his conception, and it was not something he acquired through personal effort. The significance of all this, as it bears on the coastal learned elite, is that all saints and ʿ*ulama*ʾ in coastal towns operated only through Muhammad, and thus shared in his *baraka* in various ways.[42] Likewise it was through sharing in his *baraka* that townspeople believed that the towns in which they resided were sacred. The connection between Muhammad's *baraka* and the learned leadership of coastal towns is natural and quite palpable when one recalls that the learned elite base their reputations on familiarity not only with the Quran, but more so with the *Sunna* of the Prophet. While the Quran is the primary holy book of Muslims, it is incomplete to the extent that it prescribes very little in the way of doctrine. What have become the principal sources of doctrine, in fact, are the traditions (*hadith*), whether real or spurious, based on the 'way' or 'example' (*Sunna*) set by the Prophet. It is the figure of the prophet and his *Sunna*, as set forth in local oral and written literature, which occupies the central position in coastal Islamic doctrine. It is this connection, through knowledge of the *Sunna* or through claims of actual descent from the Prophet, which gives the learned elite of the towns their moral authority. The 'right path' is the *Sunna* of the Prophet and it is to this that the learned ones of the towns are thought to adhere.

Baraka, then, can be obtained through study. However, even more powerful *baraka* is claimed by those who are said to be the physical descendants of the Prophet himself, the *shurafaʾ*. These special clans, some of whom were mentioned in the last chapter, brought to the towns in which they settled the view that they have special intercessory powers and superior claims to pronouncements on matters of law – privileges which they brought with them from the Hadhramawt.[43] By guaranteeing the efficacy of God's law, they assured the holiness and well-being (*imani*) of the towns in which they settled in the sixteenth and seventeenth centuries. As intercessors often they were among the most learned in the towns, so their charisma was not only as *shurafaʾ*, but as ʿ*ulama*ʾ.[44] Particular *sharif* clans became associated with particular towns.[45] Over several generations they intermarried with local families, became heavily immersed in local

71

traditions and society, and contributed much, in fact, to coastal literature after the mid-eighteenth century. Among the more notable of these were the Husayni of Pate, a clan which produced several notable literati both in Swahili and in the Arabic language, as well as numerous religious scholars. Other such clans were the Mahdali of both Lamu and Mombasa (and of Kilwa in the Middle Ages), the Shatiri of Mombasa and Mafia, the Jamal al-Layl ('Night Camel') of Pate and Lamu, and the al-Masila Ba Alawi of the Comoro Islands and Vumba Kuu.

Again, local customs and usages entered into the flavour of local Islam by becoming identified with the *Sunna* of the Prophet. Since it was the learned elite who determined whether or not a certain action was consistent with established legal doctrine and methods of procedure, devices (*hiyal*) were employed by coastal jurists in classifying such actions according to their supposed conformity with the *Sunna*.[46] Thus, local customs became identified with the Prophet himself, largely through the actions of local *ulama* who encouraged such a tendency by their piecemeal admission of customs whose strict conformity with 'mainstream' legal thought is at least questionable. In fact, there is evidence from the recent past that Muhammad himself may have been confused by some coastal Muslims in regards to his national origins and even his race. Some people went so far in their identification of Islam with coastal Islam that they became convinced that Muhammad was not an Arab, but an African.[47] While it is not demonstrable that this particular controversy might have been in circulation during the eighteenth and nineteenth centuries, nevertheless it is consistent with a logical development of the spirit of town Islam, particularly as it unfolded before about the middle of the nineteenth century.

UUNGWANA

In towns of the East African coast such as Lamu and Mombasa, convictions concerning the nature of Islam and 'civilization' are intimately related. Thus, to get a better idea of town Islam, it is now opportune to consider the character of town civilization and, in the next chapter, to demonstrate its meaning in socio-economic terms and in further discussions about traditional Islamic ideology on the coast.

'Civilization', for the period roughly before the middle of the nineteenth century, was rendered by the word *uungwana*. This word embodied all connotations of exclusiveness about town life as well as its positive expressions. It specifically referred to African coastal town culture even to the exclusion of 'Arabness'. 'Civilization' and Arabness, in fact, seem to have become finally associated only after the middle of the nineteenth century when the Arab Busaidi dynasty of Zanzibar began to have a cultural, as well as a political, impact on coastal communities. It was sometime after the 1860s and 1870s then that 'civilization' was characterized less and less by *uungwana* and its implications concerning parochial concepts of Islam, and was replaced gradually by the word *ustaarabu* – that is, to be like an Arab.[48] Therefore, particularly for the period before about 1850, to be civilized one had to be a coastal townsperson and a Muslim. To be called a civilized person meant being called a *mungwana*.[49]

To be considered a Muslim one had to be steeped heavily in local culture, *uungwana*. *Uungwana* included much more than the written Islamic tradition and was on very intimate grounds with non-Islamic mainland culture despite townspeople's disavowal of this culture overall as 'barbarity' (*ushenzi*). Notwithstanding the easy transition made by townspeople from living, say, in thatched, one-story houses to multi-story *majumba*, despite alterations in their modes of living, types of clothing, and in their public behaviour, *uungwana* was derived from mainland culture at least as much as from imported paradigms, and town Islam was evolved as much from non-Islamic African religions. Therefore, the transition from a mainland life style to that of a coastal townsman was not difficult, as old habits of thought and symbolic meanings applied similarly in both settings (see Chapter 5).[50]

A *mungwana* was a person who dressed in a certain way, ate certain foods, earned his livelihood in certain ways, attended to his prayers assiduously, lived in certain types of houses, behaved in certain ways in public, and, above all, spoke the vernacular Swahili well. While some European visitors to the coast, for example, spoke and wrote disparagingly of the *mungwana* and his ignorance of Arabic and the finer points of Islamic law (as these Europeans understood it, at least),[51] such criticisms were based as much on these Europeans' ignorance of coastal language and culture as on their own mastery of Arabic and positive accomplishments in comprehending Islamic law. Indeed, probably no greater error can be made than in taking approaches to coastal history and culture principally through Arabic. While it is useful to know, for example, that Swahili writers of popular epic literature have borrowed from 'the general matter of Arabian legend', and have duplicated Arabic verse forms in Kiswahili, it is more important to know what specific local patterns of thought and symbolism are reflected in such compositions.[52] Swahili is not Arabic and coastal culture is not Arab culture, though both have borrowed some elements from the heartlands of Islam. Townspeople certainly recognized these facts in the past and, significantly, asserted the primacy of their language and civilization in the face of Arab pretensions time and time again.[53]

Language more than anything is a paradigm of culture. Therefore, it should hardly be surprising that the Swahili language was the embodiment of town culture and learning. A town Muslim was said to be *mswahili sana* – that is, very knowledgeable of local language, culture, and history. To be *mswahili sana* implied sophistication, wittiness, and subtlety of mind and intellect, especially in the use of language as the complete symbolic construct of *uungwana*.[54] This implied that for one to be civilized, he had to be fully in command of *Kiswahili cha ndani* (Metaphorical Swahili), often in verse form with all its historical, ideological, and social allusions. To Kiswahili as a lexical and grammatical discipline was added Kiswahili in each of its local dialect forms (Kiamu, Kimvita, Kiunguja, etc.), the cultural side of the language. The townspeople were proud of coastal civilization and Islam, particularly of the local varieties of which they were members and adherents. And just as they guarded and defended local culture, history, and belief, so then did they cultivate the subtleties of their language. Language was both 'a weapon of rivalry and emulation' at the same time, as explained by Nicholls.[55] For, just as their civilization was paradoxical in its conflicts of ideas and schizophrenic in its cultural and religious heritage, so was the language, itself a blend of Bantu grammar and vocabulary along with a high proportion (25–35 per cent) of vocabulary borrowed by the nineteenth century from Arabic. Yet, despite borrowings from neighbouring, ancestral, or imported ideas, and despite apparent contradictions of meaning and usage, both coastal civilization and language were positive realities, unique in their own right, which took elements from other related cultures and reinterpreted and reapplied them to fit the environmental, social, and spiritual exigencies of life on the coast.

5

Wealth, piety, justice, and learning

The previous chapter was devoted to doctrinal aspects of the fusion between the African and Islamic religious traditions which took place in coastal towns. This chapter considers the economic and sociological underpinnings of leadership in the towns, with particular emphasis on the relationship between religious and political authority.

AFRICAN MATERIALISM AND THE 'RIGHT PATH' IDEAL

What is real in most pre-industrial societies is what works best in assuring their material well-being. Hence, in the past, African civilizations evolved as adaptations to prevailing environmental conditions, and these adaptations largely were the result of the dialogues people established with their natural surroundings. Thus, the character of a particular African civilization and the ideology which derived from it were influenced heavily by what worked best in that particular environment in bringing material comfort to human society and the resources people had on hand for its mastery. Naturally, among such resources was the collective knowledge of the world as it was handed down generation after generation and which formed a large part of a society's historical tradition and religious beliefs. Historical tradition, religious belief, and wealth were all directly linked.

An idea common among Africans, whether or not they were Muslims, was that the person who had wealth had *baraka*, whereas he who was impoverished was 'wrongly guided' and 'had no power with God'.[1] The world-view underlying this was one which viewed the natural and supernatural worlds as correlative and reciprocal sides of the same reality. One whose fortunes prospered in one sphere was expected to prosper in the other. Conversely, one who failed in one world was expected to fail in the other. On the coast, this is revealed by the fact that a poor man, even if clever, was thought to be ignorant by fellow townsmen, and his fortunes were thought to be doomed to lasting frustration. On the other hand, a rich man, even if dull-witted, was listened to and his advice given weight wherever people gathered.[2] The social implication of having wealth is revealed in this poem:

Poverty is a difficult thing fashioned by the Creator.
The great are made low and the hero becomes a coward.
A poor man has no shelter; for him good goes unrewarded.

I bow my head to think, then raise my hand in supplication;
Even your brothers chase you away and think you mad.
What the poor man says is a fantasy; thought comes not to him[3]

What was to be believed, then, was what brought material benefits. He who brought them, in any form, was considered to have God's favour (that is, he had *baraka*) and to have known Truth.

Wealth and the attainment of wealth stood at the centre of all social arrangements. How wealth was obtained was an important function of social and ideological diversification. One scholar, for instance, has wrestled with the apparent contradictions of social arrangements in Lamu and has concluded that it is very difficult to impose order on the available data. Confusion arises over the use of both Bantu and Arabic social terminology, sometimes with exactly the same meaning, and at other times only with approximately similar meanings.[4] In attempting to arrange town societies into definite social hierarchies in which 'tribes', clans, or houses are treated as autonomous, unrelated social atoms, such as Prins has attempted, one runs into trouble. Yet Prins himself notes the plethora of kinship terminology and its ambiguity of meaning. Within town society, of course, an individual exists and lives within a web of social relationships of various categories, some of which are African in origin and others which have legal implications and stem from the written Islamic tradition. Thus, one individual can belong to a particular *jamaa* (social 'action' set), *kabila* ('tribe' or patrilineal descent group), *taifa* (eponymical 'tribe'), *tumbo* (kin born to the same man or woman), *mbari* or *mlango* ('tribal' subdivisions), and *mji* (kinship unit based on a common place of residence in a town and traditional claims to farm plots in the bush). Social references are manifold and the key to understanding them lies in knowing how particular descent groups fitted into the community economy. In other words, different social categories often implied different means by which people obtained wealth, their resources in terms of tools and collective knowledge which they exploited to obtain wealth, and the consequences which these might have on their world-view. Because town societies were economically diverse, then, so too were they religiously diverse. People were grouped not only horizontally by how much wealth they had, but vertically by how wealth was earned and the types of wealth they possessed.

One basic division in coastal town society seems to have been between the 'haves' and the 'have-nots' (between *na* and *hana*).[5] Thus, in eighteenth- and nineteenth-century Lamu and Mombasa one would have found three categories into which society was arranged horizontally: at the top were the 'Arabs', consisting of a few *sharif* clans and wealthier *waungwana*, followed by poorer *waungwana* (for example, Wayumbili at Lamu), and at the bottom were non-Muslim *washenzi*, Muslim newcomers or 'foreigners' (*wageni*).[6] (Mainlanders and *wanyika* were replaced by the end of the eighteenth century by imported slaves.) However, more germane to this discussion is Bujra's observation that these economic strata corresponded roughly with ascriptive categories into which town societies were (and are) arranged. That is to say, in coastal towns ascriptive status corresponded roughly with economic status, and social strata were not discrete groupings so much as they were socially ascriptive integrals.[7] What this means is that if a man came from a certain descent group or 'tribe', particular modes of thought, behaviour, means of earning a living (for example, see the 'terms of settlement' discussion in Chapter 3), and relative wealth were expected of him simply by virtue of the socio-economic standing of his descent group in town society as much as by virtue of his personal talents and motivations. (One must be careful in not going too far with this model, however. Even the most evolved coastal communities never possessed formal caste structures such as were found in India, for example.)

This viewpoint is supported by Allen's observation that relative wealth in a Swahili town implied the assumption of new modes of behaviour and habits of thought.[8] Thus, the people who lived in large, multi-story *majumba* were expected to own several large coconut plantations (*shamba*), they often would have been merchants having a long (albeit embroidered) genealogy, probably they would have claimed to have been long-term residents of the community (or else *shurafaʾ*), and would have been deeply learned in local traditional lore and the Shariʿa. Mainland farms would have been important to these stone house dwellers as sources of trade goods. By the end of the eighteenth century (and probably much earlier) the *mungwana* would have inherited usufruct rights to portions of the mainland and bush, but the actual task of farming these shifting bush plots (called *mahonde*) would have been left to clients, debtors, or slaves. The person who dwelt in a single-storey, thatched house (*nyumba*) would have owned perhaps one or two small *shamba*. Probably, too, he would have earned a significant portion of his livelihood as a fisherman or an artisan, or through cultivating on the mainland. He might not have claimed a long genealogy or, at best, he claimed one which was questioned by his fellow townsmen. He was familiar with local mythology and historical traditions, though some would have doubted his wisdom and it is unlikely that he would have been considered an important authority on local lore. It is very unlikely that he would have been able to read or write Kiswahili. He would not have known much Arabic beyond what he knew of the Quran, and it is unlikely that he would have been very familiar with the Islamic written tradition. The non-Muslim newcomer or slave would have lived in a single room (*chumba*) of his patron's house for part of the year, and in a mainland *banda* during the planting and cultivating seasons. He would have raised a portion of his crop of cereals, beans, cow peas, and bananas for his patron/master, but he would have been permitted to keep a portion for himself.[9] Other slaves and clients laboured in their master's or patron's household as domestic servants, concubines, or perhaps as shipmasters. They would have been (comparatively) short-term residents of the town of at most three generations, tracing their ancestry to neighbouring *nyika* peoples or, if they were slaves, their ancestry would have been with the more distant interior of slave ports like Kilwa Kivinje or Bagamoyo. These people would have known relatively little local tradition, mythology, history, or written religious tradition. Their religion, even if they were Muslim converts, would have resembled mainland beliefs, practices, and usages more than one which reflected knowledge of written *hadith* literature, legal commentaries, or Quranic exegesis.

It will be noted, however, that all these economic, ascriptive categories shared common traits. All or most townspeople, for example, were Muslims, though they exhibited varying degrees of learning in the local and written traditions. All but some newcomers or slaves might have owned *shambas*, though their size and numbers differed. Finally, all were dependent on bush cultivation, dryland or bush (*nyika*) crops, and ties with mainland or *nyika* neighbours to some degree and, thus, were open to mainland ideological influences as well as to the influences of the written tradition imported from overseas. In short, town life retained a certain flexibility. Wealth was understood as being obtainable through sundry means and from a variety of places. There were no clear-cut distinctions among the overseas trade, island cultivation, bush cultivation, and mainland social ties. The town's economy was multiform: and just as it was varied, so were the world-views of its inhabitants. Yet, there was no formal system of authority relations.[10] As one author has pointed out, people could move with relative ease from a mainland *banda* to a *nyumba*, or from a single-storey *nyumba* to a stone mansion.[11] Wealth was the key, and however wealth was earned ultimately was unimportant. After all, all shared at least certain values and vocational practices. The critical point here is that along with wealth came a certain ascriptive status to which all aspired. This 'ascriptive' status is what has been described already as *uungwana*. Modes of behaviour, etiquette, family alliances, the house in which one lived, attention to religious duties, devotion to learning, and even genealogy changed fluidly with the achievement of wealth.[12]

The most important source of identity to which people referred in a town was their 'tribe' (*kabila* or *taifa*) or descent group. These units were not really so much true blood groupings as popular agglomerations which shared common ethnic backgrounds, eponymous founding ancestors, and dependency relations. They represented the vertical divisions into which town life was organized socially, into which the town was arranged spatially, and roughly into which it was ordered vocationally. A particular descent group was organized socially and economically around a network of linkages through which wealth and vocational resources of the group were distributed.[13] Wealthier units, of course, enjoyed greater prestige not only for the added luxuries to which they had access, but through the larger size of the dependency network which they supported and the amount of community resources over which they had control.[14] Such groupings were held together by *kutunga*, 'caring' for each other materially in terms of widespread distribution of wealth through gift-giving. At the top of these networks were the wealthy and learned merchants, while at the bottom were the common fishermen, artisans, farmers, and client peoples. The networks created social links with other descent groups or clans through intermarriage, and they won social prestige by 'helping' the people.[15] Other peoples of the town having lesser means at their disposal tended to imitate the wealthier descent group and clans as they were the style-setters, perceived as living close to the 'right path' ideal. Existentially, they simply were 'bigger' than other people.

Spatially, descent groups were associated with particular *mitaa*. Indeed, each *mtaa* had a shared genealogical core. Life in the *mtaa* centred around its mosque, intermarriage, and common celebrations of funerals and circumcisions.[16] Insomuch as descent groups tended to be situated together spatially within the town, so too were mainland associations arranged by descent group. Farm plots on the mainland (*bara*) or bush (*nyika*) were parcelled out by the *mitaa* and their residents. Inheritance of usufruct rights on the *bara* and bush remained within the group. Client relations with particular mainland neighbours, too, tended to be organized in the town by descent group. The client relations of various Mombasa tribes, for example, were with particular, individual Miji Kenda peoples. At Lamu, the Bauri and the Kinamti, of course, had ancient associations with the Pokomo settled around Ozi, while the Maawi held most of the *bara* land around Mpeketoni and social ties were with Bajun and Somali living on the mainland.[17]

Individual clans or descent groups were noted also for their specialization in certain vocations. Since knowledge strongly tended to be kept within kin groups, vocational specializations of a descent group usually reflected their ethnic origins and ties – or at least their claims to such ethnic ties. At Mombasa, political rule belonged to the Awlad Uthman bin Abdallah clan of the Mazrui increasingly throughout the eighteenth century. In the nineteenth century, most of Mombasa's 'high' *culama* were from the Awlad Abdallah bin Nafi[c] clan of the Mazrui. Political leadership of the Three Tribes seems to have been in the hands of the al-Malindi (Bauri). Mombasa's vocational structure, however, does not appear to have been as formally arranged as it was at Lamu where wealth and vocation even came to be preserved in the town's oral traditions, as was seen in Chapter 3. The Wayumbili were 'assigned' less prestigious occupations while also being given ritual leadership.[18] The Maawi (Bwana Gogo) were the *khatibs* of the Friday mosque and became wealthy businessmen. The Makhzumy/Kinamti likewise were wealthy tradesmen and political leaders of the Suudi faction, along with the Bereki (Barayk).[19] The Bakari were navigators and shipbuilders, as well as merchants.[20] Latecomers like the Husayni *shurafa* (who arrived from Pate in the late eighteenth century), were poets, *culama*, and merchants, while the Bwana Mshuti Waziri and the Jahadhmy were keepers of the town regalia.[21] As will be discussed below, learning and types of learning, too, tended to be concentrated within certain clans or descent groups according to their vocational specializations.

These horizontal and vertical divisions in town society were reinforced from four directions in wealthier, more developed societies like Lamu, and in at least two ways in smaller, less affluent towns. All towns tended to isolate houses and kin groups spatially within quarters, for one thing, and secondly, descent groups and classes tended to be endogamous. Being

Islamic societies, preferential kin marriage was the ideal, while at the same time hypergamy was practised among the most prosperous clans.[22] People's world-view reinforced social distinctions, also. Townspeople considered themselves to be racially dissimilar to their non-Muslim *nyika* neighbours, and within the towns themselves it was thought that there were similar differences between *waungwana* and *sharif* families.[23] Such views received further succour among the wealthy, upper class clans who believed that there were definite existential distinctions between individuals of one clan and those of another. Certain groups of people (practising certain vocations) were seen as being ranked on a definite scale of existential 'bigness' according to the putative nobility of their ancestors. One simply inherited one's place in society through birth. Islamic fatalism, coupled with socio-economic realities of town society, resulted in the supposition that people were ranked by the will of God himself.[24] Thus, one's place in society had to be accepted without choice, and Islam itself and proper adherence to its principles were equated with fear of God and acceptance of his will concerning social arrangements. This was borne out even in the idea that familiar spirits, in the form of personal angels, were ranked socially.[25] Every individual, it was believed, had an angel of the right who was responsible for one's good actions, and an angel of the left who was the evil side of one's conscience. As these angels were thought to desire association only with their equals, town society then had to be stratified. Thus, individuals were thought to be existentially different from one another; they were created by God and placed by him in a universe which was stratified by his design, and it was the sole duty of everyone as a good Muslim to accept his place in God's great plan.

The final way in which social stratification and social divisions received support was through the limited educational opportunities open to most townspeople. Recent converts and most *waungwana* were permitted to learn the basic tenets of the faith, but their knowledge of the written tradition and Arabic extended only as far as what was taught in the Quran schools (*chuo*, pl. *vyuo*).[26] Such an education lasted only two or three years, after which most boys were initiated into the vocational arts of their fathers and forefathers. Even children of the wealthier and more prestigious houses were permitted to attend only a few *darasas* offered by local *walimu* for the wider community. Usually such classes were offered in the *mwalimu*'s home or in the mosque at appointed times of the day.[27] Knowledge of most advanced Islamic sciences, in their local versions and with what texts were available, was open only to the scions of certain clans which were recognized for their specialization in these areas. Thus, in Lamu the Maawi were known as the clan which produced the town's *walimu* and *khatibs*, whilst in Mombasa the Mazrui, Maamiri, and Mandhry clans made up the town's learned elite. *Shurafa'* also brought detailed knowledge of the Hadrami tradition in religious sciences wherever they settled. Usually knowledge of written texts was passed from generation to generation within these clans in special tutorials offered only at night or in early morning hours and in the private chambers of the master's home. In any case, a child usually followed the profession of his clan or descent group because such a calling was thought to be most natural and suitable for one of his birth. What was perceived as 'natural and suitable', of course, depended on the ascriptive status of his clan. Thus, the profession one followed and the attendant knowledge and skills that went with it were ascriptive just as persons born into certain socio-economic groups were expected to exhibit certain talents and modes of thought and behaviour.

As a final note, the ascriptive statuses of certain descent groups had a strong bearing on the local notion of justice and its proper administration just as it had on other aspects of town culture. What was considered to be just, of course, was whatever reinforced local Islamic traditions and norms. And, as one might expect, justice abetted the social hierarchies of the towns and, in turn, social stratification influenced court proceedings. Islam itself was inherently biased in not allowing a non-Muslim to testify against a Muslim, while a Muslim's word carried more weight with a *qadi* than that of an unbeliever. In a Swahili court, the word of one who was thought to be living closer to the requirements of the Shari^{c}a and the 'right path' ideal had more influence than of one who was thought to enjoy less of God's favour. 'Religious integrity' (Ar. *adala*; Sw. *adili*) was a factor in the acceptance of testimony and the weight given it by the *qadi*. *Adili* in turn was affected by the *heshima* of an individual (that is, his honour, dignity, position), and *heshima* of course depended on adherence to prescribed modes of thought and behaviour – that is to say, by established custom. The law, then, did not apply equally to all, as various eyewitnesses of the past and informants in the present have observed.[28] All the rules which conduced social integration were present, including gift-giving to the elder or *qadi* deciding the appeal. Thus, *qadis* who lived off gifts received in deciding cases[29] usually were accused of bribery by European observers who failed to understand the dynamics of town social structure and how they bore on the implementation of religious law.[30]

One can conclude by saying that coastal towns were economically and vocationally diverse. Wealth was a prime factor in determining an individual's or clan's standing in the community. How wealth was acquired was not so important ultimately so long as the means were considered honourable. However, wealthy clans tended towards certain vocational activities, as well as towards certain ways of thought and public behaviour which were considered exemplary. In fact, town society was divided vertically into descent groups or clans which often were ascribed not only certain vocational activities, but even certain life styles. Thus, individuals born into particular clans were expected to inherit definite behavioural and intellectual predilections simply by virue of their birth. Naturally, historical factors decided which clans became wealthy, but local traditions sometimes buttressed socio-economic and vocational divisions in society by making it appear that such divisions were constituted at the society's founding. In addition, support was given to those divisions in the belief that such ascriptive categories and social arrangements were part of the divine order of things, and acceptance of one's place in this scheme was equated with 'orthodox' Islamic practice.

Town society itself was arranged into an ascriptive hierarchy by which particular groups were thought of as having varying existential statuses based on 'bigness'. Some descent groups were thought of as 'bigger' than others by virtue of the wealth they commanded and the prestige of their vocational activities (for example, being a *shamba* owner was more prestigious than being a bush farmer or fisherman). The most obvious aspect of Islamic practice which was affected by this local ascriptive hierarchy was the way Islamic justice was administered. The notion of *adala* found throughout the Islamic world found its counterpart on the coast in the word *adili*. A person's *adili* affected the worth of his testimony in local court proceedings, and of course this was defined locally as being dependent on the ascriptive status of the clan from which the witness in question came. Thus, the practice of Islamic law and its execution by *qadis* in coastal towns were heavily subject to local customs and usages.

ERUDITION AND CHARISMATIC LEADERSHIP

Just as a wide range of vocational specializations was recognized as beneficial to a town's welfare, so then was the definition of learning a broad one. Before the middle of the nineteenth century, for example, terms used to designate learned individuals were vague and generally overlapping. A person noted as a religious scholar could have been called many things, while at the same time all persons who were considered learned were expected to have at least a minimal knowledge of locally practised religion (see Figure 1). Generally speaking, learned members of the town simply were designated as *wazee* or *washehe* (elders or grandees). A short discussion of these terms alone reveals much concerning local perceptions of the relevance of learning to the social and economic interests of the community, for a *mzee* or *mshehe* was a community leader who was pre-eminently knowledgeable of all affairs of importance to the welfare of the town. The appellation and 'position' were partly heritable and charismatic in their implications in that the *wazee* or *washehe* almost always came from descent groups 'recognized' in the community and were people who achieved distinction in ways that were lauded by their fellow townspeople. In the wealthiest, most developed communities like Lamu and Mombasa, *washehe* (as in Mombasa) and *wazee* (as in Lamu) were the formal representatives of their *mitaa* in town political gatherings and were responsible for civic and judicial duties carried out in the *mitaa*.[31] Certain descent groups, however, were noted for producing *wazee* or *washehe* who specialized in certain types of learning. Some *wazee* from certain clans thus were especially influential in town politics. At Mombasa, for instance, the al-Malindi were the political representatives of the indigenous Twelve Tribes in Mazrui councils. In the distant past, probably before the eighteenth century, the Kirume clan, from among Lamu's WaTikuu inhabitants, were considered the town's 'owners of

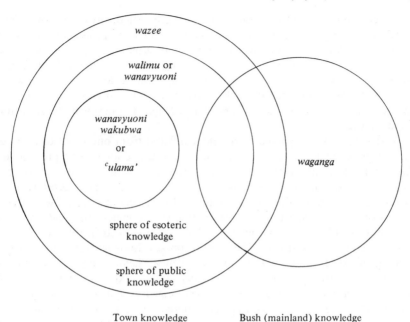

Figure 1.

the land' (*wenyewe*) whose sanction had to sought by all strangers wishing to settle in the town and who were responsible for community rituals.[32] By the eighteenth century, a position called the *mwenye mui* had emerged which was rotated among the 'recognized' Twelve Tribes of the town. The *mwenye mui* seems to have acted as a sort of chairman to Lamu's town council (the Yumbe). By the nineteenth century, though, the Bakari and the Makhzumy came to dominate the office of *mwenye mui*.[33] It appears that by about the early nineteenth century the *mwenye mui* functioned in a manner very like the *diwani* of Bagamoyo. In both cases, the ruler had authority over lands and fields and, interestingly enough, they administered the laws of the town in most situations where disputes arose among the clans of the town. Other *wazee* and *washehe* who were not learned in the written tradition seem to have served only as advisors in deciding such cases.[34] Similarly, within the *mitaa* it was the *wazee* of the tribe or clan who adjudicated disputes.[35]

The town elders, above all, were typical 'pillars of the community'. The formal nature of their position within local society varied from town to town. In most instances, it appears that the socio-political structure of the community was relatively informal and open, whereas at Lamu political authority was somewhat more institutionalized in the form of the Yumbe and its head, the *mwenye mui*. (Mombasa, of course, presented a unique situation where political influence was distributed informally among the Twelve Tribe elders, but was led after the early eighteenth century by a clan holding the title of *liwali*, namely the Mazrui.) Their functions essentially were community-related. Among them were adjudication of some legal rows, providing political leadership, calling town meetings (*kupiga pembe*), organizing dance competitions (*ngoma*), and supervising the religious and ritual events which were crucial to the community interests.[36] Naturally, then, people were recognized as *wazee* or *washehe* and were empowered with such community responsibilities to the extent that they were judged to possess the necessary skills and knowledge to perform these duties competently.

Just who was recognized as an elder differed from one town to another. As certain clans became prominent in the town, of course, their prestige and wealth made it likely that these clans would produce more leaders than others. The appellation itself was not so much a title in most cases as it was a respectful term of address which accrued to a person once he was judged to possess certain attributes, skills, or knowledge which were valued in the community. Thus, all town grandees had to be learned in reading, writing, and the local oral tradition. They had to possess knowledge of town history, clan genealogies and relationships, as well as having at least a working knowledge of the Shariᶜa as it was locally understood and applied.[37] Above all, an elder had to be one of the 'recognized people of the town' (*ayan bilad*) whose public actions were considered to be paradigmatic for all.[38]

The informal means by which individuals gained recognition as *wazee* or *washehe* partly grew out of the social and spatial arrangements of the town and its pervasive spirit of competition. The ordering of the town into quarters coincided with its division into descent and ascriptive groupings. Each *mtaa* was a tiny community unto itself with its own mosque and elders. These social and spatial divisions along descent and ascriptive lines engendered a feeling of rivalry and strife among the *mitaa*, and particularly between the moieties. The usual channels by which this competitive spirit was directed was through harmless and even socially reinforcing ways such as dance and poetry duels (*ngoma* or *mashindano*). Besides being culturally reinforcing, of course, these *mashindano* were rhetorical platforms in which inter-ethnic and clan grievances were aired. Given this, it is not surprising to learn that people who were recognized (addressed) as *wazee* frequently included those who enjoyed reputations for their poetic skills in the local dialect and for virtuoso performances in leading their *mitaa* to triumph in dance competitions.[39] Having skills as a poet in these rivalries meant possessing a thorough command of local tradition as well as a forensic mastery sufficient to represent one's clan forcefully in town politics. Often, however, these peaceful outlets for ethnic and class tensions gave way to open strife and, here again, a person could make a reputation for himself as the leader of a victorious clan or faction.[40]

Poets often were privy to other individuals and other clans who were involved more directly in town politics. Their skills made them useful orators and propagandists, and their mastery of locally received wisdom made them useful counsellors. Noteworthy examples of such poet propagandists are Bwana Muyaka al-Ghassani and Suud b. Said al-Maamiri, both of Mombasa. Bwana Muyaka was a Nine Tribesman who allied himself with the Mazrui in the last few decades of Mazrui hegemony in Mombasa. His early poems of support earned him the right to eat at Mazrui tables at Fort Jesus,[41] and later he became privy to their inner councils.[42] It was he, for example, who advised the *liwali* (governor) Abdullah b. Hamid against defying Sayyid Said b. Sultan openly: he counselled against Mazrui meddling in the politics of the Lamu archipelago; he criticized and warned the Mazrui for their fatal tendency to quarrel openly over succession to the *liwali*-ship.[43] His close friendship with the *liwali* Salim b. Hamid Mazrui cost him a great deal of humiliation at the hands of the Three Tribes *wazee*, Sh. Jabir, Sh. Muhammad b. Hamis, and Sh. Mshirazi, after Mombasa fell to the sovereignty of the Busaidi Sultanate of Zanzibar and Oman in 1837 with the complicity of the Three Tribes.[44] *Mzee* Suud b. Said was a scion of one of Mombasa's Omani families who supported the rebellious Sh. Mbarak b. Rashid Mazrui in his struggles with the Zanzibar Government in the 1870s. In particular, he took an active part as a propagandizer when Sayyid Barghash's *liwali*, Muhammad b. Abdullah Bakashwaini ('Al-Akida'), strove to bring Sh. Mbarak to heel between 1870 and 1874. Various other poets rallied around Suud, including Muhammad b. Ahmad al-Mambassiy (Mvita), and propagandized a mission to Zanzibar undertaken by Suud to seek Al-Akida's dismissal.[45] When Al-Akida attempted to ensnare Mbarak through false promises of peace negotiations, Suud managed to get the news to Mbarak, even though Al-Akida restricted his movements, by improvizing metaphorical (*abjadi*) lines at a dance competition which reached the ears of the *shaykh*. It was Suud and his allies who denounced Al-Akida before the Sultan, and in the end it was their unceasing propaganda among Mombasa's townspeople which led to Al-Akida's final disgrace and removal.[46]

Most people received recognition as *wazee* or *washehe* through the acquisition of knowledge and exhibitions of public behaviour which marked them as exemplary *waungwana*. That is to say, the learning which they acquired and their public actions were valued highly in town society and were the distinguishing standards of coastal urban civilization, *uungwana*. However, it must be pointed out that much of this knowledge of local civilization was readily available to all freeborn townsmen and even to slaves and strangers to a certain extent. In other words, within town society there was a 'sphere of public knowledge' which was accessible to all who lived in the community, the essentials of which had to be mastered by all who hoped to be accepted as *waungwana*. What seems to have set off many as grandees was the superior degree of their mastery of this corpus of publicly accessible knowledge.

The 'sphere of public knowledge' had both its formal and informal aspects. For example, on one hand all children of *waungwana* were expected to master the written tradition to a minimal extent by being able to recite the Quran and to read it in Arabic. For this purpose, every town had several Quran schools (*chuo*, pl. *vyuo*) which children attended at a 'trifling expense' until they knew the Holy Book by heart, after which they went on to study more advanced sciences or to take up the trade of their clan.[47] The informal side of publicly available knowledge was that which sociologists would call the acculturative process. Sanctioned behaviour, of course, was learned from infancy onwards, whilst the accumulation of local history, myths, fables, and traditional lore was obtained informally through example and word of mouth. As in most African societies, children gathered daily with their elder relations around work places or nightly around a warming fire to be entertained by stories which both regaled and taught a lesson. Adults too shared oral traditions with their social equals during evening *barazas* held in the foyers (*sabule*) of their homes or in nightly visits among women.[48]

Town society, however, was not only characterized by forms of learning which was available to all, nor did all *wazee* obtain enlightenment by strictly oral means. There were varieties of specialized knowledge which were vital to community life and which were the exclusive preserve only of certain descent groups. Thus, within the sphere of public knowledge there was a 'sphere of esoteric knowledge', and included among the town elders were its specialists. Such specialists were known either as *walimu* or *wanavyuoni*, and their knowledge included much of what Westerners would call religious education (though this characterization is not necessarily employed by townsmen, as will become clearer below). Several features distinguished specialized, 'religious' knowledge from publicly accessible learning. First of all, usually it was retained in certain clans. Second, it appears to have been transmitted more formally. Third, its written content often was greater than was the case with publicly available knowledge. Fourth, and last, since such information was kept within descent groups, to a certain extent it was mixed with the particular history, ethnicity, and world-views of the clans who mastered this specialized knowledge.

The key to understanding the various categories of specialized erudition is to realize that religious knowledge and practice were viewed by townspeople as constituting a vocation much as other secular crafts were.[49] As such, religious learning and its applications were not only personally enlightening as a means to stay in God's grace, but were personal sources of income to religious practitioners. Naturally, then, the more exclusive the nature of such knowledge and the higher its social value, the greater the income it could fetch.

Every clan possessed a certain reserve of knowledge, skills, and resources which constituted a vocation exploitable by the group as a source of income. This corpus of knowledge and skills usually was kept secret within the descent group itself, and it was taught within the home where parents and grandparents passed it on to sons and daughters as part of the clan patrimony.[50] Generally, it can be asserted that the precise nature of the vocation followed by a clan was determined by the varieties of resources within the clan which made up its patrimony. In clans which were noted as craft specialists, this patrimony consisted of particular skills and tools. Examples of clans noted for special craft skills include the Bakari of Lamu who were carpenters and shipbuilders, the Maawi who were farmers, the Changamwe of Mombasa many of whom were 'medicine men' (*waganga, falaki*, or *tabibs*) and herbalists, and the Husayni of Pate and Lamu who were skilled poets as well as merchants and religious scholars.

Taken in this sense, then, certain descent groups of *waungwana* can be said to have been especially 'skilled' in the religious sciences which were just as vital to the community welfare as were such secular crafts as carpentry, silversmithing, shipbuilding, or farming. For 'religion' often was medicine, and 'medicine' in the coastal town, as elsewhere in Africa, consisted not only of the physical treatment of ailments, but ministering to their psychological and 'spiritual' causes as well.[51] Since 'medicine' consisted of following closely prescribed rituals and the use of medicinal plants, in a sense it can be viewed as a skill requiring a specialized body of esoteric information and a related collection of materials which comprised a patrimony within certain clans which had to be transmitted from generation to generation.[52] Thus, where tools and skills formed such a patrimony in artisan families, in houses which produced *walimu*, clan patrimony consisted of secret formulas, esoteric knowledge of the religious sciences (Ar. *fanun*; Sw. *fenni*), and, above all, knowledge of sacred texts (*vitabu*).

At present, there is relatively little available information on just when particular texts were introduced into coastal communities, nor on what texts might have been used in the distant (that is, pre-nineteenth century) past. As a general rule of thumb, though, it is reasonable to say that a very high proportion of the texts mentioned by Becker as having been in use by the early twentieth century can be assumed to have come into existence or to have arrived on the coast during the period of the Busaidi Sultanate.[53] Given the rough correlation between wealth and erudition in the written tradition (due to the greater leisure necessary for *darasa* attendance), however, it seems not unreasonable to assume that before the middle of the nineteenth century wealthier towns such as Siyu, Pate, and Lamu contained a comparatively large number of written sources.[54]

Nevertheless, in most coastal communities written religious materials were relatively rare before the 1860s or so. Few but the wealthiest houses possessed anything besides a Quran, and rarer still was literacy in Arabic.[55] As such, *vitabu* were a scarce resource and the ability to read and interpret them an even more precious commodity needed to protect the *imani* of the town. Holy books were among the resources only of certain clans and, to a degree, of certain communities. Thus, while the children of most *waungwana* were trained to memorize the Quran, instruction in the advanced sciences (*fenni*) was the exclusive domain of the few descent groups who possessed additional written resources which formed part of the clan patrimony.[56] The rarity of *vitabu* itself contributed to the parochial character of local Islam since, obviously, a community or clan which had trained *wanavyuoni* and books on certain sciences among its resources (for example, *fiqh*, law; *tafsir*, Quranic exegesis; *tasawwuf*, sufism) acquired reputations for the particular *vitabu* and sciences which they had mastered.[57] Also, certain texts were considered locally as being more authoritative than others.[58] All this means that a student of written religious sciences had to study particular books more than particular subjects, *per se*, and his reputation was based on his acquisition of certificates (*ijaza*) for each text he mastered.[59] Because different *wanavyuoni* were noted as specialists in certain individual sciences and were the masters of particular texts, usually the student had to obtain the permission of these respective masters to study privately under their tutelage. In this way, then, learning in the advanced sciences tended to be divided by families or clans according to the resources and specializations of these houses. Only the offspring of a few clans who had an established reputation for learning were allowed into private sessions with the recognized masters as only members of these descent groups were believed to have the ascriptive capacities to master the Arabic language and advanced texts.

However, *vitabu* were valuable not only for their rarity, but also for their importance in 'symbolic magic'. The use of the Quran (and other holy books) in amulets (*hirizi*) and in other types of preventive and curative medicine goes back to the eighth-century debate over the createdness of the Quran.[60] According to Asharite thinking, which became the 'orthodox' point of view among Sunni scholars, the language of the Quran has existed autonomously, regardless of human agency and speech, since the beginning of time. 'The Book,' as one missionary put it, 'is everything. The man is but the mouthpiece of the Book. It is God who wrote the Book, not Muhammad. The human element is reduced to a voice that repeats a lesson committed to memory.'[61] In other words, the Arabic language is God's language, and specifically, the Quran and its language are extensions of God himself, taken Neoplatonically.[62] For Swahili urbanites this itself implied that the Arabic language, God's name uttered in Arabic ('Allah'), and especially the Holy Quran, all had *baraka*. As already discussed, what had *baraka* was what was attuned above all to the divine order, and as long as something conformed to this overarching order, it might be expected to bring material benefits.[63] Thus, in a large sense *baraka* was a potential commodity. This means that the sources of *baraka*, whether it was in the form of descent from the Prophet, in knowledge of God and his universe, or as holy books, likewise were to be guarded, passed on as patrimony from one generation to another, and to be distributed for a price.

THE NATURE OF RELIGIOUS LEADERSHIP

Religious training, however, was not always in the 'advanced' sciences which involved the written Islamic tradition, nor did the written tradition originate purely from non-African sources. Indeed, those who specialized in the study of the advanced written texts formed a relatively exclusive minority among the *walimu* and *wanavyuoni*, and were dignified by several epithets, included among which were *wanavyuoni wakubwa* ('great' *wanavyuoni*), *maalimu*, or the Arabic *ʿulama*ʾ. (The last term, however, might have become current with the tendency to identify erudition with the written tradition, especially with imported written materials, with the 'Arabs', or with those who claimed Arab descent during the Busaidi period and later.) The crucial point, though, is that before the last quarter of the nineteenth century, when the Omani presence really began to be felt along the coast, there were very few places where *walimu* were extensively knowledgeable in the written tradition.[64] Again, it was the rarity of written texts which made them so valuable. Therefore, there were few *ᶜulama²*, in the strictest sense of the term, yet there certainly were *walimu* and *wanavyuoni*.

Religious knowledge was diverse, esoteric, and socially reinforcing, making extensive use of oral sources as well as the few written resources there were. It borrowed much from a town's African traditions and environment, and somewhat less from the imported written tradition. Also, while traditions were mixed unconsciously and in varying degrees from one individual to another, there was a certain conscious distinction made between native-born knowledge and knowledge which was imported from other Islamic lands across the ocean. What is interesting is that certain sciences were allowed to be taught in mosques because they were considered to be properly 'religious', while others had to be taught elsewhere because they were not accepted as such, though they clearly were taken from the *African* religious tradition. The town's learned were divided into categories of *ulama wa dini* (*ᶜulama²* of religion) and *ulama wa dunia* (*ᶜulama²* of the world).[65] What this entailed, of course, was a distinction between the sorts of problems faced by townsmen in their religious life as they interpreted them in terms of the sorts of remedies they required. One view emphasized the problem of maintaining the 'sacredness' of the town *umma* through properly adhering to God's laws, especially in their written form, and through the conscientious attention to essential religious duties (that is, profession of faith, prayer, fasting, alms giving, pilgrimage). The other view derived more from the locally evolved world-view and was directed more at divining and settling the spiritual causes behind difficulties encountered in day-to-day living. The latter view was more activist in its philosophy and spiritual concerns and centred more on ritual matters than did the former view. In short, the coastal townsperson implicitly recognized the distinction between absolute and relative views of transcendence.

The dividing line between ideologies born in the African environments of the towns and the imported varieties followed the economic and vocational distinctions between the coastal towns and the *nyika*. Among *walimu*, some specialized in sciences which borrowed more from imported wisdom, while others' learning came from the accumulated wisdom of the town's *bara* and *nyika*.[66] Thus, there arose a rough distinction between 'town' learning (*elimu*) and 'bush' learning (*uganga*). (However, many *walimu* were known to be *waganga*. It was *uganga* which was thought to be non-religious, while *elimu* was 'religion', properly speaking, to townspeople even though *elimu* itself included much that was African.) Town learning was considered religion, while knowledge which came from non-Islamic regions adjacent to the coast simply was 'medicine'.

Having come from the mainland and bush, 'medicine' largely was the product of the accumulated experiences of both townspeople and their non-Muslim neighbours. It was divided into three categories according to the types of problems it was intended to solve and by the methods used to solve them. One type was that aspect of local practice which treated ailments by physical means. Usually this involved skin cutting, cupping, the use of hot and cold surfaces, and, especially, knowledge of drugs.[67] These drugs mostly included fats and fleshes of sundry animals, as well as the roots, bark, and flowers of locally grown (that is, usually native) plants. Knowledge of the plants and animal products that were useful for treating specific illnesses originally was attained through a thorough knowledge of the town's botanical and zoological environment and, just as in farming the *bara* and the *nyika*, through experimentation.[68] Individual *tabibs* (*walimu* who specialized in medicine) were noted for being especially skilful in treating certain conditions. One informant, for instance, provided a list of nineteenth- and twentieth-century *walimu* who were, individually, specialists in treating tuberculosis, dropsie, rheumatism, skin disorders, headaches, eye cataracts, and in mending broken bones.[69]

Three points are especially germane to this discussion, however. First, it is important to emphasize here as elsewhere that herbal recipes for the treatment of specific disorders as given above were kept secret within certain descent groups or clans. Medical practice was hereditary, and skills and recipes were frequently passed from parents or grandparents to family offspring.[70] Such knowledge and skills were part of the family inheritance. The second point is that medicine was divided into categories of *uganga* or *elimu* according to its source. *Uganga*, as discussed above, was medical knowledge that made use of non-Islamic knowledge from nearby mainland or bush country.[71] Town society, in its efforts to maximize physical survival, exploited the coastal and island physical environments not only for economic purposes, but also for medical reasons. Just as social relations with mainland and bush peoples served as avenues by which the non-Islamic ideological environment found its way into the religious practices and assumptions of the towns themselves, so then did the exploitation of the nearby non-Islamic environment serve for medical reasons. This, in turn, leads to the third point to be raised here, namely that medicine, as it was practised in the towns, was not wholly physical in its approach. It shared one overriding conceptual characteristic with the medical/religious practices of neighbouring non-Muslims (and with popular Islamic medicine everywhere, by the way). This shared ground was that all ailments were thought to have supernatural causes as well as physical ones. It was this belief which was the basis of the two other aspects of medical practice.

Medical practice in East Africa's coastal towns involved an essentially relative view of transcendence. Implicit in this was the notion that behind all natural events were unseen, supernatural causes. Whenever things remained normal it was assumed that the townspeople were 'rightly guided' and that the community was in a state of *imani*. But when something untoward happened, it was assumed that God or the spirits of the dead were offended. Hence, divination was called for to ascertain such things as the causes of illness, the reasons for natural catastrophes, as well as to augur future happenings to identify propitious moments for the enactment of crucially important events.[72] Usually, this was accomplished through interpretations of dreams or the casting of sticks, bones, or pebbles much as in the tradition of the mainland bush.[73] In some centres, however, where written sources were available on the subject, there was some knowledge of the Greek medical tradition and astrology which had been preserved in Islamic sciences.[74] Given the special charisma of *vitabu*, portions of them were employed for divination or for amulets. Also, certain written works on astrology and divination were available in the nineteenth century – and possibly even earlier. One of these was the *Sawt al-Khabar*, a popular medical manual of uncertain origin. Interestingly enough, while works like the *Sawt al-Khabar* made use of the *baraka* of written Arabic and various forms of Islamic numerical and symbolic magic, one knowledgeable informant emphasized their strongly African character as evident in their use of local formulas, syntax, and terminology.[75] Thus, again, mainland non-Islamic beliefs and usages found their way into what were supposed to be essentially Islamic works.

Two especially interesting forms of divination which indicate further mainland and bush influences on town Islam can be seen in the offices of the *mkuu wa pwani*, the maritime ritual expert, and of the bushland 'guardian of the soil'. Both offices were occupied by townsmen and were divinatory in character. Methods and resources used by the *mkuu wa pwani* are not available at this time, but what is known is that the office was occupied by one who had sufficient seaman's skills to ascertain the most opportune time to set sail on fishing expeditions and how to plan for overseas commercial voyages. In Lamu the clan which was especially noted for maritime skills and which monopolized the position of *mkuu wa pwani* was the Bakari.[76]

The position of 'guardian of the soil' went by various names in different places, such as *mvyale* (Hadimu in Zanzibar), *mwizi* (Pemba), *mwinyi mkuu* (Tumbatu), *jumbe la wakulima* (Pate), or just as a plain *mwalimu* (Lamu).[77] Likewise, these experts appear to have varied slightly in function from location to location, and in fact it seems plausible that their duties might have been shared by more than one person. Generally, though, their duties appear to have included divining the most propitious time for planting, selecting the best areas of the bush for cultivation, and setting the planting season schedule by a solar calendar which they computed.[78] Equally important (and interesting, considering the fact that they were Muslims) were their efforts at communicating with spirits thought to reside on the land selected for farming in order to appease these spirits and to obtain their blessings for the vital tasks about to be undertaken.[79]

Closely associated with divination were the cures for the supernatural causes of disease and disaster. Such therapy often was aimed at psychological or psychosomatic disorders and centred on rituals called *pungwa wa pepo* (driving out a spirit, *pepo*, or exorcism). The belief was that mental derangement or certain physical disorders were caused when a spirit took possession of a person, while of course such disturbances had their grounds in social or family disturbances. As such, 'Divination,' as observed by Bohannon and Curtin, usually 'is one of the specialties most likely to attract the person with an intellectual bent. Diviners must have an excellent intuitive knowledge of the societies in which they live.'[80] *Pungwa* rituals always called for sacrifices of numerous cocks, goats, and bullocks, plus generous amounts of food for the *walimu* and their Quran reciters during the several days of treatment. Along with these came constant dancing and drumming, day and night, and frequent consultations of *vitabu* such as the *Sawt al-Khabar*.[81] The place of the *mwalimu* in these rituals actually was as a therapist of sorts whose task was to seek out the psychological and social causes of the disorder. Indeed, as one informant put it, 'if someone is inquisitive and knows all the news of the people, it is [considered] very dangerous... They say, "Take care of that [one]; that [one] is a *Sawt al-Khabar*. Don't do anything in front of him. He'll go and tell the people."'[82] Thus, the 'cure' in these cases eventuated when the *mwalimu* had aired and resolved all attendant social problems, 'in the course of seeking to counter and divine manifestations'.[83] Therefore, it is not as astonishing as it was to Stigand to learn that 'the victim of the *pepo* almost invariably regains sanity at the expiration of the ceremonies'.[84]

A final few words have to be added here concerning the relationship between the *mwalimu*'s efforts at affecting cures through physical means and his use of 'magic' for the same ends. One of the points which has been stressed in various ways has been the close relationship between the natural and supernatural worlds in the relative view of transcendence implied by coastal medical practices. While the 'guardian of the soil' or the *tabib* resorted to 'magic' and incantations to cure his patient or to augur future events, at the same time he employed methods and drugs based on a collective empirical knowledge he and his fellow townspeople had of the environment which they inhabited.[85] More than anything else, it was the presence of town intellectuals, such as the *walimu*, in their African physical, social, and intellectual settings which affected uniquely the character of town Islam. It was their inescapable involvement in this world, as farmers practising shifting agriculture in *nyika* and *bara* lands for part of the year, which was the main venue by which African ideas and usages continued to influence Islam in the coastal towns, especially before about the 1860s.

While many scholars would note the *mwalimu*'s skill and 'intellectual bent' as an observer and practitioner who based his work on his observations, some might portray him also as a charlatan who specialized in deceiving others through the employment of meaningless 'mumbo jumbo' alongside his 'real' work as an observer and scientist of sorts. It is submitted here that such criticism is patently unfair and patronizing, especially when one notes similar tendencies among so-called Christian faith healers. While the African *mwalimu* might have observed the world about him and based his practices on these observations, he also sought to systematize his observations into a coherent world-view. As in the case with European metaphysical systems, for example, such a world-view essentially amounted to a projection of his empirical experiences of the natural microcosm in which he lived onto the unseen and unknown. To the extent that these metaphysical models were consistent with the observable world, they can be considered as having been rational and even 'proto-scientific' in a Western sense. Given this, these models can be said to have been irrational only inasmuch as they might have been inconsistent with knowledge which was obtained empirically. The irrational, then, simply was what reflected the imperfections and anomalies in the cosmic model. This occasional slipping back into total irrationality was considered to be witchcraft.[86]

To the African coastal townsperson the borderline between the rational and the irrational was clouded. There was a fuzzy border region around the hard core of observable knowledge which separated it from the irrational and unobserved.[87] One simply did not slip from the rational to the irrational realms directly. Rather, one reached the irrational only by passing by degrees into worlds entirely alien, worlds where physical and social stimuli were so new and strange and unpredictable that they could not be assimilated to past experiences and relatable knowledge. Perhaps *uganga* belonged to this epistemological nether region in that, while it consisted of a corpus of knowledge which coastal Africans had obtained by empirical means, it was a knowledge which was no longer, nor completely, meaningful to them in an ultimate sense. While on one hand, for example, economic, vocational, and ideological diversification was useful for community comfort and survival, there were significant differences between island or coastal environments and the lands of the drier *nyika*. Thus *uganga* was fully appropriate to the *bara* or *nyika*, but was a partial anomaly in the coastal town itself. *Uganga* was not 'religion' – that is, ultimately meaningful – because one's environment was not only physical and social, but traditional and historical too. Knowledge was not only directly experiential, then, but a heritable knowledge and wisdom. Thus, *uganga* was also an anachronism in the town. But to the town it was useful, a 'non-religious' anachronism and anomaly.

SOCIAL CONNECTIONS OF THE *WALIMU*

Consistent with this view of the *walimu* as the most intelligent and socially attuned members of the coastal community is the fact that they usually were the 'pillars' of town society and politics. For one thing, most of the descent groups which were noted for siring religious experts also tended to be among the wealthiest clans in their respective communities. At Mombasa the Mazrui had extensive power and landholdings. The Awlad Zahur branch owned *shambas* at Takaungu, while the Awlad Nafi^c, who produced most of the most notable scholars after the 1840s, possessed clove plantations at Pemba.[88] The Changamwe, who produced most of the 'little' *wanavyuoni* among the Three Tribes in the nineteenth century, had both *shambas* and mainland plots (*mahonde*) where coconuts, mangoes, citruses, and some cereals were grown for export to India and Arabia.[89] At Lamu, extensive mainland *mahonde* holdings around Mpeketoni and ties with such mainland peoples as the Bajun and sedentarized Somali brought the Maawi and Bakari wealth through trade by the eighteenth century.[90] Somewhat later, in the eighteenth century, this wealth was augmented by the acquisition and employment of huge numbers of slaves.[91] Finally, the *sharif* clan of the al-Husayni were noted, similarly, for the extraordinary wealth which they garnered from *shamba* ownership and from commercial activities.[92]

Of course, the coincidence of wealth and learning is to be anticipated. Only wealth could afford individuals the leisure time and a descent group the patrimony consisting of the written sources and collective learning requisite for scholarly pursuits. This view is further reinforced by the fact that within these clans there was a conscious effort at singling out the most promising younger members for training in the sciences, while other children were charged with carrying on the group vocations in trade or farming.[93] It was this 'business' branch of the descent group which was expected to support the learned ones, the clan 'lawyers'.

The nature of the training given to prospective *walimu* reflects their 'family' interests in perpetuating the economic and social status quo of the communities in which they lived. In addition to being steeped in local history and lore,[94] all *waungwana* appear to have been trained in the simple elements of arithmetic for use in business matters as part of their primary, Quran school education, for example.[95] Those who were trained as *walimu* generally were educated in all sciences which qualified them for leadership roles in both religious and 'practical' areas of community life.[96] The ethnic and class origins of most *walimu wakubwa* are betrayed by the fact that instruction in commercial skills and law was a *sine qua non* of advanced training. Generally, most *walimu* seem to have been experts in matters concerning buying and marketing of merchandise to the extent that some even served as investment brokers for others in their communities.[97] Their involvement in town commerce and their concern for property and property rights are shown by the emphasis which was given to *fiqh* and inheritance law in coastal Islamic education.[98] Closely allied to direct financial concerns and training in sciences related to commerce was the priming given in matters concerning marriage and divorce. *Mkutu* ('equality' in marriage alliances), of course, was rooted firmly in the socio-economic status quo of the town and implied concern for the preservation of property and investment 'capital' within the town and especially within certain clans. Also, given the connection between material well-being and world-view, preservation and transmission of capital in the community and its wealthy, intellectually skilled clans suggest a local concern for ensuring the cultural and ideological continuity of the town – that is, of the character of town Islam. Therefore, the second important area of 'religious' education in coastal towns was in matters concerning marriage and divorce. It was the business of the *mwalimu* to know 'all the news of the people' and part of this knowledge included local history. Knowledge of history meant familiarity with local genealogies and myths concerning supposed places of origin and time of settlement of each clan of the town where social status was figured largely in terms of prior claims of residence in the town or through claims of descent from the Prophet.[99]

Thus, it is interesting and significant to note the strategic importance of the mosque and attendant mosque functionaries in the life of the town and the quarter. Where each *mtaa* was a residential quarter for a given descent group, the mosque served as the focal point of ethnic identity, while the quarter's *walimu*, *wazee*, or mosque attendants acted as guardians and repositories of ethnic heritage and patrimony. Furthermore, the town as an ethnic and historical conglomerate of sorts was represented in the Friday mosque(s), and there was a corresponding role played by the *khatibs* and the clan from which they came in relation to the community as a whole. Therefore, Velten's informant wrote of the type of *mwalimu* 'in the ancient tradition' (*kama iliyokuwa zamani*) who was associated with the mosque to pray and keep abreast of the events of the *mtaa* and of the town.[100] It was the mosque which was the social centre of the *mtaa* and of the town, a place where elders gathered informally late in the day to exchange news of the town and quarter and where others sought advice from the town sages. The mosque *walimu* provided 'practical' information and sanctions for proposed undertakings couched in the traditional and religious idioms associated with the descent group, the town, and the mosque. It was the mosque which was the cultural and educational centre of *mtaa* and town activities. It was there where the most important decisions were made in respect to clan and community welfare. That it was so only indicates once again the inseparability of town vocational, economic, and social practices and the meaning which they gave to town religion. It was the *mwalimu*, the one who sat in the mosque praying and gathering 'news of the people' and possessing knowledge of town affairs past and present, who was indispensable in guaranteeing the well-being of the quarter or town and whose sanction of marriage alliances, fishing expeditions, commercial deals, or mainland farming was essential.[101] Seen in this way, the 'parish' phenomenon associated with the mosque and the *mwalimu* takes on new meaning. Not only were the *walimu* religious virtuosi in the strictest sense, but community caretakers who controlled institutionalized Islam at the local level and, through their control over education and the Shari'a, 'inculcated the norms and values of their style of Islam'.[102] In performing vital community and clan functions and in providing the expertise needed in deciding matters concerning planting, fishing, trade, war, and dealings with commercial associates from overseas and with mainland clients, the *mwalimu*'s 'style of Islam' had a tremendous political base of a distinctly local colouring. It was to him that the townspeople turned for advice in the practical affairs of daily life, for it was his sanction that assured any undertaking of success in a secular sense and of 'blessing' (*baraka*) taken in a wider, universal sense.[103]

It was this concern for divine sanction of actions undertaken and the place of the *mwalimu* as the functionary who supplied the *baraka* through his religious and secular knowledge which determined the place of the religious specialist in town judicial and political decisions. The significant fact here is that, before the Busaidi period, there were few towns on the coast which had genuine *'ulama'*.[104] This suggests the essential informality of town politics and the *ad hoc* and traditional nature of judicial decisions. Also, as is frequently the situation in African communities, political advantage started with the power to arbitrate. Hence, the coexistence of both politics and law and the tendency of both to inhere within the same classes and clans. However, where the two came together naturally, political power definitely predominated. Thus, it was the political authority in the town, such as the *diwani* at Bagamoyo and the *wazee wa Yumbe* at Lamu, who held court to adjudicate internal problems between descent groups of the town.[105] *Wazee*, as previously mentioned, were learned in the law and were in a position to decide cases on the bases of local Islamic usages. However, some *wazee*, and *walimu*, were more learned in the written tradition and it was their place to advise in judicial proceedings and to give them their sanction.[106] Concern was for the sanctions which the written tradition might render to actions heavily based on local custom. Written tradition, as such, tended merely to serve as an integument which contained and gave form to local ideas and usages which formed the substance of town Islam. (One can attribute this, again, to the relative scarcity of written legal sources and the low level of literacy in Arabic among most coastal scholars before the end of the nineteenth century.) Yet, it was the written tradition, the *vitabu*, and knowledge of them possessed by the religious specialists and their interpretation of these sources in accordance with the 'right path' which brought *baraka* to the little coastal communities, and assured them of the security and comforts of earthly success and divine salvation at the end of time.

6

The Zanzibar Sultanate, 1812–88

So far, this book has depicted the evolution of coastal culture up to the late eighteenth century. Attention has been focused more narrowly on East African coastal Islam as a religion which was fixed in this wider cultural framework. The remainder of this work will demonstrate how this cultural and religious edifice was reduced to relative unimportance in the early history of the modern East African nations. What this entails, especially, is an analysis which centres on one overriding problem: how did the gradual imposition of the Busaidi Sultanate at Zanzibar and European imperialism affect culture and Islam on the coast in the nineteenth century?

THE POLITICAL SITUATION, 1698–1888

To appreciate better the cultural and religious changes which took place under the Busaidi Sultanate, a summary of political developments in the eighteenth and nineteenth centuries is useful at this juncture. However, since such an undertaking is helpful solely as a way of further illuminating cultural and religious history, only the barest description is needed. The reader who is interested in greater (and perhaps more precise) detail is referred to some of the works by Bennett, Coupland, Gray, Nicholls, and Ylvisaker listed in the bibliography.[1]

With the temporary eclipsing of Mombasa in the sixteenth century, Pate became the greatest Swahili power on the coast. Nevertheless, the Portuguese remained as great a problem for Pate as they had been for Mombasa. Despite the fact that she led several revolts against the Portuguese, Pate never succeeded in casting off the Lusitanian menace completely of her own accord. This had to await the considerable assistance of the Yarubi Imams of Oman. However, once the Portuguese chose to withdraw all their nationals to Mombasa, following an uprising in 1631, Pate seems to have enjoyed relative liberty to enhance her commercial and political circumstances. Her commercial and cultural pre-eminence probably continued well into the eighteenth century. New crises arose in the early eighteenth century when a pro-Lamu group among the ruling Nabahani, with kinship ties to Lamu's Zena faction, was opposed both at Pate by an anti-Lamu clique and at Lamu by the Suudi faction. Succession disputes between these cabals broke into open civil war in 1763. In the six years between 1769 and 1775, it appears that destruction at Pate was so severe that damage to its trade network, political power, and prestige thereafter remained permanent, a condition described most remorsefully by Sayyid Abdallah Ali Nasir in his *Al-Inkishafi*.

Lamu was both a partial cause and an obvious beneficiary of the Nabahanis' decline. While, for example, Pate's already mediocre 'harbour' (a creek) silted up in the eighteenth century, Lamu's favourable location and supply of sweet water made it an especially attractive port of call for dhows plying the routes between Southern Arabia and East Africa. It also was advantageously located to tap the Bajun coasting trade, as well as the products of *bara* cultivation. This situation was equally apparent to the 'pro-Lamu' Nabahani (for example, Sultan Abubakari b. Muhammad and his descendants), who kept a stake in Lamu by continually renewing kinship ties with their Waungwana wa Yumbe relations (Bakari and Jahadhmy), and to the Suudi 'Arabs' at Lamu who favoured a 'forward' policy of independence from Pate. The Stigand version of the 'Pate Chronicle' thus mentions several eighteenth-century attempts by Lamu to break free from Pate. A conclusive victory which finally gave Lamu its freedom was won between about 1812 and 1814 at the famous Battle of Shela, where Suudi and Zena managed to forget their rivalry long enough to defeat a combined Nabahani and Mazrui (Mombasa) force sent to subjugate the town.

The most important new ingredient in coastal politics, however, was the Omani Arabs. It was the Yarubi Imams of Rustaq who, with British help, led the counter-offensive against the Portuguese both at Oman and in East Africa. Possession of Muscat was regained in 1650 by Sultan b. Saif Yarubi and, in a famous siege which lasted from 1696 to 1698, the Portuguese and their Faza allies were driven out of Mombasa's Fort Jesus and the coast north of Cape Delgado. In the next thirty odd years, though the Omanis kept small garrisons at Mombasa, Pemba, Zanzibar, and Kilwa, preoccupations with domestic politics made it too difficult for them to maintain an effective presence in East Africa. Consequently, the Portuguese succeeded in retaking Fort Jesus, and held it from 1726 to 1727. Once the Omanis retook possession though, a stronger governor (*liwali*), Muhammad b. Uthman Mazrui, and a garrison were stationed in Mombasa. This move was fateful. Large numbers of Mazrui followed Muhammad b. Uthman to Mombasa, and a second development further hardened the Mazrui entrenchment there: suffering a Persian occupation in 1741, the Yarubi were driven from power in Oman by the Busaidi, who in turn rooted out the invaders. When Muhammad b. Uthman Mazrui refused to recognize the new Busaidi Sultan as his sovereign, the difficulties of establishing their claims at home prevented the Busaidi from retaliating. Throughout the remainder of the eighteenth century these persistent domestic concerns made control over their East African 'possessions', with the notable exception of Zanzibar, beyond the reach of the Busaidi Sultans.

Unbridled by control from Muscat, the Mazrui led Mombasa to a renewed pre-eminence as the greatest power on the northern half of the coast. With close ties to Mombasa's Three Tribes confederation, the al-

Malindi clan, and the neighbouring Miji Kenda, by the 1770s they had managed to extend their influence from Ras Ngomeni in the north to Pemba and the Pangani River in the south. Three things, however, eventually undermined their position. First, beginning with the reign of the fourth *liwali*, Masud b. Nasr (1753–75), they began meddling in the treacherous politics of the Lamu archipelago. The second was their fatal tendency towards internecine in-fighting over succession which seems mostly to have involved two out of the eleven Mazrui sub-clans, namely the Banu Nasr b. Abdallah and the Banu Uthman b. Abdallah. In the reign of the sixth *liwali*, Ahmad b. Muhammad (1775–1814?), blood actually was shed among the clan. The final source of their undoing was their inordinate pride and overconfidence. Thus, in 1814, when called by the youthful Sultan Sayyid Said b. Sultan al-Busaidi to submit to his sovereign, *Liwali* Abdallah b. Ahmad Mazrui answered with a challenge consisting of a coat of mail, a grain measure, powder, and shot.

Sayyid Said b. Sultan himself was an extremely capable ruler and a dangerous intriguer. Clearly, he was not someone with whom one trifled, and Abdallah b. Ahmad's act of bravado probably stiffened the Sultan's resolution to rid himself of the Mazrui and to gain possession of Mombasa and the rest of the coast. Previous Sultans, of course, had been in no position to act in far-out East Africa and, had a previous Mazrui governor acted as Abdallah b. Ahmad had, Sayyid Said's predecessors would have been forced to accept the insult unchallenged. However, Said b. Sultan enjoyed a stronger 'hand' than his predecessors. While other coastal centres had fallen away from Busaidi control throughout the eighteenth century, Zanzibar had remained steadfastly loyal and control over Kilwa had been reasserted in 1786. The toe-holds in these two crucial bases gave Sayyid Said important staging points for the conquest of the coast and, with their growing trade in ivory and slaves, much needed sources of revenue. A third important position was won in the Lamu archipelago at about the time Abdallah b. Ahmad sent his ill-considered message of contumacy. Fearing Nabahani and Mazrui reprisals after the resounding victory at Shela, Bwana Zahidi Ngumi of Lamu's Suudi alliance extended an invitation to Said b. Sultan to send a governor and a Baluchi garrison to occupy the newly built fort there. Following this, the Busaidi managed to occupy both Siyu and Pate at various times from 1824 onwards. The growing unpopularity of Mazrui rule at Pemba also enabled Sayyid Said to put a garrison and governor on that island sometime between 1819 and 1824. Most important of all, though, is that by 1820, Said b. Sultan had achieved a secure position in Oman. This was due to the efforts of his grandfather, Ahmad b. Said, and to agreements forged with the British both by his father, Sultan b. Ahmad, and by himself which guaranteed continued British interest in sustaining the Busaidi position at Muscat against the assaults of Ibadi and Wahhabist extremists from the Omani interior.

The final curtain was drawn on Mazrui independence in Mombasa in 1837. Relatively unmolested throughout the reigns of the first four Busaidi Sultans of Oman, Mombasa had become a focus of Sayyid Said's growing expansionist designs in East Africa, as well as a threat to his personal authority. It was the final bulwark against Busaidi hegemony over the coast and clearly had to go. By 1822, Sayyid Said was prepared to storm Fort Jesus, but a brief interlude of British involvement from 1822 to 1824, usually known as Owen's Protectorate, forestalled events. Once the Foreign Office refused further involvement, though, a Busaidi assault was inevitable and a compromise treaty was arranged which permitted a small Busaidi garrison in the fort and theoretical governance of the town. However, discovery of secret attempts to augment this garrison resulted in the forcible removal of the Busaidi troops and *jamadar* in 1828. The strong leadership of *Liwali* Salim b. Ahmad Mazrui made any further attempts at taking Mombasa impossible for the time being.

After this events moved dramatically. The old folly of Mazrui disunity over succession, added to increasingly autocratic practices in their style of rule, finally alienated the Three Tribes from the Mazrui. After the imprisonment of the Kilifi *shehe*, a secret agreement was struck with Sayyid Said which allowed him to occupy Kilindini and use it as a base from which to attack Fort Jesus and the Kavani moiety. By 1837, the Sayyid again had Fort Jesus garrisoned and there was firm control of the town. What followed was a kind of 'Barmakid feast'. To eliminate finally any remnant of Mazrui pretensions (and to frustrate possible Three Tribes duplicity), various Mazrui elders were invited singly into the fort in observance of the ᶜId, whereupon they were seized and bound over for imprisonment in far-off Banda Abbas. Never were they heard from again and Sayyid Said's position in Mombasa was made fast.

While Sayyid Said was in total control of the principal coastal towns – Kilwa, Zanzibar, Mombasa, and Lamu – Busaidi authority over the entire coastal strip remained incomplete until 1895. Nabahani and Mazrui resistance, for example, continued to threaten the Busaidi position even in the towns where their control seemed most secure. Busaidi control over Lamu and Pate town was fairly unquestioned by 1856, but Sayyids Majid, Barghash, Khalifa, Ali, and Hamid b. Thuwain had to contend with the mainland rebellion of one scion of the Nabahani house. While recognizing Busaidi power in the islands, in 1856 one Ahmad 'Simba' Nabahani fell back upon Pate's mainland allies and mounted a resistance to the Busaidi at Lamu by seizing control of Ozi and taxing all Pokomo produce passing down the Tana River for Lamu. Though he was expelled from Ozi, Simba simply moved further inland to Witu where he founded a new Nabahani 'Sultanate' which served as a base of rebellion until it finally was destroyed in 1895. Similarly, when Mazrui control of Mombasa passed to the Busaidi in 1837, many of the clan abandoned the town and relocated in Gazi and Takaungu. From these locations, Mbarak b. Rashid Mazrui was able to threaten the Busaidi positions at Mombasa, Malindi, and Mambrui. As in the case of Simba's rebellion, Mbarak's activities came to a conclusion in the 1890s when a combined force of the British and the Sultan's troops finally drove him and his supporters out of the British East Africa Protectorate (Kenya) and into German East Africa (Tanganyika).

What must be borne in mind is that these well-known rebellions did not take place in a vacuum. Clearly, Simba and Sh. Mbarak b. Rashid had popular bases of support both in the towns from which they came and among the mainland peoples who traditionally had been allies of the old Nabahani and Mazrui dynasties.[2] It was the nature of this support and the reasons for it which reveal a great deal about the Zanzibar Sultanate and its control over the coast, as well as how some people felt about the Sultanate (or, more appropriately, about the Sultans). For it was one thing for townspeople to accept hegemony over the entire coastal strip (and the economic benefits which this hegemony brought), but it was quite another matter for them to accept more than the smallest manifestations of local control by Busaidi *liwalis* and the implications of this control by way of interference in town sovereignty and traditional ways of handling local affairs (that is, in power relations within the existing social structures).

The reactions of townspeople to the Sultanate appear to have been determined by two factors. The first was their religious and perceptual differences from the Omanis and the Sultans. Not only were there sectarian differences – of Sunnis in juxtaposition to Ibadis – but also significant differences in the worlds from which the two peoples came. That of the townspeople was centred on the local community and what this implied in terms of local history, traditional ways of doing things, and traditional values, all of which had an oral base of legitimacy and an oral mode of transmission from generation to generation. This, of course, meant that local *Weltanschauung* and the character of local religion were uniquely adapted to the local physical setting, local history, local social structure and power relations, and local modes of production. The Omanis, on the other hand, came from the literate, cosmopolitan, ascetically inclined world of Kharijite eastern Arabia and the Indian Ocean. So while the Sultanate enjoyed great prestige at times because of the positive opportunities it brought to the coast for material improvement, the arrival of the Omanis and their British allies put considerable strains on town-based institutions and old viewpoints. These changes will be discussed in detail in Chapter 7. In the meantime, it should suffice to say that religiously inspired resentment of the Busaidi was present on the coast at least as late as 1875 and lingered long afterwards.[3]

The last factor which influenced how Swahili reacted to the Sultanate was its very nature and how heavily it bore on the personal lives of townspeople. The Sultanate did change as the nineteenth century wore on, and the strength of its impact on the various communities along the coast clearly was affected by the respective distances of these communities from Zanzibar.[4] At the outset at least of Busaidi rule, authority appears to have been vague and diffuse, hence its part in the social and religious lives of the townsmen for several decades was more paternalistic than autocratic in character. Such, then, is a useful introduction for a discussion of the Zanzibar Sultanate and some of the changes which it brought to coastal life.

MONEY, POWER, AND THE SAYYIDS

At the very core of the Zanzibar *hukuma* (power structure) stood the Sultan: it is more accurate than not to say that he was the *hukuma*.[5] His position and political strength had three bases, two of which are related and will be discussed together. These two include the traditional relationship between the Sultans and their subjects as it existed originally in Oman, as well as in Zanzibar, and the Sultans' personal attributes and how they affected these relationships. The third base upon which the Sultan's position rested was his personal wealth and how it was used as a political instrument.

The Sultanate was both personal and informal in character. As stated by one envoy to the court,

> The Sultan himself is the government and it is necessary that I should do my business with him. All his subjects without distinction go to him, and if an English or American merchant should go to him with any complaint the Sultan would not refer them to their *own Consul* but decide for or against them as suited his own pleasure.[6]

At least before 1891 there was no formal structure in the sense that, 'There were no departments, no ministers.' Most decisions were strictly in the hands of the Sultan himself.[7] Generally the government functioned informally as a sort of royal magistracy which, as did the traditional councils of elders of the Swahili towns prior to Busaidi rule, listened to people's complaints or squabbles and decided them on the spot.[8]

The nature of the Sultanate and the Sultan's place within it had their roots in the original Imamate of Oman. (In strict Ibadi terms, there legitimately existed only the Imamate.) The Ibadi Imamate saw itself, like the city-states of the coast, as an *umma*, a community of believers which maintained its special position of grace with God by walking the path of righteousness. Also like the coastal communities, the Ibadi Imams pursued the 'right path' through adherence to God's laws as interpreted by a body of educated jurisconsults and *qadis*. The Imam was an elected charismatic leader who was at once head of state and principal interpreter of Holy Law. However, while the Imam was thought to have a special claim to interpreting and administering God's laws to the faithful, his position in this regard was rigidly circumscribed and subject to the closest scrutiny of the community.[9] As pointed out by Badger, for Ibadis, the *umma* had priority over the Imamate itself. Indeed, the *umma* could function without an Imam in that the people themselves, without superior authority, could apply the Shari'a.[10] The tribal *mashayikh* and *'ulama'*, as representatives of the *umma*, elected Imams on the basis of their personal merits and popularity according to established standards. Often the election and the legitimacy of the chosen one's claims were disputed by some of the tribes. Unanimity was rare and the Imamate was not continuous, at least before the Yarubi Imams.[11] By the time of Yarubi rule, however, the tendency was for succession to the Imamate to be based on a strong preference for members of the current ruling house over the claims of outsiders.

After the succession of Ahmad b. Said al-Busaidi, the informal recognition of a single ruling line was implied in the application of the special title of Sayyid only to the offspring of the ruling Imam. The innovation gave the house of the Sayyids a 'corporate dignity and pre-eminence over all other ruling chiefs and grandees'. The house of the Sayyids, then, became a recognized dynasty with prior claims to succession to the Imamate.[12] The final separation of rule from the religious institution of the Imamate came in 1791 when Sultan b. Ahmad seized control of the coastal port of Muscat from his brother, the Imam Said b. Ahmad.[13] Thereafter, the successor no longer necessarily was an Imam; the rulers of Muscat only assumed the title of Sayyid or Sultan and, eschewing claims of religious pre-eminence, succeeded to supreme authority in civil and political matters.[14]

With the establishment of a Sultanate of Muscat, as opposed to the old Imamate of Oman, the Sayyids' power base shifted somewhat. No longer enjoying the religious aura and charisma of their forbears, Sayyids Sultan b. Ahmad and Said b. Sultan increasingly relied on their command of the developing shipping industry out of Muscat as a source of revenue and power.[15] This state of affairs, in fact, already had begun to take shape under the Imams. In addition to the traditional rights of Imams to collect the *sadaka* and the *zakat*, the proceeds of which went to religiously enjoined purposes, the Sayyids also began receiving customs dues on imports at various ports of their domain which were used for general purposes of administration, including support of a bevy of court dependants and hangers-on. This additional source of income, then, gave the Sayyids a source of political leverage independent of the old religious establishment and the old desert tribes of the interior who formerly could make or break an Imam.[16]

Sayyid Said continued to rely on personal wealth as a basis for his power when he relocated his capital to Zanzibar. A precedent for this was set in 1821 when, as terms of their submission to the Sayyid and independence from the Mazrui, the Tumbatu of Pemba agreed to a 5 per cent excise duty on their exports and an annual head tax (*zakat*) of two Maria Theresa dollars.[17] Once ensconced in Zanzibar, the Sayyids' wealth derived from an amazing range of sources. One of these, seemingly customary among Middle Eastern potentates, was the exercise of royal monopolies.[18] Trade and clove cultivation, however, were the Sayyids' principal sources of income. At an early date, Sayyid Said's agents regularly began collecting cowrie shells from Kilwa, Zanzibar, and Lamu which he exported to Calcutta and the Persian Gulf on his own account.[19] By the 1840s, also, the Sultan was taking advantage of the burgeoning caravan trade. An American reported, for example, that Said b. Sultan annually sent 'one-hundred men' inland to collect ivory for him.[20] The Sultans took advantage of the commercial ventures of others, too. Signing commercial treaties with the Americans, the British, and the French in turn regularly gave Sayyid Said 5 per cent customs dues on all imports into coastal ports by nationals of these countries. As a result of these treaties, customs revenues rose from $39,000–$40,000 in 1807–8, to about $200,000 in 1862.[21] Clove cultivation,

Table 5: *The Sultans of Zanzibar*

Said b. Sultan (1806–56)
Majid b. Said (1856–70)
Barghash b. Said (1870–88)
Khalifa b. Said (1888–90)
Ali b. Said (1890–3)
Hamid b. Thuwain (1893–6)
Hamud b. Muhammad (1896–1902)
Ali b. Hamud (1902–11)
Khalifa b. Harub (1911–60)

however, probably was Said b. Sultan's most notable contribution to the economy of Zanzibar. Cooper shows, for example, that Said managed to acquire forty-five plantations during his reign.[22] Waters reported that, in addition to extensive clove cultivation, the Sayyid also experimented in raising other cash crops, such as coffee and nutmeg.[23] Finally, while the facts and figures tell something only of Sayyid Said's personal wealth, there is little reason to assume that his successors, at least from Sayyids Majid through Ali b. Said,[24] suffered any major diminution in income.[25]

The Sayyids' personal wealth was the keystone of their government. It was the lubricant which facilitated their rule of the Arab tribes of Zanzibar and the coast, as well as the coastal towns of their realm. Even in Oman the Sultans' control over their subjects was highly precarious, especially in view of the questionability of their claims to religious leadership and the factional differences between them (who were Hinawi) and the supporters of their Yarubi predecessors (who mostly seem to have been Ghafiri). As Burton stated,

> Throughout Oman the rival tribes still occupy separate quarters; they will not connect themselves by marriage, and they seldom meet without a 'factional fight'. Even at Zanzibar, where the climate has softened them, they rarely preserve the decency of hate which is due by Arabs of noble strain to hereditary and natural enemies.[26]

Over these quarrelsome rival tribes and old enemies the Busaidi barely maintained a military advantage by which their word could be enforced.[27] Several Omani clans, such as the Mazrui, the Mandhry, the Harthi, and the Barwani, had ties to Zanzibar and the coast which predated effective Busaidi rule. Most of these owned plantations and numerous slaves.[28] In general, many clansmen were loyal first to their *shaykhs* and, therefore, were 'uncommonly likely to rat or revolt' when required to obey their Sultan.[29] Even as forceful and strong-willed a Sultan as Barghash was described by one observer (early in his reign) as little more than a *primus inter pares* among the Arab *shaykhs* whose word was circumscribed by the 'wants, wishes, usages, and prejudices of his own Arab race and of some influential classes of his subjects'.[30]

The Sultan continuously had to walk a fine line both in his personal conduct and in matters of state in order to avoid conflicts with his subjects. Ostentation and any sign of 'conspicuous consumption' had to be eschewed out of deference to his Omani subjects' Ibadi puritanism.[31] Whenever a new measure was introduced by the Sultan, invariably it met with the disapproval of some of the clansmen – any of whom was permitted in the Sultan's presence – who assembled and addressed him 'more as an equal than as a superior'.[32]

Often the power of the *shaykhs* rivalled that of the Sultan. One such example was Sulaiman b. Hamid al-Busaidi. Born around 1785, Sulaiman served in various unofficial capacities at the courts of Sayyids Sultan b. Ahmad, Said, Majid, and Barghash. His influence over the mainland towns actually was 'above that of the Sultan himself'. A threat to Barghash's authority in the early part of his reign, he was one of the *shaykhs* who violently opposed the Frere mission to impose a new anti-slave trade treaty in 1873.[33] Another example was Muhammad b. Juma al-Barwani al-Harthi, who was sent by Sayyid Said to relieve Mafia after it had been sacked in 1818 by the Betsimisaraka of Madagascar. The success of his mission led to Sh. Muhammad's appointment as *liwali* of Mafia afterwards. However, fearing Barwani wealth and influence on the mainland,[34] within a year Said replaced him and his son, Nasir, with another appointee.[35]

Out and out resistance to the Busaidi Sultans, in fact, was not uncommon before the 1880s. The examples of the Mazrui and the Nabahani have been covered already. While these instances took place on the mainland and at considerable distances from the capital of the Sultans, resistance did occur even at Zanzibar. What seems to have made this possible were the slave armies of rival clans. Burton mentions that,

> Sometime a noble, when ordered into arrest at Zanzibar, has collected his friends, armed his slaves, and fortified his house. One Salim b. Abdallah, who had a gang of 2000 musketeer negroes, used to wage a petty war with the Sayyid's servile hosts.[36]

Since the Busaidi were Hinawi, often support for such rebellions was given by Ghafiri tribes who kept, 'little castles armed with guns which [were] mere robbers' dens'.[37] Also, with the removal of Muhammad b. Juma al-Barwani from his sinecure at Mafia, both the Harthi and Barwani clans mounted considerable opposition to Busaidi authority which came to a climax during the Sultanate of Sayyid Majid. While Said b. Sultan enjoyed a reputation for firm rule and a 'fair hand' neither Majid's personal eminence nor administrative skills matched those of his gifted father. His standards of right and wrong differed from those of Said: consequently, there was greater corruption in the *qadis*' courts, law and order were less consistently maintained, and there was more court intrigue.[38] All this reflected on the Sultan's personal character and attributes, so the situation was ripe for rebellion. The Harthi numbered about eight hundred and owned 'many' slaves.[39] Resistance broke out in small ways, like the refusal of the Barwani to allow Majid's retainers to set foot on their lands.[40] Abdallah b. Salim al-Harthi and one Salim Bahiri were arrested on 7 July

1859 for acts of sedition against the Sultan. Ahmad b. Salim al-Harthi was imprisoned for giving a $3,000 bribe to the *jamadar* of Zanzibar Fort to assassinate Majid, and allegedly he was murdered while imprisoned at Lamu under Majid's instructions. Several Harthi and Barwani were bastinadoed and deported (eventually they resettled at Tabora and Mwanza).[41]

Recognizing their precarious position in the towns, as with the tribes of Zanzibar, the Sultans abstained from interfering in town institutions and with local customs as much as possible. Though Sayyid Said is said to have remarked that, 'his orthodox [that is, Shafii] subjects would people [heaven] but poorly',[42] he is described as having been 'amiable, liberal, and just. He not only tolerates but protects all subjected to him or within his dominions without regard to their religious creed or observances, and even pagans and Hindoos are amongst his most confidential servants.'[43] In order not to offend the townspeople, the Busaidi avoided proselytization.[44] Local customs had the force of law, as Ward explains:

> The Sultan and his people profess to being governed by the laws of the Koran, and certain customs which have grown up among them from circumstances or necessity ... If when at any time the Sultan makes a custom for the occasion, his people do not speak of it to Europeans. Custom, however, has all the force of law ... In all cases, a simple notification by any of the head men, as they are called, seems to have, from custom, all the force of a complaint.[45]

Furthermore, in order to guarantee non-interference in local customs, *qadis* could be appointed and paid by the Sultan, but had to have the approval of town elders. At Mombasa, for example, a separate *qadi* was appointed for each of the two Swahili confederations and for the Omanis, but the tribes reserved the right to select their own *qadi* if they chose not to go to the court of the Sultan's appointee.[46]

As Nicholls points out, theoretically the town *wazee* were under the Sultans' tutelage and the *liwalis* were their personal appointees, yet little effective control was feasible at the more distant locations. In 1839, for instance, the Sultan's *liwali* and Baluchi garrison were murdered by irate townspeople at Pate. In similar fashion, in 1841 a Somali force descended on several Benadir towns where they robbed and murdered several of the Sultan's subjects.[47] The position of the Sultan's governors, then, often was precarious. While he was 'supreme in all important matters ... [he] generally concerned himself only with the affairs of his Arab followers and foreign merchants, committing all affairs connected with the old, local population to the management of their ruling families in the town and asserting but little authority at a few miles distant from the town'.[48] Furthermore, as Boteler remarked of Said b. Hamid al-Busaidi, the governor of Lamu in 1824, 'Like the generality of Arab governors, he made but little display of his official dignity, and he could never be distinguished from those by whom he was surrounded.'[49]

The Sultans' relationships with town *wazee*, of course, were uneven, differing from location to location and changing over time. At Zanzibar, for example, the old Ba Alawi *Mwinyi Mkuu* was treated as a subject of the

1. *Mwinyi Mkuu* of Zanzibar *c.* 1850.

Sultans. His area of jurisdiction included only the eastern part of the island farthest from Zanzibar town. Recognition of his authority extended to granting him a portion of the head taxes he collected, along with continued rights to being mentioned in the *khutba*.[50] At Mombasa, it is clear that few changes were made. Relations between the *wamiji* and the Sultans had something of a constitutional character. First of all, representatives of the

107

two tribal confederations, called *tamims*, and a *shaykh* of the Arab clans were appointed by the Sultan.[51] As pointed out by Berg, the *tamims'* letters of appointment tended to be regarded by townspeople as charters defining their status within the Sultanate which touched on the rights and obligations of the Tribes.[52] At Lamu, the *Yumbe* continued to meet and, alongside the *liwali* (though the relationship is not clear), the clan *wazee* continued to govern the affairs of their kinsmen according to local forms of Islamic law.[53] In all cases, the rights of the local populace and their elders were recognized as paramount. The elders from each town went yearly to Zanzibar to greet the Sultan and to reconfirm their loyalty. Semi-official recognition of their authority was given in the form of gifts of clothing (open robes called *johos*, and turbans), and for this reason town *wazee* came to be called *kwa jihi* in Mombasa and *vijoho* in Lamu.[54] While *liwalis* did administrative and some judicial work, they were restricted by the Sultans from interfering in affairs which were considered purely local – that is, as properly the affairs of the *wazee*. Whenever an action or judgement of a *liwali* was disliked by the townspeople, they had the right to send delegations of elders to the Sultan as a court of final appeal.[55]

With all the independence of their subjects, then, how did the Sultans maintain effective order and command the loyalty of townspeople? Quite simply, the entire government of Zanzibar and of the coast under the Busaidi rested on the personal reputation of each Sultan for even-handedness in dealing with his subjects and in bringing them wealth. His rule was seen, for example, as firm and just. One Swahili said of his Sultan,

> When the Sultan comes to the audience, he is fierce as a lion, terrible to behold. He has a sword in his hand and a fine scimitar. Even a brave man would be afraid and fear would come on him. When he puts on his turban and sits like a lion, the strongest shrinks under his accusation. His character is quiet and untroubled. This Sultan has no doubt or hesitation. His judgement is noble: if you go to him you will receive justice. An eye for an eye, an ear for an ear, a tooth for a tooth and a life for a life.[56]

More than anything, patronage was the glue which kept everything together. To be sure, the economic changes which the Sultanate brought to the coast benefited people of all classes, but it principally was the judicious application of his personal wealth in the form of largess which kept the Sultan's subjects loyal to him.

Largess took various forms. The first was the Sultan's purchase of the loyalty of the tribal *shaykhs* and town elders who visited his court. In this connection, Owen reported that the loyalty of the *Mwinyi Mkuu* of Zanzibar, and that of other town elders, was secured by an annual stipend of $15,000.[57] Especially troublesome tribes, like the al-Harthi, were pensioned.[58] Furthermore, besides letters of appointment, the *tamims* of Mombasa were salaried,[59] and town elders, as mentioned previously, received various presents whenever they visited Zanzibar. Secondly, even common people were beneficiaries of the Sultan's purse. One form was through 'big entertainments' given annually in observation of religious holidays, such as the feast for 'several thousand' mentioned by Waters.[60]

Then, of course, there were the little presents of food and clothing described by the admiring poet:

> The Sultan is a good man and generous. If you go to him and speak, you receive your request. How many of the poor receive food from the Sultan! You go to the city, you receive and you take away ... How many retainers has he who do not work but live free at his expense! How many tribes are there which he does not leave to perish if they are involved in war! How many receive from him good food and clothes; to how many does he give presents![61]

Most interesting, however, were the people of the Sultan's court. While elaborate rituals were followed at each afternoon's *baraza*, in which the Sultan took notice of each one in attendance according to the honour due his person and rank, the Sultans maintained a large number of functionaries and hangers-on. They were a mixed lot. There were *wazirs*, tribal *shaykhs*, *qadis* and *muftis*, clerks and scribes, *imams*, prayer and Quran readers, attendants, and a vast host of relatives and guests.[62] To support them there was no regular system of collection and expenditure, no books kept, no fixed wages, and no budgets. Their presence served two purposes: they were useful to the Sultan in giving advice on religious questions and on controlling the unpredictable towns, and they often gave added prestige to the court. That said, however, most of these courtiers never worked, yet they received money and 'were the cause of innumerable brawls and disturbances and a constant danger to the public peace'.[63] About Rs 18,000 were being spent, in short, on a system of government which was hardly more than, as one put it, 'a crude system of patronage'.[64]

THE *LIWALIS*

Socially and politically, the story of changes in town life in the nineteenth century revolves around the waxing of Busaidi influence. As mentioned already, for example, the town elders came to be subsidized by the Busaidi and thus to occupy intermediary positions between Zanzibar and their kinsmen. In addition, representation before the Sultan's officials changed from one where the elders represented the *mtaa* to one where they simply represented their respective clans.[65] Similarly, sometime before the 1890s the town *qadis* became salaried officials of the ruling family.[66]

It is the history of the *liwalis* which illustrates, however, the changing status of the Sultanate and the power of the Busaidi in the towns. Locally, these officials were the direct representatives of the Sultans and it was through them and their actions that townspeople perceived the nature of the Sultanate. It is not surprising, therefore, to learn that the *liwalis* are remembered for having come 'as brothers', who helped the poor by inviting them to eat with them and to hear their complaints. Based on this, the Sultanate is remembered for being concerned with 'the needs of the people, to defend them and prevent hunger'. The *liwalis* shared their wealth, building mosques for Sunnis (that is, the townspeople) and not interfering with their beliefs.[67]

There is another side to some people's recollections of what life was like under the *liwalis*, however. While the Busaidi came 'as brothers' and maintained a low profile in the early decades of the Sultanate – when it was less securely established – such was not always the case. The greatest danger, both to townspeople and to the Sultans, was that *liwalis* could use their position to establish an independent power base. To avoid this threat to some degree, *liwalis* usually were selected first from among the royal family.

Yet, even this was not enough, as *liwali*-ships tended to be treated as sinecures and local ties increasingly came to be established through intermarriage with local families. One problem was that, though they were salaried, several *liwalis* were able to establish local sources of income independent of their suzerain's purse. One reads, for example, of one *liwali* who possessed a monopoly of the slave trade at Zanzibar and of others who received allowances out of customs duties they levied on goods embarked or landed at Zanzibar and at Lamu.[68] An even greater source of wealth to *liwalis*, however, was the accumulation of large landholdings in the towns in which they were established. The two clans most notorious for this practice were the Banu Salim b. Khalfan al-Busaidi of Malindi and Mombasa and Banu Hamid al-Busaidi of Lamu. Both one field informant and Cooper indicate that Salim b. Khalfan and his son, Ali b. Salim, used their positions as *liwalis* to lend money to landowners who were out of pocket during the lean years after the 1850s when the coastal economy experienced a series of depressions (see Chapter 9). Large tracts thus were acquired through foreclosures on unrepaid loans.[69] At Lamu, between 1865 and 1903, the Banu Hamid held office for a total of thirty-five out of thirty-eight years. Patterning themselves after a precedent set by Sulaiman b. Hamid in the time of Sayyid Majid, they made it a practice to intervene in local land disputes between clans, often seizing the land in question for themselves (as 'crown' land, therefore[70]), leaving only the slaves and a money settlement for the disputants. Informants usually pointed out Suud and Abdallah b. Hamid as having been particularly guilty of such practices.[71]

Another reason for *liwali* independence and power in their districts was their marriage ties to local families. According to el-Zein, it appears that the early Busaidi governors of Lamu, at least, remained aloof from the local population by building their own mosques, holding on to their Ibadi beliefs, and bringing their wives from Oman.[72] By the time of Sayyid Barghash, though, things began to change. The powerful Suud b. Hamid married locally to a Jahadhmy, and another Busaidi even managed to take one of the aristocratic Husayni *shurafa'* for a wife.[73] According to óne reliable informant, things began to alter so much in Lamu that even the powerful Maawi eventually found it necessary to intermarry with the Busaidi to legitimize their rising social and political star.[74] By the 1890s, matters had progressed to the point that at least some of the *liwalis* at Lamu had been locally born and reared. *Liwali* Abdallah b. Hamid was thus described by Simons:

> He was born here, and although an Arab is essentially a Swahili on the female side, he is thus connected by marriage with most of the principal people of the place and his interests and sympathy are entirely Swahili.

He is desirous of being on a perfectly friendly and happy footing with all
here and therefore anxious to keep himself clear of all questions touching the
– to them – vexatious raid made by us against slavery.[75]

The net effect of all these actions by the *liwalis* was the gradual
replacement of leading *waungwana* houses at the top of the social and
political scale by the Busaidi. Already by the 1850s, Guillain noted the
considerable freedom and power being exercised by the *liwalis* through their
position as intermediaries in local disputes.[76] Armed with the rights of
intervention in local quarrels and the power of imprisonment and seizure of
property, they often succeeded in enriching themselves and in playing off
local clans against each other.[77] Suud b. Hamid went so far, in fact, that at
least temporarily during Sayyid Majid's reign he managed to ban all
barazas in Lamu on the grounds of suspected sedition against himself. In
1890 Suud's mere arrival from Zanzibar was sufficient to put down a
nascent rebellion at Lamu against Imperial British East Africa rule at Witu
and the 1890 slave decree.[78]

As indicated by local reactions against unpopular measures such as those
mentioned above, the *liwalis* did meet with some local resistance. In 1889,
feeling the decline of their pre-eminence at Lamu in the face of Busaidi
power, the Maawi declared themselves to be under German protection. In a
case where one of their kinsmen, Abdallah b. Hamid Maawi, was killed
accidentally by Shehu Ghalib b. Shehu Abdu'r-Rahman, they were unable
to obtain sufficient blood money from the *liwali* Abdallah b. Hamid and
from Sultan Khalifa. That they accused the *liwalis* of taking the sides of
other tribes 'with whom they have cases' against them, indicates the
growing compromise in their position at Lamu *vis-à-vis* that of the Busaidi.[79] Finally, the *liwalis* used their power to 'suggest' appointments to
religious offices, thus setting a precedent that later would be followed under
British rule. To undermine the position of their rivals at Lamu, the Maawi
informants related how the *liwalis* 'opposed' the house of the *khatibs* and
introduced 'certain changes' by appointing scions of the Mahdali clan to the
qadi-ships. There is little wonder, then, that, while poorer clans claim the
Busaidi came as 'brothers' to Lamu, Maawi memory of Busaidi rule is one
of harshness and oppression.[80]

IMMIGRATION

The second great factor which had social and, it will be seen, economic and
religious impact on life in the coastal towns under the Sultanate was
population movement and immigration. One such migration involved the
Thelatha Taifa (Three Tribes) at Mombasa, a large body of people who
originally lived on the mainland in villages to the west and northwest of the
city. Sometime in the Middle Ages they constructed a village on Mombasa
island at Twaka, and later another settlement at Kilindini. However, most
of the Three Tribes settlements were destroyed in the final battle between
the Mazrui and the Busaidi in 1837, so they began occupying Kizingo
quarter soon afterwards.[81] Somewhat later (after 1850?), they settled in
Kavani (around Fort Jesus), praying in the Shikely, Mnara, and Mandhry

mosques.[82] This move, as will be seen, was a decisive factor in the conversion of the remaining Ibadis of Kavani to Shafii Islam.

Another significant relocation of people involved the Comorians. Over the centuries, of course, there had been regular contact between the Comoros and the coast principally because of the cowrie trade and the resettlement of *sharif* clans like the Jamal al-Layl and the Abu Bakr b. Salim in Comorian villages. In addition, Comorians had been settling seasonally in other coastal towns as petty traders, rope makers, and fishermen.[83] However, this pattern of resettlement increased dramatically as the prosperity of Zanzibar waxed under Sayyid Said. Besides the lure of Zanzibarian affluence, other factors accounted for this as well. For example, Burton pointed out the endemic 'intestine divisions'; attacks from Madagascar which ravaged the southern islands and Mozambique between 1815 and 1822; and the French slave emancipation at Mayotte in 1847 which 'set a large class free to travel'.[84] In Zanzibar, 'they came in by their dhows or fishing smacks at the beginning of every southern monsoon, sometimes with their families and cargoes of cattle, merchandise, and slaves'.[85] At Lamu, some originally came as slaves and all settled in Langoni quarter. At Zanzibar they settled in Shangani, Mji Mpya, Malindi, and Ngambo quarters, where they remained detached from the local Swahili and socially beneath the Omanis. There they preserved their customs and frequently engaged in the petty quarrelling characteristic of their homelands.[86]

Chaotic conditions in southern Arabia led, again, to one of the occasional emigrations of those 'Swiss of the East', the Hadramis, sometime in the late eighteenth century and again, apparently, after 1870.[87] People of all classes seem to have emigrated to the coast and Indonesia, but those who came in greatest numbers and who had the greatest effect on coastal society and economy were the peasants (*da^{c}if* and *maskin*), artisans, and merchants. The *da^{c}if* class, accustomed to menial labour, were industrious, hardworking, and willing to remain on the lower strata of the social scale while slowly enriching themselves. They remained as loners, despised for their lowly occupations, such as water carriers, and often without their own mosques in which to pray.[88] In addition to the services of unskilled labour, East Africa benefited from the influx of experienced Arab merchants. In their native Hadramawt, merchants were organized into guilds governed by statutes (*qanun*) which constituted a corpus of law complementary to religious law. Using these statutes, *qadis* settled disputes among merchants involving customs and religious/legal questions. In peaceful times the system worked well. But periodically, merchants and skilled workers were subjected to exactions from powerful tribal chieftains, which sometimes even included house searches and confiscations.[89] Usually, the net result of such actions was the emigration and loss of their talents to places like East Africa and Malaysia. In their new homelands, the Hadramis worked as petty capitalists and entrepreneurs, engaging in the sort of commerce and financial dealings which, increasingly, many wealthy and socially superior *waungwana* disdained in the later nineteenth century.[90]

The immigrations of the Hadramis and Comorians had socio-economic repercussions over the long term. Hadrami merchants and labourers held a different, non-stratified view of society than did the *waungwana*. Labourers moved around a great deal and, therefore, had little or no roots in the coastal communities. Consequently, they had no vested interest in the existing social status quo wherever they settled.[91] Other Hadramis, such as the merchants who settled in one place, established small victual shops and, like the *da^cif* families, did not deserve local rules on marriage and were excluded from traditional vocations wherever possible (for example, *shamba* ownership and bush farming).[92] Consequently, they tended to support those like themselves who were not part of the local social establishment. Not surprisingly, at Lamu they backed the interests of the Busaidi and (later) the British against local nobility like the Maawi and the Bakari. With their wider trade contacts and readily available cash, they supported other 'non-established' peoples like the Bajuni and Indians who settled alongside them in Langoni. Indeed, with the arrivals of these various groups of newcomers, Langoni market came to rival the older *Utukuni* market controlled by the Maawi.[93] Finally, some of these families accumulated enough wealth to live comfortable lives devoted to learning, and were able to marry local women who formerly would have been socially inaccessible to them.[94] Clearly, their religion, like their world-view, extended beyond the sometimes constricted, parochial town Islam of the *waungwana*. It was this religion and new wealth, like that of the Hadramis and the Comorians, which came to threaten town Islam on the coast in the nineteenth century.

The Comorians, like the Hadramis, had little to gain by accepting the values of the old coastal social order. Having little interest in things as they were, they had much to gain from change. Although not the shopkeepers and merchants that many Hadramis were, they did share their industrious, enterprising spirit as well as an appreciation of what wealth could do. They worked hard as small artisans, beach combers, fishermen, and menials in the houses of the well-to-do.[95] They were competitive and adaptive because they strove hard to achieve social equality with their superiors. In addition, extensive travel as fishermen and petty traders put them in touch with a wide range of ideas which, especially after 1870, made them aware of the 'needs of modern life'.[96]

ECONOMIC GROWTH

A salient feature of coastal economic history under the Sultanate was the dramatic expansion in coastal agriculture and trade. Except for clove cultivation, most of the elements, and indeed the beginnings, of this growth were already present and operating in the late eighteenth century, especially at Lamu and somewhat less so at Mombasa and the Benadir ports. Clearly, extensive population shifts behind the immediate areas of Mombasa and the Lamu archipelago, which involved the Kamba and the Somali respectively, had much to do with this. Yet the arrival of the Busaidi gave an impetus to this expansion which, perhaps, might not have occurred otherwise. Said b. Sultan and his successors were merchant princes in every

113

sense of the word. They engaged in trade personally and used their profits and customs dues to advance their political interests. More so, they promoted the development of agriculture and business activities. Sayyid Said encouraged Indian financiers to settle on the coast; he introduced Indian *pice* as a much needed unit of exchange; and it was he who concluded the treaties with the Americans, the British, and the French which assured the continued growth of the coast's export trade.[97] More importantly, he was the principal founder of the Zanzibar clove cultivation which became one of the corner-stones of coastal trade after the 1840s.

This expansion in coastal economy had a varying impact on different areas of the coast. Zanzibar, of course, was the hub of the international trade. While the 'coasting' trade brought the ivory and slaves for export to Zanzibar from the various towns, it was Zanzibar which was the point of embarkation for the ships from Europe, India, Asia, and America.[98] In addition, Zanzibar and (after 1872) Pemba were the principal sources of cloves. The mainland towns were the staging points for the inland trade and specialized in a more traditional sort of crop cultivation than in the cloves of Zanzibar. The increased stability and unification of coastal trade brought on by the leadership of the Busaidi were responsible for the shift of the Yao ivory and slave trade away from Mozambique to Kilwa Kivinje after the 1780s.[99] Nyamwezi and Luguru enterprise, too, led to the opening up of the Bagamoyo and Saadani hinterland sometime already by the late eighteenth century. Trade expanded in the Vanga area in the 1860s out of the friendship between the Diwan Rugas and their Digo and Segeju neighbours.[100] When Maasai raiding cut off the 'northern' route in the 1850s, a new one was established between Mombasa and Mount Kilimanjaro in the 1860s. Thereafter, routes from Mombasa were extended steadily inland, skirting Kamba and Kikuyu country, and advanced north and westwards through Maasailand, up to Mumia's in Baluhya country, and eventually all the way to Buganda.

From Mombasa north, however, trade was not the principal *métier* of coastal entrepreneurs since no long-distance inland routes developed. Instead, commercial agriculture thrived. At Mombasa, the Swahili clans continued cultivation and trade in cereals from their *honde*, while Arab clans like the Mandhry and Mazrui engaged in grain cultivation on *shambas* owned at Pemba, Kisauni, Changamwe, and Takaungu, as well as from *mahonde* worked around Kilifi.[101] Malindi and Mambrui were settled by Omanis, Washela, and Hadrami migrants in the 1870s and soon developed into the foremost cereals-producing region on the coast. In 1897, Hardinge described the area as, 'the most productive on the coast, the fertile zone extending far into the Nyika'.[102] The area extended through a string of villages with surrounding *mashamba*, along the coast from Takaungu to about 5 kilometres north of Mambrui. Malindi and Mambrui together supported a population of about 9,000.[103] Finally, Lamu continued the prosperity begun in the late eighteenth century based on her trade with the Pokomo. Both sides of the Tana River were under grain cultivation. Kau and Kipini on the Tana were centres of cultivation and, by the 1870s, staging points for caravan routes up the river farther into Pokomo and Oromo country, while Lamu also was a centre for the slave re-export trade northwards and engaged in some ivory trade with her Dahalo neighbours.

One very noteworthy consequence of coastal people's growing affluence in the nineteenth century was the increased reliance on slaves for the performance of all manual labour in the towns and on the farms.[105] Furthermore, some slaves were trained in skills which enabled them, in time, to take over the operations of their masters' trades and to captain their ships, leaving the wealthy *waungwana* with even more time to pursue their leisure activities.[106]

Wealth and slaves, then, went even further in creating a new leisured class. As Cooper points out, the caravan trade which had sprung up by the early nineteenth century provided capital for reinvestment in less risky enterprises like *shamba* ownership. A new, even larger landed class of leisured Swahili and an Arab aristocracy appeared whose choice of investment in clove *mashamba* or cereals-producing *mahonde* reflected an opting for the more laid-back style of plantation life.[107] The evolution of the slave system is an obvious sign of this. Whereas most slaves were imported (7,000–10,000 per annum) into Zanzibar only to be re-exported in 1811, by 1854 half of these were being kept for employment on local estates and successive anti-slavery treaties forced this figure even higher.[108] Profits from these estates were put to political uses. For example, Bujra claims that wealth was used, 'to create and support a network of linkages of which [the landowner/entrepreneur] is the centre'. Money was used to expand a wealthy person's network of dependence through reinvestment in land, employment of others (slaves or clients) to work the land, or usury.[109] Wealth brought leisure and ever greater influence.

However, wealth also brought changing views on landownership and land use. If indeed the idea of the *shamba* predated the nineteenth century (perhaps as 'sacred' coastal or island land protected from the invidious and pagan spirits of the bush), the idea of *mashamba* as land which has been alienated for personal use, as opposed to land to which one could claim only usufruct rights based on ancestral claims, certainly received its greatest boost under the Sultanate. The Omanis benefited from differences between landownership as defined by written tradition and landownership as it was perceived locally.[110] Hence, it was the Busaidi *liwalis*, such as the Banu Khalfan and the Banu Hamid, as well as Indian money-lenders, who subtly introduced the concept of legally defined landownership and alienation when, in lending money, they took land (which *waungwana* presumably understood as usufruct rights) as collateral. At Zanzibar the system was most advanced. Where, before the 1840s, land was largely for growing fruits, cassava, rice, and millet, clove cultivation revolutionized matters. There whether or not 'fraud' or force was used to remove the local Wahadimu, the introduction of a perennial money crop like the clove required a very different relationship of the 'user' to the land than formerly had been the case.[111] Landownership, as opposed to rights of usufruct, simply could have been a difference of perennial crop cultivation versus crop husbandry which required traditional shifting cultivation techniques.

CONVERSION OF IBADIS TO SHAFII ISLAM

The Sultanate affected changes in religion along the coast in different ways and to different degrees. Generally speaking, however, just how people reacted to the Sultanate and the changes which it brought in their lives and in their perceptions depended greatly on their respective relationships with the Busaidi before Sayyid Said arrived on the coast. Also, because the power of the Sultanate waxed over time, these responses tended to intensify accordingly.

One way the Sultanate brought about religious change was through the conversion of many Ibadis to Sunni beliefs. The reasons for this lay in the precariousness of the early Sultanate (pre-1870s) and the loose means which it employed to retain the allegiance of the many coastal locations. As seen above, the Sultans' governors were sent only to protect the towns, promote trade, and adjudicate disputes among the towns' many clans and ethnic minorities. Field informants were quick to point out that because the Busaidi were invited into their communities, they were not allowed to interfere in local affairs. Because, 'they came only for government', as one man put it, proselytization was not permitted them.[112] At Zanzibar, too, because of the great variety of sects and religions, tolerance was required of the Omanis.[113] At the courts of the Sultans themselves, religious debating apparently was indulged so long as matters were kept on a detached, scholarly level, and no disputation was countenanced. In addition, *qadis* of both the Ibadi Shafii sects were consulted in legal matters.[114]

The net effect of this atmosphere of religious liberality, especially in cosmopolitan Zanzibar, was a certain amount of free association of ideas among Ibadis and Sunnis. Many Ibadis, in addition, were partially out of touch with the strict scholarly tradition of their native Oman and, as Burton pointed out, many had 'little education and no learning'. Within one or two generations, they lost Arabic as their primary language and some lost it altogether. All this meant that, as 'food for their own cravings of belief', many Ibadis were forced to borrow 'from the Sunnis' commentaries (*tafsir*) and other religious works' by such standard Shafii pundits as al-Bukhari, al-Baghawi, and the Jalalayn (ubiquitous on the coast).[115] At the same time, various Sunni ʿulamaʾ studied under Ibadis whose reputations for scholarship in certain sciences were pre-eminent.[116] Also, in an apparent effort to engender good will, wealthy Ibadis built mosques which they either shared with Sunnis or which they built outright for Sunni use.[117] Finally, it should be mentioned that for many Ibadis who were not schooled in the finer points of their religion, there were few, if any, distinguishable cult differences between their sect and Sunni practices.[118] It is for such reasons, therefore, that many Ibadis, even the families of *liwalis*, like the Busaidi of Lamu, began converting to Shafii Islam after a generation or two.

Another point which seems to account for the conversion of many Ibadis was the social integration of Omani clans and the Swahili townspeople among whom they lived. At Mombasa, this had been going on for several generations before the inception of the Sultanate. Families like the Mandhry and the Shikely, for instance, came to Mombasa as poor merchants who took African wives and, being without mosques, converted to the persuasion of local Muslims whose mosques they shared. However, the process appears to have affected the wealthy and socially elite clans like the Mazrui rather late. Apparently, it was only after their erstwhile Three Tribes allies began moving into the Kavani, around the 1840s and 1850s, that some Mazrui began converting. Once this process began, Three Tribesmen and Arab clans like the Mazrui and the Mandhry began praying together in the Mazrui, Mandhry, Azhar, and Mnara mosques.[119]

As early as 1856, however, observers of the coastal scene already could discern the most obvious rationale for the conversion of many Ibadis to the Shafii beliefs of their *waungwana* neighbours. By then, feuding between old elite families, like the Mazrui and the Barwani, and the new Busaidi elite had gone on long enough for Burton to cite this as a prime factor for the conversion of the former.[120] This resistance, however, was not all of one variety.

From the very beginning of Busaidi rule, there was a general reluctance of some (especially Ghafiri) clans to accede to Busaidi claims to overall leadership of the Omani community. As indicated above, it was for this reason that the Mazrui of Mombasa broke with Ahmad b. Said al-Busaidi when he assumed the Imamate in the 1740s. Thus, as one informant stated, the East African Ibadis 'were excluded from Oman', and were unable to pray on Fridays because, 'They [had] to be ordered by the Imam. But there [was] no Imam. The religious leader [was] the Sultan, and this Sultan of Zanzibar is [*sic*] no religion.'[121] As late as the 1870s, many Ibadis continued in this practice (not praying) out of a conviction that the Sultans were unjust and did not rule by strict Ibadi law and custom.[122]

As would be expected, it was the Mazrui again who led this resistance to Busaidi pretensions, both secular and religious. After Sayyid Said seized Mombasa, large numbers of the clan and their clients, retainers, and slaves fled from the city to resettle at Gazi and Takaungu. The earliest Mazrui *ᶜalim* of whom we hear, and who fled from the Busaidi, is Shaykh Abdallah b. Nafuᶜ Mazrui. The information on Sh. Abdallah is meagre, but what is certain is that he founded the redoubtable Banu Nafuᶜ branch of his clan which, above all others down to the present, has been noted for its intellectual leaders.[123] In 1837 he fled Mombasa with his son, Ali, and made his way to Mecca. There, he and his son remained until 1846, studying under several Shafii *ᶜulamaᵓ*. Thus, Abdallah b. Nafuᶜ and Ali b. Abdallah were the first (known) Mazrui to convert.[124]

Sh. Abdallah never made it back to Mombasa, as he died at Shihr on the return journey in 1846. However, Sh. Ali b. Abdallah Mazrui did return to Mombasa and became one of the most accomplished Sunni *ᶜulamaᵓ* on the coast in the second half of the nineteenth century. He served as official *qadi* of Mombasa under Sayyid Majid (1856–70), returning to Mecca for additional studies in 1859, and subsequently authored several scholarly texts.[125] His most notable work was as an apologist, defender, and proselytizer of his Shafii beliefs – and it was these activities which eventually landed him in trouble. When Sh. Muhammad b. Ali Mandhry, the Ibadi confidant and advisor to S. Majid, published a work criticizing Shafii views on the homomorphism of God, Sh. Ali b. Abdallah engaged him in a public debate on the issues and wrote another work in response.[126] Sh. Ali, however, ran into Sayyid Barghash's prejudices in his efforts to convert his kinsmen and other Ibadis to Sunni beliefs. As pointed out by one source, Sh. Ali's position as an *calim* gave him enough charisma to be feared by the Busaidi and, of course, his growing personal reputation would have been intimidating even if he was not a Mazrui.[127] The final scenario occurred in 1887 when Sh. Ali began *darasas* at Pemba which produced some conversions. For these actions, Sayyid Barghash imprisoned Ali b. Abdallah where he remained until the Sultan's death in 1888.[128] Sh. Ali b. Abdallah's animus towards the Busaidi also is evident in the support which he gave to Mbarak b. Rashid's rebellion. Informants claimed that he journeyed 'up and down the coast' to confer with Sh. Mbarak, to render advice and moral support, and to act as an intermediary between him and the Sultan's *liwalis.*[129]

It was not only the general phenomenon of Busaidi rule which induced many Ibadis to convert to Sunni Islam, but the prejudicial actions of Sultan Barghash in particular. The evidence on this is quite clear. One European, while noting Barghash's 'remarkable good sense' in most matters, also was compelled to remark upon his obstinacy and his way of being 'personally inclined to bigotry in religious matters'.[130] Another source mentioned how one convert to Christianity was imprisoned by the Sultan for three and a half years, 'scorning all offers of freedom at the cost of his religion'.[131] It was at the inception of his reign, especially, when Barghash was most intolerant. At that time, he came under the influence of a reformist party of Ibadi *culama*ɔ called the *mutawwiun*, who counselled him in his personal religious habits as well as in state matters. Apparently, their fundamentalist views included the banning of tobacco, commonly used by many *waungwana* and Arabs alike; banning Friday prayers among the Sultan's Sunni subjects; and other matters.[132] These *culama*ɔ were described by British Consul Churchill thusly:

> A council of priests is to direct the affairs of state, the law of the Koran is to be revived, and there is now talk of making the Zanzibar dominions an appanage of the Imamate of Muscat as it was in Seyed Saeed's time.[133]

While Barghash 'threw off' these pretensions in 1872, when he performed the *hajj*, and in 1873, when he came under increased pressure from the British anti-slavery party, nevertheless his prejudicial attitudes remained manifest throughout his reign. In addition, he continued to keep one *mutawwi*, Sh. Hamud al-Furahi, as a confidant for some time afterwards. Finally, as will be seen, he established a printing press to disseminate Ibadi views as a counter to growing Sunni beliefs among his Omani subjects.

Barghash's ire was roused most noticeably in the events which surrounded the conversion of two influential personalities among the Sultans' old rivals, the Barwani. The conversion of Sh. Ali b. Khamis al-Barwani was personally painful to Barghash in that Sh. Ali formerly had been privy to the Sultan. While still a boy, Sh. Ali had been given entry into Barghash's *barazas*, and he grew up studying under some of Zanzibar's most prominent Ibadi *culamaɔ* of that time: Sh. Yahya b. Khalfan al-Kharusi; Sh. Muhammad Sulaiman Mandhry; and Sh. Khamis b. Sliyim al-Khasibi, a noted Omani grammarian.[134] By the time he was thirty years old, Sh. Ali was a competent specialist in Arabic grammar (*nahw*) and morphology (*sarf*) and had been associated with the Sultan's press. However, not long afterwards, he was converted to Shafiism by a Lamu *calim*, Sh. Muhammad b. Salih al-Farsy. As if this was not enough, Sh. Ali's conversion took on some interesting class overtones through his association with a certain Sh. Khamis b. Salim al-Khasibi, an Omani of the *biswari* class – a class of low social status somewhat akin to the Hadrami *duacfaɔ*. However, because he was a *qadi*, Sh. Khamis refused to address the Sultan as Habib, as was customary among the *biswari* class, but insisted on calling Barghash by his usual title of Sayyid. Barghash threatened to imprison Sh. Khamis for his insolence, so the *qadi* fled to Oman where he composed verses attacking the Zanzibar Sultan. In addition, Sh. Khamis retaliated by arranging a marriage between Sh. Ali b. Khamis al-Barwani and the daughter of a wealthy *biswari* with the intent that Sh. Ali b. Khamis could use his new wealth to proselytize other Ibadis into becoming Sunnis – behaviour which Sh. Khamis knew would nettle Barghash.[135]

Sh. Ali b. Khamis's conversion once again brought out the worst in Barghash. Initial persecution gave way to imprisonment at Zanzibar, threats, then eventual deportation to Oman. The Ibadi *mufti* of Barghash's court, Sh. Muhammad Sulaiman Mandhry, was sent to persuade Sh. Ali to relent, but to no avail. Eventually, Sh. Ali was forced to repudiate his beliefs, but soon after his release he died.[136]

While Barghash 'lost' a highly learned *calim* in Sh. Ali b. Khamis, a worse blow was the conversion of Sh. Muhsin b. Ali al-Barwani. Sh. Muhsin was the *shaykh* of the entire Barwani clan at Zanzibar and was influential in clan and community, so when he converted all male members of the Zanzibar Barwani went with him. A row ensued with Barghash, and Sh. Muhsin subsequently became a pupil of the noted Shafii *calim*, Sh. Abdallah Bakathir.[137]

Another major embarrassment to Barghash were the activities of the *tariqa shaykh*, Sh. Abdu'l-Aziz b. Abdu'l-Ghany al-Amawi. Sh. Abdu'l-Aziz's popularity as a *tariqa shaykh* apparently won many converts to Shafii beliefs and interest in Qadiriyya *dhikrs*. Among these converts, it was rumoured, was the Sultan's estranged brother, Sayyid Khalifa b. Said. Because of Sh. Abdu'l-Aziz's activities and his friendship with Sayyid Khalifa, Barghash took away Abdu'l-Aziz's *qadi*-ship and tried to prevent his followers from saying their Friday prayers. Abdu'l-Aziz, however, mustered opposition to the Sultan's interference by coming armed, in the company of his students, to Friday prayers. Though he did not escape arrest for his defiance, in the end Abdu'l-Aziz's popularity was too extensive for Barghash to make the charges against the ᶜ*alim* stick. Abdu'l-Aziz was released and the harassment ceased.[138]

The result of all these conversions was that, whereas most Omanis were Ibadis before 1870, by 1907 few Ibadis were still to be found in Zanzibar.[139] By then there were so few Ibadi ᶜ*ulamaʾ*, for example, that the British authorities were experiencing difficulty in finding replacements for deceased Ibadi *qadis*. Judge Peter Grain was forced to recommend that the criminal courts of appeal discontinue employing Ibadi *qadis*. Because of the paucity of Ibadis by then he saw 'no good reason for keeping alive these two schools (both Ibadi and Shafii) of law'.[140]

NEW MAGICO-RELIGIOUS SKILLS FROM OMAN

Two other noteworthy shifts in town Islam emerged under the Sultanate. One of these involved new magico-religious skills picked up by the Swahili townsmen, ostensibly from the Omanis, which appear to have played an interesting part in Swahili initiatives in upcountry travel and trade.

Although Ibadis, most Omanis who came to East Africa in the eighteenth and nineteenth centuries were not fanatical purists or fundamentalists: relative as well as absolute views of transcendence can be found even among Kharijites. This would be true especially for seafaring Arabs like the Omanis. Sayyid Said himself is reported by Burton to have believed in metamorphosis of the soul, to have believed in ghosts and spirits, and was not altogether sceptical of the powers of *waganga*.[141] Emily Reute (née Salama bti. Said al-Busaidi) commented on the high susceptibility of the Omanis to many 'superstitions' resembling those of the *waungwana*.[142] Various factors account for this. Foremost among these, of course, was that many East African Omanis were somewhat distanced from the more literate Islam of their homeland, and, especially as more of them converted to Shafii Islam, remaining Ibadis had relatively few ᶜ*ulamaʾ* in their midst to stem their ignorance of the written Islamic tradition (that is, so-called orthodox Islam). Apparently, even the Sultans' courts were not free of illiteracy. Reute, again, commented on limitations in the religious training of the courtiers and the Sayyids themselves, citing by way of example their dependence on court *qadis* to carry out their written correspondence.[143]

However, there is another reason which accounts, at least, for a certain type of superstition. Many Omanis (and other Arabs) who came to the coast to trade or to live were merchants or seafarers. As seamen, these merchants had to rely on ancient systems of navigation which were based on astronomical observations and calculations. While these practices, called ᶜ*ilm al-falak* in Arabic, had some scientific bases in actual observations handed down from the Greeks, they also had their pseudo-scientific side. ᶜ*Ilm al-falak*, in fact, means both astronomy and astrology in Arabic.[144] Thus, *falak* was an important science for the seamen of the East, and Oman itself was said by Burton to have 'teemed' with these specialists in magico-religious activities which had grown out of the written Greco-Islamic tradition. On the East African coast, at the time of Burton's visit in the 1850s, *falakis* were feared for practising what local peoples still thought was a form of sorcery.[145]

The connection between medicine based on the written tradition and the Omanis is indicated in evidence obtained from a number of informants. *Tibb*, a type of (coastal) medicine which employed *falak* along with other techniques, was said to have been based on medicines imported from Arabia and the employment of written materials. The distinction that *tibb* was imported medicine based on the written sciences, as opposed to local or bush medicines, was clearly distinguished by two informants.[146]

The *waungwana* perceived this same distinction, and in efforts at reconciling themselves to the changing world around them under the Sultanate, they tried to pre-empt some of this Arab 'magic'. Thus, they distinguished between *mizimu*, ancestral or locality spirits which lived in the trees and caves of the lands on which their forefathers had lived, and the Arab *pepo* spirits. The Arab *pepo*, called *jinni*, like the Arabs were said to have come from and to have inhabited the sea. More interesting still is that some *jinni* were considered harmful to *waungwana*.[147] Psychological pre-emption of the potential threat which Arabs and Arabness (*ustaarabu*) posed to town life on the coast manifested itself through spirit possession rituals similar to older *pungwa wa pepo* ceremonies discussed in Chapter 5. In one ritual, *tari la ndia*, an Arab spirit or *tari* took possession of the victim. In the process by which the *tari* was placated (note, *not* exorcised), the victim became an Arab spiritually and thus pre-empted the power of the potentially inimical Arab 'otherness' represented by the *tari*. Even in form the person possessed became an Arab by ritually eschewing his old clothing for a turban, a scimitar, and a *kanzu*.[148]

Thus the townsperson absorbed Arab magic, medicine, and techniques and turned them to constructive purposes. *Falak* was one of the most useful contributions to local magic and medicine made (at least ostensibly) by the Omanis. It is possible, for example, to see how townspeople at Mombasa used Arab additions to their medicine kits to make needed adjustments in their economies following the successive restrictions placed upon the slave trade. By the 1870s, new anti-slavery treaties concluded between the Sultans and the British began to make the old plantation life on the coast increasingly difficult. For this reason, among many of course, many *waungwana* of Mombasa increasingly turned to upcountry trade as an alternative source of income.[149] Where food items and ivory formerly could be obtained in local markets, loss of slave labour and impediments placed by the Kamba in the way of direct overland trade from Mombasa forced *waungwana* to develop southerly routes.

Falak became the favourite medicine employed by caravan guides, thus 'navigating' the unknown interior just as Omani seamen had employed it in charting the unknown dangers of the sea. Muscat remained the principal school of *falak*, apparently, as several *waungwana* actually journeyed there to learn the new science.[150] Once the science caught on and people ceased fearing it, it was learned in the *barazas* and all respectable caravan guides were expected to know it. It was not taught in the mosques because 'it wasn't considered religious'. At Mombasa, certain clans became famous for their specialization in astrology, but each used it for different purposes.[151] Mzee Muhammad Ahmad Matano explained, for instance, how his ancestor, Mwinyi Matano wa Kombo, taught *falak* in his home to his sons, Mwinjaka and Mtondo, after which Mwinjaka passed on the secret lore to his nephew, and Muhammad Ahmad's father, Ahmad Matano. Both Mwinjaka wa Mwinyi Matano and Ahmad Matano became noted caravan guides and *falaki* from the time of Sayyid Barghash onwards.[152] Before setting out for the interior, the caravan would gather at Mwembe Tayari where *falak* and *raml* were employed to determine the propitious day and hour for departure.[153] In addition, the Timami clan, especially one Rigezi al-Timami, became specialists in setting out the calendar for the coming year through employing *falak* and the *Sawt al-Khabar* mentioned in Chapter 5.[154]

The final change in town religion generally had to do with the changing nature of the *ᶜulamaᵓ* themselves. While this is a topic which can be dealt with better in the context of Chapter 8, discussion of at least certain manifestations of local reactions to these changes are in order here.

At the start of Busaidi rule, appointment of *qadis* was largely in the control of the townspeople. While done by the Sultan or *liwali*, official appointment was governed by the principle that 'The tongues of the people are the pen of God.'[155] However, with the growing power of the Busaidi in local affairs, the *liwalis* played an ever greater role in the selection of *qadis*, so consequently the *qadis* increasingly became the instruments of the Sultanate. In general, *liwalis* became bolder in their attempts at interfering in local religious matters. For example, it was mentioned above how the Busaidi at Lamu, as rivals to the Maawi, opposed the choice of the Maawi as *khatibs* and recommended that certain Mahdali be appointed in their accustomed place. At Mombasa around the 1870s when Ibadi revivalism was popular at the court in Zanzibar, some *liwalis* apparently tried to prevent dancing or the use of tobaccos and certain local varieties of intoxicants (*tembo ya kali*).[156] By then, too, the *liwalis* were becoming the principal figures in choosing the *qadis*, overshadowing even the town *wazee* in the selection process.[157] As one informant pointed out, it was the *liwalis*, along with other *ᶜulamaᵓ*, who made the recommendation to the Sultan for the appointment.[158] While it might be thought that the *ᶜulamaᵓ* themselves continued to represent the *waungwana* and their religious views, this, however, was no longer entirely the situation.

The growing tendency, in fact, was for the local *ᶜulamaᵓ* to cooperate with the authorities. A new type of *ᶜulamaᵓ* emerged under the Sultanate who derived recognition, if anything, through association with the 'big men' of their times. Indeed, stature as an *ᶜalim* was based essentially on the recognition and homage paid by others. The great *ᶜalim* was one who tended the *barazas* of the rich and powerful who, in turn, visited him and paid him honour. When the recognized *ᶜalim* died, too, he left behind a legacy which reinforced values accepted by the socially and politically elite.

The funeral of the great *ᶜalim*, like that of any great person, was well attended by the people who mattered in the community.[159]

In this vein, el-Zein gives some excellent examples of how the *ᶜulamaᵓ* under the Sultanate were pressured into cooperating with the powerful, even when they might have chosen otherwise. He tells how the Busaidi at Lamu slowly began abandoning Ibadism, and how, in 1883, one of them decided to take a wife from the al-Husayni, one of the town's most prominent *sharif* clans. Naturally, most of Lamu's old elite opposed any recognition of this match, but to avoid strife the *khatibs* and the *ᶜulamaᵓ* were coerced into declaring for the marriage. The blow was hard for Lamu, but it was intensified soon afterwards when the *ᶜulamaᵓ* sanctioned another alliance between another Busaidi and a Jahadhmy.[160] A social upheaval was in the making. So, on the heels of these marriages, the poorest and most downtrodden class at Lamu (the Wayumbili) allied themselves with the Busaidi and, with the new state of affairs, laid all their past misfortunes at the feet of the elite Maawi and Makhzumy. The old *ᶜulamaᵓ* and *khatibs*, the Maawi, were accused of guilt by association for having supported the old order (at least as it had emerged in the seventeenth and eighteenth centuries). Thus, as el-Zein concludes, the entire ideological basis to the class structure at Lamu, as represented and supported by the *ᶜulamaᵓ*, was tottering.[161]

In addition, the entire old system of Quranic justice was 'corrupted' by the Busaidi. Burton describes, for instance, the 'rough and ready law' which was meted out by the local *liwali* and three 'patriarchs' at the fort of Zanzibar in the years before Sayyid Said moved permanently to East Africa.[162] Afterwards, under the Sultanate, *qadis* cooperated in a system in which punishments 'more or less severe' were dealt out even for lesser crimes. More telling, though, was that, 'Fines and confiscations, which have taken the place of the Koranic mutilation, are somewhat common, especially where impudent frauds are practiced upon the Prince's property.'[163] It would appear, then, that some *ᶜulamaᵓ* cooperated in the confiscation of property which enriched some Busaidi *liwalis*, such as the Banu Khalfan and the Awlad Hamid.

A similar example of Busaidi control over the *ᶜulamaᵓ* can be given in the case of a lawsuit between the firm of Jairam Sewji and an Arab, Ali b. Uthman, which took place in 1877. In this instance, Barghash ordered his *qadis* not to hear Jairam Sewji's case – that is, a boycott was ordered.[164] In a similar case, when Sewji tried to foreclose on a delinquent loan made to another Arab, one Muhammad b. Salim, it was reported that 'hostility and unfairness [was] shown towards the petitioners by the khazi appointed by and acting under the direct orders of the Sultan'.[165] In other cases involving inheritances it is said that, 'His Highness Syed Barghash is a keen man of business and makes almost an invariable practice of appointing himself executor of any of his subjects who may die possessed of means.'[166]

Clearly, this sort of tampering, both in Zanzibar and in towns like Lamu and Mombasa, had to elicit some reaction from *waungwana*. The first visible instance of hostility to the Sultanate by townsmen came in 1875 with the

McKillop Pasha expedition. This was an adventure organized by the Scot, Captain H. F. McKillop, whereby various towns along the Benadir coast and the Lamu archipelago were seized by Egyptian troops in the service of the *Khedive* Ismail of Egypt.[167] The reaction of some *waungwana* at Lamu and Mombasa to this temporary occupation clearly revealed the hidden sentiments of some Swahili towards the Busaidi. Aside from the expected support of renegades like Ahmad Simba and Mzee Saif of Siyu, both Lamu and Mombasa were astir with anticipation of an Egyptian victory. People were responding to the Egyptian aggression on the heels of the 1873 anti-slavery treaty; hence, some were willing to believe rumours that the trade would be restored in exchange for their support of the invasion.[168] Furthermore, some chose to believe the propaganda that the Egyptians were sent to 'protect the poor Musulmans in East Africa and to resist the aggression of Syed Barghash who had abandoned himself to the influence of the Christians'.[169] While there were overtones of a personal dislike of the Sultan for his high-handedness and his 1873 treaty, there also were vague religious and inchoate Pan-Islamic aspects to Swahili reactions. Some townspeople, for example, were receptive to Egyptian pronouncements that they were sent by the 'Sultan of the Muslims' in Istanbul, and, therefore, their mission deserved the support of local Muslims since they, with the Turks and Egyptians, were all of the same sect (Sunni, as opposed to the Ibadism of the Omanis).[170] Furthermore, in Mombasa, it was said that Twelve Tribesmen who were 'accustomed to pray in their mosques on Fridays for the Sultan of Turkey as head of their religion look to events with interest'.[171]

CONCLUSION

Coastal Muslims in East Africa were coming under the influence of a new government after about the 1820s, and as has been seen, some strains were gradually introduced in their relationship with this government. These were greatly accelerated during the reign of Sayyid Barghash (1870–88) due to the changes in the position of the Sultan and the power of the Sultanate which resulted from the 1873 treaty. While coastal Muslims had been slowly, almost unconsciously, pulled into a more universal system of economy and society by the centralized government at Zanzibar, their views also were becoming more opened up and universalized. Finally, as hinted above, so too did they find a new sort of intellectual elite in their midst who increasingly were different in their views and practices from the old-style town *waganga* and *walimu* discussed in Chapter 5. This 'opening up' in modes of thinking for coastal Muslims and the presence of new-style *ᶜulamaᵓ* among them as a partial result of these changes are the subject matter of the next two chapters.

7

New secularism and bureaucratic centralization

The coming of the Busaidi Sultanate marked a new departure for towns-people from purely local concerns and views to a new internationalism. Certainly this was true in the realm of economics for most towns, and was true of Lamu before the 1820s. Yet, what started in coastal economy slowly worked its way into the social and ideological spheres. Local reactions to these alterations, as should have been apparent in the preceding chapter, were ambivalent, even contradictory. While some chose to embrace the new order of things from the start, others were slow to reconcile themselves to the changes. And while a new social condition was of obvious benefit to newcomers and outsiders in the towns, as Mannheim explains matters, the old elite found accommodating themselves a more difficult matter.[1]

Although changes were being introduced from the time of Sayyid Said onwards, matters advanced by several quantum steps in the reign of Sayyid Barghash. While Said b. Sultan simply introduced the prevailing political and economic order of Muscat to his new capital at Zanzibar, Sayyid Barghash conscientiously and actively sought changes in the ideological realm. It is for this reason that he is remembered on the coast as the first modernizer in coastal history, and it is to his reign and those of his successors that the subject matter of this chapter is especially applicable.

THE SECULARISM OF THE SULTANATE, ITS PRESTIGE AND IMPACT

As was seen in the previous chapter, with the reign of Sultan b. Ahmad al-Busaidi, the Sultanate became distinct from the Imamate. Indeed, Sultan b. Ahmad had been considered a rebel by the Imamate, and Sayyid Said seized power by assassinating his cousin, the *Imam*-elect, Badr b. Saif (1804–5).[2] Power and force had become the paramount factors which determined succession, not religious charisma. The Imams and their allies among the tribes of Oman's interior were powerless to oppose the Sayyids effectively. Thus, at Oman there evolved a theoretical separation of religion and state, although the state retained most of the religious and civil prerogatives which formerly had been exercised by the Imamate.[3]

In addition to receiving the *sadakat* and the *zakat*, which were intended for religious purposes, the Sayyids based their authority on customs dues from imports at Muscat and other Omani seaports. Thus, a source was found

125

for the rule of the realm that was independent of income derived from religious sanctions. Sultan b. Ahmad's and Said b. Sultan's popularity increasingly became confined to Oman's coastal region and her merchants and seamen. Their rule became increasingly secular in its foundations and could be characterized more as a Sultanate of Muscat than an Imamate of Oman.[4] It was for this reason, therefore, that Sayyid Said faced extreme opposition from the more traditional inland tribes, several of which had become involved with Wahhabism, during the first two decades of his reign.[5]

Sayyid Said, however, did not at first give up his claims to religious leadership of the Ibadis. Owens reported that in 1824 he showered treasure on the *sharifs* of Mecca in an attempt to gain their recognition of his claims to the Imamate, but to no avail.[6] Thereafter, he relinquished his claims to the title and, because of a lack of true religious leadership and for the sake of expediency, his reign and those of his successors (save Barghash in a few instances) were noteworthy for their religious liberalism. Matters had progressed so far by the 1890s, for example, that Sayyid Hamid b. Thuwain is once said to have remarked that, 'The wise men who made the Law, Christ and Muhammad, lived a very long time ago and made the Law according to their lights, but they did not know many things that we know now and the world has moved on further since their Law was made.'[7]

Once relocated on the coast, the secularism of the Sultanate, if anything, was enhanced. As merchant princes, the Sultans ruled over a commercial empire and placed their capital at the centre of a far-flung network of human intercourse. Berg's 'Zanzibar system' graphically illustrates the truly cosmopolitan flavour of what Zanzibar society must have been like under the Sultanate.[8] According to his scheme, Zanzibar's commercial nexus brought coastal townspeople, particularly Zanzibaris, in contact with Africans from such modern-day countries as Tanganyika, Kenya, Uganda, Zambia, Malawi, Zaire, Somalia, and Ethiopia. External contacts existed between Zanzibar and merchants from southern Arabia, India, Egypt, the East Indies, North America, and Europe. At various times of the year, slaves, merchants, seamen, and diplomats from all these countries might be found in Zanzibar or in other coastal towns.

DEVELOPING INTERESTS IN FOREIGN IDEAS

With this background in mind, it is not surprising to learn of the international character of court life at Zanzibar. Besides the comings and goings of American and European diplomats and merchants, the Sultans employed Indians in their customs service and among their most confidential advisors.[9] Furthermore, the viewpoints of the Sultans and their associates were influenced by the fact that also among the Sultans' advisors were sea captains (*nahodha*) whose contacts with other cultures certainly were extensive.[10] These *nahodhas* mostly were trained in Bombay, Calcutta, and Muscat. However, some also had been sent to Britain, 'where', Burton informs us, 'they showed no want of attention or capacity', but who upon their return to Zanzibar, almost all, 'went to the bad', dying of 'drunkenness and debauchery'.[11] Foremost among these *nahodha* ministers were Ahmad b. Naᵓaman, called Wajhayn (the 'two-faced'), and a 'Captain' Hasan b. Ibrahim. Both these men attained their positions because of their facility in English and their experiences with Europeans who increasingly were becoming the foundation of coastal prosperity under the Sultanate. Wajhayn, especially, is noteworthy because of a visit in 1840 he made as Sayyid Said's personal envoy to the USA. Later in life, he undertook intelligence work of an unspecified nature at Zanzibar for the British.[12]

The Busaidi took a lively interest in Western objects and ideas, particularly where they involved trade and military matters. In his talks with the American consul, R. P. Waters, it is reported that Sayyid Said, 'talked about America, what a large country it was, and made many enquiries which I was pleased to answer'. The Sayyid centred much of his attention on commercial affairs and on American politics and society. It is said he requested translations from American newspapers from the consul and from his personal translator, Ahmad b. Na'man.[13] Sayyid Barghash, too, appears to have shared his father's interest in the West. Badger reported that the Sultan's library included, besides religious works, information on the comparative power, resources, and military and naval strength of the various European states. In addition, Barghash took a lively interest in the modernization programmes being carried out in Egypt by the Khedive Isma'il.[14] He interviewed the Khedive during his 1875 visit to Egypt and made it a point to visit the medical college, to browse through the Khedive's library, and to garner information on Egypt's Western-style armed forces.[15]

From the beginning, too, the Busaidi introduced Western and Indian inventions, objects, curiosities, and styles of dress to the coast. Burton relates that the palace of Said boasted, 'a few dingy chandeliers, and three rows of common wooden bottomed chairs'.[16] In her book, Reute makes constant references to Western and Indian artifacts and inventions commonly found in 'Arab' houses at that time. Sayyid Said's eldest son, Khalid, especially had a 'predilection for France and everything French'. His villa, at 'Marseilles', featured walls covered with large, imported, European mirrors; black and white tiled French floors; European clocks just coming into vogue; glass globes; 'large round quicksilver balls'; and other 'works of art'.[17] Again, it was Barghash, though, who went the farthest in introducing Zanzibar and *waungwana* to the West. With revenues obtained from increased taxation of the clove industry, he brought in a modern, fresh water supply system to Zanzibar, gas lit Zanzibar's streets, bought steamships and set up a service in competition with the British East India Line, established a uniformed police force, and later introduced a standing army drilled and trained in the European manner under the Englishman Lloyd Mathews.[18] His most notable construction projects included the clock tower at Zanzibar and his personal residence, the famous Bayt al-ᶜAjaᵓib ('house of wonders'), which featured a large array of European objects, fashions, and inventions. The impression made by all these things on the local population typically was described in Reute's remark that 'Truly, the Christians are devils!'[19] Swahili reaction to Barghash's innovations are summed up in the poet's words concerning the Bayt al-ᶜAja'ib:

> The palace where he lives would amaze anyone; it gleams with bright fabrics.
> The covers are silk, scarlet and green. Wherever you look you are dazzled.
> Jewels and glass I cannot describe to you; you cannot look at them, they are
> so bright. His audience chamber is a mass of gold. It would amaze you how it
> is furnished. It is strongly built and excellently adorned.[20]

THE PRESTIGE OF THE SULTANATE

Because of his modernization efforts, it was the reign of Barghash more
than that of any other of the Sayyids which established the prestige of the
Sultanate in the eyes of coastal *waungwana*. The Sultan (any of the Sultans,
that is, the Sultanate itself) was characterized as 'a good man and generous'.
He was 'unmistakable; he is beautifully built; I have not seen his equal'. He
was 'fierce as a lion, terrible to behold' in his majesty, yet, 'His character is
quiet and untroubled', as befitted a man in harmony with God and His
Laws. Indeed, 'His judgement is noble; if you go to him, you receive
justice.'[21]

The prestige of the Sultanate reached its highest point in the fêtes and
displays staged by the Sultans for every great public event. Such were the
occasions for the firings of cannon and muskets, *ngoma*, salutes from the
Sultan's men-o-war in the harbour, march-pasts, singing, and displays of
fireworks. All this culminated in the grand *baraza* at the palace, attended by
the town *wazee*, leading *mashayikh*, principal Asian merchants, and the
consular representatives of all the great nations of the West – all of whom
came to pay their respects publicly to the Sultan. On these occasions,
people from up and down the coast flocked to the capital where they
observed the proceedings 'with open-eyed wonder, and exclamations of
astonishment and delight [which] frequently broke forth from members of
little groups amidst the crowds of Swahilis'.[22] The feelings of the
waungwana perhaps were expressed best by one old Somali who declared
that, 'nothing in the world could possibly excel such a show; not even in
Bombay or Europe could such wonders be seen, surely Zanzibar was the
grandest place in the world'.[23]

It was the age of Barghash which modern-day informants remember as
having represented the Golden Age of the coast. It was Barghash who
brought 'civilization' (*Arab* civilization, *ustaarabu*) to the coast.[24] As one
informant remarked, 'He was *very* famous.' Further, people from all over
the coast travelled to Zanzibar to search out their Sultan, 'to look at him'
and his wondrous palace, to visit him, and to seek his opinion.[25]

Zanzibar of the Sultans, consequently, attracted people from all over,
Mombasa and the Comoro Islands especially. It was the Paris of the coast.
Those who owned *shambas*, slaves, or ships – people of some leisure – spent
their time at Zanzibar. When they returned to their respective communities,
they brought back the best cloth (imported) for *kanzus*, and the latest
fashions set by the Omani ruling class: the turbans, *johos*, *juba* vests, and

swords, along with the perfumes, imported from India, and manufactured items brought from Europe and America. Consequently, those who visited Zanzibar came back home more 'civilized' in the Arab fashion (*-enye kustaaribika*).

All of this, of course, meant that upper class Omani Arabs acquired enormous social prestige on the coast. The nature of civilization itself in the coastal towns underwent a change, as Allen has observed. Increasingly, to be 'civilized' was not to be a *mungwana*, but an Arab. Thus, it appears that sometime between the 1830s and 1870s (probably closer to the latter date, considering the impact made by Barghash's years of rule) the Swahili word for civilization was altered from *uungwana* to *ustaarabu* – 'to assimilate oneself to the Arabs, to become an Arab, to adopt the customs of the Arabs'.[26] With this psychological shift, then, the Omanis became the fashion setters. As seen by Europeans, the 'Natives endeavour to follow the Arabs in their customs, not so much from religious convictions as from the *heshima* thus acquired.'[27]

> So the Swahili has found no difficulty in assimilating himself to the varied conditions of life which have influenced the east coast of Africa during the last two thousand years. He has rubbed shoulders with all kinds of people and nations, has absorbed some of their virtues and some of their vices in proportion to the extent and length of association, and we find him today a full-blown Moslem, with his mosques in every village and taking as his pattern of life his superior the Arab.[28]

USTAARABU

The most indicative sign of the Swahili shift towards Arabization was in their assumption of Arab-like *nisbas*. This is evident most clearly in Mombasa where the Kilindini began calling themselves al-Kindy, the Kilifi took the *nisba* al-Kufy, and the Tangana took the name, noble in Islamic history, of al-Taif. Interestingly enough, too, the informant who related this information recognized that, along with the imitation of the Sultans and Zanzibari Arab society, people began changing their names and identities in a negative sense due to the declining social value of *uungwana*.[29]

Mimicry of Arab fashions found its way into the design of people's homes, furniture, and clothing. Architecturally, for instance, Allen points out that there was an abrupt change of style about the 1820s:

> In Lamu town itself there was frantic competition to adopt foreign styles: eighteenth century houses perforce remained, but no new ones were built in the former style, and in smaller items such as furniture and kitchen utensils there was a scramble to acquire the Indian or Indian-type models which the al-Busaidis brought with them to Zanzibar.[30]

In architecture, this stylistic change essentially amounted to a simplification. Houses were larger and closer in style to those found in India and the regions of the Persian Gulf.[31] Mosques were built without minarets. All this may have been done by *waungwana* as a concession to Ibadism, or, as in the case of the mosques, because they actually were built by Omanis.

129

One other innovation which seems to have been introduced in architecture at that time was the 'Zanzibar' style in carved doors. These more floriated patterns in wood carving supplanted the older, more stylized Bajun forms found throughout the northern islands at Pate, the Bajun isles, and at Lamu.[32] Inside these more simply designed structures, coastal townspeople took to furnishings which included carved chairs imported from India, canopied Indian beds, and the lacquered *vitanda vya hindi* (which replaced the familiar *ulili* flat-bed).[33]

The other most notable change in people's life styles came in the clothing they wore – again in imitation of Omani styles. The most noticeable innovation of this period was the *joho*, or braided open robe worn by Omanis, which soon became popular with some townsmen. As related by Pearce,

> The Zanzibar Arab clothes himself when in public in a dark blue *joho*, or open robe, decorated along the edges with gold, red, or black braid. In the old days of Seyyid Said, when the puritanism of the Ibathi sect was rife, the decoration of the men's clothes was very scant, and it was not until Seyyid Barghash's reign that the braiding became broader and the patterns more elaborate.[34]

A smaller version of the *joho* was the *juba* which, cut in the same fashion as the *joho* and also braided, resembled more a vest. Although skull-caps had been popular before the Busaidi, the familiar embroidered *kofia* (embroidered cap) was introduced at this time.[35] Another fashion popularized during the Sultanate was the turban or *kilemba*. The sort commonly worn was one of 'mingled red, yellow, and blue stripes'. Members of the royal family, however, wore turbans of a distinctive style which was peaked over the forehead.[36] Colours of *vilemba* and other clothing, too, indicated a person's class. *Shurafaʾ*, for instance, usually clothed themselves in black or green, whereas *ʿulamaʾ* and others 'noted for piety' commonly wore whites. Indeed, while most *ʿulamaʾ* knew the wisdom of moderation even in matters of dress, some pedants went so far as to adorn themselves completely in white, so immaculately that, 'a fly would not so much as light upon them'.[37]

NEW LITERACY

As was emphasized in previous chapters, town culture and religion had an oral base. That is to say history, literature, and legal practices, rights and obligations among coastal townspeople were preserved orally from generation to generation. Written history, literature, and law appear to have been virtually non-existent among the majority of coastal townsmen at least up to the early nineteenth century. Books were rare treasures possessed by the precious few who had the wealth to acquire the   and the leisure to read them. Islam itself, as a religion based on a rich and massive written legacy, did not take on the ritualized, highly formalized aspects in the isolated coastal communities which commonly were to be found in, say, Egypt, Syria, or Iran. Even in taking into account his vious prejudices, Burton probably was right when he remarked that most *waungwana* knew little of Islam's usual formalities and obligations beyond the profession of faith and that few could read even a simple letter in Arabic.[38] Even those who knew some Arabic spoke it imperfectly or in a pidgin form.[39]

Things, however, began to change in the nineteenth century under the tutelage of Hadrami *ᶜulamaᵓ*, especially those who were *shurafaᵓ*. One elderly informant, particularly, recognized the Arab contribution to literacy on the coast when he mentioned that coastmen could not read nor write prior to Busaidi times. His claim was that the 'Africans' started becoming familiar with the written Islamic tradition, thanks to the Arabs, in the days of the Sultanate.[40] The affluence of the times contributed to this. Wealth gave people the time to learn Arabic and to read, as well as the mosques where such learning was transmitted. This is partially discernible, for instance, in the large numbers of *vyuo* (Quran schools) built at Zanzibar in the nineteenth century.[41]

Foreign born *ᶜulamaᵓ*, such as certain *shurafaᵓ*, especially were responsible for bringing a written tradition to the coast. The fact that *sharif* clans like the Jamal al-Layl and the Abu Bakr bin Salim came to the coast learned in *fiqh* and *tafsir* and frequently were noted literati in Arabic, qualified them as experts in the Islamic written tradition. In addition, they usually enjoyed high social standing in the communities where they settled, so their example was to be emulated.[42] Lyndon Harries has indicated the important role which the *shurafaᵓ* played in 'establishing the tradition of Swahili [written] versification'. He points out that nearly all early examples of written Swahili poetry were the work of Hadrami *ᶜulamaᵓ*. Their influence derived from their involvement in religious education in coastal towns and from their prolific output of works which were 'nearer the people' than those of Ibadis.[43] Due to their Hadrami origins, early (c. 1820s) written Swahili works often paraphrased didactic and homiletic verses in Arabic.[44] Hence, Harries indicates the irony that, despite the African origins of the language medium employed by the early translators, 'its real essence is Arabian. Its lexis is deeply rooted in the belief and practice of Islam [which, one must be reminded, was not necessarily Arabian].'[45]

One figure who was involved in translation activities was Sayyid Abu Bakr b. Abdu'r-Rahman al-Husayni (Sayyid Mansab). Born at Lamu around 1828, Sayyid Mansab was an early 'reform' figure and proselytizer on the northern coast. Sh. Abdallah Salih Farsy, for example, says that he built a small mosque at Chwaka, Pemba, where he taught and proselytized to eliminate 'heresy' among the *waungwana* there.[46] A one-time pupil of various Hadrami and Hijazi *ᶜulamaᵓ*, later in life he turned to writing adaptations of Arabic religious works (for example, the *Durar al-Bahiyya*) in Swahili for purposes of instruction among coastal Muslims.[47] Once, he attempted to have a collection of his translations published, but the work was 'lost at sea' while being shipped to India for printing.[48]

Another figure of note was a Punjabi *sharif*, Sayyid Muhammad Hasan, who once commissioned a Sh. Muhammad b. Abdallah Wazir Msujuni to translate the Quran into Kiswahili. Again, the copy was to be printed and sold for the edification of local Swahilis. However, as happened in the case of Sayyid Mansab's efforts, certain conservative *'ulama'* prevented the manuscript from getting into print.[49]

This relatively new tradition of publishing religious works of a didactic nature continued through the Busaidi period and into modern times. Partly, this was encouraged by Sultans like Barghash who, as mentioned already, established a press to distribute Ibadi propaganda with an educational and informative intent. Harries writes that *tendi* (epic) literature came into vogue only with the introduction of written verse by the *shurafa'* and what he feels was a growing sense of nationalism and self-awareness among *waungwana* during Busaidi times.[50]

In more recent times, other Sunnis have carried on this tradition of publishing religious works. The East African Muslim Welfare Society in Mombasa has printed various informative little pamphlets written by such luminaries as Sh. Al-Amin b. Ali Mazrui, Sh. Muhammad Qasim Mazrui, Sh. Abdallah Salih Farsy, in addition to works by less well-known scholars. In the early days of the twentieth century, one Mwisha Hali wa Mwinyi Ngwame wrote a little work covering various aspects of the hajj, and which was distributed among those preparing to make the pilgrimage.[51] Sh. Ali-Amin b. Ali Mazrui established a printing press and newspaper and devoted himself to teaching the basics of the faith, preserving Islamic institutions, and maintaining certain aspects of traditional Islamic education.[52] In recent years, Sh. Muhammad Qasim Mazrui has taken up where Sh. Ali-Amin left off with a newspaper entitled *Sauti ya Haki* (Voice of the Truth), which is distributed monthly.

All this new literature and emphasis on resuscitating Islamic written education in East Africa appears to have had its effects on the *waungwana*. Ingrams mentions how 'revivalist' movements occasionally appeared in the nineteenth century and in the early years of colonial rule among rural Swahili. As one example, he relates the story of a young *mungwana* named Daudi Musa who had attended *darasas* in Zanzibar, and, 'in a campaign of earnest preaching he told his people that their regard for the devils [*sic*] of their ancestors was wrong and that they should throw down their altars and return to the worship of the one God'. As a result, 'the dwelling places of the *Mizimu* [spirits] and the *Wamavua* [rain spirits] in a few villages were deserted and thickets where formerly spirits dwelt were cut down and crops planted'.[53]

Muhammad Ahmad Matano told of another ancestor of his, Mwinyi Ngwame wa Mwinyi Mkuu, who was an *'alim* and a *khatib* in the Mnara (Basheikh) mosque. His son, the above-mentioned Mwisha Hali, was versed in the written tradition and a specialist in *fiqh*. Apparently, Mwisha Hali understood the differences between some local practices and the injunctions of literate Islam as he openly opposed *falak* and *uganga* in his *khutba* sermons. Labelling such practices *haram* (sinful), he publicly spoke out against them and opposed their inclusion in the mosque-school curriculum, much to the displeasure of some members of his own clan (for example, his cousin, Babu Kombo, abused him).[54]

132

While many Swahili were happy to make use of the newly available religious literature, not all were ready to reject old beliefs as had Daudi Musa or Mwisha Hali. As will be seen, for a number of reasons the growing popularity of 'reformist' teaching among the elite was repudiated by many townspeople who introduced new institutions in defence of the religion of their ancestors.

TIGHTENING OF CONTROL AND JUDICIAL CENTRALIZATION

More than any single event, Frere's negotiations with Sayyid Barghash during 1872–3 revealed precisely the tenuous nature of the Sultans' relations with the Arab *mashayikh* and town *wazee*. Barghash's principal reservation about signing the new treaty which imposed further restrictions on the slave trade, apparently, did not concern loss of personal income, but compensation for the Arabs.[55] Consequently, his fears for his personal safety and position became clear to the British envoy in the course of the negotiations. By 17 January 1873, Badger realized that the Sultans already had been pushed about as far as they could go with the 1828 and 1843 treaties, and that any agreement by the Sultans for further British interference in the commerce of their subjects would require that the British protect them from their counsellors and subjects. Under pressure from a stronger power, Barghash is reported actually to have begged that the English Queen order him to sign the treaty, thus removing all culpability for the action from his shoulders.[56] In effect, then, Barghash placed himself and his Sultanate under the protection of the British from that time henceforth.

Other events, too, contributed to Barghash's decision to request British protection. Aside from fear of his subjects in Zanzibar, he also had to retain the loyalty of the other towns of the coast after signing the 1873 treaty. It was reported by the *liwali* of Kilwa that efforts were being made to tear down the proclamation announcing the treaty and that the town, facing a Rs 120,000 per annum loss, was on the verge of open defiance. As late as 1880, considerable 'disaffection' was felt at Lamu towards the Sultan, and it is clear that only British support for the Sultanate kept the town from actual rebellion.[57] Then, too, there was the abortive McKillop Pasha expedition, mentioned previously. Again, in this situation Barghash found himself to be clearly helpless and dependent on the British to remove the Egyptian interlopers.

The effects of the 1873 treaty and the Egyptian occupation on the personal power of the Sultan were most noticeable. Now with British might at his back, the Sultan's position no longer was that of a *primus inter pares* at Zanzibar. Evidence concerning this is quite apparent in the testimony given by Reute. In the first part of her autobiography, in discussing her early years, she mentions very little about British involvement in the interior affairs of Said's and Majid's governments. She makes clear the changes which occurred under her brother, Sultan Barghash:

> At that time [that is, before Barghash] the English did not possess the supremacy that they have at present in East Africa; they had as little to do with the inner affairs of Zanzibar as the Turks or the Germans. It is only since 1875 – thanks to their slave police – that their power has greatly increased....[58]

As observed by Kirk, the Sultan's rule became more autocratic; he enjoyed a 'personal authority unknown before'.[59] He acted more as a sovereign now, 'and the others as his subjects'.[60]

With this new power, Barghash and his *liwalis* could do all sorts of new things. One of these, for example, was the Sultan's increase in the clove tax from the former 5 per cent to 25 per cent. Even as far away as Lamu the new strength of the Sultan was felt. There, Suud b. Hamid al-Busaidi's iron-fisted rule kept the town peaceful in the face of the 1873 treaty and the 1875 McKillop invasion. In the latter instance, Ylvisaker relates that Suud, with Kirk's assistance, was able to muster three hundred local merchants into a force meant to discourage possible Egyptian designs on Lamu and to restore the Sultan's authority in Kismayu. Unfortunately, it was also the new strength of the Sultanate that enabled Busaidi governors like Suud b. Hamid and Abdallah b. Hamid to impose unauthorized taxes on Lamu meant for their personal profit.[61]

With enhanced political control came an effort by Barghash to exercise greater control over the judicial system in the coastal towns. As has been emphasized, it was the policy of Sayyids Said and Majid to allow the internal affairs of the subject towns to go relatively untouched both by themselves and by their representatives. In most towns it was normal practice that, within the *mitaa*, the *wazee* arbitrated all disputes. In situations involving persons from different *mitaa*, each town had its own institutions for dealing with these matters. Such situations involved not only strictly judicial considerations, but also matters that, to a Western eye, would have been classified as political. Some towns like Lamu had a body of *wazee* who met officially to decide town and clan matters. Others, like Vuga and, later, Lamu, had one principal figure who, with the counselling of the *wazee* and *walimu*, adjudicated matters.[62] In all cases, however, the important fact was that such affairs were settled on the basis of recognized traditions and legal claims as the law was locally conceived and practised.

The 'hands off' policy in force under Sayyids Said and Majid appears, for the most part, to have left such practices pretty much as they always had been. In the towns, the *qadis* heard cases submitted to them by litigants of their own free will and by mutual agreement. At least in some cases where something like 'criminal' wrongdoing was involved, the *qadis* passed sentence, often carrying it out personally and on the spot.[63] As described by Burton, frequently, 'Instant justice is the order of the day', and every *shamba* (or *mtaa*?) had its own stocks where justice was applied in impromptu fashion. Yet cases also were brought before *liwalis*. Greffulhe relates that at five o'clock daily a *baraza* was held at Lamu where the governor, with the assistance of the local *wazee* and two *qadis*, settled cases – probably in the manner of the old *Mzee wa Mui*.[64] Before Said b. Sultan moved his capital to Zanzibar, the *liwalis* there meted out a 'rough and ready law' at the gate of the old Portuguese *gereza* with the help of three 'patriarchs with long grey beards, unclean white robes, and sabres in hand'.[65] Under the Sultanate, however, the gravest cases were dealt with by the Sultans themselves and they served as the final court of appeal for disputes left unsettled to everyone's satisfaction by town *wazee* or *liwalis*. Less weighty cases were settled by the Sultan's heir-apparent or by court *qadis*.[66] Yet, the very informality of the Sultanate made enforcement of the law or execution of decisions made even by the Sultans very difficult. Because there were no regular police, few jails, little control of affairs directly outside Zanzibar town itself, convicted persons often got out of prison, 'and once upon the mainland … laugh[ed] at justice'.[67] In situations involving powerful or truculent tribes, such as the al-Harthi, or distant towns, like Lamu or Mogadishu, control was tenuous, indeed.

Barghash's decision to alter this state of affairs seems to have been based as much on political considerations as on any personal abhorrence he might have had for local practices. For one thing, the Sultan was very much under the influence of the *mutawwiun* from the very inception of his reign. It was in the interests of Barghash to adhere to their doctrines to avoid the accusations of *shirk* (heresy) which they had been wont to level at his father, Said b. Sultan. It should be remembered, for example, that Said and Majid faced bitter opposition not only from the tribes of the interior of Oman, but from some of the Ghafiri tribes of Zanzibar and the coast who sympathized with the *mutawwiun*.[68] By thus siding with these followers of the revivalist ʿ*alim*, al-Khalili (see Chapter 10), Barghash might have hoped to head off the religious opposition which his father and brother Majid had faced from tribes like the Mazrui, the Barwani, and the al-Harthi mentioned in the previous chapter. (It will be recalled that the opposition of the Mazrui and the Barwani was expressed in religious terms. This led many to abandon Ibadism — and thus reject the Busaidi claims to overall religious leadership of the Omani.)

In addition, by adhering to *mutawwah* (defined, by the way, as 'one who enforces obedience'[69]) doctrines, Barghash appears to have been trying to lay claim to the Imamate. The story behind this began in Majid's reign when the Sultan of Oman, Thuwain b. Said, was killed by his sons, Salim and Abduʾl-Aziz, and his brother Turki was imprisoned. While it enjoyed the succour of the Bombay Government, Salim's rule was corrupt and unpopular. In 1868, Salim's cousin, Azzan b. Qais, led a revolt of the tribes of the interior under Sh. Salih b. Ali al-Harthi and the Ibadi reformer, Said b. Khalfan al-Khalili, and managed to force Salim into exile. Azzan was chosen as the new Imam by his *mutawwah* supporters for his devotion to fundamentalist principles and his campaign against the use of silk and tobacco. In the meantime, Turki had been released from prison and had fled to Gwadar where he seized power. In 1871, with gold he had received from Majid in Zanzibar, he defeated and slew Azzan and seized the Sultanate.

While he remained in this position for a long time, Turki's hatred of the *mutawwah ʿulamaʾ* cost him the support of the hinterland tribes and throughout his reign he faced continual rebellion and intrigue.[70]

While Majid had supported Turki and the anti-*mutawwah* party, Barghash chose to support the other side. During the struggle between Azzan and Turki, it was said that Barghash, 'makes no secret of his inclinations to the fanatical party of which the headquarters are at Muscat'. The same source reveals the motives behind Barghash's actions where he mentions that, 'there is now much talk of making the Zanzibar dominions an appanage of the Imamate of Muscat as it was in Sayyid Said's time'.[71] Barghash's personal ambitions in all this were revealed by Kirk when he mentioned that, had the *mutawwah* party won out at Oman, Barghash was hoping that he would succeed as Imam both for Zanzibar and Oman.[72] Although Turki managed to hold on, and Barghash abandoned the *mutawwah* cause in Oman, it is certain that Barghash remained a devout Ibadi. His religious intolerance and continued support of revivalist Ibadism bears this out.[73]

To break the influence of the old town elite and the tribal *mashayikh*, then, Barghash had to consolidate his position in East Africa. This required, for one thing, that the Sultan throw his support to groups of newcomers to the coast, such as the Hadramis, Comorians, and Indians, against the entrenched position of the old town elite. As pointed out by Wilson, this meant that something had to be done to remedy the judicial imbalance in the towns which, because of local practices and standards, heavily favoured the old aristocracy.[74] Thus, to break the old *wazee*, we are told the Sultan placed the towns under 'ordinary Arab law' and appointed his own *qadis* to oversee its 'proper' application.[75] At Zanzibar itself, the island was divided into *wilayets*, each of which was placed under a *liwali* and the legal administration of *qadis* who, because they were court appointed, were strictly answerable to the Sultan and not to the people among whom they lived and worked. While *qadis* formerly had been selected by popular consent, in the towns it is likely they increasingly became creatures of the Busaidi. While there is no direct evidence to support this view, with the waxing power of the Sultanate and the Busaidi, one suspects that the Sultans and *liwalis* became more autocratic in selecting *qadis*. Thus, when one informant mentioned that the first official *qadis* were appointed in Busaidi times, it appears likely that he was referring to the years after 1870.[76]

The sorts of abuses exercised by some Sultans indicate just how strong their control over the judicial and religious institutions became. In 1892, Portal reported that *qadis'* decisions often were overturned by the Sultan, that he sometimes sat and decided cases in which he or members of his household were defendants, and that his decisions sometimes were capricious and arbitrary.[77] Another observer pretty well summed up matters when he said,

I beg to point out that the 'Arab courts' are but another name for His

Highness the Sultan, he is the head judicial authority in Zanzibar dominions, without his knowledge and consent no judgement of the least importance is given, and he can and does reverse any judgement he does not approve of.[78]

The Sultans after Barghash exercised this control, of course, by making *qadis* their personal dependants and by systematizing and coopting the *ᶜulamaᵓ* and the administration of Islamic law. Such is the subject of the next section which, in addition, discusses how this new order of things, this emphasis on uniformity of legal practice, contributed to the appearance of a new *ᶜulamaᵓ*.

NEW *ᶜULAMAᵓ* AND THE WRITTEN ISLAMIC TRADITION

The period of the Sultanate was, above all, a period when the coast opened up to new influences and novel ideas. This was affected primarily by the arrival of new peoples from other parts of East Africa. Of these immigrants who introduced new forms of Islam and new (or lost?) perceptions of the faith espoused by coastal Africans, the groups who, besides the Omanis, had the greatest influence on coastal Shafiis and who contributed the most to change were the Hadrami *shurafaᵓ*, the Comorians, and Benadir coast people.

The *shurafaᵓ* have been mentioned in various parts of this book already since they, as other Hadramis, have been coming to settle the coast at least since the thirteenth century. However, the period beginning with the early nineteenth century witnessed one of those periodic recurrences in the cycle when the Hadrami and Comorian population shifts reached a zenith. It was from the early to the mid-nineteenth century, for example, that forebears of *ᶜulamaᵓ* who later were to play very important parts in the coastal scene arrived on the coast from Hadhramawt. Therefore, it would seem useful at this point to review some important information concerning the history of the *sharif* migrations and to bring matters up to date as they stood in the era of the Sultanate.

First, it is important to point out that, because they were descendants of the Prophet and because they were families especially learned in the written tradition, the influence of the *shurafaᵓ* was primarily spiritual. As Van den Berg explains,

> les *Sayyid* ne portent pas d'armes, et que leurs *Munshib* n'ont, par consequent, aucun moyen de constraint, si l'on refuse d'obeir à leurs ordres. De même que les *Sayyid* en général ne conservant leur influence sur le reste de la population que par le respect qu'ils inspirent à cause de leur origine, de même l'autorité des *Munshib* sur les membres de leur famille et sur les tribus dont ils sont les chefs spirituels, ets purement morale.[79]

While this sort of charisma had little direct political impact in the Hadhramawt, the situation in East Africa was sometimes different. There, with their pedigrees reinforced by their long genealogies, they commanded great respect and were guaranteed an influential voice in the affairs of any town where they settled (see Chapter 3). This came despite their (normally stigmatic) status as strangers and their religious views considered unorthodox in the eyes of *waungwana*. This sort of religious aura could work either for or against them, depending on the situation. As Lienhardt points out, the political elite in some towns quite plausibly took them as a threat to their own position, and the fact that they often stood outside local rivalries sometimes discouraged supporters.[80] On the other hand, some local dynasts, wishing to invest their position with an 'aura' of theocratic rectitude, married into their families. In turn, the offspring of such alliances were able to take over existing political structures or create new states with a stronger religious base.[81] Examples will follow which serve to illustrate both extremes.

Over the centuries, the *sharif* clans which were most influential in coastal religious history were the Mahdali, the Abu Bakr bin Salim, the al-Husayni, the Jamal al-Layl, and the al-Massila Ba Alawi. In the nineteenth century, the Shatiri and the bin Sumayt were added to this list. The Mahdali were the earliest *sharif* clan to have played an important part in coastal history. Originally settling on the Benadir coast, they established the Abuʾl-Mawahib dynasty at Kilwa just before 1300. Afterwards, they settled at Mombasa and Lamu and, with the passing of the centuries and loss of their written genealogies (*silsilah*), they lost much of their former prestige.

The Abu Bakr b. Salim have been discussed in Chapter 3. According to Martin, one of the clan, Salim al-Muhajir, settled at Anjouan in 1676.[82] Once there, the clan established ruling dynasties at Matsumudu and Domoni and, in relative isolation, became heavily Swahilized.[83] By the nineteenth century, a number of chiefs at Anjouan and Grand Comoro were descendants of the Abu Bakr b. Salim. Among these was one Sh. Ahmad of Bambao, Moroni.[84] This Sh. Ahmad warred with Msa Fumo of Itsandara, Grand Comoro, and his kingdom was destroyed. Many of his subjects were killed. Those who survived emigrated or were sold as slaves to various coastal towns, the most notable among those being Lamu and Zanzibar.[85]

The Husayni are descended from a *sufi shaykh* by the name of Muhammad b. Sh. Ali b. Abu Bakr al-Alawi al-Husayni (d. 1610/11). According to one source, the founders of the East African branch of the clan, Sh. Khan b. Husayn and Sh. Ahmad b. Husayn, originally settled at Pate and at Siyu where they were known as as-Saqqaf.[86] Coming to Pate as 'strangers', ethnically separate from the *waungwana*, the Husayni, as well as the Jamal al-Layl, were permitted little voice in local politics. However, they married into the ruling Nabahani clan and, because of their position as *shurafaʾ*, they enjoyed a *de facto* authority among *waungwana* as religious authorities and teachers. Their influence, however, became a threat to the Nabahani during the period of the Pate civil wars when one of their clan, S. Ahmad b. Alawi al-Husayni, embroiled himself in a religious dispute with the Sultan over the treatment of a slave. Fearing that S. Ahmad would become 'king', the Nabahani assassinated him and began persecuting the *sharif* houses.[87] Shortly thereafter, both the Husayni and the Jamal al-Layl emigrated to Lamu and Grand Comoro.

According to Professor Martin, the Jamal al-Layl originated in Tarim and settled in Pate, at the invitation of the Husayni, in 1543–4. Another cadet branch had settled at Mogadishu, from whence they migrated to Tsujuni, Grand Comoro, where they established a ruling house in 1650. The Pate branch, as already mentioned, emigrated to the Comoros due to political persecution they endured there between 1777 and 1809.[88] It appears, however, that even in the Comoros the Jamal al-Layl were not entirely welcome. One informant claimed, for instance, that they later re-emigrated to Lamu because local rulers created obstacles to their religious teachings and made it difficult for them to marry local women.[89]

Under the Sultanate, the *shurafaʾ* were able to bring about religious change for two overriding reasons: their widespread contacts, especially with the Islamic heartlands, and their involvement with the Alawi *tariqa*. To start with, many of them were wealthy merchants. The Husayni were the most visible example of this, but other affluent clans were the Shatiri and the bin Sumayt.[90] Trade put them into frequent contact with many ports up and down the coast, as well as with distant Hadhramawt, India, Oman, and even the East Indies. It is for this reason, therefore, that these *sharif* clans were extraordinarily mobile and usually had many relatives not only all along the coast, but inhabiting the entire Indian Ocean periphery. The Husayni had branches in Pate, Lamu, and Zanzibar, in addition to the Hadhramawt and even Sumatra were they were known as the Banu Umar b. Hasan and the ash-Shihab ad-Din. Likewise, the Jamal al-Layl had groups of clan members in Pate, Kilwa, Pemba, Zanzibar, Anjouan, and in Indonesia where they were called the al-Qadri.[91] Finally, one of the most noteworthy examples of widespread trade connections involved the bin Sumayt. Sayyid Abu Bakr b. Abdallah bin Sumayt migrated to Grand Comoro from Shibam, Hadhramawt, sometime around the middle of the nineteenth century. Sayyid Abu Bakr was a *nahodha*, owner of seven dhows, and learned in various Islamic sciences, who became wealthy plying between various coastal ports carrying cargo during the decades when the Sultanate was most prosperous. His son, Sayyid Ahmad b. Abu Bakr bin Sumayt, however, achieved fame as one of the most erudite Shafii *ʿulamaʾ* on the coast. Like his father, he spent his early years as a *nahodha* and visited ports-of-call, so claims Farsy, all over the Indian Ocean.[92]

The fact that the *shurafaʾ* were so mobile and enjoyed extensive contacts with the world outside the coast meant that their knowledge of the religious sciences was not of the parochial variety discussed in previous chapters. At least two reliable informants pointed out, too, that the *baraka* possessed by *shurafaʾ* like the Abu Bakr b. Salim and the bin Sumayt was because their knowledge derived not from local sources, but from the Hijaz and the Hadhramawt.[93] In fact they were more familiar with the written Islamic tradition than were coastal townspeople. This was due, especially, to their involvement in the exclusive Alawi *tariqa* which, as Martin explains, 'served to keep *sayyids* and *sharifs* in touch with each other and tended to reinforce their importance as a group'.[94] Part of their programme for maintaining their elite status was through maintaining distant, supra-local ties with each other and by keeping certain types and degrees of religious expertise out of the hands of most *waungwana*.[95] In short, this religious knowledge was generally non-local and elitist in character. It had to be that way since it was the only way, along with their putative genealogies, that the *shurafaʾ* could preserve their unique identity and social statuses whereever they settled.

COMORIAN AND BENADIR *ʿULAMAʾ*

Another 'external' influence on town Islam came from Comorian and Somali *mashayikh* who migrated to coastal towns such as Lamu, Mombasa, and Zanzibar during the years of Busaidi rule. As alluded to previously, these Comorians usually migrated to escape the intestinal quarrels which marked Comorian history in the nineteenth century, or, not escaping, they were enslaved and sold to other coastal towns. Partly from religious teachings of immigrant *shurafaʾ*, these Comorians possessed some knowledge of the basic Islamic sciences.[96] At Lamu they were considered *ustaarabu* Muslims (Arab-like and learned in the *vitabu*). Consequently, they enjoyed a special status at Lamu even as slaves. Some did only domestic work, whilst others were employed by the elite clans as *nahodhas* due to their talents and the high degree of trust placed in them. As sailors and skippers, Comorians also had the opportunities to keep in touch with distant places like southern Arabia, the Benadir ports, Zanzibar, and the Comoros where as el-Zein mentions, they could stay abreast of developments abroad.[97] Furthermore, with their reputation for religious learning, they were allowed to have their own mosque, the Ras al-Heri, to which many *waungwana* sent their children for instruction in the basics of religious studies.[98] Treated almost as 'relatives' (*ndugu*) by the Maawi, one informant asserted that they came from the Wambudi ('pious', 'religious') people of Grand Comoro. While most taught only the poorer *waungwana* and other Comorians, some *shurafaʾ*, like one Mwinyi Alawi Shatiri and a Mwinyi Sayyid Ali (Jamal al-Layl?), were recognized as fully fledged *wanazuoni* (namely, *wanavyuoni*).[99]

At Zanzibar, Comorians also had some influence as *ʿulamaʾ*. According to Ibuni Saleh, the first Comorian 'mullahs' arrived in Zanzibar at about the time they first came to Lamu – that is, during the reign of Sayyid Said. Also, as in Lamu, most were not 'great' *ʿulamaʾ*, but Quran school teachers, *walimu*, and a few *wanazuoni wa katikati* ('middle level' *ʿulamaʾ*) who, despite their humble social standing and limited knowledge of the written sciences, eagerly proselytized among the 'pagan' *waungwana* of Zanzibar's and Pemba's rural villages.[100] Sh. Farsy's book affords some intelligence on a few of these first generation immigrants who managed to achieve a measure of status as learned *shaykhs*. Besides S. Abdu'l-Hasan b. Ahmad Jamal al-Layl mentioned already, the two most reputed Comorian *ʿulamaʾ* of this generation were Sh. Hasan b. Yusuf Mngazija and Sh. Abdallah b. Wazir Msujuni. Little information is available on Sh. Hasan except that he was trained in the Comoros and helped popularize interest in the religious sciences until his death in 1895. Sh. Abdallah Wazir (?–1904) was one of the few Comorians who attained a position of real influence at Zanzibar. He was close to Sayyid Ali b. Said al-Busaidi and served as a *wazir al-awqaf* (minister of endowments) during the latter's reign (1890–3). However, in the reign of Hamid b. Thuwain (1893–6), he fell out of favour and was forced to his native isles until Sayyid Hamid died. Other Comorians of this generation who had some authority in religious circles were S. Fadhl b. Ali Mngazija Mbangwa (?–1885), who was one of Sh. Abdallah Wazir's mentors, and S. Ahmad b. Salim Abu Bakr b. Salim (?–1870), who was born and trained in Grand Comoro and became the personal *qadi* of the wealthy Shatiri clan.[101]

In general, the Comorians of common birth did not enjoy the same religious prestige as their fellows who were *shurafaʾ* or who enjoyed greater social standing in their respective communities. Frequently, therefore, they were closer to the lower class, non-Arab *waungwana* among whom they had settled and it was to these people that they appealed as religious leaders. Even the Maawi at Lamu looked upon them as 'brothers' and sent their children to them for training, as mentioned already. Doubtless, they had more in common with them and felt them to be less threatening than the aloof, more literate *shurafaʾ*. Indeed, some of the Comorian *wanazuoni* are said to have disputed the special status and privileges claimed by the *shurafaʾ*. For example, Sh. Abdallah Wazir was a great nemesis of one Sayyid Hasan b. Muhammad Jamal al-Layl who, because of Sh. Abdallah's attacks, was compelled to write a book (*Al-Ajwibatuʾsh-Shamila* – 'Complete Answers') defending the traditional claims of the *shurafaʾ*. Similarly, Sh. Abdallah Wazir and his son, Sh. Muhammad Abdallah, busied themselves with translating religious works into Kiswahili to make them accessible to ordinary *waungwana*. This was done to undermine the *sharifs*' monopoly of Arabic and the religious sciences. It will be remembered that it was Sh. Abdallah Wazir also who translated the Quran only to have the manuscript stolen before the last two *suras* were completed.

The influence of the *ᶜulamaʾ* from Barawa and Mogadishu appears to have been fairly sustained since the Middle Ages. In modern times, this preponderance essentially stemmed from the activities of various *sufi shaykhs*, especially from those associated with the Qadiriyya. Professor Lewis explains that the Qadiriyya was established in Harar sometime before 1508–9 by one Sh. Abu Bakr b. Abdallah al-Aydarus. Among the Somali it traditionally functioned as an educational institution devoted to Islam's literary, rather than propagandist, tradition. Congregations of Qadiriyya brethren trained Somali *wadad* (*mashayikh*) who functioned as 'bush teachers' and rain-making specialists. In the latter capacity, these *wadad* led classes in prayer, the Quran, and in elementary Arabic. They acted as unofficial *qadis* among Somali clansmen, both sedentary and pastoral.[102]

Testimony obtained in Mombasa indicates that some of the Somali *wadad* were active in introducing the rudiments of the written tradition to the Bajun islands and the Lamu archipelago. One informant told how the moieties at Siyu actually invited several *wadad* to teach some of the *fanun* to 'the people'. The informant related these *ᶜulamaʾ* came actually as masters of *dhikr* who taught one selected science to each group of ten people who, in turn, passed on its particular speciality to the other groups. Competition very like the traditional *mashindano* was struck up between the moieties in displays of religious erudition.[103] By employing such measures, towns like Siyu (besides being a major centre for the production of Qurans in the eighteenth century) earned reputations for their learning, and other coastal towns like Mombasa sometimes relied on *wanazuoni* from the Lamu region or from the Hijaz for their especial expertise in sciences which otherwise were not locally known and taught.[104]

Three examples of *ʿulamaʾ* who were trained either in Somalia or by Somali and Bajun *ʿulamaʾ*. Among these were a Sh. Uthman b. Shaykh Ahmad as-Saqqaf ('Mwinyi Abudi'), Sh. Muhyi ad-Din al-Qahtani al-Waʿil, and Sh. Abdu'l-Aziz b. Abdu'l-Ghany al-Amawy. The first of these, S. Abdu'r-Rahman (1844–1922), was born and trained at Siyu by various Somali and Bajun *ʿulamaʾ*. Among these were Sh. Uthman b. Shaykh Msomali (who taught him *fiqh*), Sh. Ali b. Umar Msomali (*nahw* and *sarf*), Sh. Faqih b. Uways Msomali (*tafsir* and *hadith*), and Sh. Lali b. Vai Mbajuni. Originally a *qadi* at Siyu who fought alongside Muhammad b. Bwana Mataka against Busaidi control, he later was appointed to the newly created position of *Shaykh al-Islam* by the British administration. At Mombasa, he played a major part in training lower class *waungwana* in the basic written sciences.[105] More will be said about him in Chapter 10.

Sh. Muhyi ad-Din (1794–1869) was born and educated in Barawa by Somali *ʿulamaʾ*. For a while he lived at Lamu in the company of other *shaykhs* and *sharif ʿulamaʾ* for which Lamu was famous all over the coast before the middle of the nineteenth century. After moving to Mombasa, he composed verses supporting the Mazrui in their rivalry with Sayyid Said. He changed his allegiance, though, when it became clear to him that the Busaidi ultimately would be the winners.[106] He served as a Sunni *qadi* at the courts of Sayyids Said and Majid, in which capacity he sometimes mediated in the continuing struggles between his Busaidi masters and those who continued offering resistance to them. He composed several works in Arabic, including a small book on *tawhid* (proofs of God's unity), a commentary on the *khutba* of the *Minhaj at-Talibin*, a work on *sarf* (Arabic morphology). In addition, he composed several poems in Swahili, including a prayer for rain (*Dua ya Mvua*) and an *utenzi* epic on the *miʿraj* of the Prophet. Sh. Muhyi ad-Din's most important contribution to coastal Islam, however, appears to have been the tradition he helped establish for learning in the written sciences among a large number of pupils who themselves later became important *ʿulamaʾ*. Among these were another Somali *ʿalim*, Sh. Abdu'l-Aziz b. Abdu'l-Ghany; Sh. Muhammad b. Ahmad al-Moroni; and three of the Comorian *ʿulamaʾ* mentioned above, Sh. Hasan b. Yusuf Mngazija, Sh. Fadhl b. Ali Mngazija Mbangwa, and S. Ahmad b. Salim Abu Bakr bin Salim.[107] Finally, he was one of the first native-born *ʿulamaʾ* of the nineteenth-century coast to re-establish the tradition of travelling abroad and performing the *hajj* to maintain links with the great *ʿulamaʾ* of the Islamic heartlands.

Sh. Abdu'l-Aziz b. Abdu'l-Ghany al-Amawy (1834–96) was a student of Sh. Muhyi ad-Din, as well as of a *sufi shaykh* from the Hijaz, Sh. Ahmad al-Maghribi. Born in Barawa, he received his entire education there, most of which appears to have been in *tasawwuf* – literary sufism largely based on Ghazzali's works.[108] After leaving Barawa as a youth, at one point he travelled to Mombasa where he tried to introduce the Qadiriyya *tariqa*. However, he was unsuccessful in this, principally because of his poverty and the opposition of Sh. Ali b. Abdallah Mazrui, who enjoyed far greater repute locally than a stranger like Abdu'l-Aziz could hope to muster.[109]

Having failed at Mombasa, however, Sh. Abdu'l-Aziz did succeed in Zanzibar. By 1848, Sh. Muhyi ad-Din chose him to be a *qadi* of Kilwa, and he became a *qadi* of Zanzibar sometime during Barghash's reign. In addition, he was a regular attendant at the *barazas* of all the Sultans from Sayyids Said to Hamid b. Thuwain. More importantly, though, his *sufi* teachings and *dhikr* attracted widespread interest among the *waungwana* of Zanzibar and Pemba.[110] His influence was great enough, in fact, to have 'converted' Barghash's brother, Khalifa b. Said, to Sunni Islam or at least to have given him sympathy with the Sunnis. His popularity and the success of his *dhikr* eventually brought him into conflict with Barghash. Though the Sultan could not put a stop to his activities, he ultimately did deprive Sh. Abdu'l-Aziz of his *qadi*-ship.[111]

Sh. Abdu'l-Aziz's halcyon years were under Sayyids Khalifa (1888–90) and Ali b. Said (1890–3). His friendship with Khalifa began when Barghash banished his brother to 'exile' at a *shamba* eight miles removed from Zanzibar town. There Sh. Abdu'l-Aziz visited Khalifa regularly and arranged to be secretly informed in the event of Barghash's death to pass on the intelligence to his friend and patron. Needless to say, his *qadi*-ship was restored to him when Khalifa finally succeeded.[112]

Abdu'l-Aziz was a faithful servant to both Sayyids Khalifa and Ali. Unlike many court *culama'* and *wazirs*, he stuck by Khalifa during the time of the Anglo-German blockade and during the years when the British East Africa Company was assuming control over what would become Kenya. Under severe criticism from the Omanis and the *waungwana* for his inability to take action in the face of European aggressions, Khalifa suffered a series of nervous relapses. Often he was forced into seclusion, remaining accessible only to his three most trusted advisors, Sh. Abdu'l-Aziz, Peera Dewji, and Sh. Muhammad Muhammad Bakashmar. Apparently with the advice of Sh. Abdu'l-Aziz, he finally decided to restore Zanzibar completely to the letter of Islamic law to cut short further criticism (something Barghash had tried to do under the tutelage of the *mutawwah culama'*).[113] This measure included summary executions for confessed homicidals who, in some cases, had been imprisoned for years in Zanzibar fort. However, this action was blunted through the complicity of the Sultan's Arab foes and the British consul.

In addition, Abdu'l-Aziz actively fought against all European political and cultural inroads among the *waungwana*. The Germans expressed a feeling that, 'he was in the habit generally of thwarting their desires and

143

acting inimically to German interests' in East Africa. The British, equally distrustful of him, felt he 'was (as is almost universally believed) on terms of confidential intimacy with the German consulate'.[114] Consequently, he often was in trouble with both contenders for power and empire in East Africa. The Germans threatened him several times with deportation, while the British consul, Euan-Smith, likewise tried to pry Abdu'l-Aziz from the side of Khalifa.[115]

The fact that he stoutly defended coastal Islam against Christian missionary efforts also exposed him to criticism. He publicly debated and maintained a continuous discussion of religious subjects with Bishops Tozer and Steere and with Father Godfrey Dale of the UMCA mission in Zanzibar. Sh. Farsy claims that,

> Indeed, there has not been an ʿ*alim* who has proven so effective in debating with the missionaries of Zanzibar as did Sh. Abdu'l-Aziz, for his arguments were the most strident, nor were they mere boastings and hysterical clamourings. His arguments were like the point of a gun: whatever stood before them could not escape destruction.[116]

In the end, the British managed to rid themselves of Sh. Abdu'l-Aziz's nay-saying. As a condition of their support for Hamid b. Thuwain's succession, the consulate insisted that certain 'leading Arabs' who had 'spread lies' about British officers in the reign of Ali b. Said and who had given Sayyid Ali 'bad counsel' leave the palace and not be permitted in the *baraza* unless summoned. Among the 'leading Arabs' so designated were the two court *qadis*, one of whom was Sh. Abdu'l-Aziz b. Abdu'l-Ghany al-Amawy.[117]

8

A new literacy

The secularity of the Sultanate, the increasing availability of religious texts, the appearance of new *ʿulamaʾ* from other parts of the coast and from abroad, and the new contacts established from expanding trade opened up coastal towns to changing religious perceptions. Religion became less parochial in the nineteenth century; Islamic perceptions and practices became less reflective of the individual town.

The impact of religious beliefs produced by such an opening up of society has been studied by Professor Monica Wilson, and her observations seem especially appropriate to the situation of the nineteenth-century coast. In general, the phenomena which Wilson considers to be characteristic of societies experiencing such an expansion include problems of accommodating a local judiciary to the needs and claims of immigrant strangers, an increased specialization of local productive forces and an ensuing secularization of society, and a gradual abandonment of locality spirits and a growing monotheism.

Concerning the first point, Wilson shows the problems frequently encountered by local judges in introducing testimonies of strangers into courts and the consequent difficulties of forming legal opinions on the basis of evidence so provided.[1] When viewed in such a context, one easily can imagine how towns like Mombasa, Zanzibar, and Lamu in the nineteenth century would have required less localized bases for *qadis* to make judgements in cases involving immigrant strangers. Such *qadis* would have needed access to legal source materials which had a wider cultural and historical scope than would have been present in most coastal towns previously. This would imply that a new sort of religious leadership itself would have been needed in communities experiencing such growth and changes in social composition and ideological vision. As will be demonstrated in the following pages, just such a new *ʿulamaʾ* did emerge.[2]

Regarding the second and third phenomena associated with growth and expansion in a society, Wilson also hypothesizes that such a society becomes more specialized in its productive modes, while at the same time people become materially better off. Where specialization occurs a greater range of choice of vocation, knowledge, and perspectives open up for people living in such a society. The result is that they experience a greater autonomy of thought and action, leading to an expanded range of choice in beliefs and values.[3] It becomes increasingly possible for people to reject 'magical attitudes' associated with their society's or kin group's particular founding figures. They become free to abandon ritual forms no longer felt to be relevant to new values of materialism and individualism. Where the old spirits are abandoned, Wilson sees a shift to a monotheistic principle where God alone is thought to create life. Life is perceived less in terms of reproduction and promulgation of the kin group and more in a concern for life in the here and now. Conversion to a more transcendent view of God and creation takes place when greater closeness to a 'high' God is perceived in terms of a higher form or quality of life.[4] It is useful to test these ideas against the evidence from the East African coast.

WRITTEN VERSUS ORAL TRADITION

Traditional Islam of the pre-Busaidi towns was the offspring of local history, physical environment, technology, and social structure. What changed this was contact between townspeople and new peoples such as those discussed in the preceding chapter, as well as with new ideas. Especially, it was contacts with southern Arabia and with the holy cities of the Hijaz which were thought to be prestigious among *waungwana*. Consequently, religious ideas and attitudes emanating from these places had significant influences on coastal religion. The Husayni were regarded in Pate and Lamu as great authorities on religion, possibly equal in another sense to locally trained *wanazuoni*.[5] This knowledge was supplementary or alternative to local knowledge to the extent that it was not concerned with local history and ancestral spirits, but with God's laws as they were written down and practised from books obtained from abroad. In cases like the quarrel that occurred between the *shurafaʾ* at Pate and the Nabahani, such alternative knowledge was viewed as threatening. Yet, in cases requiring an even-handed sort of justice, regardless of class or kin, *shurafaʾ* or new *ʿulamaʾ* schooled in written law, who remained outside local rivalries, could be a boon.[6] That their erudition derived from the holy cities, especially, was something to be regarded highly. Thus it was that all the most prestigious *ʿulamaʾ* on the nineteenth-century coast at some time or another performed the *hajj* and studied in centres in Arabia which were famous for learning in the written Islamic tradition. Among these great *ʿulamaʾ* were Sh. Muhyi ad-Din al-Qahtani, Sh. Abdallah b. Nafuʿ Mazrui, Sh. Ali b. Abdallah Mazrui, Sh. Abdallah Bakathir al-Kindi, Sayyid Abu Bakr b. Abduʾr-Rahman al-Husayni, Sayyid Abduʾl-Hasan b. Ahmad Jamal al-Layl, and Sayyid Ahmad b. Abu Bakr bin Sumayt. A new *ʿulamaʾ* emerged who were influential partly because they were strangers to local rivalries and because they possessed personal character and religious knowledge of a non-local, written legal tradition.

Often, the reason why many of these *ʿulamaʾ* adhered to a new, written religious tradition was that they came as strangers to the coast and rarely married into local clans. The tendency towards hypergamy among the *shurafaʾ*, as well as among such aristocratic families like the Mazrui and Busaidi, accounts for this. In societies which had become increasingly stratified socially and materially from the sixteenth century onwards, marriage alliances were carried out with a keen eye to class considerations based on a historical and legalistic tradition of relative nobility. In this sort of circumstance, it was one of the most important functions of local *wanazuoni* and *walimu* to uphold such class distinctions by sanctioning carefully chosen alliances and giving them the appearance of fitting into an assumed universal order. Accordingly, as related by one informant, pre-Busaidi *wanazuoni* were 'appointed by the people' expressly to perform marriages and whose formal knowledge of (written) Islam was limited to prayer, fasting, and a memorization of the Quran.[7] Obviously, then, families who did not marry locally would have had little need to know local history and ideas about pedigree.

One notable example of a clan which divorced itself from local traditions concerning the proper functions of a learned religious elite were the Mazrui. For one thing, it will be remembered that the founders of the Banu Nafuᶜ, Sh. Abdallah b. Nafuᶜ and Sh. Ali b. Abdallah, both benefited from education abroad and managed to establish this as a tradition among the Mazrui *ᶜulamaᵓ* who followed them. Among the last were Sh. Sulaiman b. Ali Mazrui, Sh. Muhammad Qasim Mazrui, and Sh. Al-Amin b. Ali Mazrui. The more 'bookish' knowledge obtained by these men was kept exclusive largely among themselves and a few, hand-picked pupils. They did not attempt to teach the *waungwana*. Yet the townspeople of Mombasa also did not seek them out for their knowledge, because it was not 'useful' knowledge that could be applied to 'practical' situations like marriage; nor were the Mazrui in the habit of supervising marriages themselves.[8] In certain instances, too, the Mazrui and their pupils opposed ancestor veneration and magico-religious practices performed by Swahili *waganga* and *falaki*, claiming that such beliefs constituted idolatry. Their beliefs were more passive, less manipulative, closer to a more transcendent view of God than those of the *waungwana*.[9] Occasionally, there arose conflicts between the 'great' *ᶜulamaᵓ*, like the Mazrui, and the *waungwana* over matters of belief and practice. In these instances, it is noteworthy that *waungwana* dismissed the Islam of the new *ᶜulamaᵓ* as not 'orthodox' (*-enye imani*) because such beliefs and practices were not followed by their ancestors.[10] (All this indicates, once again, that 'orthodoxy' is a slippery concept in religion and depends on which foot the shoe is made to fit.) In the end, many townspeople felt ill-served by *ᶜulamaᵓ* like the Banu Nafuᶜ and rebelled against them through requests that they be given other *qadis* by their Government – *qadis* who would minister to their social and spiritual needs better and whose ideas about Islamic orthodoxy were closer to their own.

Probably no other institution, though, did more than the *tariqas* in promoting literacy in East Africa.[11] The Qadiriyya, for example, already has been discussed in connection with the influence of the Benadir *ᶜulamaᵓ*. In addition to promoting *dhikr* exercises, the Qadiriyya gave some emphasis to teaching the fundamentals of a few religious sciences.

However, the Alawiyya *tariqa* seems to have been the one most popular among the new *ᶜulamaᵓ* and the one which was most responsible for the new standards of scholarship. The important part which this *tariqa* played in

147

advancing knowledge of the written sciences in East Africa is illustrated by the fact that the most influential and learned of the new ʿulamaʾ were associated with it and espoused its teachings. Among these adherents were most of the Hadrami *shurafaʾ* of the Abu Bakr b. Salim and the Jamal al-Layl clans, as well as Sayyid Ahmad bin Sumayt, Sh. Abdallah Bakathir al-Kindi, and Sayyid Salih b. Alawi ('Habib' Salih of the Riyadha *madrasa* in Lamu).[12]

The Alawi brotherhood was different from other *tariqas* in several important respects. First of all, it was south Arabian in origin, having been founded by the Hadrami *shurafaʾ* primarily as an institution to maintain social ties among them and to serve their group interests. Therefore, it largely reflected the stringent religious attitudes of its adherents as described by Van den Berg:

> L'Islamisme y a un caratère trop mâle, ou à vrai dire trop Arabe, pour admettre de déviations de cette nature, dues au mysticisme maladif des Persans et des Turcs. Les *Sayyid* ... ne cachaient pas leur mépris pour les chefs actuels des derviches hurleurs et danseurs ... Ils les traitaient d'imposteurs qui enseignent des cérémonies, peut-être louables à l'origine mais ayant, de nous jours, perdu toute raison d'être.[13]

Indeed, one can imagine that the Hadrami ʿulamaʾ felt the same towards the traditional Islamic beliefs and practices of East Africans as they did towards the 'chefs actuels des derviches hurleurs et danseurs'.

Though many besides *shurafaʾ* followed the Alawi way, its core was composed primarily of Hadrami *shurafaʾ*. It lacked formal organization since its aims were literary and educational rather than political. Only loose, informal ties were maintained between mosques and towns, though the ʿulamaʾ of one town or mosque had kinship ties or intellectual friendships which could extend as far away as Arabia.[14] Unlike other *tariqas*, *dhikr* exercises were not a central feature of Alawi activities in East Africa since it was thought that the potential 'excesses' in *dhikr* activities had to be avoided even if the exercises themselves were not excluded altogether.[15]

Essentially, the Alawiyya and its members emphasized ʿilm (religious erudition) and instruction in all the *fanun* (sciences) as its centre-piece. In the 1850s, Sayyid Muhammad b. Ahmad ash-Shatiri initiated a world-wide programme of opening Quran schools and *madrasas* for training students in *tafsir* (exegesis), Arabic grammar (*nahw*) and morphology (*sarf*), law (*fiqh*), *hadith* (the Sunna of the Prophet), and *tasawwuf*. As the last science indicates, the Alawiyya appears to have been a *tariqa* more in the benign, conservative tradition envisioned by Ghazzali – a tradition which balanced love and adoration of God with a conscientious programme of coming to know His word as found in the Quran (hence, *tafsir*) and as exemplified in the way (*Sunna*) of His Prophet.[16] This would have been consistent with the Alawi ideal concerning worship of God and the proper life style for a Muslim. As mentioned, the former was thought to consist not so much of the usual *dhikr* exercises as of ritual prayer (*awrad*) and 'being fearful of God'.[17] As explained by Serjeant,

> No ʿAlawi may go counter to the Pious Ancestors, but act with humility,

148

piety, and lofty motive, with the Prophet for his model. The ᶜAlawi sufi must love obscurity, dislike manifestation, withdraw from the madding crowd, but he must warn against neglect of religious duties. He must show kindness to wife, children, neighbors, relations, to the tribes. and to all Muslims.[18]

Such, then, serves as a useful introduction to the 'high' ᶜulamaᵓ who appeared on the coast in the years of the Sultanate.

THE NEW ᶜ*ULAMA*ᵓ AND GREAT MEN OF THE COURT

Whereas the old religious elite of the towns essentially were exponents of town history, lore, and (oral) traditions, now a new class or type of learned elite appeared in the great trade centres. While little information on the subject exists, it appears that the original homeland of the new type of ᶜulamaᵓ was in the commercially active Lamu region. As they were associated (originally) with Lamu's 'golden age' of trade and wealth, they already were present in the Lamu archipelago by the 1850s, and probably as early as the sixteenth century (see Chapter 3).[19] By the second half of the nineteenth century, though, Zanzibar became the cultural and intellectual capital of the coast, if intellectual greatness can be measured in terms of numbers of ᶜulamaᵓ, rather than in the extent of their (known) erudition.

In reading Sh. A. S. Farsy's manuscript, 'Baadhi ya Wanavyuoni wa Kishafii wa Mashariki ya Afrika', it is apparent that this new class of religious leaders was distinguishable by four essential characteristics, some of which have been mentioned already. The first of these was that the ᶜalim usually was a person who travelled a great deal in his lifetime and whose intellectual horizons extended well beyond the community in which he lived. With a few exceptions, most ᶜulamaᵓ of the nineteenth century were Hadramis or had Hadrami masters. Therefore, a considerable number mentioned in Farsy's manuscript (perhaps twenty) performed the *hajj* and several journeyed to the Hadhramawt for instruction. Almost all the ᶜulamaᵓ, whatever their origins, received at least some of their training from other mentors outside of the town in which they were born or reared. This contrasts significantly with the old town elite, who nearly always were schooled locally by locally recognized masters and they themselves usually came only from houses recognized in their community as religiously pre-eminent.

Secondly, they were trained in at least one of the traditional written sciences. Among these were *fiqh* (law), *faraydh* (inheritance law), *hadith, nahw* (Arabic grammar), *sarf* (morphology), *bayan* (rhetoric), *mantik* (logic), *tawhid* (theology), *tafsir* (exegesis), and *tasawwuf*. An ᶜalim had to be proficient to some degree in Arabic. For example, he often was a poet in Arabic and commonly also in Swahili.

A student of ᶜilm (sciences, religious knowledge) learned certain subjects by copying, word-for-word, certain texts from a recognized master who dictated the text and provided some commentary. Once the pupil mastered the text in question, he received a certificate, an *ijaza*, from his master which testified to his achievement and from whom he received his training. Thus, the student benefited from the knowledge so acquired and from his masters' *baraka*. Naturally, the more *ijaza* a student accumulated and the greater the number and fame of his masters, the greater his own reputation became.[20] The importance of his teachers to a prospective ᶜ*alim*'s own reputation often was decisive. For example, to hold a *darasa* of his own, the student first had to receive permission from his own *shaykh*. Once the student began his own classes, too, he still was required to continue returning to his master's *darasa* to receive help with any difficulties or questions encountered in his classes. Sometimes, too, an instructor's own *shaykh* might attend his classes 'to give ... incentive (ili kunitia hima)'.[21] Indeed, a student and his *shaykh* were very close. In some cases the student lived in his master's house, married his daughters, and continued supporting the old master in his old age.[22] Finally, the student sometimes even imitated his masters in mannerisms and style of dress (*mwendo*).

Thirdly, a new terminology of address was introduced for the new elite. Where the town elite usually were referred to as *shehe, walimu, waganga, wazee*, or simply as *wanavyuoni*, the great *shaykhs* of the nineteenth-century coast were given the Arabic title of ᶜ*alim* (pl. ᶜ*ulamaᵓ*) or its derivative, *maᶜalim*. Differences between *shaykhs* were signified through special terms of qualification. A 'great' *mwanachuoni*, for example, was a *mwanachuoni kabisa* (learned 'in all the sciences'), or a *mwanachuoni mkubwa*. This contrasts with a town *mwalimu* who was a *mwanachuoni mdogo* or, perhaps (grudgingly), a *mwanachuoni wa katikati* if he had some training in a *fann*. Only rarely, for example, does Farsy apply the word *mwalimu* to an ᶜ*alim*. Other terms of reference or qualification, in addition, were applied to the new learned class. For instance, the ᶜ*alim* was supposed to be a 'pious' person; therefore he was 'God-fearing' (*mcha Mungu*). He was 'Arab-like'; therefore he had to be learned in Arab ways (*ustaarabu*). Perhaps he was even called an Arab (*Mwarabu*). Farsy commonly employs other apt phrases in speaking of an ᶜ*alim*, such as 'he was honoured' (*alitukuzwa*) or people 'honoured him for his learning, piety, dignity, etc. (wakimsifu sana kwa ilmu, ucha Mungu, na ukarimu, na wengineyo)'. The final judgement seems to have been passed when it was said that, 'They say that he was one of the East African coast's greatest gentlemen (wakisema ni miongoni mwa mabwana makubwa sana waliokuwako pande hizi za Mashariki ya Afrika)'.

Finally, after 1870 especially, many of the new religious leaders became connected with the Sultanate in various ways. There was a certain new consensus, for instance, among great ᶜ*ulamaᵓ* by which, in fact, individuals were recognized as belonging to this inner circle of the most distinguished on the coast. It was through the recognition accorded his masters that an ᶜ*alim* began to establish his own reputation. Furthermore, in the course of his studies, he came to know and be known by other 'recognized' individuals, who through greeting and visitation habits all became part of that special social circle of the elite. ᶜ*Ulamaᵓ* also were on friendly terms with many other important people of their times, such as *wazirs* and consuls, as well as with the Sultans themselves. An ᶜ*alim*'s fame was enhanced by those who, through their public actions, paid him honour. Finally, the greatness of an ꜥalim was gauged at his death by the legacy he left behind which reinforced socially accepted values, and to which tribute was paid by the many notables who attended his funeral to praise him on that last occasion.[23]

COURT ꜥULAMAꜣ

Besides social ties with people of the Sultans' courts, many ꜥulamaꜣ were bound to the Sultanate as dependants. As has been mentioned, control was increased steadily over the ꜥulamaꜣ, especially with Barghash's reign. Thereafter, all *qadis*, even in the remotest towns, were hand-selected by the Sultans or their *liwalis* and were paid directly out of the Sultans' purse. Selection involved no examination and was done informally. Sometimes the Sultan personally made the appointment, but in most cases it was made with the advice of other ꜥulamaꜣ, court favourites, or in distant ports like Kilwa or Lamu through agreements between town *wazee* and the *liwali* who, in turn, made their choice known to the Sultan.[24] Sometimes too, there was disagreement over the choice of a *qadi* and, in the case of the wealthy Shatiri or of the Three Tribes at Mombasa, clans or families appointed their own *qadis*. There were only two *qadis* in places like Mombasa and Lamu: one Ibadi and one Sunni. Yet, at Zanzibar there were many *qadis* of both sects and people had a choice as to which one they might present their cases.[25] It was for this reason, therefore, that class or ethnic prejudice or residual town pride entered into selections of *qadis* – people simply chose the *qadi* whom they thought would sympathize with their appeal, and usually this would be a kinsman or fellow townsman.[26]

Qadi-ships, as did learning itself, however, tended to run in families or clans. At Lamu, the Maawi continued as *khatibs* and *qadis*, while at Mombasa appointments of Sunni *qadis* were taken from the Mazuri clan. At Zanzibar, the sons of *qadis* frequently succeeded their fathers. Burhan b. Abdu'l-Aziz al-Amawy succeeded as Chief *Qadi* under the British administration and, later, Umar b. Ahmad bin Sumayt, too, became a Chief *Qadi*. The Ibadi *mufti* of Zanzibar usually was chosen from among the Mandhry clan. Farsy's manuscript abounds with similar examples.

Yet, to exert control over their *qadis*, the Sultans and their *liwalis* occasionally tried to break the grip of some clans over religious offices. The case of the appointments of some Mahdali to *qadi*-ships at Lamu has already been detailed. The exact date when this occurred is not known, but one informant was certain that it was, as one would expect, under Barghash.[27] There were similar incidents in the reign of Sayyid Hamud b. Muhammad. The most notorious of these involved the *liwali* of Mombasa, Ali b. Salim al-Busaidi, who appointed Mwinyi Abudi as Chief *Qadi* (*Shaykh al-Islam*) of Kenya to thwart the Mazrui hold over *qadi*-ships. Afterwards, though, the position fell to Sh. Sulaiman b. Ali Mazrui.[28]

At Zanzibar itself, control was strongest and the judicial and religious institution most elaborately developed. Everything there revolved around the life of the court. All or nearly all ꜥulamaꜣ were members of the Sultan's personal retinue and, aside perhaps from presents received customarily from court petitioners, essentially they lived off the court. To control and institutionalize the scholarly class, Barghash and his successors created a semi-official system of *qadis* and court advisors. There were many *qadis*. These were arranged more or less by prestige and seniority into a hierarchy with an Ibadi *mufti* and a Sunni *qadi al-qudat* (Chief *Qadi*) at the top. Moreover there was some assignment of jurisdiction, although, as has already been pointed out, people were free to choose their own *qadis*. For example, there were two Chief *Qadis*, a *qadi* of Pemba, *qadis* attached to each quarter of Zanzibar town, a *raᶜis al-awqaf* (head of *waqfs*), a *qadi* of the *askaris*, and at least one *qadi* of the rural regions. In this arrangement, the Ibadi *ᶜulamaᵓ* were better paid by the Sultan and were considered more influential at court than were their Sunni counterparts. Generally, the role of the Sunni *qadi al-qudat* was as principal advisor on Sunni matters, whereas the Ibadi *mufti* was directly involved in matters of state policy in addition to the Sultan's daily administrative and personal affairs.[29]

Of the Ibadis, the only *ᶜalim* on whom any information is available is Sh. Sulaiman b. Ali Mandhry. His most noteworthy characteristic, at least to the extent that one can trust the available material, is that he was an opportunist who took advantage of court factionalism and Sayyid Majid's failing health to enrich and arrogate power to himself. Reute claims that, 'He was a crafty, selfish man, who gradually contrived to get all the power into his own hands, and to reduce the other ministers to mere ciphers...' Power was obtained by Sh. Sulaiman when,

> in secret he managed to incite all brothers and sisters one against the other in order to increase his own power. He succeeded too well in his plots everywhere; quarrel upon quarrel took place in our family, many notables were insulted and neglected, and things grew gradually so bad that people began to murmur and complain aloud.[30]

Specifically, Sulaiman took sides with Sayyid Majid against Barghash in the struggle for the throne. It was Majid who won out at first, of course, but in the end Barghash got his revenge on Sulaiman when, in 1870, he ascended to power and forced the wily old *ᶜalim* to take flight to India.[31]

Sulaiman used his position, too, for personal enrichment. Reute tells further how he sued for and won the hand of one of Said b. Sultan's concubines – a Circassian named Fatma – in order to gain control of her rather sizeable endowment.[32] Also, he took bribes from the British consulate and a variety of court petitioners in return for representing their interests before the Sultan.[33]

SAYYID AHMAD BIN SUMAYT AND SHAYKH ABDALLAH BAKATHIR

The first influential Sunni *ᶜulamaᵓ* of the court were Sh. Muhyi ad-Din and Sh. Abdu'l-Aziz b. Abdu'l-Ghany, both of whom have been discussed previously. However, from several sources of information, the two most venerable of the great *ᶜulamaᵓ* of Zanzibar were S. Ahmad b. Abu Bakr bin Sumayt and Sh. Abdallah b. Muhammad Bakathir al-Kindi. A close

2. Sayyid Ahmad bin Sumayt (d. 1925).

examination of their lives, alone, reveals in considerable detail the nature of court life and the religious institutions at Zanzibar under the Sultanate and in the early colonial era.

Aside from the disproportionately large amount of space Farsy devotes to these two ῾ulamaʾ, the measure of their venerability is given witness by Farsy in four different ways. The first is the other ῾ulamaʾ whom they

153

trained.[34] From these lists it is clear that, like many *shurafa*, S. Ahmad confined his teaching to a favoured few who later bore his reputation by the fame which they themselves garnered. Sh. Abdallah, on the other hand, had an enormous number of pupils from all over the coast. In addition, it was he who instituted the practice during Ramadhan of offering public lectures on the basics of the faith. Doubtless, the differences in the educational philosophy of both men were due to the differences in their social backgrounds: while S. Ahmad was a *sharif*, Sh. Abdallah came from an impoverished Hadrami family and was very much the 'self-made man'.

Secondly, it is clear from their circle of acquaintances that both were very much men of their times. Among Sh. Abdallah's friends, for example, were three Sultans, Hamud b. Muhammad, Ali b. Hamud, and Khalifa b. Harub, as well as several *liwalis, wazirs*, and men of wealth and influence.[35] S. Ahmad's circle of acquaintances, however, was even wider. Farsy mentions that various Busaidi were in the habit of visiting him at his home even before they became Sultans. Among these were all the Sultans from Khalifa b. Said (1888–90) through Khalifa b. Harub (1911–60). Also, he was personally acquainted with the Ottoman Sultan, Abdu'l-Hamid; various Hadrami *shaykhs* of the al-Ghayti tribe; scores of the leading *ulama* and *shurafa* of the Hadhramawt; the Grand *Mufti* of Mecca, Muhammad Said b. Muhammad Babsayl; various Egyptian *ulama*; and three British appointees to the Zanzibar Court of Appeals, Sir James Murrison, Judge Peter Grain, and Justice Reed.[36]

Next, some idea of what helped establish an *alim*'s reputation is afforded by Farsy's discussion of the legacies of these two men. Among the things for which S. Ahmad is remembered, aside from his students, are his learned children, especially S. Umar b. Ahmad, who later became a Chief *Qadi*; his various scholarly works; his poetry; and his tables for calculating the correct times of prayer that are found in all of Zanzibar's mosques. Sh. Abdallah's legacy also included a learned son, Sh. Abu Bakr b. Abdallah. Again though, Sh. Abdallah's efforts in instructing other *ulama* and the poor are evident in the things for which he is remembered. Among these are, again, his afternoon Ramadhan classes; the superrogatory Witr and Tarawih prayers which he introduced for Ramadhan; and the Ukutani *madrasa* for advanced religious studies.[37]

The final gauge of an *alim*'s reputation is the number of people, particularly 'great' people, who attended his funeral. Both Sayyid Ahmad's and Sh. Abdallah's funerals (1925) were attended by Zanzibar's notables and several of them participated directly in the funerary rites. Thus, a glimpse of a great *alim*'s popularity is rendered by Farsy's description of the scenes that attended S. Ahmad's last rites:

> Zanzibar had never witnessed a funeral which was attended by more people than that of Sayyid Ahmad. Official word went out that these funerary services were to take place in the Malindi Friday Mosque. A great line extended from the front of Sayyid Ahmad's house to the graveyard of the Friday Mosque, as well as inside the mosque and even on the floor. There was not even space for one's feet. If someone got up to move about, he could go

neither forward nor backward. The cloth which covered the funerary bed was sought by everyone in attendance. Every person wanted to leave with a piece of it, even if it was only a tiny scrap. What a pushing and pulling there was! Everyone's intention was to get whatever he could.[38]

Despite the fact that these two men came from different places – Sh. Abdallah from Lamu and S. Ahmad from the Comoros – they had much in common. Both were Hadrami and, consequently, adherents of the Alawiyya. Sh. Abdallah (1860–1925) spent his youth as a poor orphan who earned his livelihood by embroidering caps (*kofia*). However, being a Hadrami, he was able to study under the leading Hadrami *shurafa°* of Lamu at that time. Foremost among these was the popularist of Islamic teaching (see Chapter 10), S. Salih b. Alawi Jamal al-Layl ('Habib' Salih), as well as the poet, S. Abu Bakr b. Abdu'r-Rahman al-Husayni (Sayyid Mansab), and S. Ali b. Abdallah Jamal al-Layl. S. Ahmad's (1861–1925) early training was under Alawi masters such as his father, S. Abu Bakr b. Abdallah (the *nahodha*), and S. Abdu'l-Hasan b. Ahmad Jamal al-Layl, both of whom have been mentioned already.

Both men, too, were well travelled, studied under the same Hadrami *°ulama°*, and had a strong mutual respect. Through the promptings of his father, S. Ahmad journeyed to Hadhramawt three times, the first time in 1881, to study under the leading Alawi *mashayikh* of that time. There he travelled to Shibam, Du°an, Ghurfa, and al-Hawta (Inat?) where he obtained *ijaza* from 'the greatest of the Hadrami masters of the past century', S. Aydarus b. Umar al-Hibshi, and a host of other *°ulama°* of the Hibshi, at-Attas, bin Sumayt, and Abu Bakr b. Salim tribes.[39] Meanwhile, Sh. Abdallah had obtained an introduction to S. Ahmad from his old master at Lamu, Habib Salih b. Alawi. He went to Zanzibar in 1888 and struck up a friendship with S. Ahmad which was to last until both of their deaths in 1925. Sh. Abdallah, Farsy says, held S. Ahmad in such veneration that,

> he would not sleep in the same room as S. Ahmad, nor even in the same house nor at the same location. Sh. Abdallah acted in S. Ahmad's presence the way a child acts in his father's presence; for, indeed, religious and intellectual parentage is superior to parentage by blood. He would not take any action unless it was approved by S. Ahmad, nor would he reply to any religious or legal queries while S. Ahmad himself was in Zanzibar.[40]

From S. Ahmad, Sh. Abdallah obtained a letter of introduction to many of the Hadrami *°ulama°* under whom S. Ahmad himself had studied. At Hadhramawt, he read principally under S. Ali b. Muhammad al-Hibshi, while at Mecca he studied under one Sh. Umar b. Abu Bajunayd, as well as under other leading *mashayikh* and leading *shurafa°* of both places.

Finally, both men travelled widely, studying under many masters; benefiting from a wide range of ideas current among Shafii *°ulama°* around the entire Indian Ocean periphery at about the turn of the century; and, in turn, disseminating what they had learned among many students of their own. As a *nahodha*, for instance, S. Ahmad plied the Indian Ocean ports from Madagascar to Lamu. His studies and travels brought him to Zanzibar, Hadhramawt, Mecca, Medina, Egypt, and Istanbul. Besides his training in

Zanzibar and the Hadhramawt, Sh. Abdallah learned and taught in the Hijaz, Java, at the court of the *Kabaka* of Buganda, and in Capetown, South Africa.

S. Ahmad served as a *qadi* of Zanzibar briefly under Barghash in 1883–6, but because of the low status and salaries given Shafii *qadis* at Barghash's court, he resigned his position and fled to the court of the Ottoman Sultan, Abdu'l-Hamid. There he was received by S. Fadhl b. Alawi b. Salih, described as a former *wali* of Dhofar. According to Martin, however, S. Fadhl planned and promoted Pan-Islam in sub-Saharan Africa along with the more notorious Jamal ad-Din al-Afghani. Before returning to Zanzibar, after the accession of Khalifa b. Said in 1888, S. Ahmad received medals of honour and a stipend from Abdu'l-Hamid.[41] S. Ahmad's contacts with Pan-Islam and Islamic reform extended also to Cairo, where he studied briefly at the Azhar *madrasa* at the time when reform thought was gaining popularity among its scholars. Finally, through Sh. Ahmad b. Muhammad Mlomri, S. Ahmad carried on an irregular correspondence with the leading theoretician of the Salafiyya reform movement in Egypt, Sh. Muhammad Abduh.[42]

S. Ahmad's fortunes varied considerably upon his return to Zanzibar in 1888. His *qadi*-ship was restored to him by Khalifa and his standing grew rapidly. He authored several works in Arabic and he became recognized as the foremost scholar on the coast. While the new *ʿulamaʾ* generally were distrusted by *waungwana*, Judge Peter Grain was forced to admit that,

> Sheik Hamed bin Smeit [*sic*] even among the natives, is looked up to as a learned, honest, and just judge. I say 'even among the natives' because it is a common practice among the natives, if a decision goes against them, to say that the judge was bribed.[43]

S. Ahmad's relations with the Sultans reached a zenith under Sayyids Khalifa and Ali b. Said (1888–93), but took a turn for the worse after that. S. Hamid b. Thuwain (1893–6) plotted to seize power in Oman from Faisal b. Turki, who had assassinated Hamid's brother, Salim b. Thuwain. This scheming was done with the encouragement and assistance of numerous Ibadi *ʿulamaʾ* who poured into Zanzibar during the crisis.[44] All this opened a Pandora's box of intrigue at Zanzibar which resulted, in the end, with S. Ahmad being implicated and discredited by the Sultan.

By 1894, Hamid b. Thuwain had been alienated from the British consulate after having had the Kenya coastal strip and Rs 200,000 taken from him with the collapse of the British East Africa Company (see Chapter 9 for details). Partly in reaction to this and to events in Oman, Hamid removed his pro-British *mufti*, one Muhammad b. Saif, and replaced him with Sh. Hilal b. Amr, who was deeply involved with Hamid's manoeuvrings in Oman. In addition, Hilal b. Amr was connected with Ali b. Abdallah Hinawi who had been entrusted by Hamid with seizing the lands of deceased *waungwana* in Pemba. S. Ahmad's downfall came, apparently, because of a mere friendship between his son, Umar, and the ex-*mufti*, Muhammad b. Saif, and because he chose to defend the rights of the *waungwana* of Pemba against the predatory Sultan and his henchman,

Hilal. The result was that the Order of the Brilliant Star medal that had been presented to him in Istanbul was taken from him, as well as access rights to the Sultan.[45]

S. Ahmad's most famous peccadillo, however, involved him in a three-way quarrel with S. Ali b. Hamud (1903–11) and the Chief *Qadi*, Sh. Burhan b. Abdu'l-Aziz al-Amawy. Sh. Burhan, son of the Qadiriyya *shaykh*, Abdu'l-Aziz b. Abdu'l-Ghany, himself was active in Qadiriyya activities in Zanzibar. Sayyid Ahmad, in the true Alawi tradition, issued a *fatwa* opposing the *tariqas* and their *dhikrs* at Zanzibar.[46] This decision, possibly, plus jealousy over S. Ahmad's greater popular renown (S. Ahmad was considered the 'unofficial' Chief *Qadi* by many), caused Sh. Burhan to encourage S. Ali b. Hamud to demote S. Ahmad and to rusticate him as the *qadi* of the *shambas* (rural villages).

Enmity between Ali b. Hamud and S. Ahmad reached a crisis when S. Ahmad cooperated with the British efforts to remove the traditional rights of the Sultans to decide appeals cases from Sayyid Ali. Educated in England, S. Ali was too unfamiliar with Islamic law to form proper judgements in the eyes of his subjects. In addition, he was a spendthrift who frequently journeyed to Europe to vacation. He saw much in East Africa that he wished to change, including many of his subjects' beliefs, which he considered superstitious. People thought that, 'He did not care about things.' His headstrong resistance to increasingly iron-fisted British control over his personal prerogatives as Zanzibar's Sultan caused growing friction with the English consuls. The British propagandized against the Sultan by trying to represent him as a drunkard and a religious backslider. Ahmad b. Sumayt was taken in by this propaganda, and in the end he was persuaded to sign a petition to the Foreign Office, along with thirty or forty other prominent citizens, to ask that the Sultan's rights to hear appeals cases be taken from him.[47]

Ali b. Hamud scolded S. Ahmad for allowing himself to be used by the British and had him banished as *qadi* of the *shambas*. While serving in this position, S. Ahmad continued to face the opposition of the pro-British party who were behind his nemesis, Sh. Burhan b. Abdu'l-Aziz. On several occasions these people had sought to have S. Ahmad replaced in his position by his only rival in erudition, Sh. Abdallah Bakathir. Farsy relates how the plaintiffs in a case once refused to accept a decision made by Sh. Burhan and the Ibadi *qadi*, Sh. Nasr b. Salim ar-Ruwayhy. They went to the British appeals judge and asked that the matter be put before a *mufti* for a decision. Informed by Sh. Burhan's followers that Sh. Abdallah was the greatest ᶜ*alim* in Zanzibar, Sh. Abdallah was sent for to render a pronouncement on the case. Yet Sh. Abdallah, as was his manner, refused to give a decision, declaring, 'The only one who can answer these questions is my *shaykh*, Sayyid Ahmad, not I his pupil. I can only answer questions concerning prayer and fasting.'[48]

Finally, the judicial reforms which resulted from Judge Peter Grain's report of 1907 led to S. Ahmad's restoration to the position of *qadi* of Zanzibar. Judge Grain proposed that an examination be given to all *qadis* to identify the most capable ones. When the results of these exams came in, Grain was informed by his court translator that, 'There is no one who can answer these questions except that one whom you have thrown as a rural sweetmeat to the people of Ngambu! [the 'native' quarter of Zanzibar town].' The answers were sent to Egypt where the *'ulama'* of the Azhar issued replies which concurred with bin Sumayt's. Subsequently, S. Ahmad was restored and given an office in which to work. He continued as an official *mufti* until his death in 1925.[49]

Beyond what has been said of Sh. Abdallah already, there is only a little to add on his Alawi involvements and teachings. Sh. Abdallah travelled everywhere to teach. While studying in Mecca under Sh. Umar b. Abu Bakr Bajunayd in 1888, he was sent by his mentor to Java to teach the sciences. He journeyed also to Capetown in 1913 to settle a row among Cape Muslims, and to Buganda in 1914, along with various pupils, to teach. In 1892, he established a series of *darasas* at the Msikiti Gofu which he continued leading until 1902. In 1902, he purchased a house in Ukutuni quarter of Zanzibar – where the Gofu mosque is located – and continued his classes there until his death. He started out by teaching his classes in the vestibule (*sabule*) of the house, but soon had to expand by constructing a larger antechamber especially for his classes in advanced sciences and Alawi traditions. His two special pupils, who resided at Ukutuni with him, were Sh. Muhsin b. Ali al-Barwani and Sh. Muhammad b. Umar al-Khatibu. Both these men took over Sh. Abdallah's work as a teacher. The former did so in 1917 by taking Sh. Abdallah's morning classes at Ukutuni, and, with his master's death in 1925, he continued with all of Sh. Abdallah's major classes both at Ukutuni and at his *shamba* at Kitundu. Sh. Muhammad b. Umar was a tutor for some of Sh. Abdallah's classes at Ukutuni, then took over his own 'small' classes. He was made the *imam* of the Witr and Tarawih prayers introduced principally by Sh. Abdallah. Later, he assumed direction of the classes at Msikiti Gofu when the old master grew too feeble. Finally, it was Sh. Muhammad who conceived the idea of endowing the Ukutuni *madrasa*. This *madrasa* became so famous that, in the end, it was supported by the colonial government, taking on the new name of the Ukutuni Institute.[50]

THE SWAHILI REACTION

As a final point, it must be said that the appearance of the new class of *'ulama'* basically was an elitist phenomenon, largely stimulated by ideas foreign to the *waungwana* and represented by Hadrami and Comorian *'ulama'*. Some coastal townspeople, apparently, accepted some of the views presented by the written Islamic tradition and studied under the new masters like Sh. Abdu'l-Aziz, Sh. Muhyi ad-Din, Abdallah Bakathir, and S. Ahmad bin Sumayt. Farsy's 'Baadhi ya Wanavyuoni', for example, mentions a considerable number of *'ulama'* who, by their names, obviously were from old coastal clans. Among these were Sh. Muhammad Umar al-Khatibu, one of Sh. Abdallah's two protégés, as well as several Maawis (Abdallah b. Ali, Abu Bakr b. Muhammad, and Ali b. Muhammad),

Makhzumy (Faisal b. Ali and Muhammad b. Abdu'r-Rahman), Sh. Abdallah b. Muhammad al-Khatib, and Muhammad Ahmad Bereki – all from Lamu. At Mombasa, there was Mwinyi wa Mwinyi Ngwame ('Mwisha Hali') who studied *fiqh* under Sh. Ali b. Abdallah Mazrui. Characterized by a kinsman as an *ᶜalim wa dini* (as distinct from an *ᶜalim wa dunia*, a *mganga*, or *falaki*), Mwisha Hali became a *qadi* of the Three Tribes and a *khatib* of the Mnara (Basheikh) Mosque.[51] Finally, Farsy briefly mentions Sh. Said b. Ahmad Mkilindini, who studied *fiqh* and became a *qadi* of Takaungu.[52]

It should be noticed that, except for the last two, all these *ᶜulamaᵓ* came from families which traditionally had been recognized for their religious leadership at Lamu. Through their social connections and as 'owners of the soil', they had been able to penetrate the social exclusiveness of *sharif* clans, like the Jamal al-Layl, at Lamu and had benefited from the knowledge gained. Beyond these few, however, the remaining *waungwana* mentioned in Farsy's manuscript seem to have acquired their learning not so much through the new tradition introduced by the Hadramis and the *shurafaᵓ* as through the Qadiriyya brought from Somalia. Several are mentioned, for example, who bear *nisbas* like al-Shirazi, Mbaluchi, or al-Kilindini. Yet the two most notable among these for their involvement in *tariqa* activities were Sh. Shauri b. Hajji Mshirazi (d. 1913) and Sh. Shehe b. Sero (d. 1909). The former was born at Donge, Pemba, and studied under Sh. Muhyi ad-Din al-Qahtani. Among the sciences, he was especially noted for *tafsir*, but he was more heavily involved in *dhikr* activities. After founding his own branch of the Qadiriyya, called the Kirama *tariqa*, he popularized *dhikr* around Tumbatu. He left two students to continue his work, Sh. Hajj b. Vuai Mshirazi (d. 1937) and Sh. Ali b. Umar Mshirazi (d. 1925). In addition, much of what he knew about *sufism* and elements of Islam he taught to his wife, Mwana Alama, who helped popularize his *dhikr* among the women of northern Zanzibar.[53] Shehe b. Sero studied under Sh. Ali b. Abdallah Mazrui and, due to his long life and great energy, popularized Islam and *sufism* around Tanga.

While the Qadiriyya, popularized by Sh. Abdu'l-Aziz b. Abdu'l-Ghany and Sh. Uways from Somalia,[54] and *falak* caught on rapidly among *waungwana*, some of the excesses associated with them offended the new *ᶜulamaᵓ*. The great *shaykhs* stuck to a more fundamentalist and transcendent form of Islam and occasionally conflicted with devotees of *dhikr*, *uganga*, and *falak*. The attempt by S. Ahmad b. Sumayt to banish *dhikr* and imprison its followers has been cited already. At Mombasa, Sh. Ali b. Abdallah Mazrui was the principal obstacle to *sufism* there during his lifetime. Mwisha Hali, too, supported Sh. Ali in this, preaching against *dhikr*, *falak*, and *uganga* in his Friday sermons, while Sh. Muhyi ad-Din composed verses in which he vilified *uganga* and *falak*. One of these, 'Wapungaji' (Against Exorcists), goes as follows:

> Study only the books, open and read them
> And show me there those who have been cured by these, the spirits of dancing.
> All these of which people talk are lies.

Those lies have no basis in truth: they are lies invented by the deceitful.

It is for naught that you pay them; they have no powers.
They perform only their tricks; their patients do the curing.
And he who denies this is one who walks in ignorance.
The first is the *pungwa* of Kitanga, and the second is the *pungwa* of Kitimiri.

My words are true, as I shall explain.
Because, as people say, the truth is always bitter.
Don't be hurt, my brother, if you would deny this.
Tell me the truth, then, for it will bring you pain.

The situation of these *waganga* is this: they are all Barmakids.[55]
Makoikoi and Pangwa, no spirits come to their heads;
Madungumaro and Ringwa are especial liars.
They are Muslims in name only, the former are the *matari pungwa*.

The evidence is this, if you want to be told:
When they are in their rituals, on the day when the spirit seizes hold of them,
They become more like devils and they increase their lies.
The spirit of Dewa is a liar, [as is] the spirit of Madogari.

If you want my advice, those of you who listen,
Stop them with fetters, all those who claim these cures.
And those who are rightly-guided shall avoid these people.
And those who deny this are not Muslims, but heretics.[56]

Even though he was trained by Qadiri *shaykhs*, Sh. Abdu'l-Aziz, too, advocated moderation in the performance of *dhikr* and a more fundamentalist Islam. He too spoke out against the excesses of some *dhikiri* in this poem:

He who speaks the name of God does not leap and cough.[57]
This is not the religion of the Prophet, but innovation.
This requires examination; the opinion of the *ᶜulama᾿* should be sought.
Where was this worship of coughing invented?

I ask for proof, even if it angers you.
The Beneficent One usually is beseeched, and his praises are spoken,
But today you clap and sway your necks.
Where was this worship of coughing invented?

Often I see women carrying banners.
They drag their beads and shake their breasts.
This religion is harmful, for it harms the chest.
Where was this worship of coughing invented?

You [*dhikr*] *shaykhs* who peer into holy books,
Your *dhikr* is dancing. Why only dancing?
It might be Lelemama or Kimarua.
Where was this worship of coughing invented?

First it came from Sh. Husain when it was brought here.[58]
In his hands it was true worship, not a play like this.
But in your hands it is competition, noise, and derision.
Where was this worship of coughing invented?

'Dha nadiya li saluti' – all of you know this –

As well as the Friday prayers which God enjoined.
This that you're doing is changing the worship of God.
Where was this worship of coughing invented?

After every prayer you must call upon God
by reciting the Tahlil [99 names of God] and praising His name.
But now you exorcise these spirits and offer them food.
Where was this worship of coughing invented?[59]

Most 'great' *ᶜulamaᵓ* sympathized with the views expressed in these poems. They felt that saint worship and exorcism were *shirk* (innovation) because they put people equal to God. Their view was that men were only slaves to the Almighty; they emphasized fatalism in place of the more manipulative religion of the *waungwana*.[60]

Fundamentalism of this sort, however, was irrelevant to many townspeople and the life they knew. As explained by one missionary observer, Islam 'is interwoven with the social life and traditions of the people. It may not exert much influence on life [?!]; it may be for most only a convention; but no one is harder to convert than the man who has never taken his own religion seriously.' In this case, of course, the author was wrong: townsmen took their religion seriously enough. Their Islam simply was not the Islam of the books which he had expected to find. Further on, he remarks that, 'Men are willing to listen to debates on Christianity and Islam, and are not shocked or even angry when the arguments are against them. They find the argument interesting in itself and the conclusion unimportant.'[61]

The arguments and proofs found in textbooks, of course, were unimportant for the Swahili for whom Islam was a living religion. Most were ignorant of Arabic and too poor to study the necessary texts, so the debates of the sort alluded to above could not help but pass right by them. The Islam of the new *ᶜulamaᵓ* was foreign Islam for most: it did not play an important part in daily life as they knew it. However, when the traditional socio-economic structures of the townspeople were threatened, their social attitudes and dispositions towards traditional Islamic education did change. El-Zein cites a case at Lamu where *waungwana* and the *shurafaᵓ* conflicted over religious doctrine, especially where it concerned marriage and hypergamy. While the *shurafaᵓ* maintained that genealogy determined social status, the *waungwana* claimed that it was *heshima* and *uungwana* – that is, adherence to local traditions and norms. The result was that the *waungwana* began questioning the *baraka* (charisma) of the *shurafaᵓ*, as well as the general validity of their social and religious views.[62]

Similarly, at Mombasa quarrels between the *ᶜulamaᵓ* and the local *waganga* and *walimu* broke out over questions of religious practice. Local *ᶜulamaᵓ*, like Mwisha Hali and the Mazrui, refused to permit *falak* and *raml* (geomancy) to be taught in the mosques. Consequently, as did the *waungwana* of Lamu, the *wamiji* of Mombasa sought outside religious leadership. They threatened to send their children elsewhere (besides the homes of local *ᶜulamaᵓ*) for their religious instruction, and they took over all mosque functions from the reform-minded *ᶜulamaᵓ*. Such dissatisfaction eventually led some to request the (British) Government to enforce an examination of all candidates for the position of *Shaykh al-Islam* in an effort to thwart Mazrui aspirations of winning the appointment. It was this examination which brought Mwinyi Abudi to Mombasa (Chapter 10).[63]

Two other factors caused many Swahili to reject the new *ʿulamaʾ* and their teachings: traditional distrust of foreign *wanazuoni* and distrust of the Government *qadis*. The former has been discussed before and needs no elaboration. Distrust of *qadis* appointed by the Busaidi stemmed from their alleged use as a cat's-paws by the ruling family to claim the lands of deceased *waungwana*. This was especially true of Zanzibar where much of the island was appropriated by the Omanis for their clove plantations. Also, the written Islam accepted in *qadis'* courts was not the Islam of the *waungwana*. Oral evidence, in the form of a poem, for example, of Swahili claims to land (use), probably had no more legal basis in a *qadi's* court than it later did before European magistrates.[64] These topics, however, will be dealt with at greater length in the following chapters.

9

The early colonial era, 1885–1914

It is as difficult in East Africa as it is in other parts of Africa to say exactly when the colonial era began. European influence had been waxing long before 1885. The Sultans of Zanzibar signed successive anti-slave trade treaties with Great Britain in 1828, 1873, and 1876, for example, in addition to treaties of trade and friendship with America (1832), Britain (1839), and France (1844). For decades, these treaties had made European sailors, merchants, and consular officials increasingly familiar sights in coastal towns like Lamu, Mombasa, and Zanzibar. However, 1885 usually is considered to mark the formal onset of the colonial phase in East African history, since it was in 1885 that Kaiser Wilhelm issued the *Schutzbrief* taking under German protection the territories acquired by Karl Peters through treaties.[1] This single action perhaps more than any other ignited Anglo-German rivalry on the coast and in the interior.[2]

Colonial rule did as much to transform coastal life as anything else in the previous history of the coast. Stated directly, the East African coast was transfigured radically and permanently. Furthermore, the most crucial changes occurred in the initial years of actual colonial rule, 1885–1914. In these three decades, the British managed to affect gravely the relationship of the Sultans to their subjects; to re-create the form and function of the old Sultanate to resemble something more like the European notion of a proper governing institution; and, finally, to alter the essential socio-economic underpinnings of life within the coastal towns. As will be seen, coastal peoples reacted to the resulting crisis in their daily lives, as well as to the overall threat to their very civilization, in two basic ways. Some sought to protect the old life by rejecting all that was new and (supposedly) inimical to local institutions and habits, while others sought to preserve the status quo by selectively choosing what aspects of changing conditions could serve their material needs while not affecting basic values.

BILKING AND BREAKING THE SULTANS

Whether or not it was their original intention to do so, the British concept of 'proper' government in Zanzibar and on the East African coast meant driving a wedge between the Sultans and, first, their principal advisors and cronies and, later, the generality of their other subjects.

A whole series of measures, plus innumerable incidents associated with them, contributed to the breakdown of the Sultanate. In Zanzibar, as elsewhere in Africa, Britain had been content with exercising 'paramount influence' before the 1880s. However, beginning with the forced cession of all coastal ports of Tanganyika to the Germans and the accession of Kismayu to Italy in 1888, along with the rebellion of Abushiri, Britain felt constrained to take decisive actions towards creating a formal empire in East Africa and Zanzibar.[3] Based upon an aborted series of negotiations which had taken place in 1877–8 for the cession of the entire East African interior to a private company, in 1888 the Imperial British East Africa Company was chartered by the British Government and given rights by Sultan Barghash to 'open up' the Kenyan hinterlands. Along with this went another agreement that a coastal strip ten miles wide, reaching from Vanga to Kipini, was to be rented to the Company.[4] The next step was a declaration in 1890 of a formal protectorate over Zanzibar. As explained to Sayyid Ali b. Said, its purpose was purely 'defensive' – a measure to pre-empt any German designs on the island kingdom. Initially, promises were made to the Sultan that no interference in Zanzibar's internal affairs was intended if only he would agree to protectorate status.[5] Finally, with the collapse of the IBEA Company in December 1895, Sultan Hamid b. Thuwain was prevailed upon to accept an agreement whereby rule of the Kenya coastal strip was to be entrusted to officers appointed by the Foreign Office – that is, Zanzibar and the Kenya coast were now formally under the 'protection' of Her Majesty's Government.[6]

Promises notwithstanding, within barely a year of the declaration of the Protectorate status of Zanzibar, British Consul Gerald Portal already was initiating a series of 'reforms' in the Zanzibar Government. Having come to Zanzibar from Cromer's Egypt, Portal and his successor, Rennell Rodd, understood but little the principles of informal rule on which the Zanzibar Sultanate ran. What they saw was a 'government' which had no system for the collection and expenditure of state funds, no fixed schedule of wages for *liwalis* and *qadis*, no accounts kept, no ledgers, no budgets, and too many court hangers-on – in short, 'a satire on the assumption of the British Protectorate'.[7] Repelled by what he perceived as, 'the corruption of the officials, the venality of the judges, the lack of public works, the lavish life of the court', Portal's first measure was to create autonomous departments of the treasury, the army, the police, the customs service, a post office, and an office of public works, each of which was to be directed by a European.[8] In addition, a street cleaning service was started, along with harbour improvement and modern street lighting in Zanzibar town. Complete control over the Sultan's finances was assumed and salaries for the Sultan's officials were fixed, while the personnel themselves were put under surveillance. Finally, the entire government was placed under the direction of an English officer, Sir Lloyd Mathews, 'irremovable by the Sultan', who was answerable not only to the Sultan himself, but to the British Consul.[9] When Portal left for Uganda at the end of 1892, Sultan Ali b. Said attempted to rid himself of his 'First Minister', Mathews, but Rodd was of the same mind as his predecessor and pressured S. Ali to retain him.

When S. Ali b. Said died, Rodd took advantage of the usual ambiguities over the succession to appoint as Sultan a person of his own choice, Hamid b. Thuwain, over Khalid b. Barghash. Using his powers to the full, he forced S. Hamid b. Thuwain to accept conditions which reduced his authority merely to the level of a ceremonial functionary. Furthermore, he lessened the size of the Sultan's personal bodyguard and cut him off from the anti-Mathews faction at the court. Finally, the bureaucratization of the government was refined even further with its reorganization around four principal departments: Administration, Military Forces and Police, Post Office, and Customs and Revenue Collection. The administrative heads of all four departments were to be appointed by the Protecting Power, and all four heads were to attend Ministerial councils under the chairmanship of the Chief Minister, Mathews.[10]

The shabbiest incident, however, took place in 1895 when the Foreign Office virtually bilked Hamid b. Thuwain out of £200,000 which had been paid over to the Zanzibar Government (that is, supposedly by the Sultan) in return for their mainland possessions. Originally, the funds had been invested in securities in the name of the Government of Zanzibar. However, with the collapse of the IBEA Company, the Foreign Office decided that the Company's £250,000 in debts should be covered, partly, through the repurchase of the coastal strip which had been leased to the Company: £150,000 was to cover the purchase and an additional £50,000 was to be used to buy up Company capital goods. To make matters worse, however, once the matter had been forced on the Sultan, it was decided that title to the strip was to be transferred from the Sultan to Mathews or to the (by now) Consul-General A. H. Hardinge, and that actual rule over the strip was to be directed by the Foreign Office rather than by the Zanzibar Government. The Sultan was to be paid £10,000 per annum in 'rent', in addition to 3 per cent interest on the £200,000.[11] Perhaps Hardinge best described the position into which the Sultanate had fallen when he wrote that Hamid b. Thuwain,

> was merely a little bird in the claws of an eagle, and as the eagle either could release the little bird or rend it to pieces, so England either could give back to him or tear away from him his dominions as she thought fit.[12]

The final blow to an independent voice for the Sultans in their own Government came in 1896 with the death of Hamid b. Thuwain. Then, for the second time, Khalid b. Barghash attempted to seize the Sultanate from the British by force. The entire incident probably came as close to a full-scale popular revolt against a domineering European presence as had occurred in East Africa since the Abushiri rising against the Germans. According to Cave, Khalid was supported by the Sultan's bodyguard, plus 1,500 to 2,000 supporters whom Khalid had recruited over a period of about three years. The palace was seized by Khalid and a message was sent to Cave that it was to be abandoned.[13] With no reply forthcoming and defensive positions assumed by Khalid's supporters inside, British naval ships bombarded the Sultan's palace. Five hundred of Khalid's retinue were killed, martial law was imposed on Zanzibar, and several Omani *mashayikh* suspected of supporting Khalid were arrested and deported to Machakos.[14]

It is little wonder, then, that the next nominee to the Sultanate was completely supine before British interests. As Hamilton described it, S. Hamud b. Muhammad 'was devoted to the English; his only desire was to please them and to do all they wished', while Pearce regarded him as 'a very intelligent ruler, and intensely English in his sympathies'.[15] Given this situation, it was in Hamud b. Muhammad's reign that Zanzibar is remembered for having 'changed from an Oriental state, governed purely on Eastern lines, to its present condition'.[16]

The greatest change occurred when the administration of the coastal strip and the entire hinterland of British East Africa was put into the hands of Arthur Hardinge, who acted both as Consul-General of Zanzibar and Commissioner for British East Africa. Furthermore, all the senior officials in Zanzibar were formed into an Advisory Council to Hardinge.[17] Hardinge made certain that Europeans secured control over all senior positions, but he also retained all the old *qadis* and *liwalis* who had been appointed under the Sultanate and the brief period of IBEA Company rule in Kenya. Partly in an attempt to absorb personnel from previous administrations, partly due to personal prejudices, and partly because of ideas concerning colonial administration current at that time, Hardinge began a policy of 'native administration' which was distinctly racialist in its assumptions. While recognizing the blows that had been suffered to their prestige over loss of political and social status under British rule, Hardinge sought to establish an efficient civil service staffed by Arabs and Swahili 'of good family'. These were to be employed in judicial and administrative capacities not only on the coast itself, but also in the interior.[18]

Two final administrative upheavals took place prior to 1914. In 1904, with the departure of Hardinge and Mathews, the Governments of British East Africa and Zanzibar each were placed under their own respective Consular representatives.[19] In Kenya, Sir Charles Eliot began a policy which shifted the focus of administration away from the coast and the 'Arabs' to Nairobi and a position which favoured non-Muslims in the recruitment of civil service trainees and employees. Similarly, at Zanzibar, Edward Clarke, head of the Foreign Office's Africa Department, initiated a concatenation of measures, the basic intent of which was to improve the efficiency of the Government at the expense of the privileged position accorded the Arabs. Following up on the recommendations of C. E. Akers that further public works projects were needed for the island and Pemba, Clarke simply had to cut corners and rid the Government of some lower echelon native employees to meet expenses for the new projects.[20]

In 1913, finally, the British Government used the occasion of Clarke's death to formally transfer rule of Zanzibar from the Foreign to the Colonial Office. Thus, all pretence of any sovereign voice for the Sultan in his own Government was removed. This is apparent in the decision to abolish the office of First Minister and the creation of the post of British Resident. These measures combined all the former functions of First Minister and

Consul-General under the general supervision of the Governor of the East African Protectorate, who himself was answerable directly to the Colonial Office.

THE CIVIL LIST IMPOSED

The other means by which the Sultanate was dismembered was through limitations placed on the Sultans' personal expenditures and support of court favourites. As a corollary to this, certain 'undesirables' among the Sultans' personal retinue and advisors were banished from the court or simply jettisoned from the list of court dependants.

The principal instrument by which the Sultans' personal control over expenditure was curtailed was the imposition of the 'civil list'. This first was instituted in 1891 as part of Portal's wider programme for bringing Zanzibar's finances and administration under control. Portal's view of how government should be organized was, of course, that it should be departmentalized, with each department fiscally responsible for its own programmes. The Sultan and his court appears to have been, in Portal's mind, simply a necessary, though inconvenient, institution which had to have a place somewhere in his scheme. Hence, the Sultan and his court were to become another 'department'.[21] In addition, Portal was critical of the patronage system for its inefficiency and slack organization and as it was an independent source of power to the Sultan which could remain outside his (Portal's) control. He criticized, for example, the Sultan's habit of lending out his 'good many' personal properties to his retainers and hangers-on 'free of rent as a crude system of patronage'.[22] Elsewhere, he expressed dismay over the numerous 'irregular soldiers', 'armed slaves', retainers, and dependants of all kinds who never worked and who drew a regular income, yet 'were the cause of innumerable brawls and disturbances and a constant danger to the public peace'. In this connection, he felt that the Sultan's income, in the amount of Rs 18,000 a month, merely was being used for bribes 'to keep the peace'. Thus, the Sultan's income had to be trimmed to Rs 17,283 per month, representing about half the total income of the Government of Zanzibar – still too much in Portal's opinion, since it stood in the way of his pet public works projects and a proposed take-over of the administration of British East Africa from the Imperial British East Africa Company.[23]

Generally, the British consuls used their support of each new successor to the Sultanate as a lever to extract concessions for further reductions of the civil list. By October 1892, for example, Portal again was talking about another reduction as a means of further manipulating S. Ali b. Said and his advisors and confidants. Naturally, Sayyid Ali resisted and suggested that, rather than dismiss his retainers, it would have been better to get rid of 'all the European officers who had been introduced into the administration during the last year'. However, Portal managed to reduce expenditures to Rs 10,000 per month. No trouble from the five to six hundred court retainers was expected, though, as most of them feared that the property they held at Zanzibar could be seized by the Government. Those who resisted and did not own property simply were to be 'sent back in dhows to their native country of Muscat'.[24] When Ali died, and Hamid b. Thuwain was being pushed as the new Sultan, part of the conditions for which British succour was to be given was,

> That the Sultan's Private Purse [*sic*] for the present be restricted to 10,000 Rs monthly, and the subsidies to His highness's relations and pensions be continued but subject to strict investigation. Any reductions afterwards decided on in the Royal Establishment to be agreed to.[25]

While the British permitted an additional Rs 3,000 to be restored to the civil list in 1895 to sweeten their use of Zanzibar funds to cover the IBEA Company losses in Kenya, they again used the accession of a new Sultan as another occasion for deeper cuts.[26] Cooperative in matters concerning his court expenses as he was in all things, Hamud b. Muhammad agreed to stay within prescribed limits on his personal expenditures. Cave reported that 'he has put down the more useless part of his predecessor's establishment', that there were no more 'big entertainments', and that it was Mathews, in fact, who now governed the purse.[27] Also, not appreciating the charismatic nature of the Sultan's style of rule, it had been agreed that the Sultans no longer would have the right to bestow expensive medals or gifts of money gratuitously on whomever they wished.[28] Willing to sacrifice almost anything to see his son, Ali b. Hamud, succeed to the throne after him, Hamud b. Muhammad agreed to a fifth reduction in 1901 in exchange for guarantees from the British.[29] The final alteration in the civil list took place in 1905 when, in return for administrative rights to the Sultan's 'crown lands' (that is, personal *waqfed* property), Ali b. Hamud's civil list was increased by Rs 1,600 per year.[30]

What all this means is that between 1891 and 1901 and through five cuts, the Sultans' personal expenditures were reduced roughly from about Rs 36,000 a month to something under Rs 10,000 per month, with a slight rise to between Rs 10,000 to Rs 12,000 in 1905. Besides losing almost all voice in the management of their own government, 'the vast horde of servants, parasites were weeded out' with a 67–70 per cent reduction in the monies over which they formerly had control. Naturally, foreign meddling in the relationships that had prevailed between the Sultans and their entourage did not go unresisted. Administrative and fiscal measures of the sorts delineated above were devised specifically, in fact, to jettison the numerous 'undesirables' with whom the Sultans surrounded themselves and who counselled resistance to further expatriate meddling in the Sultans' domains. While smaller, less threatening fry fell by the wayside, it is quite obvious in their correspondence with the Foreign Office that successive British consuls were pursuing bigger fish in the formulation of their policies at Zanzibar. Since at least two of these figures were ʿulamaʾ who have been mentioned at various other parts of this book, it would be especially useful at this juncture to discuss the political entanglements in which they had become ensnared since such involvements were central features of their stories.

All these personalities share one characteristic which has made them such visible figures in the available source materials, namely, they resisted European efforts at control, not to mention European cultural influences, and they all suffered various forms of exile as a consequence. Three of these were Ibadi *°ulama°* and *wazirs* and, unfortunately, nothing much except their names is known about them. Ali b. Salim Meskiri, one Yorubi Deremki, and Abdu'l-Aziz b. Muhammad Deremki all were large land and slave owners who were removed from the court of Ali b. Said for giving the Sultan 'bad counsel'.[31]

While little is known about the above individuals, considering the time when they were banished from the court, the conditions of their exile were probably quite similar to those which led to the banishment of Sh. Abdu'l-Aziz b. Abdu'l-Ghany, Peera Dewji, and Muhammad Muhammad Bakashmar. Two facts seem to emerge in looking at the stories of all these individuals. First, they all were ostracized about the same time, c. 1889–90, when Anglo-German rivalry was at its height. Second, in at least two known cases there was an obvious change of British attitudes towards these men as concern over possible betrayals to the Germans began to surface.

Sh. Abdu'l-Aziz was encountered above in the discussions of the various Benadir *°ulama°*, so only a few additional words are necessary here. As mentioned already, Sh. Abdu'l-Aziz served as *qadi* of Zanzibar from the time of S. Barghash, but, since he was a close personal friend of S. Khalifa b. Said, the years in which he was most influential were during the reigns of Sayyids Khalifa and Ali b. Said (1888–93). Along with Peera Dewji and Bakashmar, he was one of the 'three favourites' among those closest to these two Sultans.

Also, as in the case of Peera Dewji, his final undoing in 1893 involved suspicions of his complicity with the Germans. This was a rather interesting conclusion to a bizarre series of events which reflect the nature of the tense, three-way power struggle among the Sultans, Britain, and Germany which was enacted between about 1885 and 1893. At first, almost no mention of Sh. Abdu'l-Aziz appears in official British correspondence, despite the many years which he had spent at the courts of all the Sultans from Barghash onwards. When first encountered in this correspondence, he appears as a reactionary 'kazi' who advised Khalifa to execute all criminals in Zanzibar prison and to restore the island completely to the letter of Islamic law. This followed the traumatic series of events which resulted in Portuguese, German, Italian, and English seizure and parcelling up of all the Sultans' mainland 'empire'.[32] In the correspondence following these incidents, it is clear that it was Abdu'l-Aziz, along with Peera Dewji and Bakashmar, who was counselling resistance to the Anglo-German blockade based on a complete restoration of the Sultans' possessions to Quranic law. Euan-Smith, for example, reported that Khalifa was 'in the hands of low advisors who virtually ruled the State', and that, 'he had now determined to rule and be guided solely by the precepts of the Koran'.[33]

Abdu'l-Aziz was in and out of trouble in the years that followed. When next we hear of him, it is the Germans who are threatening to have him deported from Zanzibar since, 'he was in the habit generally of thwarting their desires and acting inimically to German interests'.[34] The occasion this time was a German effort to get Sultan Khalifa b. Said to grant them full rights to the ports of the Mrima coast at a reduced rental rate.

Sh. Abdu'l-Aziz managed to stay on longer at court than did Peera Dewji and Bakashmar, but again it was the enmity of the British establishment which undid him. Pressure had begun mounting already by 1890 when, following the departures of Peera Dewji and *Shaykh* Bakashmar, Euan-Smith opined that,

> the Sultan's character is such that unless some generally trusted person of weight and position succeeds in attaining such a post near his Highness, the direction of affairs and control of the executive ... will inevitably fall into the hands of [Abdu'l-Aziz and one Ahmad Amari] and a state of affairs similar to that which existed in the time of Bakushmar and Peera Dewji will thus be recreated.[35]

By March 1890, Euan-Smith suspected that the *ᶜalim* was reporting all daily correspondence between the Sultan and the British agency to the Germans and was 'on terms of confidential intimacy with the German Consulate'.[36] After this, it was only a matter of time before Abdu'l-Aziz was out of the picture. While he managed to stay on until the death of S. Ali b. Said, the British again used their support for Hamid b. Thuwain as leverage to finally securing an agreement for his dismissal.

Though he figures prominently in official correspondence *c.* 1888–9, little substantial material is available on Peera Dewji. An old enemy of Princess Salme bti. Said, she remarked that he was a Hindu and had served as head of Barghash's personal espionage network.[37] A former lamp cleaner, he was 'extremely clever, capable, and unscrupulous' and rose through stealth to become a 'jack-of-all-trades' to Barghash and Khalifa b. Said.[38] Writing very unflatteringly of him, Reute mentioned that he devoted 'his services to the sovereign of Zanzibar in the highest and lowest positions'. He was in charge of all diplomatic affairs and, she alleges, sold his influence to the highest bidder since he was paid a miserly $30 a month.[39]

Euan-Smith felt that he was 'a standing danger to the best interests of the Sultan of Zanzibar', and that as a British Indian subject he should be deported to Aden. This he managed to procure by early 1889 when he reported that 'the consensus of opinion on his head ... leaves in my mind no doubt whatever that in the person of Peera Dewji, English interests in Zanzibar ... have an active and uncompromising enemy'. As in Abdu'l-Aziz's case, suspicions that he was trying to ally himself with the Germans 'in open hostility to the English' produced his removal from the side of Khalifa b. Said.[40]

Of the three individuals discussed here, perhaps Muhammad Muhammad Bakashmar's career is the most interesting. Like Abdu'l-Aziz, he enjoyed a long career and was an *ᶜalim*. Originally from the Hadhramawt, he started in the service of S. Thuwain b. Said of Oman who, because of his usefulness, recommended him to his father, Said b. Sultan, under whom he began his career in Zanzibar. He subsequently was put in charge of court finances under Sayyids Majid and Barghash. He travelled widely and, among other things, visited Britain several times as Barghash's representative to purchase men-of-war for the Sultan's navy.[41]

It is again interesting to see that as circumstances changed, so did British attitudes towards this man. In 1868, Churchill described him as 'a shrewd, intelligent man who was much appreciated by my predecessors'. Indeed, his relations with the British had been so amicable that he is said to have fallen into disgrace at one time for having been 'too friendly' with Colonel Playfair.[42] By 1872, however, Kirk claimed that, fearing to become involved in disputes between the British agency and Barghash, he was refusing to meet with any white man or to call on them or be sent as an emissary to their consulates.[43] In negotiations over the 1873 anti-slave trade treaty, Badger reported that as one of Barghash's two *wazirs*, he was notably courteous to the British party, 'even affectionate', taking a position in the discussions which at times supported the Sultan's point of view and at other times supported the position of the British envoys.[44]

By 1888, however, the trials of S. Khalifa over the partition of the mainland deeply affected Bakashmar's position and attitudes towards the Europeans. As first minister to Khalifa, he and the Sultan secretly encouraged the Abushiri resistance to the Anglo-German blockade and, apparently, he counselled Khalifa to renounce it publicly.[45] He came under the same proscriptions by the English and the Germans for his position as did Peera Dewji and Sh. Abdu'l-Aziz.[46] By July 1889, both the British and the Germans were seeking his deportation, calling him 'the greatest enemy in this country to progress, to the abolition of slavery, to the success of the German and English companies, and to Europeans in general'.[47] As did his colleagues, he clearly saw what had been happening to coastal society and religion. Therefore, where formerly he had been courteous, even friendly to Europeans, by the time of his exile to Aden in August 1889, Portal noted what he termed his 'narrow minded fanaticism and his hatred of all things European'.[48]

However, Bakashmar's resistance was not over. He remained an independently wealthy man and his temporary exile to Eastern Arabia apparently opened his eyes to some of the news of anti-European, Pan-Islamic activities and writings of other Muslims from other parts of the Islamic world. Within a few years he was back in Zanzibar where, along with others, he began influencing the thoughts and opinions of a new generation of East African Muslims towards accepting new modes of Islamic ideology. Coming from Egypt and Syria, this new reform movement was meant as a response to the intellectual challenges posed by the Christian West. This phase of Bakashmar's life will be described in the next chapter.

In conclusion, then, the primary administrative aim of the British at Zanzibar was the effective isolation of the Sultans from their subjects, from those who counselled resistance, and even from their own administrative machinery. Where formerly the Sultans stood at the centre of coastal political, economic, and judicial proceedings by dint of their personal wealth and charisma, by the 1890s they had been removed from the centre of public life on the coast. The exact degree of their loss of touch with their subjects can be seen in the 'coronation' scene which greeted Sayyid Hamud b. Muhammad upon his succession in 1896. Where formerly the Sultan's *baraza* consisted of his vast entourage of subject clan heads, town *wazee*, relatives, *ʿulamaʾ*, *liwalis*, *wazirs*, soldiers, and other dependants, the *baraza* which was introduced to the new Sultan by his First Minister, Lloyd Mathews, was described as, '... a motley group, Parsees, Goanese, Indians, in different richness and sobriety of costume, completely filling the Throneroom'.[49]

CIVIL SERVICE AND JUDICIAL CHANGES

During the months of crisis, 1888–9, when the Anglo-German blockade was in effect and the Abushiri rebellion was raging on the Mrima coast, MacKenzie and the IBEA Company were in a parlous situation trying to bring Company rule to British East Africa. To ameliorate local feelings against alien intrusions, the Company followed local practices in sending presents and subsidies to town *wazee* and the elders of neighbouring mainland peoples. Furthermore, an effort was made to give the impression that the Company was only acting as the agent (*wakil*) of the Sultan[50] and that no personnel changes were made in the existing administration (such as it was). Existing *liwalis* were courted and groomed as instruments of the Company. While some resisted, notables like Salim b. Khalfan al-Busaidi of Takaungu, Said b. Hamid of Malindi, Abdallah b. Hamid of Lamu, and, for a while, even Sh. Mbarak b. Rashid Mazrui of Gazi acquiesced in this arrangement in so far as they were able to reap personal benefits from it.[51]

Always an Arabophile, when Arthur Hardinge found himself dually appointed to the positions of Consul-General of Zanzibar and British High Commissioner of British East Africa, he advocated the continuation of administrative policies begun under IBEA Company rule. To exercise a form of Indirect Rule, he established a system of civil administration in Kenya which was run essentially by English Sub-Commissioners and District Officers in Mombasa, Lamu, Kismayu, and Machakos, aided by District Administrators. Placed below these were the native *liwalis* who 'still exercise side by side with the District Officers a limited jurisdiction over the native population'. Within their *wilayets* (sub-districts), they administered justice and generally acted as intermediaries between the British authorities and the Muslim population.[52]

At the lowest rung of the administrative ladder was the village *shaykh* or *shaykhs*. Where formerly each town or village had its own *wazee* who performed a variety of civic functions, now they had become paid petty officials of the State whose powers were clearly defined and circumscribed. Defined by one official as 'glorified policemen with statutory powers of arrest', they also provided mandatory labour when called for and settled small, local disputes.[53] Being a relatively minor position, that of the town *shaykh* remained essentially unaltered through the administrative changes that took place after 1901.

Hardinge's view of the superiority of the Arab–Swahili population of the

coast led him initially to advocate a system which was centred adminis-
tratively on the coast and which envisioned a special place reserved for the
'Arab' within the Protectorate governmental apparatus. As Hardinge himself stated,

> The Arab and upper class Swahilis are the only natives ... who can read, or
> who have any comprehension of politics, justice, or government. Community
> of religion, language and intermarriage gives them an influence over negro
> coast populations, which the European stranger cannot as a rule possess in
> the same degree, and even in the interior they are as Africans more at home
> than he can be. Only they have thoroughly learnt the lesson that he is the
> predominant partner, and must be obeyed as such, their influence applied
> under his control may be ... very useful: it is, I think, very important for the
> future of East Africa that a native administrative element should, if possible,
> be formed and trained up out of the Arabs and higher Swahili.[54]

Hardinge thus proposed that a school be built out of *waqf* monies for the
training of young Arabs and *waungwana*, 'so as to qualify them for posts in
the native political and administrative services...'[55]

The privileged position reserved for coastal people in Hardinge's scheme
was ended by his successors. Despite his expressed wishes, Hardinge left
neither a training institute for coastal officials nor a systematic method of
recruiting local peoples for government service. Consequently, representation of coastal Arabs and Swahili lost ground to upcountry peoples for a
variety of reasons. First of all, following the closing of the slave trade in the
1890s, there was a fall-off in agricultural production and a general erosion
in the economic power of the coast. Furthermore, at the very time when
upcountry converts to Christianity were taking advantage of educational
opportunities offered in the missionary schools, only a very few coastal
Muslims were willing to send their children to school. Consequently,
traditional coastal education in the Quran schools and *madrasas* meant
short-comings for coastal peoples in respect to modern needs.[56]

The most important occurrence which resulted in lost ground for
Muslims in the Protectorate Civil Service, however, was the official change
of policy during the administrations of Sir Charles Eliot and Sir Donald
Stewart. With the extension of the Uganda railway to Kisumu and the
subsequent relocation of the Protectorate headquarters to Nairobi, most
administrative concerns thereafter centred on problems of white settlement
of the highlands and the 'pacification' of the interior. Along with this
growing preoccupation with the problems of the interior went a policy
which favoured upcountry representation in the administrative apparatus.

A reflection of the declining position of the coast and coastal people in
the Protectorate administration was the demotion of three *liwali*-ships to
administrative posts of less importance. Due to the emigration of large
numbers of people to larger towns like Mombasa, Dar es Salaam, and
Nairobi, Takaungu and Mambrui were demoted to *mudirates* in 1905, and
in 1906 the same thing happened to Gazi.[57] In 1928, only the position of
town *shaykh* remained unaltered. By then there were no *liwalis* or *akidas*:
the only native officers between the village *shaykh* and the District Officer
were *mudirs*.[58]

THE JUDICIAL INSTITUTION

From the very inception of their involvement in East Africa, Europeans displayed a marked willingness to interfere in local religious and judicial proceedings. Part of this, of course, was due to cultural misunderstanding. At Mombasa during the period of 'Owen's Protectorate' in 1825, for example, Lieutenant Emery demonstrated his ignorance of the differences between locally perceived and administered law and the law of written tradition, as well as of local factional politics. In a dispute over what he considered the wrongful incarceration of a man found guilty of a crime by the local *qadi*, Zakaram, Emery wrote,

> Went to the fort [Jesus] and made known to the Sultan the conduct [of] Zakaram and told him it was impossible ... I then informed [him] how ignorant Zakaram was of the Koran (my being informed by some of the headmen of the place) and his unfitness to hold such a position – that it ought to be a man of the greatest integrity, so that justice should be done on both sides. He said that justice was out of the question at Mombasa, as he always acted as he thought fit, and if Zakaram did not know the Koran, he would soon learn. I then informed him, as the place is to be governed by the laws of the Koran, those laws shall not be broken while I am at Mombasa.[59]

Similarly, misunderstanding the local customs of gift-giving to *wazee* and *ᶜulamaᵓ* in exchange for justice rendered, Clifford Crawford convicted Sh. Muhammad Qasim Maamiri and the *qadi*, Sh. Sulaiman b. Ali Mazrui, of bribery and 'gross neglect of duty', in a famous case which occurred at Mombasa in 1896. For this, the *qadi* was sentenced to three months in prison, while Sh. Muhammad Qasim, accused of abetment, received one month and a fine of Rs 200.[60] Indeed, Foreign Office correspondence is rife with allegations of bribery and fault-finding of the local religious establishments. The final area in which there appears to have been misapprehension of local Islamic practices was over the slavery issue. The classic case which illustrates this concerned British attempts in the 1890s to impose a total ban on slavery and to emancipate all remaining slaves through a plan to 'repurchase' their freedom from their masters. Naturally, this failed in most instances since the Europeans did not realize that a slave could be freed only by his master, according to Islamic law, and that compensation could not be obtained for an illegal act perpetrated by a third party.

Then, of course, even where Englishmen knew and understood local customs and legal practices, they could show little sympathy where they conflicted with English law and European sensibilities. Thus, in 1898 Hardinge wrote that,

> Meanwhile, as civilization spreads and European institutions gain a greater hold in the country, these primitive individualistic conceptions ... will gradually disappear and give place to views more consonant with our own as to the rights and duties of society as a whole.[61]

Thus, a combination of cultural misunderstanding and patronization lay behind the judicial changes introduced into Zanzibar and Kenya after 1891.

In most respects, throughout this period judicial proceedings in Zanzibar and in British East Africa remained under separate jurisdictions. In Zanzibar and in Kenya, the Sultans continued to appoint *qadis*. In the Kenya coastal strip, while Islamic law was applied in its general principles under the ultimate authority of the Sultan, according to the concession of 1887, IBEA Company officials could be appointed as judges subject to the Sultan's approval. In 1889, however, the 1887 Article of Concession was altered so that such appointments would require only the consultation and confirmation of the Sultan. Even more important though was the division of jurisdiction which was proposed under these agreements: for the first time European magistrates were appointed to try 'criminal' cases, while *qadis* were to be assigned only to hear 'civil' disputes, 'such as are ordinarily tried by kathis' (implying, of course, that such was past practice).[62]

When British East Africa was taken over by the Foreign Office as a Protectorate in 1895, Hardinge stated that, while the coast would remain under the sovereignty of the Sultan, he himself would assume ultimate control of the judicial system. While *qadis* and *ᶜulamaᵓ* would be 'honoured', no clause providing for the appointment of *qadis* was included in the 1895 treaty.[63] Henceforth, the only functions of the *qadis* were to try 'civil' cases and to serve as legal consultants to *liwalis* and District Officers.[64]

Between 1897 and 1899, a number of very crucial changes were made in policy concerning the application of Islamic law both in the Protectorate and in Zanzibar. The Native Courts Regulations, under the East African Order in Council of 1897, empowered the Courts Commissioners of Kenya to make rules and orders for administration of 'native courts', including alterations in any native law or custom. By these regulations, two classes of native courts were created. One was a system headed by a High Court of Zanzibar and presided over by the British Consul-General, and assisted by two British magistrates, which administered the Indian Civil Procedure Code and the Indian Penal and Criminal Procedures Codes. This system was to follow general principles of Islamic law in civil and criminal cases tried within the coastal strip. The Regulations also instituted Provincial Courts under the title of second-class District Magistracies, held by Sub-Commissioners.[65]

Parallel to the native courts system presided over by European judges was another system of courts which, at least by appearances, seems to have been designed specifically to deal with the problems of administering justice to Muslim subjects of the Protectorate. This system was headed by a Chief Native Court of the Protectorate which met regularly at Mombasa, twice annually at Lamu, and once a year at Kismayu and Machakos. This court had appeal rights to the aforementioned High Court of Zanzibar. Below the Chief Native Court were the Native Provincial Courts, administering the full criminal code of an Indian District Magistracy; the Native District Courts, empowered to administer the codes of a second-class Indian Magistracy; and the Petty Native Courts, with the administrative authority of a third-class Indian Magistracy. As had been the case before 1897, provision was made for 'native assessors' (or *mufti*) to advise on Islamic law and to issues *fatwas*. Within this system, also, were the Courts of *Liwalis*, on which were conferred the civil and criminal powers of the Native District Courts (presided over by British District Officers), and the *Qadis* Courts with jurisdiction over matters affecting the 'personal status and religious matters' of Muslims. Besides appeal to higher courts within the Native Courts hierarchy, the *Qadis* Courts also could appeal to the court of a *Shaykh al-Islam* (at Mombasa) who was empowered and appointed under the provisions of the 1897 Order in Council.[66] Until 1907, *qadis* were appointed by the Protecting Power with the (theoretical) consent of the Sultan.

Complaining of 'irregularities' in the proceedings of *Qadis* Courts at Zanzibar and of the lack of public confidence in *qadis*' 'purity, integrity, and independence', Hardinge promoted a Native Courts Decree for Zanzibar which was issued in 1899.[67] This measure permitted the implementation of a Native Courts system for Zanzibar and Pemba on the same general order as that of the East African Protectorate. However, the major difference was that, as in days past, the Sultan's court continued to exist to which cases could be referred or to which those of the Sultan's subjects who so desired could go to settle their cases. Below this 'Supreme Court' was the Chief Native Court, called the Court for Zanzibar and Pemba, which was presided over by two *qadis*, one Shafii and one Ibadi. Next were the District Courts, presided by *qadis* in Zanzibar town and by *liwalis* in the outlying areas.[68]

Due largely to S. Ali b. Hamud's lack of training in Islamic law, the next major changes in Zanzibar's judiciary took place in 1908. As early as 1905, Cave was complaining of irregularities in the supervision of *qadis* both by the two *muftis* of the Court for Zanzibar and Pemba and by the Sultan himself. His proposal was that the Sultan's Court be put under a British barrister.[69] Taking advantage of Ali b. Hamud's unpopularity with many of his subjects (because of his European education and tastes) and of a rift between the young Sultan and S. Ahmad b. Sumayt, the British managed to get thirty or forty signatures on a petition to the Foreign Office seeking the remand of all judicial powers from the Sultan's hands.[70] The Zanzibar Courts Decree of 1908 established ultimate control of the Sultan's Court to British magistrates, with two *qadis* as assessors. At the same time, more Europeans were appointed to supervise the *liwalis*, since, 'the Arab has no idea of time or punctuality'.[71] Finally, some changes were made in the old Court for Zanzibar and Pemba. Where formerly the two *qadis* of the Court had combined powers equal to those of the European District Magistrate who sat on the Court (when requested by the Sultans or the two *qadis*), the powers of the magistrate were now increased. The 1908 decree allowed the European magistrate to sit alone on the Court, to sit without the Sultan's permission, and to decide cases with 'somewhat more extensive powers than the Arab *Kathis*'.[72]

One other example of British interference in Islamic law in East Africa is the appointment of *Waqf* Commissions in the East African Protectorate and Zanzibar. The creation of the *Waqf* Commission of Kenya is important

176

because it comprised the earliest ordinances regarding the application of the *Shariᶜa* in East Africa and it introduced a range of reforms which clearly were contrary to legal practice formerly prevalent in Kenyan coastal towns. Specifically, these ordinances were an eclectic patchwork of provisions taken from various schools of Islamic law and were applied without distinction of sectarian differences to all local Muslims.

Thus, in March 1899, Hardinge proposed the creation of a commission charged with the control and administration of *waqf* (endowed) charities in two of Kenya's coastal provinces to see that they were being utilized for the purposes specified in the *waqf*.[73] A decree creating the *Waqf* Commission was issued in 1900, appointing Salim b. Khalfan al-Busaidi, Ali b. Salim al-Busaidi, Sh. Muhammad Qasim al-Maamiri, and one Ali b. Umar as commissioners. They were to hold office until they retired or were removed.[74]

Defining two types of *waqf* – *waqf ahli* ('family' *waqf*), created for the benefit of an individual or family, and *waqf khayri* ('charity' *waqf*), an endowment made for a 'charitable or benevolent public purpose' – the Commission assumed the administration of a *waqf* under various circumstances. It could assume responsibility for a *waqf* on the application of its trustees; if there were no properly constituted trustees; or if any trustee, following an enquiry, was found to be acting in an unauthorized or improper manner. In all situations, the Commission could not act in deciding matters of endowed property without consulting a *qadi* beforehand.[75] In cases where it was determined that the trustees were mishandling property, the Commission could apply the *waqf* and its revenues, in the case of a *waqf khayri*, in a manner thought suitable for the benefit of the stated beneficiaries. In the event that a judgement was not operable, property could be sold by the Commission and the proceeds applied for the benefit of all Muslims.[76] Out of this last provision, a 'surplus fund' was created which was used by the Commission for the upkeep of various mosques which otherwise were not endowed.

In 1905 a similar *Waqf* Commission was instituted for Zanzibar. Primarily, this was created for the same reason that, later, the Sultan's Court was taken out of the control of Ali b. Hamud – that is, it was deemed that the Sultan was insufficiently trained to apply Islamic law in cases involving property.[77] The *Waqf* Commission Decree set up two Commissions, each consisting of one European government official, one Sunni *qadi*, and one Ibadi *qadi*, all of whom were to be appointed by the First Minister. Their function was to register all *waqf* and to administer all *waqfed* property for which there was 'no properly constituted Trustee or Trustees'. Furthermore, the Commissioners were empowered to call upon trustees 'of any *waqf*' to satisfy them that the property [was] being properly administered'. If it was not being 'properly administered', the Commission could reappoint alternative trustees. Any excess funds from *waqf* property would be reapplied for 'charitable purposes on behalf of the Mohamedans'. Finally, permission for the construction of any new mosque in Zanzibar had to be obtained from the Commission.[78]

Table 6: *Civil cases tried by* liwalis *and* qadis *in Lamu, 1910–17.*

Years	Liwali	Qadi
1910/11	151	71
1911/12	343	49
1912/13	137	39
1913/14	217	68
1914/15	194	53
1915/16	176	44
1916/17	114	38

COLLABORATORS

One thing emerges clearly from the various accounts of the imposition of British rule in Zanzibar and Kenya. While most lost something from it, a few of the old elite not only managed to survive these changes, but also contined to profit from the experience.

Foremost among those who benefited were a few 'Arab' clans who, in the racially constituted social hierarchy established under the English, contrived to extend their power through appointments obtained to *liwali*-ships and *mudirates*. Of course, the *liwalis* had been emerging in the new power elite on the coast since well before the onset of European hegemony. In the administration of Islamic law, for example, it will be recalled that the Sultans increasingly had come to rely on their representatives in the coastal towns in the selection of *qadis*.[79] Some field informants also related how, under the Busaidi, some *liwalis* managed by degrees to supersede the voices of local elders in town affairs at Lamu. Power in deciding legal matters, for one thing, came to be shared between the *liwalis* and the local *walimu* or *qadis*.[80]

The same trends were accelerated under the British. Certain individuals and families entrusted as *liwalis* under colonial rule took advantage of the even greater power at their backs for personal aggrandizement. Thus, where *liwalis* previously had exercised *de facto* power in deciding local disputes over the voices of local *walimu*, their power was given a *de jure* base in the judiciary introduced under colonial tutelage. Furthermore, under the British, the actual number of cases handled by *liwalis* grew at the expense of the *qadis*' courts. Tables for the number of cases, both 'civil' and 'criminal', handled by the *qadis* and *liwalis* of Lamu from 1910/11 to 1916/17, for instance, indicate that *liwalis* averaged 45.15 per cent of all cases handled, while the *qadis* averaged only 8.63 per cent.[81]

It is noteworthy that even in the category of 'civil' cases – that is, cases involving the domestic, private lives of Muslims that were originally designated the proper domain of 'religious' law in the Judicial Ordinances of 1898 – *liwalis* tried 42.46 per cent of these cases, while *qadis* handled a mere 11.54 per cent.

Table 7: *Criminal cases tried by* liwalis *and* qadis *in Lamu, 1910–17.*

Years	Liwali	Qadi
1910/11	280	—
1911/12	—	—
1912/13	145	—
1913/14	28	—
1914/15	9	—
1915/16	70	—
1916/17	30	—

Foremost among the *liwalis* to profit from European rule in East Africa were Salim b. Muhammad Muhashami, Mbarak b. Ali Hinawi, and Sir Ali b. Salim, son of Salim b. Khalfan Busaidi – all former *liwalis* of Mombasa. A. I. Salim has studied these individuals, especially Sir Ali b. Salim, and points out their one common characteristic. All three were missionary educated at a time in East Africa when most coastal families were shunning such opportunities.[82] Coming from the wealthy and opportunistic Banu Salim b. Khalfan of Malindi, Ali b. Salim followed in his father's footsteps in becoming a *liwali* of Mombasa. Ambitious, as well as being a Busaidi, both Salim b. Khalfan and Ali b. Salim collaborated with the British in every way to frustrate the position of the Mazrui. While a *liwali* of Mambrui, for instance, Ali cooperated with efforts to eject, finally, Mbarak b. Rashid from Kenya. It was also Ali b. Salim who prevented Sulaiman b. Ali Mazrui from becoming the first British-appointed *Shaykh al-Islam* of Kenya colony (see Chapter 10). Furthermore, he actively recruited soldiers in East Africa during World War I. For their efforts, the Banu Salim b. Khalfan all were decorated, paid salaries comparable to those drawn by Europeans in the administration, and, while other *liwalis* were being demoted to *mudirs* or *akidas*, the Banu Salim b. Khalfan were being cited as the exception to the 'incapable or effete' Arab administrative officers under the British and were allowed to retain their *liwali*-ships.[83]

Needless to say, in the hierarchical society of British Kenya, 'Arab' *liwalis* like the Banu Salim b. Khalfan were atypical and universally resented. It is for this reason that, despite the good intentions that went into its implementation, the *Waqf* Commission faced growing dissatisfaction among the *wamiji* of Mombasa. With men like Salim b. Khalfan and Sir Ali b. Salim appointed as Commissioners, along with Europeans, by the twenties and thirties the Twelve Tribes were complaining openly over a lack of representation on the Commission, even though most *waqfed* land in the area belonged to them.[84]

The *qadis* themselves, of course, were affected by administrative and judicial measures introduced by the British. The new system interfered with old ways in a variety of areas. For one thing, the very law they were supposed to administer, the Indian Codes, often was alien to them. Secondly, their jurisdiction was narrowed only to matters of marriage, divorce, and inheritance. Thirdly, procedures for their appointments passed totally out of local townspeople's hands and new methods were introduced. The power of local *liwalis*, such as the Banu Salim b. Khalfan, became paramount in the selection process. Occasionally, too, new measures like written examinations were introduced for prospective candidates to *qadi*-ships.[85]

Qadis who did cooperate with the Administration often were in for a lot of criticism from their fellow townsmen. Occasionally, evidence of this appears in correspondence between field officers and the Foreign Office. In 1907, for example, C. E. Akers reported strong feelings in Zanzibar 'against certain of their countrymen serving in the administration'. Particularly, the two *Mashayikh al-Islam*, the Sunni Sh. Burhan b. Abdu'l-Aziz and the Ibadi Sh. Nasur b. Salim ar-Ruwayhi were singled out.[86] Typically, where there was criticism it involved accusations of bribery or adverse rumours concerning the competence of the *qadi* in question in matters of the *Shari*c*a*.[87]

While most *c*ulama* resisted European encroachments in some form, a few, as in the case of the *liwalis*, collaborated with the British and managed to advance their careers considerably by doing so. The first of these to appear in official British correspondence was Sh. Sulaiman b. Ali Mandhry, whose career has been discussed already. An opportunist, he served as a liaison between S. Majid b. Said and the British consulate. Frequently, he supported the British cause in their representations to the Sultan. For this, Churchill reported that Sh. Sulaiman often was the beneficiary of presents sent by the British establishment.[88] Cited by Reute for having been the 'evil spirit' who fomented the quarrel between Majid and Barghash, when the latter ascended to power in 1870, Sh. Sulaiman found himself in very comprised circumstances.[89] In this situation, Churchill felt duty-bound to protect his old ally, 'on account of the services he had rendered to His Majesty's Government during the lifetime of Seyed Majid'.[90] In the end, though, for his own safety he had to be removed to India.

Another shadowy figure, one S. Muhammad b. Saif, is mentioned in official correspondence. All we know is that this *c*alim* was a confidential advisor to Sayyid Hamid b. Thuwain. He was removed by the Sultan in the end, though, because he was 'thoroughly loyal to the protecting power'.[91]

Considering how Sh. Abdu'l-Aziz b. Abdu'l-Ghany al-Amawy was so opposed to a European presence in East Africa, it is somewhat surprising to learn that his son, Sh. Burhan, was perhaps more closely allied with British interests in East Africa than any other *c*alim*. His initial appointment and rise to a position of importance probably had to do with his personal friendship with Sayyid Hamud b. Muhammad. However, the most notable feature of his career was his running feud with S. Ahmad b. Sumayt. As is common among intellectuals, inevitably there were some who envied S. Ahmad's reputation and who, therefore, aligned themselves with Sh. Burhan. This alliance tried on several occasions to curry favour with the Protecting Power while doing everything possible to cast S. Ahmad in a bad light. Playing upon Sultan Ali b. Hamud's fears of S. Ahmad's widespread influence, they managed temporarily to have S. Ahmad rusticated as the *qadi* of the rural *wilayets* of Zanzibar.[92] Ultimately, their design failed, but Sh. Burhan was recognized as the Sunni *mufti* of Zanzibar by the British and was rewarded with the largest salary paid to any *qadi* in Zanzibar.[93]

Sh. Burhan's most notable service to Britain was his espionage activities against German East Africa during World War I. Taking advantage of people's movements between Zanzibar and the German territories, with relative ease he was able to gather considerable intelligence on German movements and activities. Finally, one of his spies was captured and the Germans tried unsuccessfully to make the British believe that Burhan was a double agent. He retired in 1932, and, in honour of his services, he was allowed to continue in the use of his old office until he died three years later.[94]

ECONOMIC CHANGES

The roots of coastal impoverishment during the colonial phase, like those of certain political developments, reached back to the salad days of the old Sultanate. This is true both in terms of the cultural impact Omani rule made on coastal peoples and in terms of the (slave) labour intensive plantation economy which attained its height in the later nineteenth century.

In his analysis of coastal plantation economy, Cooper summarizes developments as they occurred on the coast from 1873 to 1890 by observing that, 'plantation agriculture has made [some] men rich: it has left plantation regions poor'.[95] Once Barghash signed the treaties of 1873 and 1876, coastal plantation owners faced a series of crises which restricted the continued expansion in production of the sort which had occurred in the 1840s and 1850s. With British efforts to stem the trade in slaves, prices for slaves rose from the $20 to $30 a head in the pre-1873 period to a high of about $100 a head in 1890.[96] At the same time, the period was characterized, overall, as one of declining prices for cloves and steady prices for all other agricultural commodities.[97] These facts, coupled with rising taxes and interest rates, all led to under-cultivation by the 1890s. Thus, following the initial period of expansion in the clove market in the 1840s, and in the grain export market in the 1850s, the plantation economy of the coast suffered from two overriding defects. These were overspecialization on the part of plantation owners and the fact that this economy was tied almost completely to the export market. While enough cash came into some people's hands to make them rich, the failure of most plantation owners to diversify their investments spelled ruin for them in the long run.[98] By the 1890s, then, the plantation system was essentially moribund for large areas of the coast. British colonial administration only exacerbated this process of erosion.

It was not these economic developments under the Sultanate which alone led to coastal impoverishment, but the fact that they were coupled with adverse social attitudes fostered by its Omani elite. With the steady loss of political autonomy which coastal peoples experienced under Arab rule, *waungwana* suffered a markedly lost sense of the innate dignity and worth of old coastal civilization.[99] This perspective, interestingly enough, is supported by the manifest decline in local coastal initiative and creativity observed by Allen in the art and architecture of Lamu in the second half of the nineteenth century.[100]

When, before the 1870s, Omani plantation owners in Zanzibar grew richer and the Sultans disseminated largess, *ustaarabu* supplanted *uungwana* as the standard of 'civilization'. To be 'civilized' meant having to be 'like an Arab' – and usually having to be Arab-like meant having to give the appearance of wealth even where wealth did not exist. All too often, people displayed a false prosperity to give the appearance of refinement and 'civilization'.[101] While the Omanis, particularly the Busaidi, exhibited a taste for European or Indian imports, so too did all *waungwana* who wanted to appear chic. As early as the 1860s and 1870s, therefore, people were inordinately interested in luxury items. As Rigsby observed.

> Foreign trade has of late years introduced amongst them a taste for foreign luxuries, such as handsome furniture and dress, costly mirrors, china, etc. and has thus caused an outward appearance of comparative civilization.[102]

When continued expansion in the coastal export business began to stagnate in the 1870s and later, many *waungwana* and Omanis alike found it necessary to mortgage their lands or to sell them outright in order to obtain the necessary cash to keep up appearances. Often Asians lent out this cash at exorbitantly high rates of interest (25 to 35 per cent). Having gone through the boom years of the 1840s and 1850s, in the 1870s and afterwards plantation owners found it necessary to borrow cash on a future which never repeated the successes of the past. For this reason, by the 1890s many plantations already had passed to Indian money-lenders or were so heavily mortgaged as to be virtually irrecoverable. Where in 1885, then, there still existed a well-cultivated mainland opposite Lamu, producing 'large quantities' of millet, sorghum, ground nuts, and rice, by 1897 it was described as,

> a declining place, its trade having of late years been diverted to Mombasa and it is probable that its population will be stagnant even if it should not actually decrease.[103]

By 1903 it was written that the 'native quarters' (Langoni?) were half their former (1885) size and that 'the mainland was derelict – almost dead'. Most areas formerly under cultivation had reverted to bush.[104]

The story at Pemba – by 1896 the foremost clove producing region of the coast – was the same. Hardinge reported that many plantations were overgrown with weeds, with the crop only partly picked because of a slave labour shortage. Again, mention was made of indebtedness to Indian money-lenders, especially one Buddhu, who was taking 'rarely less' than 60 per cent a year and, in one case, as much as 150 per cent.[105] At Zanzibar a similar situation was reported in 1920. Remarking upon the poor business practices of the *shamba* owners and their 'perennial financial embarrassment', Pearce noted the heavy mortgages on the plantations held by money-lenders.[106]

Most of the problems which cropped up in the coastal economy under the Sultanate were only exacerbated by measures implemented under colonial rule. As difficult as the 1873 and 1876 treaties had made life for the plantation and farm owners of the coast, steps taken in 1897 and 1909 to ban the actual status of slavery made matters even worse. The failure of the British to repeal a 25 per cent clove tax originally imposed by Barghash, coupled with a labour shortage which was becoming acute by the turn of the century, was creating a growing hardship for coastal planters.[107]

For a number of reasons, too, coastal peoples began to lose control over significant tracts of land which previously had been available for their cultivation. The rebellion involving Sh. Mbarak b. Rashid and the Witu Sultanate in 1895–6, for one thing, destroyed large amounts of property around Takaungu, Gazi, and Malindi, as well as entailing the loss of many slaves who fled during the ensuing chaos. British ignorance of traditional agricultural techniques, too, led them to claim jurisdiction over large tracts of land left fallow by coastal farmers. As early as 1898–9, collaborators like *liwali* Rashid b. Salim Mazrui granted concessions of road and ferry fees, taxation rights, and rights to exploitation of ivory, mangrove, and India rubber to European companies operating around Malindi in return for Rs 2000 per annum.[108] Corporate encroachments were made in other areas, as well. At Lamu, 'Messrs Smith MacKenzie and Company obtained exclusive rights to nearby mangrove stands 'which they exploited so diligently over a period of about five years, as to render a great deal of the mangrove useless to this day [1933]'. The same source also mentions concessions made at Witu to the Witu Estates Company for the cultivation of rubber, and a short-lived cotton syndicate operating on the Tana River.[109]

On the Kenyan coast the most damaging administrative measure was the Land Titles Ordinance of 1908. In 1907, A. C. Hollis was appointed as Commissioner of Native Affairs to look into 'native' claims to land rights on the coast. To settle matters, he sought the opinions of the Crown Advocate, Judge Hamilton, and the *Shaykh al-Islam*, Sayyid Abdu'r-Rahman as-Saqqaf. While the former ruled that the lands granted by the Sultan, whether under cultivation or not, remained in the hands of the grantee, and S. Abdu'r-Rahman felt that the land was the property of anyone who cleared and cultivated it, Hollis ruled (incorrectly) that any land covered by bush was wasteland and, therefore, belonged to the Crown. It was this ruling which was the backbone of the Land Titles Ordinance.[110]

The immediate problem which arose out of the Land Titles Ordinance was the extent to which Government was prepared to accept tradition as a valid claim to land. To deal with this, a Land Arbitration Board, chaired by K. McDougall and Sir Ali bin Salim, was instituted to obtain a 'fairer' estimate of the validity of each claim. An interesting case involved the claim made by the elders of Lamu in 1915, under the Land Titles Ordinance, to around 160,000 acres of land to the southwest of the island and extending as far as Witu. The case went through the hands, and duly received the opinions, of European officers ranking all the way from the local District Commissioner to the Senior Coast Commissioner, and lasted until 1925 when a final ruling was made. The claim was argued on the basis of oral traditions which demonstrated that various patches of the area concerned had been under (shifting) cultivation by Lamuans for a generation and, as a whole, formed a complete 'economic unit'. While the District Commissioner for Lamu recognized that the land had been utilized as claimed, he urged that the claim be turned back because he felt that the *wazee* only wished to further mortgage it out. At one point, it was even recommended that 500 acres be granted, while the balance was to be leased from the *wazee* with the rent going to a trust account for the entire town. In the end, however, the community claim, except for 5,000 acres, was denied.[111]

The Land Titles Ordinance affected other parts of the coast in other ways, and various communities reacted differently to it. While Salim points out that many formerly fine plantations went to bush around Lamu, the Witu area, because of its insalubrious atmosphere, was left largely unaffected except for the aforementioned mangrove monopoly. At Malindi, the Mazrui surrendered large tracts to the Government, partly to attract investment capital to the area and partly in hopes that the Government, in exchange, would grant other, more limited, land claims made by the clan. There, about 50,000 acres were needed for land promised to Europeans 'of the best type'. In exchange, at Takaungu about 50,000 acres were alienated for the Mazrui, with 3,000 of it *waqfed* in recognition of their cooperation.[112] Traditional economies were affected most extensively at Mombasa since it was serviced by the new Uganda railway and alternative employment for many could be found in the burgeoning port town.[113]

Another factor in the decline of coastal economy was drought and the subsequent further loss of labour to bigger towns like Mombasa. Several reports from Tanaland Province, for example, give a vivid idea of the impact made by a drought which lasted from 1908 to 1913. The Provincial Annual Report for 1913 entitled 'Agriculture' mentions that 'many of the natives have had a hard time of it' because of the drought; the additional destruction of mainland crops by baboons, buffalo, and elephant; and the depredations of marauding Aweera and Somali. The net effect of all this was that, instead of the usual two crops a year, during this period only one could be produced.[114] As a result, the Report goes on to relate how the towns were losing hundreds of their youth to other areas of the coast like Mombasa, Italian Somaliland, and Tanganyika.[115]

One factor which depressed agriculture and drove additional numbers of youths to seek alternative employment in the growing cities was the hut tax. Despite clearly deteriorating conditions, for example, it is interesting to note that from 1907/8 to 1913/14, there was a net increase in the revenues collected in Tanaland Province of 60.07 per cent, with a 24.44 per cent increase for Lamu District as reflected in Table 8 below.[116]

What made matters worse is that, in addition to giving preferential

Table 8: *Tanaland revenue, 1908–14*

Year	Province revenue	District revenue
1907/8	Rs 11,637	—
1908/9	Rs 12,672	Rs 24,750
1909/10	Rs 13,425	Rs 27,495
1910/11	Rs 13,194	Rs 23,030
1911/12	Rs 15,990	Rs 27,769
1912/13	Rs 17,574	Rs 23,350
1913/14	Rs 18,621	Rs 30,800

treatment to those whom the Government recognized as 'Arabs' in terms of special socio-political rights and opportunities, class and race were extended even into hut tax collection. While the Government exempted those recognized as 'Arabs', Swahili and Bajun were taxed at the rate of Rs 3 per head.[117] The critical moment came, of course, when representatives of the Government had to decide a person's race for purposes of tax assessment. In this situation, the Government made matters even worse by entrusting collection of the tax, as well as the care of records and receipts books, to their hand-picked *liwalis* and *mudirs*.[118] Thus, as one official noted, while 'half caste Arabs evade payment', problems were encountered over collection from 'people who obviously should not pay'.[119]

While things were deteriorating in the smaller towns and rural areas, developments on European plantations and in the growing port cities introduced alternative sources of income and employment to those wishing to escape the economic realities of the old plantation life. Already in 1897–8, Hardinge noted a 25 per cent drop in taxes collected on the export of ivory and rubber at Lamu due to the widespread exodus of labour to Mombasa.[120]

Yet, even in finding alternative employment in port towns, coastal peoples encountered competition from upcountry peoples similarly seeking work. Upcountry Africans, facing many of the same difficulties with taxes as were coastal peoples, also were combing the plantations, farms, and cities for work. The higher wages paid on the coast attracted migrant labourers from as far away as the Kavirondo region. A source printed in 1912 indicates that on the highlands farms, for example, a worker could expect wages of Rs 3–6 per month plus food, whereas on coastal plantations he could earn Rs 6–9 per month plus food. Moreover, with the availability of the new Uganda railway from Mombasa to Kisumu, and special fares for migrant workers, added incentive was given upcountry workers to find employment on the coast.[121] The acute nature of the problem also was reflected as far away as the Tana River where Kikuyu and Kamba were working on an estate owned by the East Africa Cotton Syndicate. There, it was claimed 'the supply of Kikuyu labour has been so copious that Mr.

Rule ... has been able to reduce their pay and ... the men take it rather than leave'.[122]

In addition to the racially divided society created by the British, even upcountry migrant workers faced the competition of Indian immigrants in the skilled trades. One source mentions how 'skilled native labourers are practically at the present time non-existent and their place is taken by the Indian artisan', while African labour, it was felt, 'can with patience be taught ploughing and working with wagons and oxen'.[123]

Needless to say, all this did not go far in improving relations between coastal townsmen and the intruders from India and the African interior. The Quarterly Report for 1911 mentions rioting in Mombasa between rival Kikuyu and Swahili sports clubs and bands (*beni*). The same source goes on to state that 'I do emphatically deprecate the policy of quartering Kavirondo and Kikuyu askaris in an Arab Mohamedan city'.[124] Such encounters repeated themselves rather often, apparently.[125]

EUROPEAN IMPACT ON COASTAL CULTURE AND RELIGION

The most obvious means by which Europeans attempted to influence coastal culture was through missionary work. Contrary to what one might expect, Muslims did not always resist this. Initially, at least, Sayyids Said and Majid welcomed the efforts of Christian missions among the non-Muslim peoples of the littoral and interior. As early as 1842, too, Krapf and Rebmann established the first Church Missionary Society mission at Rabai, near Mombasa, where Krapf actually was assisted by one 'Sheikh Ali Ben', described as the *qadi* of Mombasa, in his translation of the Bible into Swahili for its distribution among neighbouring Miji Kenda. Furthermore, Krapf mentions one instance where an 'Arab chief from Lamu' requested a copy of the Psalms, 'and being much pleased with it begged for a complete Bible'.[126] Muslim curiosity about Christian doctrines also was manifested when the Universities Mission to Central Africa opened a new cathedral on the site of the old slave market in Zanzibar:

> The townspeople gathered at the door. The Swahili Litany followed, and in the midst the Imam of a mosque entered, followed by about twenty more. He said they were good words he heard and very much what he thought himself. A picture of the Crucifixion was hung up so that the Mohammedans could be under no illusion; but possibly they thought it a sort of Kebla for the Christians.[127]

In general, though, the presence of the missions usually was abrasive to townspeople. The CMS mission at Freretown (Rabai) especially was attacked continually for sheltering escaped slaves. On Zanzibar the Universities Mission maintained a theological college at Kiungani where African converts – who mostly were freed slaves – were taught and prepared for field missions. In addition, several lower-form schools were set up around the island.[128] Needless to say, most Muslims were suspicious of these schools and avoided sending their children to them.

While schools and centres for freed slaves were threatening enough,

186

doubtless it was Christian evangelism which roused the strongest reactions. At Mombasa, the missionary W. E. Taylor is particularly remembered. Having been remarkably proficient in Swahili, Taylor chose the market-place for his sermonizing since it was the one spot where people from both the town and the mainland gathered daily.[129] In addition, he wrote little homilies and verses which he distributed in pamphlets:

Boriti ya Isa mti wa uzima, Umetuponyoka mzigo
(Jesus is like a sturdy tree, he has lightened the burden)

Kufa kwa Imani tuliona vema, Furaha kwetu daima
(We see good in dying in the faith, happiness is ours forever)[130]

Not to be outdone, especially in their own language, responses were composed by local poets and wits, like this one from Sh. Salim b. Khalid at-Timamy:

Usijizuzeu mtu mzima, Tela zindukana ujuwe;
Ushike ibada ya Mola Karima, Sizue Tela sizue.
(Taylor, don't talk like a greenhorn, awaken to the Truth;
Seize upon God's true faith, don't tell lies, Taylor, don't tell lies.)

Yuwatangatanga na vyuo kwa pani, Atafuta mema haoni;
Ibada ya Mola haiko sokoni, Sizue Tela sizue.
(He goes about in Swahili garb looking for the Truth without seeing it;
The True Faith is not found in the market; don't tell lies, Taylor, don't tell lies.)[131]

At Zanzibar, where more learned ʿulamaʾ were to be found, missionaries like Steere, Tozer, and Father Godfrey Dale engaged individuals in learned discussions or participated in public debates. Disputations seem to have centred on such topics as the divinity of Christ versus the miracles of Muhammad or Husayn; the Crucifixion of Christ, the Holy Trinity, and Muhammad as the Paraclete whose coming was foretold by Jesus. Often, Christians took the offensive in these exchanges and one gets the impression that, especially when they were done publicly, they were carried on more in the spirit of innuendo than by reasoned discussion, with the object being, of course, the influencing of onlookers.[132] In addition, pamphlets were disseminated among Muslims with titles like 'Habari za Muhammad na Maisha Yake na Mafundisho Yake/Information on Muhammad Concerning His Life and Teachings', 'Habari za Waarabu na Islamu/Concerning the Arabs and Islam'. Judging by the complaints of some Muslims, most of these little works were intended as attacks on Islamic beliefs and on the figure of the Prophet Muhammad.[133]

Of course, such propagandizing and street harangues failed to win many converts. There are many reasons for this, but the most obvious one is that Islam was the traditional religion of the coast and its abandonment meant, for the convert, a total rejection of town society and culture – a drastic step few *waungwana* were willing to take. And those who did convert, or at least attended the missionary schools, often were not important enough socially to win over others.[134] Finally, many Christians, both African and

European, often set bad examples for people to follow. Sh. al-Amin b. Ali Mazrui, for instance, cites the 'bad behaviour' of these Christians found in coastal towns (who presumably drank alcoholic beverages, abused servants, etc.). Smith, too, betrays a racialist attitude common among European missionaries which extended even to their treatment of African clergy.[135] Such hypocrisy certainly did not pass unnoticed by Africans and made the task of missionaries that much harder.

Despite the failure of missionaries to win many converts, in areas of clothing, art, and basic habits townspeople began imitating Europeans in their tastes. As seen in preceding chapters, of course, this started with the interest shown by the Omani aristocracy in European gadgets and inventions. By 1914, this tendency had extended to *waungwana* and had been intensified by the actual presence of Europeans among coastal peoples as the new ruling elite. They were the new aristocracy. Therefore, like the Omanis before them, Europeans were to be emulated.

Again, however, it was the upper class of coastal society which encouraged this trend. Having been given an English education, for example, S. Ali b. Hamud felt uncomfortable as a sovereign ruling people whom he thought to be ignorant and backward. Thus, he established a new fashion in clothing, called the Hamudiyya style, among the upper classes. This consisted of dressing in shoes and trousers under *kanzus*, and overcoats in place of the old-style *jubas* and *johos*.[136] Also, the upper class took an interest in other European innovations which arrived on the coast from Egypt. Among these were eating from tables and chairs and the use of knife and fork. They showed a fondness for music introduced from Egypt which combined both traditional Middle Eastern and European instruments. These were 'eagerly listened to, while they [sang] their haunting songs of love and fair women'.[137]

It is quite apparent, though, that Western fashions and ideas caught on most among those who had the least to lose in traditional, old-style town culture and its passing. Some members of the lower classes, like the Comorians of Zanzibar, for example, were among the first Muslims to embrace change, especially in education. Striving hard to compete with other ethnic communities at Zanzibar, as well as extensive travelling which put them in touch with the outside world, made many Comorians aware of a 'need for modern life'. As noted by Ibuni Saleh in the 1930s, 'They were trying to grasp the situation and appreciate the immense difficulties confronting them of moving on with the times'.[138] Ibuni Saleh also mentions how, in 1905, when Ali b. Hamud opened the first Government school at Zanzibar, Comorians resented initial Government policy of allowing only those recognized as 'Arabs' to attend. By that time, the author goes on to relate, several Comorians already had received 'English' educations in South Africa, India, and Egypt. Thus, in seeking to further their community's interests, they 'eagerly attended' the day school opened by the UMCA at Ng'ambu (the 'native' quarter of Zanzibar) in 1907.[139]

At Lamu another interesting situation unfolded. There, feeling betrayed by the 1883 decision of the ʿ*ulama*ʾ to allow the Busaidi to marry Husayni women and experiencing a major social revolution in the class structure over the freedom accorded former slaves, many *waungwana* began questioning the validity of traditional religious training. Consequently, some determined to send their children to Mombasa and Zanzibar to receive a secular education. By the 1920s, several Jahadhmy and Bakari children were enrolled in the Government school at Zanzibar, and others soon followed.[140]

Most of those who subscribed to the new ways, however, were youths. It was they who imitated S. Ali b. Hamud, himself a young man, and, therefore, one who set the fashions for the youth of the coast. It was these young men and women, many of whom were formerly slaves or were the offspring of slaves, who demonstrated a predisposition to try out new things such as trousers and tarbushes. It was they who formed the *beni* of the sort described by Ranger and who took to imitating to the last detail those who, unlike themselves, had status – that is, Europeans.[141] Ingrams provides a vivid picture of these youths in the period after World War I:

> Recently, one has seen objects clad in fezzes with coloured shirts and bow ties, blue serge suits, wearing shoes and socks, wearing a monocle, and smoking cigarettes in long, gold-tipped cigarette-holders. Such caricatures are not pleasing to see, and even worse perhaps are the gentlemen who have taken to soft hats and heavy boots. Wristwatches also are in favour.[142]

However, while European fashions were catching on, the reasons why were not all positive. A void had been created by the decline of the nineteenth-century economy, the systematic and purposeful dismantling of the Sultans' leadership, the cultural disfranchisement of the *waungwana*, and the successive military defeats experienced by coastal peoples during the 'pacification' phase of colonialist rule. Thus, various sources report a 'falling standard of morality' at this time. Many youths were observed to be taken by a spirit of 'idleness and without an object in life'. Some were borrowing heavily from Indian money-lenders, using the money to buy alcoholic beverages and other varieties of imported evils.[143] Finally, Ingrams reports that, in addition to a rising crime rate, 'Many types of offense have been appearing lately in Zanzibar ... such heretofore unknown methods of crime as pick-pocketing, hold-ups on roads, and robbery by gangs are becoming known...'[144]

In conclusion, no better statement of the cultural impact of the first quarter-century of colonial rule can be found than this assessment that was offered by Colonel F. B. Pearce, himself a representative of the new order of things in East Africa:

> We English are so fond of thrusting our own ideas and institutions upon other people, without inquiry as to whether they are suited to the conditions of life of those we are so anxious to benefit, that I fear our unfortunate *protégés* sometimes live to curse instead of to bless our gift of complete personal liberty, which entitles a young man, no longer a minor, to waste his substance in riotous living, and to dissipate his fortune on the most futile objects.

The law of Islam is wiser in this respect than our own ... The Arab system of governance is that of a Royal Patriarchal Magistracy, autocratic in a measure, but strictly limited by custom and Koranic law. The Arabs still appreciate this system and the lack of a controlling discipline in their lives often leads to many difficulties and abuses and the ruin of many young men.[145]

10

Currents of popularism and eddies of reform

Through all the changes introduced after 1873, coastal townspeople and their religious leaders were not, of course, supine. Occasionally, one catches a brief glimpse of popular resistance to measures implemented by Europeans or their instruments, the Sultans. Such popular expressions of anger often were whipped up by the harangues of local *qadis*, *walimu*, and *wazee*. For example, at Zanzibar there was one case of an Ibadi *qadi*, Sh. Ali b. Msellum al-Khalassy, who dared to stand alone in open defiance against the ban on the status of slavery in 1909.[1] In addition, the 1888–90 Abushiri resistance to German takeover of the Tanganyika coast received a great deal of popular support through the Qadiriyya *tariqa*. On the northern coast, Sh. Mbarak obtained varying degrees of assistance from Miji Kenda and Swahili elders.

Such open acts of defiance, however, were doomed to failure in the face of determined efforts by the Sultans and the European Powers. Resistance, especially after 1896, largely was passive. One Provincial Report, for instance, termed the general attitude of Lamu towards colonial rule as 'not very satisfactory'. While apparently law-abiding and peaceful, Lamuans were 'nevertheless experts in the art of passive resistance'. Offences for which many 'Arabs and Bajuns who [were] more or less educated' stood accused included leaving the district to avoid taxation and failure to give assistance to 'improving the health and sanitation of the town'. Furthermore, many were said to have perjured themselves in court, 'to help a friend from well merited punishment or payment of a just debt', or to have demonstrated 'a marked absence of public spirit and common honesty'.[2]

While *qadis* were employed by the government, often they were reluctant to be seen by their fellows as acting as its representatives (which, of course, they were). One report from 1907 states, for example, that *qadis* were 'continually too ill to come [to court]. If they did come, they often were late. Sometimes they refused to come at all without an order from the First Minister.'[3] The same source makes clear why such difficulties arose, namely European interference in the administration of the Shari'a and popularly conceived notions of justice. The same report states that,

> In the absence of any provision to the contrary, I assume that if the two Kathis insisted upon adhering to their opinions they would over-rule the British Judge. Such a case has not yet happened and it is not, I think, probable. But if the Kathis are to be retained for any length of time some

precaution should, I think, in the interests of humanity be adopted to secure the preponderance of the white Judge's opinion.[4]

From a 1912 report, it is quite apparent that most *qadis* were caught between the requirements of their British superiors and the traditions and sentiments of their fellow townspeople. Therefore, they were not willing to investigate crimes 'on the spot' since 'they [were] afraid of being dragged into the "fitina" that usually ensues upon such cases'.[5]

While various forms of resistance were the means of directly confronting colonial authority, such simple, direct means were not the solution to the subtle assaults upon coastal life and Islamic traditions posed by the social, economic and cultural changes which ensued after 1873. But the reactions of townspeople were neither unified nor uniform. The specific problems presented by a Sultanate waning in power and by an increasingly visible colonial presence followed class and ethnic lines. Thus, it is the purpose of this chapter to outline how most *waungwana* perceived and responded to these problems, as well as how several of the elite, more learned in the written tradition, dealt with them.

THE RISE OF ISLAMIC POPULARISM

The examination of *waungwana* knowledge of the literate Islamic tradition made in Chapters 4 and 5 suggests that Burton's assessment of Swahili learning essentially was accurate. According to him, most townspeople knew little beyond the simple profession of faith: often they prayed irregularly and fasted only under compulsion. He reported, furthermore, that the local *walimu* were considered 'educated' once they had committed the Quran to memory and could recite a few simple prayers.[6] Rather, what knowledge was important for the day-to-day affairs of most coastal Muslims was derived from local, orally transmitted traditions. Therefore, his virulent prejudices aside, Burton's view that 'they have retained a mass of superstitions and idolatries belonging to their pagan forefathers' was fairly accurate.[7] For most coastal Muslims not living in places like Lamu, Mombasa, or Zanzibar, Islam was represented more commonly in the beliefs and practices espoused by locally trained *waganga* and *walimu* rather than by true *ʿulamaʾ* before the late nineteenth century. The truth of these views is reinforced further by the changes in local religious behaviour and practices observed by Becker between 1902 and 1905. Above all, he took note of coastal people's 'uncharacteristic' attention to the basic tenets of their religion, their 'more intensive' spiritual exercises and hitherto unprecedented efforts at spreading the faith among their non-Muslim neighbours.[8]

Between the 1870s and the early 1900s, something had happened to effect these changes. Where previously learning in Islam's literate tradition had remained the carefully guarded secret of a few elite clans, by the late nineteenth century more and more *waungwana* were assuming a new attitude concerning religious training and leadership. Many townspeople overcame old social sanctions and began seeking such expertise for themselves.

Two things went farther than anything else to alter coastal culture in the later years of the Sultanate and in the early decades of colonial rule. The first was the transformation of an agrarian economy based largely on trade or exchange of goods to a capitalist economy based on money; the second was the Uganda railroad. The penetration of a money economy had its roots in Said b. Sultan's efforts to import Indian *pice* to stimulate the expanding caravan trade and agricultural investments in the 1830s. Originally, it was the lower social strata of the towns, the newcomers who came after the late eighteenth century, whose socio-economic ascendance was linked to money and the new work ethic that went hand in hand with it. Comorians were among these. They laboured as servants to the rich and as craftsmen for money. However, they never quite succeeded on a scale comparable to that of the Hadramis.

As already discussed, the Hadramis were the 'Swiss of the East', noted by some for being 'brave and hardy, frugal and faithful ... feared by the soft Indians and Africans for their hardiness and determination'.[9] Aside from freed slaves, no other people's success was tied so intimately to Busaidi and British rule as that of the Hadramis. For example, el-Zein points out that Lamu was forced by the British to open its doors to Bajuni and Indian immigrants with whom the Hadramis had their business dealings. Therein, of course, lay the threat to traditional town society posed by the Hadramis. Basically, they were labourers and traders rather than landowning farmers and, thus, they did not hold the stratified view of Lamu society and the universe held by most *waungwana*.[10] In promoting business, they dealt with anyone without regard to social status or ethnic background. Eventually, of course, the financial success they came to enjoy extended to other communities of newcomers – ex-slaves, Indians, and Bajunis. This new expatriate society, of which the Hadramis were an important part, established an alternative market-place at Langoni which threatened the old Lamu market at Utukuni and old commercial arrangements. This put people in positions of less dependence on the older clans of the town, clans like the Maawi and the Bakari whose own rise in fortunes had been attached to the Utukuni market some fifty or sixty years previously.[11]

Along with immigrants like the Hadramis, Asians, and Comorians, slaves and ex-slaves posed a new threat to traditional society on the coast. Once slavery had become a standard feature of town economy, difficulties developed over the status of slave women and the children born of their liaisons with townsmen. Mothers of such children rarely received support from their lovers and, being without landed wealth, many were forced to turn to non-traditional sources of income, like prostitution, to survive. Children of these 'marriages' lived in their mothers' households and, rejected by free society, never were indoctrinated, nor had a use for its two principal sanctions, *heshima* and *kutunga*. A new socio-economic phenomenon with its own social principles was created, the female household unit.[12]

Similarly, once slavery was abolished in British East Africa in 1907, ex-slaves began impinging on *waungwana* society. Although it was a point of Islamic law that Muslims could not be coerced into freeing their slaves, many ignored these finer points and began acting as free men and women, frequently settling uninvited in the towns. *Waungwana* took women from these classes as mistresses and reinforced the emerging subculture of matriarchal households. Male ex-slaves, being without land, became the natural allies of community newcomers.[13]

In addition, the introduction of Western capitalism and wage-labour served as a social lubricant for the lower strata of town society. At Zanzibar, after the 1898 decrees which provided slaves with the means to seek their freedom, there followed a difficult period during which the old slave population was transformed into a new class of semi-servile tenants on their old masters' estates. Enough slaves, however, did seek their freedom to create a serious labour shortage. To meet this demand, then, free wage-labour gradually became an important feature of the Zanzibar economy. However, most of this new labour came from other towns on the coast and from the mainland interior.[14]

On the mainland, two types of employment attracted those seeking work. European-owned plantations which produced rubber, cotton, and (later) sisal sprang up both in German and British East Africa following a growth in overseas investments after 1905.[15] The Uganda railway opened up new lines inland from Dar es Salaam, and the subsequent growth of Dar es Salaam and Mombasa as ports made these cities increasingly attractive to wage-labourers. There, young Africans could find various types of work as stevedores, porters, railway employees, naval 'seedi boys', policemen, clerks, servants, and public employees.[16] An indication of this expansion in the total labour market is given by Henderson who reports that wage-labour grew from about 70,000 persons in 1909–10 to 172,000 in 1912–13.[17]

Out of this, a whole new society and framework for reckoning social status was created which entered into competition with the old society, just as it competed with the old wealth. The new money economy itself did much to bring this about. Money, unlike barter, implied a new individualism in as much as it represented a new accumulatable source of wealth which could be held outside the lineage and land, and was readily available for conversion into other forms of wealth. With it, too, capital and credit for investment purposes were more accessible. It was with money, not land and slaves, for example, that landless immigrants and ex-slaves could free themselves from local socio-economic relationships to carry on business dealings and to form and expand networks of dependence, just as many *waungwana* had done before them.[18] Money could be obtained even outside the local community. Many freed or runaway slaves and the landless illegitimate offspring of *waungwana* men could obtain wealth in the newly expanding labour markets at places like Mombasa and Dar es Salaam. Thus, a new sort of status based on the capacity to earn money came into existence which competed with inherited land, ascriptive status, and piety. Slaves and newcomers began entering into open competition both economically and socially with the old elite. Class lines became blurred and the result was social disintegration such as occurred at Lamu around the turn of the century. There it is claimed that, because marriages based on the old social criteria were no longer possible as a result of secret marriages with slaves, the town *silwa* (book of pedigree) was 'thrown into the sea'.[19]

Where traditional society had been threatened, traditional religion too came under attack. It will be remembered that at Pate the civil wars between 1776 and 1809 had led to Nabahani assaults upon the *shurafa°* of the town. About a century later, at Lamu, similar doubts about the *baraka* of the Husayni developed when traditional society began to crumble. Along with this went new doubts about the relevance and efficacy of traditional education.[20] At Mombasa, likewise, many *°ulama°* found Islamic religious training under attack as being backward and an obstacle to social 'progress'. Anxious to 'get ahead' (*kuinuka juu*) in the new order of things created by colonialist rule, many young Swahili saw traditional Islam, both written and oral, as no longer a valid way of life and thought.[21]

It was not only Islamic institutions, though, which came under attack. Increasingly alienated and impatient with the new *°ulama°* who appeared in the Busaidi period and with Government appointed *qadis*, townspeople became progressively disaffected with many of their religious leaders. As early as 1856, Burton mentioned frequent accusations of bribery in cases tried by *qadis* at Zanzibar.[22] Rigsby repeated this indictment and, accusing them also of forgery, observed that they were 'not at all respected by the people'.[23] A more telling report on the crises affecting religious leadership in East Africa came from H. M. Stanley. As he explained it, the situation clearly was exacerbated by class differences. He claimed that some *waungwana* at Zanzibar preferred the life of caravan porters (*wapagazi*) as it took them away from the 'caprice', tyranny and meanness' of the Omani ruling class. Furthermore, he stated that, 'they complain that the Arabs are haughty, grasping, and exacting: that they abuse them and pay them badly; that if they seek justice at the hands of the Cadis, judgement somehow always goes against them'.[24]

However, such alienation was not solely due to changing standards of justice. New ideology, principally in the form of greater literacy in Arabic and stricter adherence to the written law, especially as it was popularized by the 'new' *°ulama°* and the followers of the Alawiyya, accounted for this too. One Mombasan informant related how his literate great-grandfather, literate in Arabic and learned in *fiqh*, was the frequent object of criticisms from his fellow townsmen.[25] By the late 1890s, this alienation led to a partial hiatus over questions of acceptable religious practice. When *°ulama°* like Sh. Ali b. Abdallah and Mwisha Hali at Mombasa literally espoused the 'letter of the law' over many traditional practices, *wamiji* there soon learned to distrust the advice of such leadership. Finally, when Hardinge implemented his judicial reforms in 1897, rather than see one of these new *ᶜulamaᵓ* appointed as Chief *Qadi, wamiji* supported Government efforts to screen applicants by examination.[26]

ALTERNATIVE ISLAM AND ISLAMIC POPULARISM

The Prophet Muhammad, of course, always was a central figure in coastal Islam just as he was wherever people professed the faith. Traditionally, the *Mawlidi*, the birth of the Prophet, was celebrated by townspeople much as Christ's birth is celebrated by Christians at Christmas time. The 'Mawlidi Barzanji', a poem depicting Muhammad's birth in written classical Arabic, was recited among *waungwana* on successive days in the house of a different host each day to which members of his *baraza* were invited. Also like Christians, the *Mawlidi* was an occasion for feasting. At these nightly gatherings, special dishes were served, such as spiced meats (*vitoweo*), vegetable dishes (*mboga*), rice, fruits, sourdough pastries (*mahamri*), coffee, and ginger taffy (*halwa*).[27] However, along with this particular holy day, there were others of a purely local character which almost rivalled the *Mawlidi* in their importance and significance. Among these were the New Year and the birthdays of local saints and historical figures. Indeed, one gets the impression that in East Africa the Prophet was only one among several important local personalities who, taken together, were central to people's perception of their religion to the extent that it was rooted in local history and tradition.

However, all this began to change sometime in the later years of the Sultanate. With the appearance of slaves and ex-slaves in the towns, celebrations of Islamic holidays began to assume recognizable class overtones. While many of these 'Africans' were avowed Muslims, *waungwana* dismissed their beliefs and practices simply as the Islam of the ignorant. Thus, they would not condescend to celebrating the Prophet's birthday with people they saw as mere servants and clients. Consequently, a new *Mawlidi*, the Anami *Mawlidi*, was created and recited by recently converted Africans living on the coast. This 'common' version of the epic of celebration was recited in Kiswahili and resembled an ordinary *ngoma*. In this version, too, the Prophet was cast in a different light, occupying a more central position, overall, in religious celebrations. In the beliefs of the downtrodden, Muhammad was the living Prophet, an intercessor who blessed the devout poor and assured them of salvation in exchange for their trials in life.[28]

Along with the devotions of the poor, this renewed interest in the figure of the Prophet and to ritual also was a part of the beginnings of a vague response among townspeople to increasing European political and cultural pressures after the 1870s. One can see this, for instance, in the growing popularity of the *tariqas* after that time. It was about then that Sh. Abdu'l-Aziz b. Abdu'l-Ghany popularized his 'Nuraniyya' branch of the Qadiriyya in Zanzibar. It was his popularity, it will be remembered, that brought him into conflict with Barghash, and it was the highly visible nature of his followers' spiritual exercises which roused the opposition of *ʿulamaʾ* like Ahmad bin Sumayt.[29] But Abdu'l-Aziz was only one of several disciples of Sh. Uways b. Muhammad. Nimtz mentions five others who obtained their *ijaza* in 1883–4 and who later helped disseminate the *tariqa* in coastal centres like Bagamoyo, Dar es Salaam, Tanga, and inland to Tabora and as far as eastern Zaire.[30]

Finally, Hadrami adherents of the Alawiyya always had placed the Prophet at the centre of their beliefs and had emphasized ritual and erudition in the sciences as important elements in their religious devotions. When that Lamu *shurafaʾ* came under attack, and when people began querying the 'relevance' of traditional Islamic education to modern needs, *shurafaʾ* like the al-Husayni and the Jamal al-Layl moved closer to the traditional Hadrami view of the Prophet as a protector capable of interceding on their behalf.[31] By the end of the nineteenth century, then, more attention was being paid the figure of the Prophet among the elite. While this is not relevant to *waungwana* beliefs directly, it should be pointed out that the Hadramis and the *shurafaʾ* did influence Swahili townspeople in this direction. While 'great' *ʿulamaʾ* like bin Sumayt and the Maawi closed their classes to many *waungwana*, Sh. Abdallah Bakathir, himself a Lamu Hadrami, popularized new ritual prayers for Ramadhan, such as the *Salat at-Tarawih* and the Witriya *qasida* (poem) on the Prophet by Muhammad b. Abdu'l-Aziz al-Warraq al-Lakhmi.[32] In addition, it should be recalled that during Ramadhan, Sh. Abdallah opened the doors of the Msikiti Gofu to all Muslims for special classes in the essential tenets of Islam. All these contributed towards putting the Prophet back in the centre of local beliefs and encouraged ordinary *waungwana* to take an interest in learning more about their faith and its (written) heritage.

The real watershed of conversion to Islam and people's renewed interest in the positive contents of their religion followed the collapse of the Maji Maji rebellion in Tanganyika. Perhaps the single most important effect of the uprising was, as Europeans observed, that for the first time Islam was 'becoming attractive to the natives because it is linked with the cry of "Africa for Africans, and down with the intruders."'[33] It was this connection which helped convert so many mainland Africans after 1902. Particularly, this phenomenon was tied to the *tariqas* and celebrations of the *Mawlidi*. For example, Nimtz points out that in mainland towns leadership of the brotherhoods almost always went to Africans. Because of this, and the 'African' nature of worship peculiar to the *tariqas*, most Muslims in Tanganyika were converted through the influence of a fraternity, like the Qadiriyya, and 70 per cent of Tanzania's Muslims still belong to a *tariqa*.[34] Similarly, the lower class Anami *Mawlidi* processions accounted for many people's initial interest in Islam, especially where it was connected with anti-European fervour. One informant indicated the crucial part which the carnival-like atmosphere of the *Mawlidis* played in influencing people's decisions to convert. Popcorn, sugar candies, and ginger coffee were served to the accompaniment of popular railings against the missionaries and the

Government.[35] Even more important, though, was that African practices, such as dancing and drumming, sometimes were permitted to be introduced into these celebrations.[36]

For purposes here, though, the importance of this increased interest in Islam after 1902–5 was the change in the intensity of people's belief and devotion to Muhammad and Islamic scholarship. One very intriguing phenomenon which developed out of the association of Islam with African nationalism was the growing identification of Muhammad with Africa and Africans. Many new converts and lower class *waungwana* apparently identified so completely with their Prophet that some came to believe that Muhammad actually was an African himself.[37] As mentioned already, too, Becker noted people's revived interest in the tenets of their faith between 1902 and 1905, as well as the unusual intensity of their devotion. He mentions, for example, their 'strict and formal execution of the fasting practices ... during the month of Ramadan 1906', visits made to the (Ottoman) Sultan Abdu'l-Hamid by 'various prominent Arabs', and the 'living relationship which people felt to Muhammad'.[38]

At this point, three case studies of individuals who typify some of the religious developments discussed in this section, and who helped popularize Islamic literacy among lower class *waungwana*, will be presented. Such a discussion is useful and necessary in this context because all three of these personalities fostered this renewed interest in religious fundamentals in their respective communities. It was they, especially, who shaped the conservative response made by most coastal Muslims in their encounter with the modern Christian West.

The first of these men is dealt with at length in Nimtz's work on the Qadiriyya in Bagamoyo. A few summary lines on him are in order here, though, since he exemplifies how a poor man, even an ex-slave, could attain high social standing and religious stature in the fluid conditions created in coastal society during the early years of the colonial era. Sh. Yahya b. Abdallah, better known as Sh. Rumiyya, was a domestic slave to a *liwali* of Bagamoyo, Amir b. Sulaiman al-Lamki. At some unspecified time, though, he was permitted to engage in commercial ventures on his own behalf (not unusual among coastal domestic slaves), and eventually he saved enough from his earnings to buy four *shambas* comprising altogether about 2,500 coconut trees. When his enterprises had advanced still further, he had sufficient leisure to begin religious studies under one Sh. Abu Bakr b. Taha al-Jabri.[39] Eventually, he opened the doors of his own school and, with his wealth, he was able to subsidize short-term stays by poor scholars who came to study under him. By 1911, Nimtz claims, he had become acknowledged as the foremost *shaykh* in Bagamoyo, due primarily to his teachings and his efforts on behalf of the poor.[40] His reputation quickly spread and he became widely known for his activities in popularizing the Qadiriyya and converting many Africans to the faith. In 1916, he was appointed as the *likwali* of Bagamoyo. By the time he died, he was regarded not only as a *mwanachuoni* and teacher, but as a local saint who, as evidenced by his material success and generosity, possessed *baraka*.[41]

Like Sh. Rumiyya, Habib Salih b. Alawi Jamal al-Layl has been discussed elsewhere in some detail, but, again, he has a place here because he exemplifies how some *shurafa°* turned to the Alawi *tariqa* and assisted the indigent onto the road of enlightenment when they found themselves being rejected by traditional society. Born in the Comoro Islands, Habib Salih came to Lamu sometime between 1876 and 1885 and lived with his paternal uncle, Ali b. Abdallah. He studied without distinction under another uncle, one Bwanye Kai Maawi, and a Sayyid Muhammad al-Makki sometime in the 1880s – that is, about the time of the rows at Lamu over the status of slave–*waungwana* marriages.[42] As a follower of the Alawiyya who recognized the disparities between Quranic injunctions and social realities at Lamu, Salih chose to ignore traditional elitist attitudes towards the poor and recent arrivals at Lamu. It was to the spiritual and intellectual needs of these people that Habib Salih dedicated his life and work. One of the first things he realized was that most slaves and the poor were unable to improve their socio-economic circumstances while they remained ignorant of Islamic law. Therefore, he embarked first on training the children of Lamu's downtrodden in the essentials of Islam. Originally, he taught the Quran to the youngest and the basics of *fiqh* to more advanced pupils (since it is 'the most basic *fann*') in the Shaykh al-Bilad mosque. Town *wanazuoni* strongly opposed these efforts, naturally, and the breaking point soon was reached when Salih began teaching Quranic exegesis. Consequently, the *imam* of the Shaykh al-Bilad mosque was pressured into discontinuing Salih's classes.[43]

Not discouraged, Habib Salih shifted to Langoni, where he shamed Sayyid Abu Bakr b. Abdu'r-Rahman Husayni (the renowned poet, Sayyid Mansab b. Abdu'r-Rahman) into giving him some land on which to build his own *madrasa*. A critical victory came when Sayyid Mansab, no doubt suffering from the social buffetings which characterized Lamu at that period, was won over completely to Salih's cause.[44] It was Sayyid Mansab's conversion which inspired him to translate several didactic works from Arabic into Swahili verse.[45] Through their combined efforts, a mud and thatch *madrasa* was constructed where Salih continued proselytizing and educating slaves, Hadrami, and Comorians. Among Habib Salih's students was Sh. Abdallah Bakathir who, in one of his later journeys to Capetown, raised sufficient cash, gifts, and endowment money to build the larger and more resplendent Riyadha mosque and *madrasa* which stands at Lamu today.[46] Habib Salih's Riyadha programme was opened to Africans and Arabs from all over East Africa and, eventually, was expanded to a five-year course of formal matriculation which included works on *tafsir, fiqh, hadith*, Arabic, and *tasawwuf*. Like Sh. Rumiyya of Bagamoyo, Habib Salih was a noted *tabib* (physician), as well, who ministered to the impoverished. By the time of his death in 1935, his fame as a saint (*wali*) had spread all over the coast, to the Hadhramawt, and as distant as Malaysia.[47]

The final personality to be considered is interesting because his life exemplifies some of the ideological and class antagonisms between the *wamiji* and Arab *°ulama°* of Mombasa which simmered around the

199

beginning of the century. Originally from Siyu, Sayyid Abdu'r-Rahman b. Ahmad as-Saqqaf was born into a *sharif* clan which had lived in the Lamu region roughly for three hundred years at the time of his birth (1844). They long since had lost contact with their native Hadhramawt and had been steeped thoroughly in the *uungwana* tradition of Pate and Siyu. As a youth, he participated in the Famao resistance to the Zanzibar Sultanate, and in 1866 he was captured and imprisoned for six months in Fort Jesus for his part in the rebellion.[48] While there, he began studying the Quran and *falak* with the help of some of his Omani guards. After returning to Siyu, he continued his studies, receiving *ijaza* from various Somali, Qadiri and Bajuni *ʿulamaʾ* in such subjects as *fiqh*, Arabic grammar, *tafsir*, and *hadith*. Later he studied for a while under Sh. Muhammad Qasim Maamiri.[49] In 1878, Sayyid Barghash appointed him as the official *qadi* for Siyu.

As mentioned previously, many *waungwana* at Mombasa sided openly with British authorities and Sir Ali b. Salim Busaidi against some of the Arab *ʿulamaʾ* and their strict 'orthodoxy'. Deciding that this was the perfect chance to rid his clan's ancient rivals, the Mazrui, from a position of influence, Sir Ali urged the British to require all applicants for the new position of Chief *Qadi* (*Shaykh al-Islam*) to take a written test. Refusal of the proud Mazrui to submit to such an examination gave the position, in 1902, to S. Abdu'r-Rahman.

When he first came to Mombasa, S. Abdu'r-Rahman had no students. One day, however, a local *mmiji*, Ali Muhammad Mungwana, agreed to send him his son for instruction. Little by little thereafter, he managed to gather about him many pupils from among the townspeople of Mombasa who refused (and often were not permitted) to send their children to Arab *ʿulamaʾ*. He did not refuse anyone on the basis of class or ethnicity, and he devoted himself 'all day', as one informant put it, to teaching in the Sh. Mbarak mosque – that is, the mosque donated, ironically, by Sh. Mbarak b. Rashid Mazrui to the Baluchi community.[50] From these students of humble social origins, he produced several disciples who were especially noted for their mastery of *fiqh* and *tafsir*.[51] In addition, he laboured as a healer (*tabib*) among the poor and is remembered for having been a 'professional poor man' because of his generous use of his Government salary to relieve the needy. Like Habib Salih and Sh. Rumiyya, he is venerated today in Mombasa as a local saint and prayers are said over his grave beside the Sh. Mbarak mosque during the annual *Mawlidi* holiday.[52]

Needless to say, Sayyid Abdu'r-Rahman (called popularly Mwinyi Abudi) was not welcome at Mombasa as far as Arab *ʿulamaʾ* were concerned. His son claims that twice his food was poisoned out of jealousy over his appointment and his devotion to the needs of the poor.[53] In addition, there was a great ideological and social rivalry between his school and the fundamentalist Arab school of Mombasa. Often these wranglings centred on appointments to civil service positions. Some of Mwinyi Abudi's pupils, such as Abud b. Zahran and Sh. Abdullah Husnu, were deeply involved in *tariqa* activities and *Mawlidi* celebrations of the popular variety.

Of course, such associations were denounced roundly and publicly by 'new' *culamaʾ* like Sh. Sulaiman b. Ali Mazrui, al-Amin b. Ali Mazrui, and Sh. Muhammad Qasim Maamiri. The traditional marriage customs of the *wamiji* also came in for public attacks by some Mazrui. Finally, the Arabs managed to win sinecures to most of the *qadi*-ships and other Government positions – especially after Mwinyi Abudi's death – while Mwinyi Abudi's pupils landed few appointments. Consequently, there was a continual cross-examination between the two schools over points of law and theology, while the Mwinyi Abudi faction, led especially by Abud b. Zahran, continually accused the Arabs of employing unfair practices in landing such a preponderance of appointments. The result was that there were frequent street demonstrations between the two factions, often involving shouted insults and even a few spitting incidents.[54] These rivalries between reformist *culamaʾ*, most from the old elite Arab clans, and the more traditionally trained (and poorer) townsmen has continued on the Kenya coast right down to the present.

EDDIES OF ISLAMIC REFORM THOUGHT

The East African coast was not brought into the mainstream of the Islamic reform movement until the 1930s when Sh. al-Amin b. Ali Mazrui introduced some of the new ideas associated with the movement into his newspaper editorials. However, some of the historical pressures and ideological mainsprings which underpinned the development and final acceptance of reform ideas on the coast were present already by the 1870s. Therefore, some discussion of these various seeds of Islamic reform as it was formulated and articulated in the 1930s through the 1950s have a place here.

Before going ahead, however, a few words are necessary regarding what is meant here by 'reform' thought in East Africa. Although certain 'reformed' ideas concerning the place of the ancient, relatively immutable literate' tradition were espoused by the Alawiyya in the 1880s and 1890s in East Africa, it is preferable that this corpus of ideas and attitudes be labelled 'fundamentalist' Islam to reflect its distinctiveness from the 'true' (so-called Salafiyya) reform movement which came later. On the other hand, a 'reform' of sorts eventuated among some *waungwana* and African converts to Islam who turned to the figure of Muhammad as central to their beliefs and who took a 'reformed' interest in the religious duties enjoined by their faith and its literate tradition. This kind of 'reform' has been described and exemplified in the previous section. However, the latter type of Islamic reform is referred to as 'popularism' here since it differs somewhat from the usual notion of 'reformist' Islam in being non-modernist and parochial in character and aims, its main purpose being the defence of traditional values and culture.

True reformist Islam is one which is (for want of a better word) 'progressive' or modernist in its aims. Essentially, it can be characterized as having grown out of, or having been influenced principally by the teachings of Sh. Muhammad Abduh and the journalist, Rashid Rida, both of Egypt.

Its basic goal is the 'modernization' of Islamic lands on the Western model through adopting its technology, if not its culture and philosophical bases (which, of course, is impossible).[55] While it emphasizes the 'fundamental' validity of Islam as a revealed religion and way of life, it rejects the tenth-century 'closing of the gates of independent legal judgement'. In the thinking of men like Abduh and Rida, Islamic law, *per se*, is not bad since it did succeed in preserving many of Islam's original principles. What is unacceptable to them, however, is the requirement of mere imitation (*taqlid*) of past legal judgements, interpretations, and methods. Its essential aims include a return to a pristine Islam as it is imagined to have been in the days of the Prophet Muhammad and in the decades immediately thereafter when it was a religion in its simple, formative inception just encountering other peoples and modes of thought. It was at this stage of development, so the reformers realize, that Islam was still open to all possibilities in its evolution as a complete thought system and way of life in its own right.

However, a caveat is needed regarding the relationship between fundamentalist and reform Islam. Islamic reform thought is the stepchild of fundamentalism. In some respects, fundamentalism was proto-reformist, and occasionally (for example, the Ibadi reform) it even blossomed directly into 'true' reform. The Alawis were one variety of fundamentalists, for example, who shared a regard for such traits as humility, piety, love of obscurity, and abhorrence of ostentation, while they gave attention to the careful observance of religious duties and kept Muhammad at the centre of their faith above all others. Unlike reformers, they revered past generations of ʿulamaʾ and the *shurafaʾ*. Theologically; they upheld the post-Shafii and Asharite development in religious thought and in the religious institution.[56] While reform in East Africa was related to the Alawiyya in that 'reformist' ʿulamaʾ like Sayyid Mansab b. Ali and Sh. al-Amin b. Ali Mazrui benefited from religious training from Alawi ʿulamaʾ like Sh. Abdallah Bakathir and Sayyid Ahmad b. Sumayt, the reformist ideas which they eventually advocated were several steps removed from the Alawiyya *shaykhs*. This was especially pronounced in their condemnation of saint veneration. Indeed, Sayyid Mansab was criticized trenchantly by Ahmad b. Sumayt for his views and, because of them, he never was able to land a Government appointment.[57] Likewise, al-Amin b. Ali Mazrui faced similar disapproval and he was denounced as a 'Wahhabi' by the *shurafaʾ* and other Alawi followers.

What some fundamentalists shared with the reform thinkers was a reverence for the works of Taqi ad-Din Ahmad ibn Taymiyya, a fourteenth-century Hanbali who gave his life to a struggle against the degeneration in the theological institution and the worldliness of some ʿulamaʾ, in particular. Eschewing all the sophistic and spurious abstractions which led to the 'closing of the gates of *ijtihad*' and excessive reverence for the theological giants of the past, ibn Taymiyya laid stress on the original Islam as found in the Quran and as exemplified in the life of the pristine *umma* at Medina. To him, true reverence for God was the highest goal in life. This implied the simple acceptance of the Sunna and the injunctions of the Quran.[58] As for

Jslam as a way of life and the law as a prescriptive instrument for day-to-day living, he seized upon the principle of *maslaha* (welfare, utility) and the Quran as the only guide-posts needed for righteous living.[59] His concern, as Kerr states it, was for the religious origins of actions and ideas in Islam rather than for their precise modes of application.[60] He had a 'realization that the concrete "poetical" language of the Quran kept men closer to the deep springs of religious vitality than the abstractions of philosophical thinking'.[61] As such, he felt that the scholastic method, with its rigid reliance on 'authorities', had contributed to the theological decline of Islam.

Although they shared ibn Taymiyya's revulsion for the cult of saints, fundamentalists departed from reformers in their lack of interest in the methods which ibn Taymiyya had devised to escape the 'rigidity of scholastic methods and to make possible an adaptation of Islamic truth to contemporary conditions'.[62] Rather, like the Swahili popularists of Islamic erudition, they simply were trying to preserve an ideological status quo. The reformers envisioned what they felt were non-fundamental adaptations of Islamic institutions, such as reactivating *ijtihad* as a legitimate tool of theological and juristic calculation, in order to admit many of the sciences which Western culture had embraced and which had produced their technological advantages over the Muslims.

IBADI REFORM INFLUENCES

The beginnings of what became Ibadi reform were revivalist and fundamentalist in both form and scope. Both revivalism and fundamentalism dovetailed in the basic doctrines of the Ibadi sect, itself a form of Kharijite Islam. Kharijism and Ibadism were based on rejection of the political development of the *umma* following the murder of the Caliph Uthman.[63] They stressed the original purity of Islam as revealed in the Quran, as exemplified by the Prophet, and as practised in the early community. To Ibadis, the thought of any human intercessor between man and God was abhorred and, therefore, all varieties of saint worship were treated as innovation (*bidaᶜ*) and idolatry (*shirk*). In law, imitation of past practices (*taqlid*) was dismissed and the exercise of individual judgement (*ijtihad*) was affirmed. Free will and the moral responsibility of individuals were stressed while, of course, the Asharite formula concerning free will and predestination was rejected. Therefore, Ibadis believed in the importance of individual action (*ᶜamal*), effort, and strength of will (*irada*) in determining one's ultimate destiny, while passivity and stagnation were condemned along with luxury and ostentation.[64]

While the above had been the Ibadi ideal, of course Ibadis did not always live by it. The 'secular Sultanate', as described in Chapter 6, was one example of this. Another was the Ibadi merchant community in Algeria's Mzab region which went through periods when 'practice and principle' sometimes varied, leading to occasional reawakenings of reformist zeal, 'as prophetic voices called for a return to the sources'.[65]

Apparently, just one such phase of reformist zeal was touched off in Oman by the forceful seizure of the Sultanate by Sayyid Sultan b. Ahmad and by the progressive development of the so-called secular Sultanate. Salil ibn Razik tells of the assassinations of a number of non-conforming ʿulamaʾ by *mutawwiun* (revivalist ʿulamaʾ) in the reign of Sultan b. Ahmad (1791–1804).[66] By the early nineteenth century, and operating from a power base at Sohar and from the old religious capital at Rustaq, these fanatics were giving their support to the Banu Qais, cousins and rivals of those Busaidi descended from Sultan b. Ahmad. While claiming spiritual leadership of the Ibadi community, Qais b. Ahmad and the revivalist party allied themselves with the Wahhabis against the Busaidi Sultans. Out of obvious sympathy with the Wahhabi programme and ideology, the Ibadis styled themselves *mutawwiun*, after the Wahhabi *mutawwiun*, yet remained distinct in their ultimate aim of restoring Ibadism to a condition of total purity.[67]

The *mutawwah* revival in Oman was led by one Said b. Khalfan al-Khalili who appears to have been active politically between the 1840s and 1871. Originally, he recruited the support of Hamid b. Azzan Busaidi, a Qaisite who had been fighting Sayyid Said for religious control of the Ibadi Sultanate since the 1820s. After numerous rebellions, however, Hamid retired from his post as governor of Rustaq in 1840 to lead a withdrawn life of spiritual meditation and study. In his place he left al-Khalili as governor of Rustaq, and in Sohar he appointed his son, Saif b. Hamid, as *liwali*. When Saif attempted to reopen relations with the British and concluded an anti-slavery agreement with them, both Khalili and Hamid b. Azzan successfully plotted Saif's murder. Thereafter, Hamid returned as governor of Sohar in 1849, but failed to carry the revolution as far as the coastal cities of Oman.[68]

It will be recalled from Chapter 7 that Khalili again was in an insurrection in the last years of Majid's reign (1868–71). The details have been related already and do not bear repeating. However, the general course of this particular series of events resulted in the triumph of Khalili and the Qaisites, under Azzan b. Qais, over Salim b. Thuwain and Turki b. Said. Azzan was installed briefly as the Imam of Oman by his *mutawwah* supporters.[69] Eventually, Turki led a successful counter-revolution and, with British assistance, recaptured the Sultanate in 1871. Both Azzan b. Qais and Khalili were killed by the new Sultan. The *mutawwiun*, however, continued to plot against both Sultans Turki and Faisal b. Turki throughout their reigns (that is, well into the 1890s).[70]

In the meantime, a similar, though quieter, revival was taking place in the Mzab. There, according to Shinar, Ibadi merchant communities had grown lax in their religious observances over the centuries. By the 1880s a *mujtahid* by the name of Sh. Muhammad b. Yusuf Atfayyish (1820–1914) began a movement which stressed a revivification of the Quranic duties, eradication of 'heretical' practices of Berber origins, improvement of public morals, and educational reform to a system which emphasized the study and application of classical Arabic to religious studies.[71] Of special interest here were the activities of two of Atfayyish's disciples, Sh. Sulaiman Pasha al-Baruni and one Sh. Salimi, since it was these two men who were the known links between what was transpiring in the Mzab, Oman, and Zanzibar. Al-Baruni, for example, is known to have been at the court of Azzan b. Qais (and al-Khalili) in the late 1860s.[72] Sh. Salimi, on the other hand, is remembered for having been a scholar and theoretician of the same rank as Atfayyish. He had a considerable intellectual influence over both Omani and Zanzibari *'ulama'* through the agency of Baruni.[73]

In Zanzibar itself it was none other than Barghash who first took an interest in Ibadi revitalization. However, according to Burton, 'Wahhabism' (that is, Ibadi revivalism) already had been popular among many Zanzibar Ibadis by the 1850s.[74] Barghash seized upon this not only to win over the Harthi in his rivalry with his brother, Majid, but also out of a hope that, if the *mutawwiun* won out in Oman, the revolution might spread to Zanzibar where he would replace Majid as Sultan and rid himself of the meddlesome English.[75] Even after he was made Sultan of Zanzibar in 1870, the struggles between Turki and the Qaisite faction led him to entertain ambitions that he might become the Imam of Oman if the fundamentalists won out. Under the influence of six or seven *mutawwiun*, headed by one Sh. Hamud b. Hamid al-Fu'ahi, Barghash tried to cast off the British yoke and

> gave every indication of acting as a zealous religious reformer of ultra Mutawa views: the propriety of interdicting tobacco and similar sinful indulgences were seriously discussed and it was generally supposed that religious fanaticism ... would be this ruling principle.[76]

While figures like Atfayyish, Khalili, and S. Barghash all advocated a fundamentalist revival of Ibadi Islam in the 1860s to the 1880s, the movement took a turn towards actual reform under the influence of two new personalities. Again, a central figure in this development was al-Baruni, in conjunction with the nephew of Atfayyish, Abu Ishaq b. Ibrahim Atfayyish. In the Mzab there had been a long history of Ibadi resistance both to French taxation of their trade and to military conscription. Baruni himself fought against the Italians in the first Italo-Sanusi war. Thus, where Ibadis everywhere were becoming increasingly radicalized by European colonialist rule and where Ibadi fundamentalism and reform thought shared common grounds, under Baruni and Abu Ishaq Ibadism embraced reformist and Pan-Islamic ideology. By the 1920s, for example, Abu Ishaq, with Baruni's encouragement, 'steeped in Ibadi lore, combine[d] a deep attachment to his native Mzab with the ideology of modern Ibadism, Salafiyya and Islamic Renascence'.[77] At about that time or shortly before, an Ibadi weekly entitled *al-Minhaj* was published by the Salafiyya press in Cairo and edited by Abu Ishaq. As Shinar relates, this sheet was devoted 'to matters of Ibadi interest, such as Mzabi institutions and grievances against the French, the affairs of Oman and Zanzibar, thus serving in fact as a link between the widely scattered communities of the Ibadi sect'.[78] One of the foremost concerns with which this paper dealt, for instance, was British involvement in East Africa.

As mentioned already, Ibadi reform and revival had some audience in East Africa. Besides his political involvements with the *mutawwiun*, Sultan Barghash was genuinely concerned about religious revival.[79] Besides the Mzab, Oman, Tunis, and Cairo, Zanzibar became a centre for the publication of Ibadi texts and propaganda. According to one informant, this press was set up first under Barghash's aegis as part of his programme for modernizing Zanzibar.[80] This effort was continued by Ali b. Hamud with the appointment of Sh. Nasor b. Salim ar-Ruwayhy as the editor of the *Official Gazette (Jaridatuʾl-Isuriyya)*. Sh. Nasor, an Ibadi poet and the official biographer of Ali b. Hamud, devoted some space in his paper to religious questions and articles on Arabic literature and Pan-Islam.[81] Purporting to be the 'voice of the *umma* of Zanzibar', however, did not alter the fact that many Arabs refused to receive these ideas with an open mind.[82]

EARLY SHAFII REFORM INFLUENCES

Shafii reformist thought seems to have sprung from a wide range of well-springs, partly indigenous and partly external. Because it was somewhat more diffuse and came to rest from the influences of a certain few identifiable personalities, its precise ideological origins are more elusive than those of Ibadi reform. However, various signs suggest that among some East Africans reform ideas may have been making some headway as early as the 1880s. Van den Berg mentions, for instance, that by that time reformist papers like the Pan-Islamic *al-Jawaʾib* from Istanbul, *al-Watan* from Cairo, *al-Ahram* from Alexandria, and Abduh's *al-Urwat al-Wuthqa* were reaching a Shafii readership as far away as Indonesia.[83] Furthermore, it will be remembered that very early in his career, S. Ahmad b. Sumayt established and maintained ties with a few Pan-Islamicists and reform thinkers.[84]

The first solid evidence of interest in reform, however, dates from the late 1890s, when Sayyid Mansab b. Ali Abu Bakr bin Salim entertained a *baraza* of known reform-minded notables among Zanzibar society.[85] Born the grandson of a former Mwinyi Mkuu of Moroni and reared by his uncle, S. Muhammad b. Ahmad, himself a *qadi*, S. Mansab was trained in the traditional sciences.[86] However, he also was taught history and other Western sciences by Hakim Daud Ali Khan, an Indian who had studied abroad, as well as the art of drawing by an unknown UMCA missionary. He took an interest in Egyptian reform newspapers such as *al-Manar*, *al-Hilal*, *al-Muktataf*, *al-Liwa*, and *al-Muʿayyad*. In addition, it is said that he read a *tafsir* written by Muhammad Abduh.[87]

Those whom S. Mansab gathered around him, though, were even more interesting than he himself was. Among these were Muhammad Muhammad Bakashmar. According to Farsy, during his exile from Zanzibar, Bakashmar passed some time in Arabia and India where he began developing an interest in reform ideas.[88] Salim Khimry, a Hadrami, was educated in Egypt, Mecca, and Medina where he read various

'Wahhabi' (ibn Taymiyya?) works. Two Egyptians, however, appear to have been the most influential on the others' thinking and on the youth of Zanzibar. Muhammad Jamal (called Turkiyya) was a *tarbush* merchant who was active in reading and promoting reformist papers and pamphlets, such as *al-Manar*, to the *baraza*. Umar Lutfi, like Sayyid Mansab, was an active opponent of Ahmad b. Sumayt, both personally and intellectually. He was especially effective as a reformist propagandizer because, acting on his convictions, he 'gave lessons' in the Juma^c mosque at Zanzibar where he influenced various youths who were especially open to the new religious ideas he purveyed.[89]

Both Ibadi and Shafii reform, then, along with educational reforms and the malaise increasingly experienced in coastal society after the turn of the century, began having a noticeable effect on thinking among Zanzibar's young people. While older generations confined their reading to the Quran, commentaries, *hadith* literature, and law, Pearce mentions that some of the young (by inference) read the newspapers from Cairo and books on history and literature.[90]

The last major reform influence in East Africa was the 'upstart' Sultan, Ali b. Hamud. Although he has come up in various contexts throughout this book, he deserves mention again in this one. As mentioned already, Ali b. Hamud was sent by his father, Sultan Hamud b. Muhammad, to England where he received an English education at Harrow (and where he was nicknamed 'Snowdrop'). Thoroughly conditioned to Western culture and thought, yet proud and defensive about his Ibadi background, upon his return to Zanzibar and the Sultanate in 1902, he found himself in an ambivalent situation. On one side he was secretly criticized by older Muslims for his European affectations. On the other, he was emulated by the younger generation who, like him, sought to assume the garb and trappings of a ruling culture which, because it was politically more powerful than their own, was thought to be superior. Furthermore, he found himself hemmed in by a regency government imposed on him until his attainment of a majority. He chaffed especially from efforts by the British Consulate to maintain a strict control over his personal expenditures (that is, the civil list conflict). Described by his First Minister as having 'exaggerated ideas of his own importance', Ali b. Hamud quarrelled continually with his colonial masters over money matters, while he tried to run his palace and household 'on the lines of a royal court in Europe'.[91]

More important here, though, were his efforts to free himself and his Sultanate from what he felt was his 'captivity' by the Foreign Office. This took several interesting turns. Wishing to restore the Sultanate to the power and dignity it had under S. Barghash, he knew he had to seek outside help if he was going to get rid of the British. Consequently, he interested himself in Pan-Islam and considered, at one point, establishing ties with the Sultan of Istanbul. On one of his frequent trips to Europe he visited Istanbul where he was received with honour. In turn, he once received the Turkish Grand Vizier and other dignitaries from Sultan Abdu'l-Hamid.[92]

An effort to rid himself of another aspect of British control led to the establishment of the first Government school at Zanzibar in 1907. For years, Asians both inside and out of the Sultans' governments had used their status as British subjects to wrangle special advantages in their dealings with the Sultans and their *qadis*. Then, too, Asians generally had been unpopular among coastal Muslims for their sharp business practices and adroitness at dominating appointments to posts having to do with Government fiscal operations. In his efforts to reassert control over his own treasury and exchequer, Ali b. Hamud sought to replace Asians in many Government offices with Arabs and Swahilis. The assumption, of course, was that Arabs and Swahilis would be more loyal to their Sultan personally. However, the problem was that some training first would be required if qualified local talent was to be recruited. Originally, the school he funded was meant only for Busaidi. Because of the competition offered by the missionary schools, though, Muslims of other classes and even Asians eventually were allowed into the school. There, Arabic and Islamic sciences were taught by an Egyptian, Sh. Abdu'l-Bari al-Ajiz, and 'modern' subjects such as bookkeeping and various crafts were taught by a European.[93]

The significance of Ali b. Hamud's school was that it was the first of its kind in East Africa. Education more than anything was to be the key to the modernization of the East African coast, just as it was in other parts of Africa. As has been noted elsewhere throughout this work, however, many coastal Muslims were reluctant to send their children to such schools, fearing adverse effects they might have on their children's morals and religion, specifically, and probably in a vaguer sense, on their entire civilization. Such fears, of course, were not unfounded. Already Muslims could witness the effects of Western ways on coastal society, morals, and religion in the sorts of situations described at the end of the last chapter. But the trend was irreversible. The youth of the coast envied the material advantages which Western culture and technology offered. Therefore, they aspired for the very changes which their elders dreaded. And the future of 'progress' among coastal peoples, again just as it was elsewhere in Africa, was to be found through Western education. It was only through acceptance of schools like the Government school of Ali b. Hamud that coastal peoples would be able to participate fully in the new society that was being created in East Africa by colonial rule. The past could never be recaptured. The most that could be hoped for was that it might help mould the future.

Notes

PREFACE

1 T. T. Spear, 'Oral Traditions: Whose History?', *History in Africa*, 8 (1981), 165–81.
2 No doubt the best example of such a collection is J. F. P. Hopkins and N. Levtzion, *Corpus of Early Arabic Sources for West African History* (Cambridge, 1981). However, for a bibliography of Arabic and Swahili materials for East Africa see August H. Nimtz, 'Islam in Tanzania: An Annotated Bibliography', *Tanzania Notes and Records*, 72 (1973), 51–74.
3 See Randall L. Pouwels, 'Oral Historiography: The Problem of the Shirazi on the East African Coast', *History in Africa*, 11 (1984), 237–67. Also, Pouwels, 'The Medieval Foundations of East African Islam', *International Journal of African Historical Studies*, XI (1978), 201–27 and 393–409.
4 The list is growing, but two very recent publications which present opposing views are H. N. Chittick, *Manda: Excavations at an Island Port on the Kenya Coast* (Nairobi, 1984); and James deVere Allen, 'Swahili Culture and the Nature of East Coast Settlement', *IJAHS*, XIV (1981), 306–35.
5 Pouwels, 'Oral Historiography'.

INTRODUCTION

1 This was pointed out to me by James deVere Allen in a communication, 1982.
2 Such symbols appear, for example, in Swahili didactic literature; q.v. Jan Knappert, *Myths and Legends of the Swahili* (Nairobi, 1870); Knappert, *Swahili Islamic Poetry* (Leiden, 1971), 3 vols.
3 T. T. Spear, 'Oral Traditions: Whose History?' *History in Africa*, 8 (1981), 165–81.

1 THE ROOTS OF A TRADITION, 800–1500

1 Ylvisaker points out that deforestation and overworking the land on the Lamu mainland in the nineteenth century probably contributed to soil exhaustion in many areas. There are indications, too, that the entire coast might have enjoyed more rain and higher water tables before the sixteenth century. See M. Ylvisaker, *Lamu in the Nineteenth Century: Land, Trade, and Politics* (Boston, 1979), pp. 7 and *passim*; and G. S. P. Freeman-Grenville, 'The Coast, 1498–1840', in R. Oliver and G. Mathew (eds.), *History of East Africa*, vol. I (Oxford, 1963), 144.
2 Map in A. H. J. Prins, *The Swahili-Speaking Peoples of Zanzibar and the East African Coast* (London, 1967).
3 J. A. G. Elliott, 'A Visit to the Bajun Islands', *Journal of the African Society*, 25 (1925–6), 10–22, 147–63, 245–63, 338–58; V. L. Grottanelli, *Pescatori dell'Oceano Indiano* (Rome, 1955); C. W. Haywood, 'The Bajun Islands and Birikau', *Geographical Journal*, 85 (1933), 59–64; M. G. Revoil, 'Voyage chez les Bénadirs, les Somalis et les Bayouns', *Le Tour du Monde*, 49 (1885), 1–80; 50 (1885), 129–208.
4 For a full account of the archipelago, see Ylvisaker, *Lamu*, 2–7

5 Ibn Battuta in G. S. P. Freeman-Grenville, *The East African Coast, Select Documents* (Oxford, 1962), 31; 'Duarte Barbosa: An Account of the East Coast, 1517–18' in *ibid.*, 132; 'Father Monclaro: A Journey from Kilwa to Pate in 1569' in *ibid.*, 140.

6 I. M. Lewis, *Peoples of the Horn of Africa* (London, 1955), 57–9.

7 F. G. Dundas, 'Exploration of the Rivers Tana and Juba', *The Scottish Geographical Magazine*, IX (1893), 113–26; F. Elliot, 'Jubaland and Its Inhabitants', *Geographical Journal*, 41 (1913), 554–61; A. Werner, 'Some Notes on the Wapokomo of the Tana Valley', *African Affairs*, 12 (1912–13), 359–84; Ylvisaker, *Lamu*, 7–9.

8 No evidence of such early fishing activities along the northern coast or rivers has been found yet principally due to lack of investigation. However, evidence of such an association between Wilton industries and fishing has been found at Ishango. See M. Posnansky, 'The Prehistory of East Africa' in B. A. Ogot (ed.), *Zamani* (Nairobi, 1973), 64–6; J. E. G. Sutton, 'The Settlement of East Africa', *ibid.*, 85–6. Clark's investigations of the eastern coast of Somalia, on the other hand, have shown that fishermen were settled there both before and after the introduction of iron. See J. D. Clark, *The Prehistoric Cultures of the Horn of Africa* (Cambridge, 1954), 282–90.

9 See C. Ehret, *Southern Nilotic History* (Evanston, 1971), 39–41; Ehret, *Ethiopians and East Africans* (Nairobi, 1974), 7–31; Ehret, 'Cushites and Highland and Plains Nilotes to A.D. 1800' in Ogot, *Zamani*, 153–5; Sutton, 'Settlement of East Africa', 86–8.

10 Ehret, *Ethiopians*, 7–8; Ehret, 'Cushites', 153; Sutton, 'Settlement of East Africa', 86.

11 This is attested through loanword evidence given in Ehret, *Ethiopians*, *passim*, but especially 30–1. Sutton, in 'Settlement of East Africa', 86–7, mentions finds of bones of cattle, sheep, and goats, as well as grindstones, pestles, stone bowls, and earthenware pots in burial cairns he attributes to Cushites. See also C. Ehret, 'Cattle Keeping and Milking in Eastern and Southern African History: The Linguistic Evidence', *Journal of African History*, VIII, 1 (1967), 1–17.

12 Personal communication, Christopher Ehret, 28 December 1981.

13 Ehret, 'Cushites', 168; Ehret, *Ethiopians*, 34.

14 See Lewis, *Horn*, 33 and 95.

15 Lewis, *Horn*, 71; Lewis, 'Conformity and Contrast in Somali Islam' in I. M. Lewis (ed.), *Islam in Tropical Africa* (London, 1966), 253–67. Concerning the absorption of the Katwa Somali into Bajun culture, one Swahili informant remarked that they came to the coast with camels, cows, goats, millet, sorgum, maize, and bullrush millet. They introduced milking of camels and cattle, 'and every person who eats fish is not of their descent'. See 'Kurratil Ayun fi Nisbatil Bajun' in Grottanelli, *Pescatori*, 367.

16 The literature on the Bantu 'migrations' is vast. Representative of this literature, however, is M. Guthrie, 'Some Developments in the Prehistory of the Bantu Languages', *JAH*, III, 2 (1962), 273–82; R. Oliver, 'The Problem of the Bantu Expansion', *JAH*, VII, 3 (1966), 361–76; C. Ehret, *et al.*, 'Outlining Southern African History: A Re-evaluation, A.D. 100–1500', *Ufahamu*, III, 1 (1972), 9–27; J. H. Greenberg, *The Languages of Africa* (Bloomington, 1963); Peter Schmidt, 'A New Look at Interpretations of the Early Iron Age in East Africa', *History in Africa*, 2 (1975); D. W. Phillipson, *The Later Prehistory of Eastern and Southern Africa* (London, 1977), 102–230.

17 R. C. Soper, 'Kwale: An Early Iron Age Site in South-eastern Kenya', *Azania*, II (1967), 1–17; Soper, 'Iron Age Sites in North-eastern Tanzania', *Azania*, II (1967), 19–36; and Soper, 'A General Review of the Early Iron Age in the Southern Half of Africa', *Azania*, VI (1971), 5–36

18 Phillipson, *Later Prehistory*, 109–10; H. N. Chittick, 'An Archaeological Reconnaissance of the Southern Somali Coast', *Azania*, IV (1969), 122; G. G. Y. Mgomezulu, 'Recent Archaeological Research and Radiocarbon Dates from Eastern Africa', *JAH*, XXII, 4 (1981), 447.

19 Q.v. T. J. Hinnebusch, 'Prefixes, Sound Changes, and Subgroupings in the Coastal Kenyan Bantu Languages', Ph.D. thesis, UCLA, 1973; Hinnebusch, 'The Shungwaya Hypothesis: A Linguistic Reappraisal', in J. T. Gallagher (ed.), *East African Cultural*

History (Syracuse, 1976), 1–41; D. Nurse, 'Bantu Migration into East Africa: Linguistic Evidence' in C. Ehret and M. Posnansky (eds.), *The Archaeological and Linguistic Reconstruction of African History* (Berkeley, 1982).

20 See Hinnebusch, 'The Shungwaya Hypothesis', 24–5. Also see T. T. Spear, 'Traditional Myths and Linguistic Analysis: Singwaya Revisited', *History in Africa*, 4 (1977), 229–46, which attempts to reconcile the linguistic evidence with Miji Kenda traditions of origin in Shungwaya. The most recent and, probably the best statement, of this thesis is to be found in D. Nurse and T. T. Spear, *The Swahili: Reconstructing the History and Language of an African Society, 800–1500* (Philadelphia, 1985), 40–51.

21 M. Guthrie, *Comparative Bantu*, vol. 2 (Farnborough, 1971), 17–20; D. Nurse, 'A Hypothesis about the Origin of Swahili', unpublished paper presented at the Conference on Swahili Language and Society, SOAS, University of London, 20–22 April 1982, pp. 6 and *passim*.

22 P. D. Curtin *et al.*, *African History* (Boston, 1978), 29.

23 The best summary of the Miji Kenda and Pokomo traditions are in T. T. Spear, *The Kaya Complex, A History of the Mijikenda Peoples, 1500–1900* (Nairobi, 1978), Chap. 2; and Spear, 'Traditional Myths', 229–46. Material on the Katwa is found in L. Talbot-Smith, 'Historical Record of Tanaland', Kenya National Archives (hereafter KNA), DC/LAM/3/1, 44; A. Werner, 'A Swahili History of Pate', *Journal of the African Society*, XIV (1915), 157, note 9. For the Kilindini, see C. Guillain, *Documents sur l'histoire, le géographie, et le commerce de l'Afrique Orientale*, vol. II, part 2 (Paris, 1856), 240.

24 Oral traditions collected at Siyu by Mr Howard Brown, personal communication, 5 May 1982. See also, 'Kurratil Ayun', 371–2; evidence from a Bajun *vave* in D. Nurse, 'Bajun Historical Linguistics', *Kenya Past and Present*, 12 (1980), 39; F. W. Isaac, 'History of the Lamu District', unpublished MS in the possession of J. deV. Allen.

25 Q.v. V. L. Grottanelli, 'A Lost African Metropolis', *Africanistiche Studien*, 26 (1955); A. H. J. Prins, 'Sungwaya, die Urheimat de Nordost Bantu', *Anthropos*, 50 (1955), 273–82; J. Strandes, *The Portuguese Period in East Africa* (Nairobi, 1961), 204, 206, 207.

26 See discussions in previous sources. Also, J. H. van Lindschoten, *Itinerario Voyage ofter Schovaert van Jan Huygen van Lindschoten naer oost after Portugaels Indien, 1579–1592*, (s'Gravenhage, 1910–39), III end and IV end; Blaeu map of 1644 in J. Denuce, *L'Afrique au XVIe siècle et le commerce anversois* (Anvers, 1937), 112; 0. Dapper, *Naukeurige Deschrijvinge der Afrikensche Gewesten*, (Amsterdam, 1668), Frontispiece. All these sources are cited in T. T. Spear, 'Traditional Myths and Historians' Myths: Variations on the Singwaya Theme of Mijikenda Origins', *History in Africa*, 1 (1974), footnote 31.

27 Q.v. E. Cerulli, *Somalia: Scritti Yari Editi ed Inediti*, I (Rome, 1957), 254–5; R. F. Burton, 'The Lakes Region of Equatorial Africa', *JRGS*, XXIX (1859), 51 and 310.

28 Guillain, *Documents*, vol. II, part 2, p. 240, note 1, places it 'une vingtaine de milles dans le nord-ouest de Patta'; while a number of other early sources similarly placed Shungwaya northwest of Pate, such as J. L. Krapf, *A Dictionary of the Suaheli Language* (New York, 1969), 335; Krapf, *Travels' Researches and Missionary Labours in East Africa* (London, 1860 & 1868), 182; J. Rebmann and J. Erhardt, *Petermann's Mittheilungen*, II (1856), map 1; and Strandes, *Portuguese Period*, 204. Sacleux, however, placed it 'at the bottom of the Bay of Manda' (i.e. around the Mtangawanda, q.v. text below), in C. Sacleux, *Grammaire des dialectes Swahilis* (Paris, 1909), xiv. Burton simply located Shungwaya on the coast north of Lamu *Zanzibar: City, Island, and Coast*, vol. I (London, 1872), 410. See also Cerulli, *Somalia*, I, 254, note 2.

29 H. N. Chittick, 'Archaeological Reconnaissance', 115–30.

30 Spear, 'Traditional Myths', 67–84; Spear, 'Singwaya Revisited', 229–46, but especially see the map on p. 246. Regarding the strains this puts on the linguistic evidence, see Hinnebusch, 'The Shungwaya Hypothesis', 25.

31 D. Nurse, 'A Hypothesis about the Origin of Swahili', paper presented at the conference on Swahili Language and Society, SOAS, 22–24 April 1982; and Nurse and Spear, *The Swahili*, Chapter 2.

32 C. Ehret, personal communication, and T. Hinnebusch, 'The Shungwaya Hypothesis', 22–6.

33 Spear, 'Singwaya Revisited', *passim.*

34 Views presented in this paragraph and the following, concerning Southern and Eastern Cushitic linguistic influences on coastal Bantu were obtained from Christopher Ehret, 28 December 1982.

35 C. Ehret, personal communication on unpublished results of research performed in 1982 on Somali language relations and history.

36 Lewis, *Horn*, 95; Lee Cassanelli, 'The Benaadir Past: Essays on Southern Somali History', Ph.D. thesis, University of Wisconsin, 1973, 10–12; H. C. Fleming, 'Baiso and Rendille: Somali Outliers', *Ressegna di studi Etiopici* (1964), 83–90.

37 Fleming, 'Baiso', 84; and Lewis, *Horn*, 33, citing M. Colucci, *Principi di Diritto Consuetudinario della Somalia Italiana Meridionale* (Florence, 1924), 109.

38 Quoted in Cassanelli, 'The Benaadir Past', 21; and Ali A. Hersi, 'The Arab Factor in Somali History: The Origin and Development of Arab Enterprise and Cultural Influences in the Somali Peninsula'. Ph.D. thesis, UCLA, 1977, 102.

39 See evidence presented in E. R. Turton, 'Bantu, Galla and Somali Migrations in the Horn of Africa: A Reassessment of the Juba/Tana Area', *JAH*, XVI, 4 (1975), 530–4; J. A. G. Elliott, 'Bajun Islands', 10, 148, and *passim*; Strandes, *Portuguese Period*, 187, 298; L. Krapf's 'Journal', 18 March 1844, Church Missionary Society Records, CA5/016, 265. James Allen has noted how in the past Somali and Oromo could be found in mainland settlements, living in almost every stage of transformation into Swahili. See J. deV. Allen, 'Swahili Culture Reconsidered: Some Historical Implications of the Material Culture of the Northern Kenya Coast in the Eighteenth and Nineteenth Centuries', *Azania*, IX (1974), '128–31; and J. deV. Allen, 'Swahili Culture and the Nature of the East Coast Settlement', *International Journal of African Historical Studies*, XIV, 2 (1981), 322.

40 Personal communication, D. Nurse, July 1982, however, hypothesizes that the Somali influences on northern coastal Swahili came through the Bajun, rather than directly from Shungwaya. Nurse's contention of a relatively low level of Eastern Cushitic/Somali influences on Miji Kenda fits my hypothesis – as well as Hinnebusch's and Ehret's data – that most Miji Kenda, in fact, did not experience direct contact with Shungwaya.

41 Elliott, 'Bajun Islands', 147, 251–2; Talbot-Smith, 'Historical Record', 44; Turton, 'Bantu', 529; Howard Brown on Siyu traditions, personal communication, 5 May 1982. The historical accuracy of these traditions is supposed by the fact that almost all Bajun groups have Somali eponyms. See Grottanelli, *Pescatori*, 204–5; Werner, 'Swahili History of Pate', 175, note 9.

42 Guillain, *Documents*, II, 2, 237–8. It is also noteworthy that in the Miji Kenda versions, the migration from Shungwaya is associated with the founding of the age-set institution among them. Age-sets, of course, are characteristic of many of the Eastern Cushites and are found among certain southern Somali groups. Thus, the tradition could, again, represent a memory of when peoples having this institution arrived in Miji Kenda-land and introduced it there along with traditions about Shungwaya origins.

43 In connection with this, it is interesting to note that in the tenth century Mas'udi wrote that the 'land of Zanj' consisted of valleys, mountains, and deserts and stretched from the coast inland for 700 parasangs (i.e. from the Indian Ocean to the right bank of the Nile river). See Freeman-Grenville, *Select Documents*, 15. It is, of course, possible that Shungwaya could have been in the Jubba/Webbi Shebeele region and then shifted southwards over time. Thus, a series of 'Shungwayas' could have been created along the coast, just as there has been a string of Mungeas and Jundas.

44 See the traditions mentioned above, plus archaeological attestation from J. Kirkman, 'Historical Archaeology from Kenya, 1948–56', *The Antiquaries Journal*, XXXVII, 1 and 2 (1957), 16–28; J. Kirkman, 'Some Conclusions from Archaeological Excavations on the coast of Kenya, 1948–1966', in H. N. Chittick and R. Rotberg (eds.), *East Africa and the Orient* (New York, 1975), 226–47.

45 See J. Miller, 'Introduction: Listening for the African Past', in J. Miller (ed.), *The African Past Speaks* (Folkestone, 1980), 24–34, for a discussion of historical clichés, but especially 31–4 for migrations as clichés.

46 It should be remembered that the Southern Cushitic economic terms picked up by the Pokomo and the Swahili terms gotten from Somali all relate to cultivating activities and food items – and not herding.

47 D. W. Phillipson, 'Some Iron Age Sites in the Lower Tana Valley', *Azania*, XIV (1979), 155–60; Mgomezulu, 'Archaeological Research', 447–8.

48 For óne excellent illustration of how neighbouring peoples, occupying contrasting natural environmental zones, establish kinship and exchange networks as hedges against disastrous crop failures, see S. Feierman, *The Shambaa Kingdom* (Madison, 1974), Chapter 1. On alliance, kinship and exchange, see C. Meillassoux, 'From Reproduction to Production', *Economy and Society*, 1 (1972), 93–105; M. Douglas, 'Raffia Cloth Distribution in the Lele Economy', in G. Dalton, *Tribal and Peasant Economies* (Austin, Texas 1977), 103–22; and P. Bohannon, 'Some Principles of Exchange and Investment among the Tiv', *American Anthropologist*, LVII (1955), 40–70.

49 For the Gosha, see Lewis, *Horn*, 18–44 passim, and 71–5; Cassanelli, 'The Benaadir Past', 85–92. On the Pokomo, see A. Werner, 'Some Notes on the Wapokomo of the Tana Valley', *African Affairs*, 12 (1912–13), especially 360–1; R. P. A. LeRoy, 'Au Zanguebar Anglais', *Les Missions Catholiques*, 22 (1890), 496–7, 546–8, 568–73.

50 Cassanelli, 'The Benaadir Past', 9; also see Lewis, *Horn*, 95.

51 'Usulu wa Wajomvu' in H. E. Lambert, *Chi-Jomvu and Ki-Ngare*, (Kampala, 1958), 71–2.

52 LeRoy, 'Au Zanguebar', 461; C. H. Stigand, *The Land of Zinj* (London, 1913), 165.

53 Lewis, *Horn*, 95, 120–1.

54 Communications from James deV. Allen, 9 August 1982; and Mark Horton, 22 May and 2 July 1982.

55 See 'Kurratil Ayun' in Grottanelli, *Pescatori*, 366 and 367.

56 Turton, 'Bantu', 534; Ylvisaker, *Lamu*, 66; Howard Brown on Siyu traditions, personal communication, 5 May 1982.

57 Strandes, *Portuguese Period*, 186–7, 204. In another incident which took place in 1686, the Portuguese themselves sought assistance. What is especially remarkable in the context of this discussion is that an expedition was to go to Shungwaya to seek allies. There, specifically, it was Somali and Bajun (Wagunya) who were designated for recruitment. *Ibid.*, 203–4.

58 Traditions collected by Cassanelli, 'The Benaadir Past', 86; and Bajun traditions given in Turton, 'Bantu', 531.

59 See Hersi, 'Arab Factor', 134–7; Cassanelli, 'The Benaadir Past', 20–35; Lewis, *Horn*, 47. Just who or what the Ajuran were is not clear. Were they a Hawiya clan, a confederation, or a ruling Arab-Somali aristocracy?

60 Cassanelli, 'The Benaadir Past', 31–5.

61 For Miji Kenda versions of this tradition, see Spear, *The Kaya Complex*, 21. Again, I am indebted to Mr Howard Brown (personal communication, 5 May 1982) for the Famao version of this tradition. Talbot-Smith, 'History of Tanaland', and J. Clive, 'Short History of Lamu', in KNA DC/LAM/3/1. Both give a version related by Bajun historians, while another version from the Bur Gao region is given in Elliott, 'Bajun Islands', 354–5.

62 See notes 25 and 26.

63 Hinnebusch, 'Shungwaya Hypothesis'; personal communication, C. Ehret.

64 Mgomezulu, 'Archaeological Research', 447; Mark Horton, personal communication, 22 May 1982; H. N. Chittick, *Kilwa, An Islamic Trading City on the East African Coast*, vol. II (Nairobi, 1974), 320–1, 336–8; Chittick, *Manda, Excavations at an Island Port on the Kenya Coast* (Nairobi, 1984), 109–18.

65 Personal communication, Mark Horton, 2 July 1982.

66 Mark Horton, *Shanga, 1980: An Interim Report* (Nairobi, 1980), section 5.3, and personal communication. Chittick found similar mud and wattle houses in the earliest, pre-Islamic

Period Ib stratum at Kilwa, but rectangular in shape. See Chittick, *Kilwa*, I, 235–7.

67 At Kilwa, Chittick found evidence of Islamic habitation datable to about the same time or slightly later. See Chittick, *Kilwa*, I, 237–9.

68 Mark Horton, personal communication, 22 May 1982. Chittick, too, found evidence of a fish diet at Kilwa at about the same time, again; Chittick, *Kilwa*, I, 235 and 236.

69 Chittick, *Kilwa*, I, 235–6; Chittick, *Manda*, 207–12; Mark Horton, personal communication, 22 May and 2 July 1982; Phillipson, *Later Prehistory*, 155; Phillipson, 'Some Iron Age Sites', 155–9.

70 If one accepts Fadiman's hypothesis of coastal origins for the Meru, Meru remembrance of the Mtangawanda as an area 'where blacksmiths gathered' would be significant in this context. J. Fadiman, 'Early History of the Meru of Kenya', *JAH*, XIV, 1 (1973), 10–11; Sacleux, *Dictionnaire*, 61.

71 Elliott, 'Bajun Islands', 254.

72 Abu'Rayhan al-Biruni, *Kitab al-Jamahir fi Ma'rifat al-Jawahir*, edited by S. Krenkow (Hyderabad, 1355/1936–7); M. Lombard, *The Golden Age of Islam*, (New York, 1975), 179; G. S. P. Freeman-Grenville, *East African Coast, Select Documents* (Oxford, 1962), 20 and 24. Phillipson, it should be noted, argues that Freeman-Grenville might have mistranslated Malanda as Malindi, when Manda might have been meant. Phillipson, *Later Prehistory*, 155. Linguistically, this would make sense since, as Ehret notes, the intervocalic *l* has widely been dropped in Swahili. Thus Malanda would have become Manda in current Lamu or Bajuni speech.

2 THE EMERGENCE OF A TRADITION, 900–1500

1 In this category, I include works by Ehret, Fleming, Hinnebusch, Heine, and Nurse among the linguists, and Kirkman, Chittick, Horton, and Wilson among the archaeologists. For more examples of Shirazi traditions, see R. L. Pouwels, 'Oral Historiography and the Shirazi of the East African Coast', *HA*, 11 (1984), 237–67.

2 'Kitab as-Sulwa fi Akhbar Kilwa' in S. A. Strong (ed.), 'The History of Kilwa', *Journal of the Royal Asiatic Society*, (1985), 411–12.

3 For a brief, though sometimes inaccurate, discussion of some of the ways in which Shirazi has been used, see J. deV. Allen, 'The Shirazi Problem in East African Coastal History' in T. H. Wilson and J. deV. Allen (eds.), *From Zinj to Zanzibar*, (Wiesbaden, 1982), 12–14.

4 Chittick, *Kilwa*, I, 18 and 237–9.

5 J. deV. Allen, 'The Swahili House: Cultural and Ritual Concepts underlying Its Plan and Structure', *Art and Archaeology Research Papers*, Special Issue (1979), 1–32.

6 This is based on my general knowledge of the medieval sources which I have read over the past twelve years. The reader, however, is directed to the various documents in Freeman-Grenville, *Select Documents*, 8–33; and G. Ferrand, *Rélations du voyages et textes géographiques Arabes, Persans, et Turks relatifs a l'extrême orient du VIIIe au XVIIIe siècles* (Paris, 1914). The one isolated exception to this, it must be mentioned, is the thirteenth-century inscription of a Shirazi in Mogadishu's Arba'-Rukun mosque. As I have argued elsewhere, however, whatever early Shirazi there were on the coast were not Persian immigrants, but mostly local Swahili who had assumed Persian ancestry. See Pouwels, 'Oral Historiography'.

7 See Miller's discussion of the uses and meanings of the historical cliché and episode in 'Introduction: Listening for the African Past' in J. Miller (ed.), *The African Past Speaks* (Folkestone, 1980), 8–9.

8 Anthropologists have been especially at pains to point out this 'present orientation' of oral accounts. See Edmund Leach, *The Structural Study of Myth and Totemism* (London, 1967); T. O. Beidelman, 'Myth, Legend and Oral History', *Anthropos*, 65 (1970), 74–97; Luc de Heuch, *Le roi ivre ou l'origine de l'état* (Paris, 1972); B. Malinowski, 'Myth in Primitive Psychology' in *Magic, Science and Religion and Other Essays* (Glencoe, 1948).

9 Pressures from immigrant Cushitic-speaking pastoralists, both Somali and Oromo, seem

to have been the major cause of the flight of various groups, including sedentarized ex-pastoralists and Bantu farmers, out of the region. For such traditions, refer to sources cited in Chapter 1. Archaeological evidence of this abandonment of many mainland sites can be found in Kirkman's works, but especially, 'Historical Archaeology in Kenya, 1948–1956', *Antiquaries Journal*, XXXVII, 1 (1957), 16–28; and G. Mathew, 'The Culture of the East African Coast in the Seventeenth and Eighteenth Centuries in Light of Recent Archaeological Discoveries', *Man*, LVI (1956), 61–76.

10 Miller, 'Introduction', *passim*, and R. Sigwalt, 'The Kings Left Lwindi; The Clans Divided at Luhunda: How Bushi's Dynastic Origin Myth Behaves' both in Miller, *The African Past Speaks*, 126–56.

11 Burton collected two separate traditions which stated this, one at Zanzibar from the Hadimu, and another at Kilwa. R. F. Burton, *Zanzibar: City, Island and Coast*, I (London, 1872), 410–11, and II, 362. Pearce also tells of the 'Persian Sultan named Ali [b. Hasan al-Shirazi?]' who, Swahili sailors claimed, came from Shungwaya. F. B. Pearce, *Zanzibar, The Island Metropolis of East Africa*, 2nd edn (London, 1967), 29; Krapf was told a similar story, apparently by his informant, 'Bana Hamade, an intelligent and influential Swahili, chief of Mombaz'; q.v. J. L. Krapf, *Travels, Researches and Missionary Labours during an Eighteen Years Residence in Eastern Africa* (London, 1860), 182. William McKay recently collected a tradition around Vanga that the eponymous Shirazi king, Ali b. Shihiri, and his six sons came from Shiraz but settled at Kiwayuu and Shungwaya. W. F. McKay, 'A Precolonial History of the Southern Kenya Coast', Ph.D. dissertation, Boston University, 1975, 27–8.

12 S. Feierman, *The Shambaa Kingdom* (Madison, 1973), 17–18; also, B. Davidson, *The African Genius* (Boston, 1969), 54–7; C Lévi-Strauss, *The Savage Mind* (Chicago, 1966), Chapter 1; and R. Horton, 'African Traditional Thought and Western Science', *Africa*, 37 (1967), 50–71.

13 M. Sahlins, 'Culture and Environment: The Study of Cultural Ecology' in Sol Tax (ed.), *Horizons in Anthropology* (Chicago, 1964), 132–47; also, the introduction to Stephen Harvey, 'Hunting and Gathering as a Strategic Adaptation: The Case of the Boni of Lamu District, Kenya', Ph.D. dissertation, Boston University, 1978.

14 For a discussion of naive naturalist epistemology, see A. J. Ayer, *The Problem of Knowledge* (New York, 1956). For its applicability to so-called primitive cultures, see Lévi-Strauss, *The Savage Mind*, Chapter 1.

15 V. Turner, *A Forest of Symbols* (Ithaca, 1967), Chapter 1; R. Horton, 'Traditional Thought', 155–87.

16 See Chapter 1. Chittick also found evidence of grain cultivation in the earliest levels at Kilwa; q.v. Chittick, *Kilwa*, I, 235–7.

17 Personal communication, Mark Horton at Shanga; Chittick, 'Discoveries in the Lamu Archipelago', *Azania*, II (1967), 37–68, and personal communication; Chittick, *Kilwa*, I, 235–7.

18 It is worth noting at this point a meal eaten by Ibn Battuta during his visit to Mogadishu in 1331, which included, among other things, rice, bananas, meat, fish, mangoes, and milk products. See Freeman-Grenville, *Select Documents*, 29.

19 Chittick, *Kilwa*, I, 237–9; Chittick, 'Lamu Archipelago', *passim*, and personal communication; Mark Horton, *Shanga*, 5.3 and personal communication.

20 Hinnebusch, 'Shungwaya', *passim*.

21 Christopher Ehret, personal communication, November 1982.

22 Ehret, personal communication. Nurse sees proto-Sabaki as having developed into five dialects: Miji Kenda, Pokomo, Elwana, Swahili, and Comorian; q.v. Nurse and Spear, *The Swahili*, 52–5. In the context of the argument in this paragraph, a comment made in 1890 on the Pokomo language is appropriate: 'This language, like all those of related tribes, is rich and varied, though simple and naive, with perfectly drawn rules. It includes fables, songs, proverbs, and each insect, each plant, each turn in the river, everything has a name'. See LeRoy, 'Au Zanguebar Anglais', 568.

23 See Chapter 1. The Shungwaya region appears to have been a particularly important producer of iron, though iron slag has been found at the southern coast sites of Kilwa and Chibuene. See Chittick, *Kilwa*, I, 235–7; P. Sinclair, 'Chibuene – An Early Trading Site in Southern Mozambique' in Wilson and Allen, *From Zinj to Zanzibar*, 162.

24 Such products are mentioned in Mas'udi, Ibn Hawqal, and Idrisi in Freeman-Grenville, *Select Documents*, 14–20.

25 Imports at Manda were far heavier than at any other ninth to tenth-century sites, making up about 30 per cent of the total ceramic finds there. This suggests that Manda was a major ninth- to tenth-century entrepôt for the rest of the coast. See Chittick, 'Lamu Archipelago', 45–8; Chittick, *Manda*, 65–106; Chittick, *Kilwa*, I, 235–7; Chittick, 'Unguja Ukuu: The Earliest Imported Pottery and an Abbasid Dinar', *Azania*, I (1966), 161–3; T. H. Wilson, 'Spatial Analysis and Settlement Patterns on the East African Coast' in Wilson and Allen, *Zinj to Zanzibar*, 214–15, note 3.

26 Horton, personal communication; Mgomezulu, 'Recent Archaeological Research', 447; Chittick, 'Lamu Archipelago', 52–4; Chittick, *Kilwa*, II, 336–7; Sinclair, 'Chibuene', in Wilson and Allen, 153–8.

27 Horton, *Shanga*; M. Horton and C. Clark, *Zanzibar Archaeological Survey, 1984/5* (Zanzibar, 1985), 34–5; Chittick, 'Lamu Archipelago'; Chittick, *Kilwa*, I, 237–9; Chittick, 'Unguja Ukuu'; Chittick, *Annual Report of the Department of Antiquities* (Dar es Salaam, 1964); Sinclair, 'Chibuene' in Wilson and Allen; P. Verin, *Histoire Ancienne du Nord-Ouest de Madagascar* (Tananarive, 1972), 52–3; T. H. Wilson, 'Spatial Analysis' in Wilson and Allen, 214–15, note 3 and tables, 216–18.

28 Horton, *Shanga*, Horton and Clark, *Zanzibar*, 36, 39; Horton, 'Medieval Mogadishu' in Wilson and Allen, *Zinj to Zanzibar*, 54–61; Horton, 'The East Coast, Madagascar and the Indian Ocean', in J. Fage and R. Oliver (eds.), *The Cambridge History of Africa*, III (London, 1977), 203; Hamo Sassoon, 'How Old Is Mombasa?', *Kenya Past and Present*, 9 (1978), 37; J. S. Kirkman, 'The Excavations at Kilepwa', *The Antiquaries Journal*, 32 (1952), 168–84; Kirkman, *The Arab City of Gedi: Excavations at the Great Mosque, Architecture and Finds*, (London, 1954); Kirkman, *Ungwana on the Tana* (The Hague, 1966), 15–18.

29 Horton, 'Period II' and 'Period III' in *Shanga*, 5.3, and personal communication.

30 Chittick, *Kilwa*, I, 238; and frontispiece in vol. II.

31 Mas'udi mentions the presence of Muslims at tenth century Qanbalu; q.v. Freeman-Grenville, *Select Documents*, 14–17. Chittick also found a graffito in Kufic script from Period Ia levels in his excavations of the eastern courtyard of the Great House at Kilwa; q.v. Chittick, *Kilwa*, I, 131, and photo in vol. II, plate 105c.

32 Idrisi in Freeman-Grenville, *Select Documents*, 19; al-Yaqut, *Mu'jam al-Buldan*, IV, edited by F. Wustenfeld (Leipzig, 1866), 366.

33 Yaqut, *Mu'jam*, II, 75.

34 Ibn Said in Ferrand, *Relations*, I, 322–3; Cerulli, *Somalia*, I, 18; ᶜAydarus b. ash-Sharif ᶜAli an-Nadiri al-ᶜAlawi, *Bughyat al-Amal fi Tarikh as-Sumal* (Mogadishu, 1954), 42.

35 These mosques are the Friday mosque (636/1238), the mosque of Fakhr ad-Din (667/1269), and the Arba'-Rukun mosque (667/1269). See Cerulli, *Somalia*, I, 8–10; Chittick, 'Medieval Mogadishu' in Wilson and Allen, 52–4.

36 Chittick, *Kilwa*, I, 238 and personal communication. Note that these were not the familiar pillar tombs.

37 Horton, 'The Friday Mosque' in *Shanga*, 4.1–4.8, and personal communication.

38 Chittick, *Kilwa*, I, 61–3, 237–8.

39 Kirkman, *Ungwana*, Chapter II, especially Table I; Cerulli, *Somalia*, I, 45; Chittick, *Annual Report* (1964). It must be pointed out, however, that the absence of any surviving mosques or burials from earlier periods or other locations on the coast should not be construed as an argument that Muslims were not present on the coast in earlier times. For example, it is quite possible that Muslims were at Mombasa in the twelfth or thirteenth century despite lack of surviving evidence positively affirming it. See H. Sassoon, 'How Old Is

Mombasa?', 33–7. Mosques could have been built out of wood and other less durable materials, as suggested by Ibn Battuta's observations on Mombasa's mosque in 1331. See Freeman-Grenville, *Select Documents*, 31.

40 C. Geertz, 'Religion as a Cultural System' in M. Banton (ed.), *Anthropological Approaches to the Study of Religion*, (London, 1966), 7.

41 *Ibid.*; C. Geertz, *Islam Observed, Religious Developments in Morocco and Indonesia*, (New Haven, 1968), 95.

42 V. Turner, *The Ritual Process, Structure and Anti-Structure* (Chicago, 1969), 52–3.

43 Geertz, *Islam Observed*, 39

44 *Ibid.*

45 *Ibid.* Weber, of course, was the first to call attention to the tendency of mercantile activity to be associated with monotheistic religions. According to this point of view, the needs and world-views of merchants, especially those of long-distance traders, tend to support religions stressing the ethical demands of a supreme deity more than those which simply ensure the diurnal and perennial rounds of the agricultural seasons. Max Weber, *The Sociology of Religion*, cited in M. G. S. Hodgson, *The Venture of Islam*, I (Chicago, 1974), 133. This thesis has been developed in an attenuated form by Robin Horton in 'On the Rationality of Conversion', *Africa*, 45 (1965), 219–35, 373–99.

46 J. deV. Allen, 'Swahili Culture and the Nature of East Coast Settlement', *IJAHS*, XIV, 2 (1981), 324; Wilson, 'Spatial Analysis' in Wilson and Allen, 214; Kirkman, 'Historical Archaeology', 16.

47 Ivan Hrbek, 'Egypt, Nubia and the Eastern Deserts' in J. Fage and R. Oliver (eds.), *Cambridge History of Africa*, III, (London, 1977), 81–6.

48 *Ibid.*; T. Tamrat, 'Ethiopia, the Red Sea and the Horn', in Fage and Oliver (eds.). *Cambridge History of Africa*, III, 139–44.

49 Freeman-Grenville, *Select Documents*, 126. See also, B. A. Datoo, *Port Development in East Africa* (Nairobi, 1975), 43–4; E. A. Alpers, 'Gujerat and the Trade of East Africa, *c.* 1500–1800', *IJAHS*, IX, 1 (1976), 24.

50 Chittick, 'Medieval Mogadishu' in Wilson and Allen, 60

51 Freeman-Grenville, *Select Documents*, 84. Called the Mahdali on the coast, it is uncertain whether this clan descended from the Mahdali or the al-Ahdali in the Yemen. See B. G. Martin, 'Arab Migrations to East Africa in Medieval Times', *IJAHS*, VII, 3 (1974), 373–4.

52 Datoo, *Port Development*, 29–30. Among some of these feeder ports were towns like Kaole, Diani, Mtwapa, Kinuni, Kilepwa, Watamu, Uziwa, Ngomeni, Dondo, Omwe, Kiunga, Chula, Chovai, and Ngumi. Black-on-yellow wares are found rather rarely at Kilwa, but are especially common at northern coastal sites, pointing to the preponderant southwestern and southern Arab presence there. See Chittick, 'Lamu Archipelago', 64–5; Kirkman, *Gedi;* and Horton, *Shanga*, 4.3, 4.7, 5.3, 6.4.

53 Chittick noted especially the nearly complete replacement of sgraffiato wares at Kilwa by porcelains and celadons in the thirteenth century. H. N. Chittick, 'The "Shirazi" Colonization of East Africa', *JAH*, VI (1965), 286. The rise and importance of the northern ports in the fourteenth and fifteenth centuries likewise was accompanied by an influx of Chinese goods. Datoo, *Port Development*, 44–5, 47.

54 Chittick, 'East Coast, Madagascar and the Indian Ocean', in Oliver and Fage (eds.), *Cambridge History of Africa*, III, 212–14; see also Hamo Sassoon's fine description of the use of coral blocks, limestone, and other construction materials in 'The Coastal Town of Jumba la Mtwana', *Kenya Past and Present*, 12 (1980), 5–6.

55 Chittick, 'East Coast', 212–13; Kirkman, 'Historical Archaeology', 20–21; Wilson, 'Spatial Analysis' in Wilson and Allen, 207–213.

56 For examples, note the serial expansions of the Friday mosques at Kilwa and Shanga during this period. See Chittick, *Kilwa*, I, 61–99; and Horton, *Shanga*, 4.8.

57 See P. Garlake, *The Early Islamic Architecture of the East African Coast* (Nairobi, 1966), for the best descriptions of late medieval mosques. Garlake, like Chittick, argues in favour of a southern Arabian origin for post fourteenth-century mosque styles.

58 Several good examples can be seen in Horton, *Shanga*, 3.4–3.8; T. H. Wilson, 'Takwa, An Ancient Swahili Settlement of the Lamu Archipelago', *Kenya Past and Present*, 10 (1979), 7–16; J. Kirkman, 'The Great Pillars of Malindi and Mambrui', *Oriental Art*, IV (1958), 55–67.

59 M. G. Revoil, 'Voyage chex les Bénadirs, les Somalis et les Bayouns', *La Tour du Monde*, 49, 50, 56 (1885), 385–416.

60 Revoil, again, observed pilgrimages to such tombs, as did Wilson, Revoil, 'Voyage', 396; Wilson, 'Takwa', 15–16. Mathew notes evidence of sacrifices having been made at them; q.v. G. Mathew, 'The Culture of the East African Coast', 68.

61 Kirkman, 'Historical Archaeology', 24; T. H. Wilson, *The Monumental Architecture and Archaeology North of the Tana River* (Nairobi, 1978).

62 J. Allen, 'Swahili Culture', 313–14. The major problems associated with this hypothesis are: (1) Allen's theory ignores the equal possibility that the Miji Kenda graveposts might have come from the coast, rather than the other way round. (2) Many pillar tombs are found *outside* settlements, not just near mosques and within town precincts. (3) Nobody has shown that the Miji Kenda *kayas* predate late medieval coastal settlements.

63 R. Joussaume, 'Les monuments megalithiques du Harrar, Ethiopie', *L'Anthropologie*, 75 (1971), 177–99; Joussaume, 'Les monuments funeraires protohistoriques du Harrar, Ethiopie, 2me mission', *Documents pour servir a l'histoire des civilisations Ethiopiennes*, 6 (1975), 19–34; Phillipson, *Later Prehistory*, 236; Tamrat, 'Ethiopia', 136–43, especially 140.

64 Accounts by Ibn Battuta, an anonymous chronicler of da Gama's voyage, and Gaspar de Santo Bernadino in Freeman-Grenville, *Select Documents*, 30, 54, and 157.

65 A. C. Hollis, 'Notes on the History of Vumba, East Africa', *JRAI*, XXX (1900), 279–80; T. Ainsworth Dickson, 'The Regalia of the WaVumba', *Man*, 20 (1921), 33–5; McKay, 'Precolonial History', 57–62, 73; L. Harries, *Swahili Poetry* (London, 1962), 63; J. Knappert, *Four Centuries of Swahili Verse* (London, 1979), 69; A. Werner, 'History of Pate', 285–9, especially 285, note 23; Clive, 'Short History', 5; Talbot-Smith, 'Historical Record', 49; interviews, Lamu: 11 and 17 May 1975.

66 P. Garlake, *The Kingdoms of Africa* (London, 1978), 26. See also J. deV. Allen, 'The *Siwas* of Pate and Lamu: Two Antique Side-Blown Horns from the Swahili Coast', *Art and Archaeology Research Papers*, 9 (1976), 38–47; H. Sassoon, *The Siwas of Lamu* (Nairobi, 1975).

67 Hrbek, 'Egypt', 85

68 For a study of nineteenth- and twentieth-century Swahili women, see M. Strobel, *Muslim Women in Mombasa, 1890–1975* (New Haven, 1975); A. P. Caplan, 'Gender, Ideology and Modes of Production on the Coast of East Africa' in Wilson and Allen, *Zinj to Zanzibar*, 29–44.

69 Many queens are mentioned, such as Mwana Mkisi of Mombasa, Aisha bti. Muhammad of Ngumi, Mwana Inali of Takwa, Mwana Mazuru of Siyu, Queen Maryamu of Yumbwa, Mwana Miveni of Zanzibar, and (mythical?) Mwana wa Mwana of Tumbatu. See Elliott, 'Bajun Islands', 147–8; 254–5; Charles Sacleux, *Dictionnaire Swahili-Franċaise* (Paris, 1939), 639; Stigand, *Land of Zinj*, 42; F. J. Berg, 'The Swahili Community of Mombasa, 1500–1900', *JAH*, IX (1968), 42–4; J. M. Gray, 'Zanzibar Local Histories, Part I', *Swahili*, 30 (1959), 129. Strobel reports traditions that some Mombasa women were considered *wamiji*, town elders; q.v. *Muslim Women*, 80–1.

70 Strobel, *Muslim Women*, 80–4; Knappert, *Swahili Verse*, 80. Partitioned mosques from this phase indicate that women were still permitted in some mosques. On 'traditional' property rights of coastal women (*mila*), as opposed to rights permitted them by Islamic law, see Caplan's masterful 'Gender' in Wilson and Allen.

71 Knappert, *Swahili Verse*, 67–8. Inheritance and family identity through females were recorded for two Miji Kenda groups by Werner in 'The Bantu Coast Tribes of the East Africa Protectorate', *JRAI*, 45 (1915), 338–40.

72 Interview, Lamu: 9 June 1975. Evidence of medieval looting and slave raids by 'Arabs' can be found in Freeman-Grenville, *Select Documents*, 8, 9–13.

73 See Ibn Battuta's remarks on warfare between Kilwa and its mainland in Freeman-Grenville, *Select Documents* 31–2.

74 Most of the Twelve Tribes of Mombasa are descendants of those immigrant groups who came from the northern coastal towns in the sixteenth and seventeenth centuries. See Berg, 'Swahili Community', 37 and *passim*; and A. C. Hollis's notes in KNA DC/MSA/6/2.

75 Observations by Durate Barbosa, 1517–18, in Freeman-Grenville, *Select Documents*, 132; and by De Barros in reference to Mombasa, Malindi, Ozi, Lamu, Uziwa, Paremunda, and Kilifi in Kirkman, *Ungwana*, 9–10. See also quotes from Correa, Hans Mayr, Barbosa and Razende in Freeman-Grenville, *Select Documents*, 66, 108, 134, and 179–80, respectively.

76 Quoted in B. Davidson, *The African Genius*, 70.

77 *Ibid.*, 132.

78 Significantly, the Arabic word for a madman, *majnun*, is derived from the same root as *jinn*. See discussions about the behaviour of *jinnis* in Guillain, *Documents*, II, 97; J. E. E. Craster, *Pemba, the Spice Island of Zanzibar* (London, 1913), 305; W. H. Ingrams, *Zanzibar: Its History and Its People* (London, 1931), 484–85; A. P. Caplan, *Choice and Constraint in a Swahili Community* (London, 1975), 100–101.

79 Craster, *Pemba*, 305; Stigand, *Land of Zinj*, 124–5; KNA DC/LAM/3/2, p. 34; interviews, Mombasa: 28 February and 13 March 1975.

80 See Chapter 1 and Elliott, 'Bajun Islands', 255. The *nyika* again appears as a negative, anti-civilizing factor in the story of the Emozaydy in a Changamwe tradition and in a version of the Fumo Liongo epic. In these stories, Muslims are seen as losing their identity and religion when they are 'lost' in the bush, becoming rusticized 'bumpkins' (*mestizes*), forced to consume wild reeds, millet, and wild game in place of the vegetables and rice eaten by 'civilized' townsmen. See Freeman-Grenville, *Select Documents*, 83–4; Lambert, *Chi-Jomvu*, 89; and Knappert, *Swahili Verse*, 70–1.

81 For three Kilwa versions of the Shirazi tradition, consult Freeman-Grenville, *Select Documents*, 35–7, 89–91, and 221–3. The dating of the Arabic and Portuguese versions of the so-called 'Kilwa Chronicle' is crucial since they permit us to say with certainty that such attitudes of ambivalence to the outside world, especially to mainland peoples, as well as the Shirazi *genre* of traditions itself existed by the 16th century.

82 Sayyid Abdallah Ali Nasir, *Al Inkishafi* (Nairobi, 1972), 11; A. H. el-Zein, 'The Sacred Meadows: A Structural Analysis of Religious Symbolism in an East African Town', 1972, 39 – later published under the same title; B. G. Martin, 'Arab Migrations', 381; Cerulli, *Somalia*, I, 22–23; Talbot-Smith, 'Historical Record', 64; Stigand, *Land of Zinj*, 51.

83 Wilson, 'Takwa', 9 and 11; Stigand, *Zinj*, 43,

84 See traditional evidence in the 'Kitab al-Zanuj' in Cerulli, *Somalia*, I 329 and 331.

85 See Chapter 4.

3 A NORTHERN METAMORPHOSIS, 1500–1800

1 The *siwa* in question is the brass one presently housed in the Lamu Museum. The fact that there is a great deal of confusion in the traditions concerning the origin of the Lamu *siwa*, from Kinarani, Manda, or Uziwa/Mrio – and ultimately from 'Shiraz' – suggests that it was used by all these towns, just as later a *siwa* was shared by Lamu and Pate. That all these towns were so-called Shirazi towns, in recognition of common social and historical realities, reinforces this theory of a federation based on shared regalia. See Shaibu Faraji al-Bakari al-Lamuy, 'Khabar Lamu' (ed. W. Hichens). *Bantu Studies*, XII (1938), 16–17; Werner, 'History of Pate', 284, note 3; Clive, 'Short History', 5–6; Talbot-Smith, 'Historical Record', 47–49; F. W. Isaac, 'Summarized History', KNA DC/LAM/3/1, 120. Also, interviews, Lamu: 11 and 17 May, A. M. Jahadhmy.

2 Overlaps in such alliances, especially of the more informal kinds, seem to have been common and were major contributing factors towards the notorious factionalism found in most coastal towns. On the Kilwa confederation, see Morice's description in G. S. P. Freeman-Grenville, *The French at Kilwa Island* (Oxford, 1965), 135–7.

3 See R. L. Pouwels, 'Islam and Islamic Leadership in the Coastal Communities of Eastern Africa, 1700 to 1914', Ph.D. thesis, UCLA, 1979. See Chapter 3 for more details on town social organization.

4 Peter Lienhardt, 'The Mosque College of Lamu and Its Social Background', *Tanganyika Notes and Records*, LII (1959), 228–42; A. H. J. Prins, *Didemic Lamu* (Groningen, 1971).

5 T. O. Ranger, *Dance and Society in Eastern Africa* (Berkeley and Los Angeles, 1973), 19–20.

6 Prins, *Didemic Lamu*, 23, note 15.

7 V. W. Turner, *The Ritual Process, Structure and Anti-Structure* (Chicago, 1969), 83.

8 For a more detailed discussion of oral historiography and interpretation of the Shirazi tradition, see Pouwels, 'Oral Historiography'.

9 L. Bohannon, 'A Genealogical Charter', *Africa*, XXIII (1952), 302–15; T. O. Beidelman, 'Myth, Legend and Oral History', *Anthropos*, 65 (1970), 74–97; Luc de Heusch, *Le roi ivre ou l'origine de l'état* (Paris, 1972).

10 See, for example, S. Feierman, *The Shambaa Kingdom* (Madison, 1973); J. Miller, *Kings and Kinsmen* (London, 1976); J. Vansina, *The Children of Woot* (Madison, 1978).

11 Miller summarizes much of this new historiography in his 'Introduction: Listening for the African Past', in J. Miller, *The African Past Speaks* (Folkestone, 1980), 1–59. The book itself, especially Miller's introduction and Vansina's contributing chapter, undoubtedly stands as an important milestone, along with Vansina's *Oral Tradition* (Chicago, 1965), in the development in the uses of oral narratives for historical purposes. In addition, attention should be drawn again to my aforementioned 'Oral Historiography' and to T. T. Spear's 'Oral Traditions: Whose History?' *History in Africa*, 8 (1981), 165–81.

12 See Pouwels, 'Oral Historiography', and T. T. Spear, 'The Shirazi in Oral Traditions, Culture and History', *History in Africa*, 11 (1984).

13 In the text, I refer to these published traditions by number to save space. The interested reader can find them published (together) and by the same numbering system in Pouwels, 'Oral Historiography', or he can find them individually as follows:

  (1) Freeman–Grenville, *Select Documents*, 36–7.

  (2) *Ibid.*, 89–90.

  (3) *Ibid.*, 221–2.

  (4) *Ibid.*, 297.

  (5) Barbara Dubins, 'A Political History of the Comoro Islands, 1797–1886', Ph.D. thesis, Boston University, 1972, 19–20.

  (6) Elizabeth Wangari Rugoiyo, oral tradition collected at Siyu from Asmau Famau and recorded in Horton, *Shanga*, Appendix 5.

  (7) Stigand, *Land of Zinj*, 29–30.

  (8) Cerulli, *Somalia*, I, 257–61, 266–7, 334 (notes for variant manuscript L).

  (9) Hollis, 'Vumba', 282.

  (10) R. Skene, 'Notes on the Arab Clans of East Africa', KNA DC/MSA/3/1, 197, with additional information from Werner, 'Wapokomo', 366, and Stigand, *Zinj*, 44, note 1.

  (11) J. Kirkman (ed.), 'The Zanzibar Diary of John Studdy Leigh', *IJAHS*, XIII (1980), 289–90.

  (12) Amur Omar Saadi, 'Mafia – History and Traditions', *TNR*, 12 (1941), 25.

  (13) 'Kurratil Ayun fi Nisbatil Bajun' in Grottanelli, *Pescatori*, 366–7.

  (14) Freeman–Grenville, *Select Documents*, 83–4.

  (15) 'Hadithi ya Wachangamwe' in Lambert, *Chi-Jomvu na Ki-Ngare*, 89–90.

  (16) 'Usulu wa Wajomvu' in Lambert, *Chi-Jomvu* 70–1, with additional notes on 81.

14 Refer to Chapter 2, note 6.

15 M. Tolmacheva, 'The Origin of the Name Swahili', *TNR*, 70/78 (1976), argues that 'Swahili' has been in use on the coast only in the past century or so.

16 Refer to Chapter 2, note 11.

17 Such an existence continued to be lived in the 'poorer' parts of the coast throughout the nineteenth century, and can still be seen among the peoples north of Lamu. The Bajun

probably represent a fairly good example of this, as described by Elliott, 'Bajun Islands', and in Revoil, 'Voyage'.

18 Knappert, *Swahili Verse*, 66–100. According to tradition, indeed, Fumo Liongo and the Bauri clan, of which he was a member, *were* Shirazi. See text and notes below.

19 Swahili religious terms include a number of items of proto-Bantu provenance, such as words for charm, spirit, medicine, medicine man, to use medicine, dream, to diagnose illness or prognosticate by a dream, witchcraft, sorcery, to bewitch, to curse, and taboo. Guthrie, *Comparative Bantu*, 2, Appendices 8/1 and 8/2.

20 Mogadishu remains something of a question mark for this period, especially in terms of its cultural and religious life.

21 Following the line of thinking employed here, of course, it is quite possible that this arrival of Arabs in the Lamu region in the sixteenth and seventeenth centuries resulted in the creation of a Shirazi/Arab tradition in that area and at that time. The tradition, it is suggested, could very well have come from other areas of the coast which already had experienced similar periods of commercial prosperity and heavy immigration, thus giving a certain cyclic quality to coastal cultural history.

22 See Tamrat, 'Ethiopia'.

23 See Ibn Battuta on Mogadishu and Kilwa in Freeman-Grenville, *Select Documents*, 28–32; Pouwels, 'Medieval Foundations', 396–403.

24 Freeman-Grenville, *Select Documents*, 105–12 and 146–51; Datoo, *Port Development*, 101; E. A. Alpers, *Ivory and Slaves in East Central Africa* (Berkeley and Los Angeles, 1975).

25 See, for example, Nicholas T. Buckeridge, *Journal and Letterbook of Nicholas Buckeridge, 1651–1654*, edited by J. R. Jensen (Minneapolis, 1973), 45; and Freeman-Grenville, *Select Documents*, 178–86.

26 Sir John Gray, 'A History of Kilwa (Part I)', *TNR*, 31 (1951), 15, for the 31 August 1606 letter of Pero Ferreira Fagosha.

27 Sir John Gray, 'A History of Kilwa (Part I)', *TNR*, 31 (1951), 16.

28 G. Mathew, 'The Culture of the East African Coast in the Seventeenth and Eighteenth Centuries in the Light of Recent Archaeological Discoveries', *Man*, LVI (1956), 67.

29 Pouwels, 'Islam and Islamic Leadership', 63–4; Also, Strandes, *Portuguese Period*, 175; Freeman-Grenville, *Select Documents*, 157, 158, 160; C. R. Boxer and Carlos de Azevado, *Fort Jesus and the Portuguese in Mombasa* (London, 1960), 129.

30 Sir John Gray, 'A History of Kilwa (Part II)', *TNR*, 32 (1952), 17.

31 Strandes, *Portuguese Period*, 139.

32 *Ibid.*, 310, and Francis Xavier's observations in Freeman-Grenville, *Select Documents*, 136.

33 Strandes, *Portuguese Period*, 310–11.

34 *Ibid.*, 89, 92–3, 112. According to this source, indeed, throughout the sixteenth and seventeenth centuries Mogadishu remained 'the richest and most powerful town on the East African coast'. Strandes, *Portuguese Period*, 69.

35 Buckeridge, *Journal*, 45; Datoo, *Port Development*, 101. On Pate's alliances with the Aweera and the Oromo, see H. N. Chittick, 'A New Look at the History of Pate', *JAH*, X, 3 (1968), 382–3; Strandes, *Portuguese Period*, 187; C. Pickering, *The Races of Man and Their Geographical Distribution* (Boston, 1848), 212.

36 Monclaro in Freeman-Grenville, *Select Documents*, 142; Buckeridge, *Journal*, 45 and 46; Datoo, *Port Development*, 88–9.

37 Martin, 'Arab Migrations', 376–7; 'Kurratil Ayun', 371.

38 The extreme austerity of the Hadrami *tariqas* was noted by L. W. C. Van den Berg in *Le Hadramout et les colonies Arabes dans l'Archipel Indien* (Batavia, 1886), 84–5. One of the best sources in Arabic concerning the history of the *shurafa'*, especially in the Comoros, is Shaykh Burhan b. Muhammad Mkelle's history of Grand Comoro. I came across it on deposit in the archives of the East African Centre for Research in Oral Traditions and African National Languages at Zanzibar. According to this source, the first Hadrami *shurafa'* to arrive at Pate were the Jamal al-Layl who came before Vasco da Gama's momentous voyage. See EACROTANAL document EAC-003, p. 36.

39 Martin, 'Arab Migrations', 378; R. B. Serjeant, *The Saiyids of Hadramawt* (London, 1957), 17–18.

40 Serjeant, *Saiyids*, 15–18.

41 The Nabahani ultimately might have come from Oman, as is usually claimed. However, the branch that settled at Pate seems to have come via the Hadhramawt. I base this conclusion on the known presence of the Ba Barayk in the Hadhramawt and on a tradition found by Chittick in which the Pate Nabahani themselves claim Hadhramawt origins. See Chittick, 'History of Pate', 383–4; Van den Berg, *Hadramout*, 39–41; Martin, 'Arab Migrations', 376.

42 Admittedly, this dating is tentative. It is based on absolute chronology given in the Stigand version of the 'Pate Chronicle', as well as on its chronological sequencing relative to (i.e. as being roughly contemporary with) the arrival of the Abu Bakr b. Salim. Also, it is likely to have occurred somewhat before the late seventeenth century when Hatami settlement around Bagamoyo took place. See Stigand, *Zinj*, 50–1; W. T. Brown, 'A Pre-Colonial History of Bagamoyo; Aspects of the Growth of an East African Coastal Town', Ph.D. thesis, Boston University, 1971, 63–79. The relationship between the Amrani and the Hatami is discussed in Pouwels, 'Medieval Foundations', 225, 396–7.

43 'Kurratil Ayun', 371.

44 'Pate Chronicle' in Stigand, *Zinj*, 49–51. Interview of Asmau Famau by Elizabeth Rugoiyo, in Horton, *Shanga*, Appendix 5.

45 Talbot-Smith, 'Historical Record', 64; Stigand, *Zinj*, 50.

46 See el-Zein, 'Sacred Meadows', 39; Abdallah Ali Nasir, *Al-Inkishafi*, 11; Stigand, *Zinj*, 50.

47 Monclaro, quoted in Freeman-Grenville, *Select Documents*, 142.

48 Stigand, *Zinj*, 51; Brown, 'Bagamoyo', 83–99.

49 It must be noted, again, that the story of the Hatami, as related in the 'Kitab az-Zanuj' is juxtaposed with what appears to be a digression on the 'lapsed' nature of the Shirazi. See the original text in Cerulli, *Somalia*, I, 266–7, 333.

50 Martin, 'Arab Migrations', 381–3, 386; plus the traditions recorded by B. Dubins in her thesis, 'Comoro Islands', 30–1. According to Sh. Burhan Mkelle's history, the Jamal al-Layl settled at Insunjini and Ikoni, while the Abu Bakr bin Salim originally resided at Moroni. EACROTANAL EAC-003, pp. 36–7.

51 According to Martin, the Al-Masila Ba Alawi were founded by one Abdallah Ba Alawi al-Husayni; see his 'Arab Migrations', 386–7.

52 R. Skene, 'Arab Clans of East Africa', 198; W. F. McKay, 'A Precolonial History of the Southern Kenya Coast', Ph.D. thesis, 1978, 6–7, 46; Martin, 'Arab Migrations', 225. According to the anonymous author of the Arabic 'Early History of Zanzibar under Umani Arab Rule', the clan of Zanzibar's Mwinyi Mkuu claim to be descended from 'high members of Pate country'. See EACROTANAL document EAC-007.

53 Martin, 'Arab Migrations', 386–7.

54 *Ibid.*, 86–7; H. E. Lambert, *Ki-Vumba, A Dialect of the Southern Kenya Coast* (Kampala, 1957), 17–18; Skene, 'Notes', 198; F. B. Pearce, *Zanzibar, The Island Metropolis of East Africa*, 2nd edn (London, 1967); Sir John Gray, 'Zanzibar Local Histories, Part I', *Swahili*, 30 (1959), 26–30; A. E. Robinson, 'The Shirazi Colonizations of East Africa', *TNR*, 3 (1937), 50 and 81; W. H. Ingrams, *Zanzibar, Its History and Its Peoples* (London, 1931), 144–5. According to one nineteenth-century source, as of 1838 the Wahadimu still considered themselves to be subjects of the sultan of Kilwa. See F. Albrand, 'Extrait d'un mémoire sur Zanzibar et Quiloa', *Bulletin de la Societé de Géographie* (1838), 73, 79–80. In connection with this, the last Mwinyi Mkuu was an Alawi; see Robinson, 'Shirazi', 51.

55 For Vumba Kuu, see McKay, 'Precolonial History', 51; A. C. Hollis, 'Notes on the History of Vumba, East Africa', *JRAI*, XXX (1900), 282. For Tumbatu, see the stories of Alawi friction with the local headman in I. H. O. Rolleston, 'The Watumbatu of Zanzibar', *TNR*, 8 (1939), 86–7. For Ozi, see below. On Kilwa, see Freeman-Grenville, *French at Kilwa Island*, 28–38.

56 Miller, 'Introduction' in *The African Past Speaks, passim.* Nti Kuu was 'near' Shungwaya. See the 'Kitab az-Zanuj', 266.

57 Talbot-Smith, 'Historical Record', 44; Elliot, 'Bajun Islands', 255 and *passim*; E. G. Ravenstein, 'Somal and Galla Land: Embodying Information Collected by the Rev. Thomas Wakefield', *Proceedings of the Royal Geographical Society*, 6 (1884), 267; D. Nurse, 'Bajun Historical Linguistics', *Kenya Past and Present*, 12 (1980), 38–9.

58 Wilson, 'Spatial Analysis' in Wilson and Allen, 216–17.

59 'Kurratil Ayun', 371–2; Talbot-Smith, 'Historical Record', 44.

60 Personal communication on the Famao, Mr Howard Brown, 5 May 1982; also, Stigand, *Zinj*, 165. See Wilson, 'Spatial Analysis' in Wilson and Allen, 216–17 for dating.

61 A. Werner, 'Some Notes on the Wapokomo of the Tana Valley', *African Affairs*, 12 (1912–13), 363–4; M. Samson and R. G. Darroch 'Some Notes on the Early History of the Tribes Living on the Lower Tana, Collected by Mikael Samson and Others', *Journal of the East African Natural History Society*, XVII (1943–4), 247.

62 Samson and Darroch, 'Notes', 254 and 371. R. L. Bunger, *Islamization among the Upper Pokomo* (Syracuse, 1973), 12–13. The location of Mgine is vague since, as Cerulli notes, several sites exist, with one being near Barawa, another on the mainland opposite Pate Island, and even another (Mangea?) near Malindi. Cerulli, *Somalia*, I, 253, note 3; Samson and Darroch, 'Notes', map 246.

63 'Kurratil Ayun', 371–2.

64 See Miller on myths of migration in 'Introduction' in his *The African Past Speaks*, 31–4.

65 Wilson, 'Spatial Analysis' in Wilson and Allen, 216–17; Kirkman, 'Historical Archaeology', 16–17 and *passim.*

66 Elliott, 'Bajun Islands', 255.

67 Stigand, *Zinj*, 44; Knappert, *Swahili Verse*, 70–1, where Liongo is obviously very reliant on his mainland relations.

68 J. de Barros, *Decadas da India*, II, 1, ii, pp. 19–30, quoted in J. Kirkman, *Ungwana on the Tana* (The Hague, 1966), 9–10 especially. Uziwa or Luziwa is thought to have been a ruined site about 3 kilometres from Mkunumbi. Archaeological evidence indicates it thrived in about the fifteenth to sixteenth centuries. The location of 'Quitau', on the other hand, is unknown, although Kirkman guesses it to be either Ngomeni or Mwana. It is unlikely to have been the Kitao of Manda Island. Kirkman, *Ungwana*, 9, note 3; Kirkman, notes to Strandes, *Portuguese Period*, 296 and 310.

69 Mudio or Idio as a name for the area around (L)Uziwa appears on a map in W. W. A. Fitzgerald, *Travel in the Coastlands of British East Africa and the Islands of Zanzibar and Pemba* (London, 1898), 378–9. Allen's view that Hichen's identification of Mudiwo/Mudio with Idio has to be taken as a textual corruption appears to be erroneous since at least one (blind – and therefore independent) field informant made a similar identification. See Allen, 'Siwas', 43, and Chapter 3 Appendix, no. 9.

70 Kirkman, *Ungwana*, 9–10. For traditions concerning Mrio or Kiwa Ndeo, see the Chapter 3 Appendix, nos. 2, 6, 7, 8. Also, Clive, 'Short History', 4, 18–19; Stigand, *Zinj*, 151.

71 Some traditions alternatively claim that Lamu's *siwa* came from Manda; see Chapter 3 Appendix, nos. 11 and 12. Werner, 'History of Pate', 284, note 3.

72 Santos and Couto in E. Axelson, *The Portuguese in South-East Africa, 1488–1600* (Johannesburg, 1973), 181, 185, and notes 5 and 16.

73 This is based on field interviews and notes, Lamu: 11 May 1975, and additional information in KNA. DC/LAM/3/2, 'Political Records', 179–83; KNA Deposit 1, CP Bundle II MSA/6, under Kabila Lamu.

74 Clive, 'Short History', 4 and 19; F. W. Isaac, 'Summarized History', 45. Other traditions say the Kinamti came from the Hijaz. Since they do include the Mahdali, it is of course possible that there is some truth in this claim. See Chapter 3 Appendix, nos. 3–5, especially no. 4. The likelihood of African ancestry for most, however, would seem greatly higher.

75 Chapter 3 Appendix, nos. 2–4. Other informants simply say that the original inhabitants

of Hidabu Hill were '*wananchi*', or 'not Arabs'. Interview, Lamu: A. M. Mahdali, 19 April 1975.

76 Samson and Darroch, 'Notes', 247–8; Samson and Darroch 'A History of the Pokomo by Mikael Samson', *JEANHS*, XVII (1943–4), 371–2; Bunger, *Islamization*, 57–8. Based on genealogical evidence, Bunger and Werner place the time of these migrations near the end of the seventeenth century. Other traditions, however, state that they were considerably earlier, and only help to reinforce the unreliability of genealogies and kinglists as a method for dating. See Bohannon, 'A Genealogical Charter', and Werner, Wapokomo', 365.

77 J. Fadiman, 'Early History of the Meru of Mt. Kenya', *JAH*, XIV, 1 (1973), 12.

78 The Bauri clan have had an especially illustrious part in coastal history. As sultans of the old Ozi federation, they would have been rulers over Ungwana, Shaka, Mwana, Malindi, and Uziwa and, as shown in the text, they probably were related to Lamu's Kinamti. They were, of course, an important Lamu clan and supposedly were the clan of the legendary Fumo Liongo. Finally, the Shirazi sultan of Malindi who met Vasco da Gama and the Shirazi clan whom the Portuguese made sultans of Mombasa in 1593 were Bauri al-Malindi. See 'The Book of Zenj', 264, 271. Interview, Lamu: 16 April 1975, Abdallah Khatib Bauri. Though they claim to be Arabs from the Hadhramawt (Bura), in reality Bura is located on the Tana River, and they probably were Pokomo of the Bure clan. See Werner, 'Wapokomo', 67; L. Harries, *Swahili Poetry* (London, 1962), 50–1; Talbot-Smith, 'History of Tanaland', KNA DC/TRD/3/1, pp. 62–3.

79 See also Sacleaux, *Dictionnaire*, 61; Isaac, 'History'.

80 Elliott, 'Bajun Islands', 256; Cerulli, *Somalia*, I 260, note 2; Sacleux, *Dictionnaire*, 61; Guillain, *Documents*, III, 238 and 239. Yanbuᶜ is mentioned in the 'Kitab as-Sulwa' as one of the seven original Shirazi settlements; S. A. Strong, 'Kitab' in his *History of Kilwa*, original Shirazi settlements; S. A. Strong, 'Kitab' in his *History of Kilwa*, 411–12.

81 Sacleux, *Dictionnaire*, 61. Interview, Lamu: 29 April 1975.

82 Sacleux, *Dictionnaire*, 61. Stigand, *Zinj*, 145; Isaac, 'History', 8. Interview, Lamu: 29 April 1975.

83 Personal communication, H. Brown, 5 May 1982.

84 Excellent introductions to the material culture of the post sixteenth century coast can be found in Mathew, 'Culture of the East African Coast'; Usam Ghaidan, *Lamu* (Nairobi, 1975); J. deV. Allen, 'Swahili Culture Reconsidered: Some Historical Implications of the Material Culture of the Northern Kenya Coast in the Eighteenth and Nineteenth Centuries', *Azania*, IX (1974), 105–38.

85 See Chapter 4 for a discussion of the charismatic community on the coast.

86 In the Chapter 3 Appendix, no. 3, for example, representatives or 'elders' of Weyoni are referred to specifically as forty 'strong and clever' people. The deaths of the Weyoni/Tundani *wazee* in all these Lamu traditions marked the 'death' or 'conquest' of the community by the Hidabu 'Arabs'.

87 See 'mzee' in Sacleux, *Dictionnaire*, and F. Johnson, *A Standard Swahili-English Dictionary* (London, 1939).

88 Talbot-Smith, 'Historical Record', 76–9.

89 Elliott, 'Bajun Islands', 253–4, 255, 258.

90 Clive, 'Short History', 4; el-Zein, 'Sacred Meadows', 20–2.

91 Stigand, *Zinj*, 42–3, note 3.

92 *Ibid.*, 38–9. Similar references to the pride of the people of Manda exist in the Lamu Chronicle; q.v. Shaibu Faraji al-Bakari al-Lamuy, 'Khabari Lamu', 14–15.

93 Werner, 'Wapokomo', 366; Stigand, *Zinj*, 44, note 1; Clive, 'Short History', 5. Interviews, Lamu: 16 April and 17 May 1975. The Bauri, it should not be forgotten, were the Shirazi sultans of Malindi also. 'The Book of Zenj', 334, note 233.

94 Refer to note 13, tradition no. 9; also, Table 1, Set 2d See also traditions recorded in Werner, 'History of Pate', 284, note 23; F. W. Isaac, 'Summarized History', 47–9; Clive, 'Short History', 5; Hollis, 'Vumba', 282: McKay, 'Precolonial History', 32–3.

95 See Chapter 2, note 11; also, C. Sacleux, *Grammaire*, xv–xvi.
96 Stigand, *Zinj*, 165; Prins, *Didemic Lamu*, 7–8. Interviews, Lamu: 17 May and 7 June 1975. In a personal communication, H. Brown reports that no memory of Shirazi origins exist in Siyu today. Fitzgerald, however, appears to have been told in 1898 that the 'Wa-Siyu' were of Persian descent. Who these 'Wa-Siyu' were, however, is not clear. Possibly they were the autochthonous 'wazaliya' (*not* freed slaves) still found there as 'dependants' of the town *waungwana*. Fitzgerald, *Travels*, 386.
97 On the subject of the fictitious claims of origin made by Lamu groups, see M. Tolmacheva, 'They Came from Damascus in Syria: A Note on Traditional Lamu Historiography', *IJAHS*, XII, 2 (1979), 259–69.
98 See the tradition nos. 9–15 in Chapter 3 Appendix; also, the version of the 'Pate Chronicle' in Stigand, *Zinj*, 38.
99 See Allen, 'Swahili Culture Reconsidered', *passim*. 'Pate Chronicle' in Stigand, *Zinj*, 51 and *passim*.
100 Chapter 3 Appendix, no. 12; Werner, 'History of Pate', 157–9.
101 Stigand, *Zinj*, 51–4; Werner, 'History of Pate', 281 and *passim*.
102 See, for example, Buckeridge, *Journal*, 39–40, on the Comoro Islands slave trade.
103 Monclaro, while remarking on its religious leadership, also said, 'These Moors are very proud, and the worst enemies we have upon that coast...' Freeman-Grenville, *Select Documents*, 142. See tradition no. 5 in note 13, where later rulers of Domoni are said to have been married to 'Princes of Pate'. So close was the identification of these new regimes at Tumbatu and Vumba Kuu with Pate, that they took the date traditionally said to have been that of Pate's founding, 600 AH, as their own founding date. See McKay. 'Precolonial History', 41; Ingrams, *Zanzibar*, 28. It is equally significant that Pate is associated in other traditions with the destruction of the old 'Shirazi' states of Manda and the mainland. Tradition no. 7, note 13; Stigand, *Zinj*, 38–41; LeRoy, 'Au Zanguebar', 462–3.
104 Chapter 3 Appendix, nos. 13 and 15; Stigand, *Zinj*, 42–3, note 3; Werner, 'History of Pate', 156–7. Informants differed slightly on where they settled: Kivondoni quarter or Kinaoni and Madukani quarters. All agree, though, that they resided 'near' the Wayumbili. Interviews, Lamu: April and 11 May 1975.
105 Werner, 'History of Pate', 156–9; Stigand, *Zinj*, 42–3, note 3; interview, Lamu: Salim Heri, 17 May 1975.
106 Interview, Lamu: A. M. Jahadhmy, 11 May 1975. Later, when Pate and Lamu fell to quarrelling, the split loyalties of some of the Zena faction (Waungwana wa Yumbe) were to pose a threat to Lamu's security. Various accounts of the 1812 Battle of Shela mention this particular difficulty, for example. Suudi, the 'forward' party in favour of Lamu's independence from Pate, and the faction of Bwana Zahidi Ngumi, organized Lamu's preparations for war with the Nabahani and the Mazrui. See Shaibu Faraji al-Bakari al-Lamuy, 'Khabari Lamu', 18–27, especially 24–7; Stigand, *Zinj*, 72–6; 'The Book of Zenj', 280–2, 339–40; Guillain, *Documents*, III, 568; and Al-Amin b. Ali Mazrui, 'History of the Mazrui Dynasty of Mombasa' (trans. J. Ritchie), unpublished MS, Ft Jesus Museum, 31–2.
107 The Mbari Bwana Mshuti Waziri is one of the Takwa *mibari* which settled in Mombasa, for example. See A. C. Hollis's report in KNA, Deposit 1, CP, Bundle II, MSA/6, p. 45. Information related by H. Brown from Siyu, where they are called the Mui wa Mshuti.
108 Werner, 'Swahili History of Pate', 284, note 23, and 289. Interview, Lamu: 17 May 1975.
109 See, for example, the remarks on the decline of coastal piety made by some Malindi Muslims to Francis Xavier in 1542, in Freeman-Grenville, *Select Documents*, 136.
110 Martin, 'Arab Migrations', 384. The *shurafaʾ* of Lamu and Pate were *specifically* associated with coastal and international trade. Interview, Lamu: Mwinyi Nana al-Husayni, 23 April 1975.
111 Allen, 'Swahili Culture Reconsidered', 112–13.
112 Interview, Lamu: 6 May 1975. The symbolic value of the stone mansions is illustrated by

an incident that occurred in 1687. At that time, as an ultimate show of submission to the Portuguese, a Pate sultan, besides promises of good behaviour and tribute, agreed that 'within two years all the high buildings on the whole island should be reduced to one story in height'. Strandes, *Portuguese Period*, 208.

113 T. O. Ranger, *Dance and Society in Eastern Africa*, 20; and Hasani b. Ismail, *Swifa ya Nguvumali*, *The Medicine Man*, edited by P. Lienhardt (London, 1968), 20. One informant also interpreted the 'wars' this way. See Chapter 3 Appendix, no. 5.

114 Martin cites, for example, the indigenization even of the *shurafaʾ* by the eighteenth century. Martin, 'Arab Migrations', 383 and *passim*.

115 Shaibu Faraji al-Bakari al-Lamuy, 'Khabari Lamu', 8–11.

116 Interview, Lamu: Aisha bti. Nasir Bakari, 7 April 1975.

117 Interview, Lamu: Salim Heri, 17 May 1975.

118 Interview, Lamu: Muhammad Basalama, 7 June 1975.

119 Interview, Lamu: Abdallah Muhammad Bakathir, 15 April 1975.

120 Interview, Lamu: Ahmad Muhammad Jahadhmy, 29 April 1975.

121 Interview, Lamu: Abdallah Khatib Bauri, 16 April 1975.

122 Interview, Lamu: Ahmad Muhammad Adnani, 3 and 19 April 1975.

123 Interview, Lamu: Salim Heri and Amina bti. Salim, 18 May 1975.

124 Shaibu Faraji al-Bakari al-Lamuy, 'Khabari Lamu', 16–17.

125 Interview, Lamu: Ahmad Muhammad Jahadhmy, 11 May 1975.

126 Talbot-Smith, 'Historical Record', 47–9; Clive, 'Short History', 5–6.

127 Talbot-Smith, 'Historical Record', 47–50; Isaac, 'Summarized History', 120.

128 Interview, Lamu: Bibi Zena Bakari, 17 May 1975.

129 Stigand, *Zinj*, 157.

130 A. Werner, 'Swahili History of Pate', 156–9.

4 TOWN ISLAM AND THE *UMMA* IDEAL

1 Interview, Mombasa: Yahya Ali Omar, 29 February 1975. Possibly this Arabic is incorrect, and should be more like 'Kull ʿilm illaʾllah ridda'.

2 See, for example, the poem cited in the previous chapter, p. 48.

3 The degree to which this was exercised on the coast seems to have varied somewhat. Velten's informant only mentioned questions submitted by townspeople to a prospective scholar which required answering to their satisfaction. El-Zein ('Sacred Meadows', 33–4), however, mentions that in Lamu quite definite licensing procedures were followed.

4 See Prins, *Didemic Lamu*, 56; Lienhardt, 'A Controversy over Islamic Custom in Kilwa Kivinje, Tanzania' in I. M. Lewis (ed.), *Islam in Tropical Africa* (London, 1966), 377–80. Interview, Mombasa: 30 January 1975.

5 Lienhardt, 'Controversy', 377–80. Interview, Mombasa: 30 January 1975. Another interesting variation of this was observed at the rituals at Makunduchi, Zanzibar, in July 1984. In this instance, a 'hut' was constructed, townspeople placed offerings in the 'hut', they circumambulated it seven times, and finally it was burnt and stoned by all participants. Several portions of this ceremony were highly reminiscent of certain aspects of the *hajj*. According to several informants interviewed by my research assistant, Ramadhani Talib, the community was rid of evil when they 'stoned the Devil' at the conclusion. Interviews, Makunduchi: 22 July 1983, Mkwembe Makame and Suleiman Khatib.

6 Burton, *Zanzibar*, I, 410–11.

7 P. Bohannon and P. Curtin, *Africa and Africans* (Garden City, 1971), 278.

8 *Ibid.*, 274.

9 M. Mainga, 'A History of the Lozi Religion to the End of the Nineteenth Century' in T. O. Ranger and I. Kimambo, *The Historical Study of African Religion* (Berkeley and Los Angeles, 1972), 98.

10 Ranger and Kimambo, *African Religion*, 98–9.

11 This minimalization of man's ability to control his ultimate destiny through mere 'acquisition' of God's will was the Asharite answer to the Mutazilite doctrine on free will and predestination. Seen this way, man is, admittedly, a passive member of the universe. But this viewpoint does not seem to have characterized coastal society in the period under consideration here. Cf. W. M. Watt, *Islamic Philosophy and Theology* (Edinburgh, 1962), 86–8; T. J. de Boer, *The History of Philosophy in Islam* (London, 1903), 56–58; M. Fakhry, *Islamic Occasionalism and Its Critique by Averroës and Aquinas* (New York, 1969), 6–54.

12 Bohannon and Curtin, *Africa*, 274.

13 Watt, *Islamic Philosophy*, 17.

14 *Ibid.*, 34.

15 Bohannon and Curtin, *Africa*, 180.

16 N. J. Coulson, *A History of Islamic Law* (Edinburgh, 1964), 77.

17 *Ibid.*, 77–8.

18 *Ibid.*, 78.

19 *Ibid.*, 5.

20 *Ibid.*, 145.

21 *Ibid.*, 143; Lienhardt, 'Controversy', 374; Mohammad el-Awa, 'The Place of Custom (ʿUrf) in Islamic Legal Theory', *The Islamic Quarterly*, XVII (1973), 177–82.

22 Coulson, *Islamic Law*, 146.

23 *Ibid.*, 143.

24 See A. W. Sadler, 'Islam: The Parish Situation and the Vituoso Community', *The Muslim World*, 51 (1961), 198–200.

25 *Ibid.*, 199–200.

26 These terms, among others, are used by Shaykh Abdallah Salih Farsy in his 'Baadhi ya Wanavyuoni wa Kishafii wa Afrika ya Mashariki', (Mombasa, 1972).

27 K. Clark, *Civilisation* (New York, 1969), 14.

28 M. Wilson, *Religion and the Transformation of Society* (London, 1971), 10.

29 Bohannon and Curtin, *Africa*, 173.

30 Lienhardt, 'Controversy', 375.

31 *Ibid.*

32 Coulson, *Islamic Law*, 80.

33 *Ibid.*, 81.

34 Cf. J. Knappert, 'Social and Moral Concepts in Swahili Islamic Literature', *Africa*, xL (1970), 126.

35 *Ibid.*

36 Such was its characterization by C. H. Becker in 'Materialen zur Kenntnis der Islam in Deutsch-Ostafrika', *Der Islam*, II (1911), 1–48, translated in B. G. Martin, 'Materials for the Understanding of Islam in German East Africa', *TNR*, 68 (1968), 26.

37 *Ibid.*, 25.

38 G. Dale, *The Peoples of Zanzibar* (London, 1926), 48 and 67.

39 *Ibid.*, 61 and 67.

40 Samples of such stories can be found in J. Knappert, *Myths and Legends of the Swahili* (London, 1970), 65–88.

41 Dale, *Zanzibar*, 65; Knappert, *Myths*, 66–70.

42 Becker, 'Materials', 26.

43 R. B. Serjeant, *The Saiyids of Hadramaut* (London, 1957), 19.

44 B. G. Martin, 'Notes on Some Members of the Learned Classes of Zanzibar and East Africa in the Nineteenth Century', *African Historical Studies*, IV, 3 (1971), 529–30.

45 Interview, Mombasa: 6 January 1975.

46 Coulson, *Islamic Law*, 137 and 140. Where local customs and religious practices did creep into Islam as practised in the coastal towns, as well as in other communities of the *dar al-Islam*, local ʿulamaʾ countenanced such doctrines or passed over them in silence in order to preserve their claim to continuity of doctrine. This claim, of course, was important to their profession that locally evolved doctrine was essentially identical with the *Sunna* of

the Prophet and his Companions. As stated by Watt, *Islamic Philosophy*, 29, 'They were really interested in the soundness of the practical consequences of the Traditions and not in their historical objectivity in the modern sense.'

47 This is implied by the apparent necessity of explicitly stating the Prophet's supposed racial origins by al-Amin b. Ali Mazrui in 'Hidayatu'l-Atfak' (unpublished MS), 15, where the question is asked, 'What did the Prophet look like, s.a.w.? What was his colour?' Also, A. Nimtz mentions a controversy that occurred at Bagamoyo over the Prophet's racial and national affiliations during the 1930s; q.v. A. Nimtz, 'The Role of the Muslim Sufi Order in Political Change: An Over-view and Micro-Analysis from Tanzania', Ph.D. thesis, Indiana University, 1973, 446–7.

48 A number of clues suggest this hypothesis. The word for civilization in Krapf's dictionary was *uungwana*, and it is only in later lexicons that *ustaarabu* began to appear. Second, it must be pointed out that coastal peoples were known upcountry as *waungwana* and their language as Kiungwana, rather than as Waswahili and Kiswahili, in evidence presented by J. Knappert, 'Social and Moral Concepts', 128. Third, in his 1874 visit to Zanzibar, Stanley noted that coastal people distinguished between themselves, whom they called *waungwana*, and recently arrived strangers, whom they referred to as *waarabu*; q.v. H. M. Stanley, *Through the Dark Continent*, I (New York, 1879), 44–7.

49 Cf. Hasani b. Ismail, *Swifa ya Nguvumali, The Medicine Man*, edited by P. Lienhardt (London, 1968), 11–12; Knappert, 'Social and Moral Concepts', 128.

50 See Allen's discussion of the easy transition from a mainland life style to life in the stone towns in 'Swahili Culture Reconsidered', 110.

51 The most obvious such critic was Sir Richard F. Burton, as in *Zanzibar*, I, *passim*, but especially 421–3; Burton, *The Lakes Regions of Central Africa* (London, 1860), 43 and 45, where he characterizes the Swahili as 'unfitted by nature for intellectual labour', which, he claims, 'makes these weak-brained races semi-idiotic'. Also, Stigand, *Zinj*, 113–14.

52 L. Harries, *Swahili Poetry*, 27.

53 Townspeople, for example, often poked fun at Arabs for their defective Swahili, as evidenced in several conversations with informants at Mombasa in 1975.

54 C. S. Nicholls, *The Swahili Coast* (New York, 1971), 3; also, see Lienhardt's introduction to Hasani b. Ismail, *Swifa*.

55 Nicholls, *Coast*, 2.

5 WEALTH, PIETY, JUSTICE, AND LEARNING

1 See L. Harries, *Swahili Poetry*, 146.

2 Interview, Mombasa: 6 March 1975.

3 Interview, Mombasa: 10 March 1975.

4 A. H. J. Prins, *Didemic Lamu* (Groningen, 1971), 17.

5 *Ibid*, 23, note 15.

6 J. Bujra, 'Conflict and Conflict Resolution in a Bajuni Village', Ph.D. thesis, University of London, 1968, p. 5; A. H. el-Zein, 'The Sacred Meadows', 14 and *passim*.

7 Bujra, 'Conflict', 5; A. P. Caplan, *Choice and Constraint in a Swahili Community* (London, 1975), Chapters 3 and 4.

8 J. deV. Allen, 'Swahili Culture Reconsidered', 111.

9 Bujra, 'Conflict', 132–3; Shaibu Faraji al-Bakari al-Lamuy, 'Khabar Lamu', 25; J. Gray, *The British in Mombasa, 1824–1826* (New York, 1957), 61; S. T. Pruen, *The Arab and the African* (London, 1891), 209.

10 Bujra, 'Conflict', 5.

11 Allen, 'Swahili Culture Reconsidered', 111 and 125.

12 Probably the most conspicuous case of a clan changing its ascriptive status, including place of residence, family alliances, and even genealogy, involved groups of Baluchis in Lamu who, after attaining political and economic stature in the community, claimed to be Maawi. Interviews, Lamu: 7 and 19 April 1975.

13 Bujra, 'Conflict', 60–2; interview, Mombasa: 7 March 1975.
14 Again, the cases of the Maawi of Lamu and the Kilindini of Mombasa come to mind here in that these descent groups controlled large popular resources through their mainland ties and, in the case of the Kilindini at least, through their close ties with the Mazrui.
15 Bujra, 'Conflict', 62; Prins, *Didemic Lamu*, 25.
16 Prins, *Didemic Lamu*, 25; Caplan, *Choice*, 39–58; Hasani b. Ismail, *Swifa*. 13.
17 Interviews, Lamu: 3 and 16 April and 19 May 1975.
18 Interviews, Lamu: 16 and 19 April and 17 May 1975.
19 Interviews, Lamu: 7 April and 11, 17 and 19 May 1975.
20 Interviews, Lamu: 16 April and 18 May 1975.
21 Interviews, Lamu: 23 April and 11 and 17 May 1975. See also Hichens's introduction to Abdallah Ali Nasir, *Al-Inkishafi*, 13–16.
22 Bujra, 'Conflict', 104–8, 117–22; Caplan, *Choice*, 27–32.
23 Bujra, 'Conflict', 111–13.
24 El-Zein, 'The Sacred Meadows', 76–9.
25 *Ibid.*, 77.
26 *Ibid.*, 33–4; A. I. Salim, *The Swahili-Speaking Peoples of Kenya's Coast, 1895–1965* (Nairobi, 1973), 145. Interviews, Mombasa and Lamu: 21 Dec. 1974; 14 April, 1 May, and 9 June 1975.
27 Burton, *Zanzibar*, I, 405; Salim, *Swahili-Speaking Peoples*, 145; Abdallah Saleh Farsy, 'Baadhi ya Wanavyuoni wa Kishafii wa Mashariki ya Afrika' (unpublished MS in my possession), 34 and *passim*.
28 See, for instance, Simons to Euan-Smith (24 December 1890), FO 84/2063/341 encl. Interview, Lamu: 1 May 1975.
29 Interviews, Lamu: 14 and 19 April 1975.
30 Burton, *Zanzibar*, I, 263–4. British Foreign Office correspondence is full of such references, as, for example, in Portal to Marquis of Salisbury (10 September 1892), FO 84/2233/208; Cave to Landsdowne (6 September 1905), FO 367/95/8177. Also, there is the case reported in the *Gazette for Zanzibar and East Africa*, 2 Sept. 1896, involving Sh. Muhammad Qasim Maamiri and *Qadi* Sh. Sulaiman b. Ali Mazrui who were accused of taking bribes in a notorious case. As expected, both *shaykhs* justified such gift-giving as based on Mombasa custom.
31 Interview, Lamu: 19 April 1975; Prins, *Didemic Lamu*, 48.
32 Interviews, Lamu: 17 and 24 April 1975.
33 Prins, *Didemic Lamu*; interviews, Lamu: 14 and 19 April 1975.
34 Interview, Lamu: 14 April 1975. A. Nimtz, 'Muslim Sufi Order', 141–2.
35 Interview, Lamu: 19 April 1975.
36 Interview, Lamu: 19 April 1975.
37 Interviews, Mombasa and Lamu: 4 March and 19 April 1975.
38 Interview, Lamu: 19 April 1975.
39 Interview, Mombasa: 4 March 1975.
40 A notable case concerned *Mwalimu* Ahmad Matano of Mombasa. A Kilindini who was a noted Quran school teacher, a *falaki*, and a Quran reciter, *Mwalimu* Ahmad was a *mzee* widely recognized in the late nineteenth and early twentieth centuries for his aggressiveness in street brawls fought between the Somali inhabitants of the *Mji wa Kale* ('Old Town') and the Kilindini of Kuze quarter. See Hyder Kindi, *Life and Politics in Mombasa* (Nairobi, 1972), 10 and 35; interview, Mombasa: 27 February 1975.
41 Interview, Mombasa: 26 December 1974.
42 W. Hichens (ed.), *Diwani ya Muyaka bin Haji al-Ghassaniy* (Johannesburg, 1940), 5.
43 *Ibid.*, 7, 8, and 11.
44 *Ibid.*, 12 and 28–9. Another figure who gained prominence as a poet and who originally gave support to the Mazrui and later to Sayyid Said, was the *qadi* Muhyi ad-Din b. Sheikh al-Qahtani. This *mwalimu* will be discussed in detail in Chapter 7. See Abdallah S. Farsy, 'Baadhi', 1.

45 See Muhammad bin Ahmad's 'Forge Song' in Mbarak Ali Hinawy, *Al-Akida and Fort Jesus*, 2nd edn (London, 1950), 44–5, and Suud's reply, 48–51. Interview, Mombasa: 26 December 1974.

46 Mbarak Ali Hinawy, *Al-Akida and Fort Jesus*, 52–3, 55–6.

47 In the 1820s Lamu seems to have had four *vyuo*. See Boteler's journal in W. F. W. Owen, *Narrative of Voyages to Explore the Shores of Africa, Arabia, and Madagascar Performed in H.M. Ships Leven and Barracouta under the Direction of Captain W. F. W. Owen, R.N., by Command of the Lords Commissioners of the Admiralty*, II (London, 1833), 330. In the 1830s and 1840s there were only three *vyuo* in Zanzibar according to Guillain, *Documents*, II, 115. By the 1850s, Zanzibar had fifteen or sixteen *vyuo*; see Burton, *Zanzibar*, I, 405.

48 Interview, Lamu: 15 April 1975.

49 Interview, Lamu: 1 April 1975.

50 Interview, Lamu: 10 April 1975. See also Guillain, *Documents*, II, 115; Ingrams, *Zanzibar*, 443.

51 See B. Davidson, *The African Genius* (Boston, 1969), 150–9.

52 Interviews, Mombasa and Lamu: 21 December 1974; 1 and 18 April 1975. Naturally, in addition to having an ethnic and social basis, learning in the religious sciences had a class basis, as indicated in el-Zein, 'The Sacred Meadows', 33–4, and Salim, *Swahili-Speaking Peoples*, 145. Several informants, for example, recalled that religious knowledge was the exclusive domain of the 'Arab' clans, whereas 'Africans' were thought to be ignorant and their Islamic practices riddled through with the African 'superstitions'. Interviews, Lamu: 10 and 19 April and 9 June 1975.

53 Becker, 'Materials', 44–57. Also, Farsy mentions various sources the usage of which are datable from his text, 'Baadhi ya Wanavyuoni'.

54 It is suggested in Farsy, 'Baadhi', 33, where an allusion to the large number of *ʿulamaʾ* in Lamu who were learned in the written tradition is made. Also, Krapf, *Travels and Missionary Labours*, 130, reported on a *shaykh* from Lamu who was sufficiently erudite to deliver a discourse on Islamic doctrines on geography and cosmography.

55 Burton, *Zanzibar*, I, 421–2. Interview, Lamu: 9 June 1975.

56 Guillain, *Documents*, II, 115; el-Zein, 'Sacred Meadows', 33–4; Salim, *Swahili-Speaking Peoples*, 145. Interviews, Lamu: 15 April and 1 May 1975.

57 El-Zein, 'Sacred Meadows', 34; J. Knappert, 'Social and Moral Concepts in Swahili Islamic Literature', *Africa*, XL (1970), 127. Interview, Lamu: 10 April 1975.

58 For a parallel case in Indonesia, see L. W. C. Van den Berg's introduction to his edited version of the *Minhaj at-Talibin* (Batavia, 1882), vii.

59 Interview, Mombasa: 21 December 1974. El-Zein, 'Sacred Meadows', 34.

60 M. Fakhry, *A History of Islamic Philosophy* (New York, 1970), 77–9, 230–1, 309–24; W. Montgomery Watt, *Islamic Philosophy and Theology* (Edinburgh, 1962), 62–71.

61 Godfrey Dale, *The Peoples of Zanzibar* (London, 1920), 41.

62 Fakhry, *Islamic Philosophy*, 76–8; T. J. de Boer, *The History of Philosophy in Islam* (New York, 1967), 50–3.

63 For examples of the 'medical' applications of the written word, see Krapf, *Travels*, 149; Dale, *Zanzibar*, 40–1.

64 Interviews, Mombasa and Lamu: 28 February and 14 and 19 April 1975.

65 Interview, Mombasa: 13 March 1975.

66 Interviews, Mombasa: 28 February and 7 March 1975.

67 Stigand, *Zinj*, 126.

68 Interview, Lamu: 1 May 1975.

69 Stigand, *Zinj*, 126–7. Interview, Mombasa: 28 February 1975.

70 See Ingrams, *Zanzibar*, 443.

71 Interviews, Mombasa: 28 February and 7 March 1975.

72 Bohannon and Curtin, *Africa and Africans*, 180.

73 Stigand, *Zinj*, 126; Ingrams, *Zanzibar*, 500–8. Interview, Mombasa: 7 March 1975.

74 Krapf, *Travels*, 149.

75 Interviews, Mombasa: 21 and 23 January and 28 February 1975.

76 Prins, *Didemic Lamu*, 56.

77 C. Pickering, *The Races of Man and Their Geographical Distribution* (London, 1851), 80–2; A. H. J. Prins, *The Swahili-Speaking Peoples of Zanzibar and the East African Coast* (London, 1967), 62.

78 See Ylvisaker, *Lamu in the Nineteenth Century*, 44–50.

79 Interviews, Mombasa: 30 January 1975. Prins, *Swahili-Speaking Peoples*, 62.

80 Bohannon and Curtin, *Africa and Africans*, 180.

81 Stigand, *Zinj*, 125–6.

82 Interview, Mombasa: 21 January 1975.

83 Bohannon and Curtin, *Africa and Africans*, 180.

84 Stigand, *Zinj*, 126.

85 A good example of this can be found in Hemedi b. Abdallah al-Buhry, *Utenzi wa Vita vya Wadachi Kutamaliki Mrima, 1307 AH* (Dar es Salaam, 1971), 53–65. See also R. Horton, 'African Traditional Thought and Western Science', *Africa*, 37 (1967), 50–71, 155–87.

86 According to a number of informants interviewed in East Africa, the written traditions of astrology (*falak*) and geomancy (*ramli*) were unknown in East Africa before the arrival of the Omanis in the eighteenth and nineteenth centuries. However, one would expect that these pseudo-sciences would have been known to coastal *waganga* and *walimu* long before that time. According to Burton, though (*Zanzibar*, I, 422), practitioners of these arts in the 1850s were still considered to be sorcerers. As will be seen in Chapter 6, these sciences soon afterwards were totally absorbed by coastal *walimu* as part of their magical repertoire following the extensive Omani cultural impact of the 1860s and 70s.

87 Ranger implies the existence of such an epistemological nether zone in his 'Connexions between "Primary Resistance" Movements and Modern Mass Nationalism in East Central Africa, Part I', *JAH*, IX, 3 (1968), 447–448, and in 'Towards a Historical Study of Traditional Religion in East and Central Africa', East African Academy Symposium paper presented in Kampala, 1966.

88 Interview, Mombasa: 28 December 1974.

89 Interview, Mombasa: 6 January 1975.

90 Interviews, Mombasa: 8 and 22 January 1975.

91 Interviews, Lamu: 1, 6, 11, and 17 May 1975.

92 Interviews, Lamu: 23 April and 18 May 1975.

93 Interview, Lamu: 14 April 1975.

94 Interviews, Lamu: 19 April and 18 May 1975.

95 Guillain, *Documents*, II, 115; C. Velten, *Desturi za Wasuaheli* (Gottingen, 1903), 47.

96 Interview, Lamu: 8 April 1975.

97 Velten, *Desturi*, 47; also see the cases of such nineteenth-century *walimu* as Muhyi ad-Din al-Qahtani, Sayyid Mustafa b. Jafar Jamal al-Layl, and Sh. Muhammad Hirji in Farsy, 'Baadhi ya Wanavyuoni', 5, 61, and 65–6, respectively. Interview, Lamu: 14 April 1975.

98 Martin, 'Materials', 44–6. Interviews, Lamu: 14 and 19 April 1975.

99 Interview, Mombasa: 26 March 1975.

100 Velten, *Desturi*, 49–50.

101 *Ibid.*, 50–1. Interviews, Mombasa: 21 January and 26 March 1975.

102 B. G. Martin, 'Notes on Some Members of the Learned Classes of Zanzibar and East Africa in the Nineteenth Century', *African Historical Studies*, IV, 3 (1971), 526–7.

103 See A. W. Sadler, 'Parish Situation', 198–200.

104 This conclusion is applicable, strictly, only in the towns of the northern coast where research was conducted, and for the period under discussion here (post eighteenth century). However, as these communities were the largest wealthiest ones on the coast at this time, it is likely that they, at least, served as models for smaller and less affluent towns of the southern coast. See Nimtz, 'Muslim Sufi Order', 145 and 368; and Velten, *Desturi*, 50–1. Interviews, Lamu: 14 and 19 April 1975.

105 Nimtz, 'Muslim Sufi Order', 142–3. Interviews, Lamu: 14 and 19 April 1975.

106 Nimtz, 'Muslim Sufi Order', 369. Interviews, Lamu: 23 April and 1 and 24 May 1975.

6 THE ZANZIBAR SULTANATE, 1812–88

1 See also R. L. Pouwels, 'Islam and Islamic Leadership in the Coastal Communities of Eastern Africa, 1700 to 1914', Ph.D. thesis, UCLA, 1979, pp. 92–141.

2 For more details, see Chapter 5; also, Ylvisaker, *Lamu, passim.*

3 As evidence, I cite the religious disputations and attendant tensions between Sh. Ali. b. Abdallah Mazrui and Sh. Muhammad Ali Mandhry, *c.* 1870, and the support given by townspeople to the McKillop Pasha expedition in 1875–6. Both of these incidents will be discussed appropriately in the text below.

4 This, of course, was not unique to the Zanzibar Sultanate. Such was the case with the Abbasid Caliphate and the later history of the Ottoman Sultanate, for example. For discussions of these cases, see J. J. Saunders, *A History of Medieval Islam* (London, 1965), 106–25; P. M. Holt, *Egypt and the Fertile Crescent* (Ithaca, 1970).

5 I have selected the Arabic term specifically because I feel that only it can convey sufficiently the essentially informal, Middle Eastern character of the governmental 'structure' which is described herein.

6 Ward to Buchanan, 7 March 1844, in N. R. Bennett and G. Brooks, *New England Merchants in Africa* (Boston, 1965), 380.

7 Guillain, *Documents*, II, 26–7, 51; R. Coupland, *East Africa and Its Invaders* (London, 1938), 323; Owen, *Narrative*, 340–1; W. Phillips, *Oman, A History* (London, 1967), 154–5.

8 Guillain, *Documents*, II, 237; Burton, *Zanzibar*, I, 89, 163–4, and 261; also, Atkins Hamerton reported similarly in 1855, as noted by Coupland, *East Africa*, 325–6 (more on this when the subject of the court *ᶜulamaᵓ* will be taken up) and by MacDonald in a report to the Foreign Office, FO 84/1853/180.

9 Owen, *Narrative*, 340. See also (though the translation is somewhat untrustworthy) Salil ibn Razik, *History of the Imams and Seyyids of Oman*, edited and translated by G. P. Badger (New York, 1871), 373–4.

10 Phillips, *Oman*, 154; and Salil ibn Razik, *History*, 374–5. It should be noted, of course, that this view does not state *how* the Shariᶜa should be applied – i.e. who would perform such a function in the absence of an imam. Presumably, *Realpolitik* would determine such matters, and, in the end, whoever did succeed to such leadership soon would himself have been laying claim to the Imamate. In fact, this is exactly what did occur when Ahmad b. Said al-Busaidi seized the Imamate over the weak leadership of the last Yarubi Imam.

11 Phillips, *Oman*, 155; Salil ibn Razik, *History*, 382.

12 Salil ibn Razik, *History*, 377.

13 *Ibid.*, 378–80; R. S. Reute, *Said b. Sultan* (London, 1927); S. B. Miles, *Countries and Tribes of the Persian Gulf* (London, 1919), 282 and 291.

14 This is not to say that the Sayyids did not *try* to succeed to the Imamate. Owen mentions (*Narrative*, 341) that in 1824 Sayyid Said performed the *hajj* and attempted to bribe the *shurafaᵓ* of Mecca to give sanction to his claim to the Imamate.

15 See Nicholls, *The Swahili Coast*, 101–18.

16 Salil ibn Razik, *History*, 384.

17 Sir John Gray, 'Zanzibar Local Histories, Part I', *Swahili*, no. 30, p. 37.

18 Cogan to Palmerston, 6 May 1839, FO 54/3.

19 Owen, *Narrative*, 340–1.

20 Michael W. Shepard account, 1844, in Bennett and Brooks, *New England Merchants*, 263.

21 For descriptions of this commerce, see C. Guillain, 'Côte de Zanguebar et Muscate', *Revue Coloniale*, VI (1843), 520–71; M. Loarer, 'Ile de Zanzibar', *Revue de l'Orient, de l'Algerie et des Colonies*, 9 (1851), 290–9.

22 Guillain, 'Côte de Zanguebar', 550.

23 The journal of R. P. Waters, 1836–44, in Bennett and Brooks, *New England Merchants*, 201.

24 Sayyid Ali b. Said was the first to suffer the cuts made to the Sultan's 'civil list', as drawn up and implemented first by Gerald Portal. See Chapter 9 for details.
25 Said, apparently, acquired much of his landed property through confiscations, a practice which seems to have been carried on by his successors. See Guillain, *Documents*, II, 51; Holmwood to FO, 11 July 1887, FO 84/1853/110; MacDonald to Salisbury, 3 March 1888, FO 84/1906/26. The hurricane of 1872 mostly destroyed Zanzibar's clove culture, a major source of income for the Sultans; however, Barghash merely countered with a 25 per cent duty on all cloves shipped into Zanzibar from Pemba. Also, much of the clove industry simply was relocated to Pemba. Interview, Mombasa: Abdallah Salih Farsy, February 1975. F. Cooper, *Plantation Slavery on the East Coast of Africa* (New Haven, 1977), 54–75.
26 Burton, *Zanzibar*, I, 371–2.
27 S. Said had sundry difficulties in trying to exert control by force over inland tribes at Oman and pirates of the Persian Gulf. See Coupland, *Invaders, passim.* On the coast he had, of course, considerable and numerous problems in trying to overcome Swahili resistance at Pate and Siyu, and Mazrui resistance at Mombasa. At least before the creation of the *askari* force by Lloyd Mathews in 1877, he had few regular troops to keep the towns in line. See Coupland, *The Exploitation of East Africa* (London, 1939), 241. Burton reported (*Zanzibar*, I, 265) that Sayyid Said maintained a total standing army on the coast of only about 400 irregulars – 80 of whom were in Zanzibar, 250 at Mombasa, 30 at Lamu, 25 at Pate, 6–10 at Kilwa, 'and sundry pairs at Makdishu and other places'.
28 'The Book of Zenj' in Cerulli, *Somalia*, I, 333 and 335.
29 Burton, *Zanzibar*, I, 265.
30 Frere to Granville, 7 May 1873, *Correspondence Respecting Sir Bartle Frere's Mission to the East Coast of Africa, 1872–73* (hereafter *CRME*), no. 52, enclosure 1.
31 The Sayyids were permitted to retain a portion of state revenue necessary only for their simple life style, while the remainder was to be spent on the people and the state. See first-hand observations in F. B. Pearce, *Zanzibar, The Island Metropolis of East Africa* (London, 1920), 260; and C. E. B. Russell, *General Rigby, Zanzibar and the Slave Trade* (London, 1935), 92, note 1.
32 Burton, *Zanzibar*, I, 261.
33 Coupland, *Exploitation*, 237. See also the correspondence respecting Barghash's fears of his own court 'ulama' in Frere to Granville, 17 January 1873, *CRME*, no. 36, enclosures 7, 8, and 18.
34 For a summary of Barwani wealth and power, see B. G. Martin, *Muslim Brotherhoods in Nineteenth Century Africa* (London, 1976), 169; F. Albrand, 'Extrait d'un mémoire sur Zanzibar et sur Quiloa', *Bulletin de la Société de Géographie*, X (1838), 78–9.
35 Nicholls, *Swahili Coast*, 130–1.
36 Burton, *Zanzibar*, I, 262.
37 *Ibid.*, 372.
38 Coupland, *Exploitation*, 62; Russell, *General Rigby*, 93; E. Reute, *Memoirs of an Arabian Princess* (New York, 1888), 230–1.
39 Coupland, *Invaders*, 322.
40 Interview, Mombasa: 21 January 1975.
41 Russell, *General Rigby*, 85 and 94. Interviews, Mombasa: 21 January and 24 and 26 February 1975.
42 Burton, *Zanzibar*, I, 402.
43 Owen to Palmerston, 8 April 1834, FO 54/1.
44 With one exception to be discussed below – i.e., the brief period when Barghash was under the influence of the *mutawwiun*. Burton, *Zanzibar*, I, 403.
45 Ward to James Buchanan, 14 September 1846, Bennett and Brooks, *New England Merchants*, 367.
46 Interviews, Mombasa: 20 January, 26 February, and 13 March 1975; F. J. Berg, 'Swahili Community', 54; Guillain, *Documents*, II, 259–60.

47 Nicholls, *Swahili Coast*, 334.
48 Frere to Granville, 7 May 1873, *CRME*, no. 52, enclosure 1.
49 Boteler's log in Owen, *Narrative*, 388.
50 Owen, *Narrative*, 362; Burton, *Zanzibar*, I, 410.
51 Guillain, *Documents*, II, 259; Berg, 'Swahili Community', 39.
52 Berg, 'Swahili Community', 39–40.
53 Interviews, Lamu: 19 April and 1 May 1975.
54 Interviews, Mombasa: 24 December 1974; Lamu: 19 April 1975.
55 Interview, Mombasa: 24 December 1974.
56 Hemedi b. Abdallah al-Buhry, *Utenzi wa Vita vya Wadachi*, 73.
57 Owen, *Narrative*, 362.
58 Frere to Granville, 7 May 1873, *CRME*, no. 52, enclosure 1.
59 Guillain, *Documents*, II, 359; Berg, 'Swahili Community', 39–40.
60 Journal of R. P. Waters, 4 November 1842, in Bennett and Brooks, *New England Merchants*, 254; Pearce, (*Zanzibar*, 260) also mentions the Sultan's habits of giving lavish entertainments. See also Cave to Salisbury, 11 October 1896, FO 107/55/282.
61 Hamedi b. Abdallah, *Utenzi*, 27.
62 Their number, of course, varied. Portal, in 1892, however, estimated their number at 500 to 600. Portal to Rosebery, 3 December 1892, FO 84/2234/261, and 23 October 1891, FO 84/2149/277.
63 Portal to Salisbury, 22 August 1892, FO 84/2232/183.
64 Portal to Salisbury, 28 November 1891, FO 84/2150/293.
65 Interview, Lamu: 19 April 1975. As seen above, the same was true of Mombasa.
66 Interviews, Lamu: 14 and 19 April 1975.
67 Interviews, Lamu: 1 and 18 May 1975.
68 Boteler's log in Owen, *Narrative*, 372 and 387–8; Smee's log cited in Burton, *Zanzibar*, II, 491.
69 Cooper, *Plantation Slavery*, 90–1. Interview, Mombasa: 28 December 1974.
70 The Government agent, L. Talbot-Smith, made such a suggestion in 1921; see Talbot-Smith, 'Historical Record', 95; also, Guillain, *Documents*, II, 235–36.
71 'The Book of Zenj', 289; Talbot-Smith, 'Historical Record', 95; Interviews, Mombasa: 24 and 26 February 1975; Lamu: 19 April 1975.
72 El-Zein, 'Sacred Meadows', 53.
73 *Ibid.*, 63. Interviews, Lamu: 23 and 29 April and 18 May and 9 June 1975.
74 Interview, Lamu: 19 April 1975.
75 Simons to Euan-Smith, 24 June 1890, FO 84/2073/341, enclosure.
76 Guillain, *Documents*, II, 235–6.
77 See el-Zein's description of these matters in Lamu in 'Sacred Meadows', 55–60, and Krapf's comments in his journal, found in the Church Missionary Society archives, CA5/016, 329–33.
78 Abdallah Salih Nasir, *Al-Inkishafi*, 87, note 59. It should be noted, however, that the *wazee* got Majid to countermand this order – another example of the circumscriptive power of the *wazee* over their governors exercised through their rights of appeal directly to the Sultan. Simons to Euan-Smith, 1 August 1890, FO 84/2063/34, enclosure.
79 Pigott to Rodd, 17 March 1893, FO 107/18/18. This behaviour on the part of the *liwali* Abdallah b. Hamid could have been intentional.
80 Interviews, Lamu: Abdu'l-Malik b. Abdu'r-Rahman Maawi, 19 May 1975. Harith Swaleh Maawi recalled conflicts between the spheres of influence of the local *qadis* and the law as it was administered by the *liwalis*; interview, Lamu: Harith Swaleh Maawi, 19 April 1975. According to the same informant, it seems that 'certain changes were introduced' in the application of local law (by Maawi *khatibs*) when Barghash appointed some Mahdali as *qadis*. The powers of the *wazee wa mui* gradually were superseded by the *liwalis*.
81 Interview, Mombasa: 1 March 1975.
82 Interview, Mombasa: 23 December 1974.

83 Ibuni Saleh, *A Short History of the Comorians in Zanzibar* (Zanzibar, 1936), 6.

84 Burton, *Zanzibar*, I, 341 and 342; Ibuni Saleh, *Short History*, 3.

85 Ibuni Saleh, *Short History*, 6.

86 *Ibid.*, 7; Dubins, 'Comoro Islands', *passim*.

87 See R. F. Burton, *First Footsteps in East Africa*, 2nd ed. (New York, 1966), 57–8. The exact details of these later migrations seem to be disputed. Martin, 'Arab Migrations', *passim*, places their beginning around 1750, whereas Serjeant, *The Saiyids of Hadramawt*, places them closer to 1800. Steam navigation brought an 'enormous development' in emigration after the 1870s, according to Van den Berg, *Le Hadramout et les colonies Arabes dans l'Archipel Indien* (Batavia, 1886), 105.

88 Serjeant, *Saiyids*, 25–6.

89 Van den Berg, *Le Hadramout*, 39.

90 *Ibid.*, 114; see also Cooper's discussion of one such wealthy Hadrami, a Bashrahil, who made his way as a landowner at Malindi despite the opposition of the local *liwali*, in Cooper, *Plantation Slavery*, 81–97.

91 Abdallah Bujra, *The Politics of Stratification: A Study of Political Change in a South Arabian Town* (London, 1971), 42.

92 El-Zein, 'Sacred Meadows', 92–3.

93 *Ibid.*, 103–5.

94 Van den Berg, *Le Hadramout*, 115.

95 Burton, *Zanzibar*, I, 340–2.

96 Ibuni Saleh, *Short History*, 14–15.

97 See J. Gray, 'Zanzibar and the Coast, 1840–1884' in *History of East Africa*, I, edited by R. Oliver and G. Mathew (London, 1963), 216–19.

98 Nicholls, *Swahili Coast*, 77–80, 360–4.

99 E. A. Alpers, *Ivory and Slaves in East Central Africa* (Berkeley and Los Angeles, 1975), 189–90, 234–8.

100 Salim, *Swahili-Speaking Peoples*, 32.

101 Interviews, Mombasa: al-Amin b. Said Mandhry, 8 January 1975; Y. A. Omar, 28 December 1974. According to these informants, also, many Mombasans, including Twelve Tribesmen, later profited from clove cultivation at Pemba. See also Salim, *Swahili-Speaking Peoples*, 37–8.

102 Sir A. Hardinge, *Report on the East Africa Protectorate, 1898*, PP, LX, 9.

103 *Ibid.*; and Salim, *Swahili-Speaking Peoples*, 37.

104 For a summary, see Salim, *Swahili-Speaking Peoples*, 24 and 39.

105 Guillain, *Documents*, II, 115; Shaibu Faraji al-Bakari, 'Khabar Lamu', 25.

106 Salim, *Swahili-Speaking Peoples*, 33–4; interview, Lamu: 10 April 1975.

107 Cooper, *Plantation Slavery*, 38–9.

108 *Ibid.*, 43–6.

109 Janet Bujra, 'Conflict', 60–2.

110 While class differentiation may have reached its greatest heights at Lamu by 1850, it is interesting to note that one Maawi claims that endowments (*awqaf*) did not even exist before the Busaidi arrived – which, perhaps, made seizures of disputed lands all the easier for the Banu Hamid. Clearly, community-owned land, coming under the control of the suzerain, could be, and was, reclaimed by the suzerain, representing the community, in matters where usufruct was disputed. Interview, Lamu: Abdu'l-Malik A. Maawi, 19 May 1975.

111 Cooper, *Plantation Slavery*, discusses various aspects of this problem on 57–8.

112 Interviews, Lamu: 1, 18, and 24 May 1975. Burton (*Zanzibar*, I, 403), however, correctly points out the non-proselytizing nature of Kharijite Islam.

113 Muslims of various sects were found at the Sultans' courts, along with Hindus, Christians, and representatives of traditional African religions. Burton, *Zanzibar*, I, 400–2; Guillain, *Documents*, II, 95; Owen to Palmerston, 8 April 1834, FO 54/1. Interview, Mombasa: 7 February 1975.

114 Interview, Mombasa: 7 February 1975.
115 Burton, *Zanzibar*, I, 405. The *Jalalayn* is a Shafii *tafsir* (Quranic commentary) on the two Jalals: Jalalu'd-Din Mahalli and Jalalu'd-Din Suyuti. It, along with the *khutba* of the *Minhaj* by al-Nawawi and the *Fathu'l-Muin*, is one of the most commonly read religious works on the East African coast.
116 A. S. Farsy mentions five Sunnis of varying reputation who studied under Ibadi *mashayikh*; see 'Baadhi ya Wanavyuoni wa Kishafii wa Mashariki ya Afrika' (Mombasa, n.d.), 27, 62, 63, and 65.
117 Interviews, Mombasa: 7 February 1975; Lamu: 18 May 1975.
118 Burton, *Zanzibar*, I, 403. Interview, Mombasa: Muhammad Rashid Mazrui, 22 February, 1975.
119 Interview, Mombasa: Yahya Ali Omar, 21 December 1974.
120 *Ibid.*
121 Interview, Mombasa: Muhammad Rashid Mazrui, 22 February 1975.
122 Accusations of this sort were levelled at Barghash by Sh. Abdu'l-Aziz b. Abdu'l-Ghany Amawi in a quarrel over one of the Sultan's notorious attempts to interfere in the religious practices of his Sunni subjects. Interview, Mombasa: 5 March 1975.
123 Professor Ali Mazrui of the University of Michigan is the latest notable scion of this learned line. Sh. Abdallah b. Nafu^c would be Professor Mazrui's great-grandfather.
124 A. S. Farsy, 'Baadhi', 9. Interview, Mombasa: 22 and 24 February 1975.
125 A. S. Farsy, 'Baadhi', 9–14. His compositions included *Ad-Durur as-Sabigha*, commentaries on *Dala'i'l-Khayrat* and *Shamaili't-Tirmidhi*, and an interpretation of the *Ahl Badr*.
126 A. S. Farsy, 'Baadhi', 13–14, and interview, Mombasa: 7 February 1975. The debate, in keeping with the rules of the court however, was friendly. It centred on the Sunni belief that God would be seen after death.
127 Interviews, Mombasa: Kamal Khan and Charo Shambe, 11 January 1975. According to these informants, Sh. Ali was popular enough, and therefore powerful enough, to have quarrelled with some *liwalis* over certain administrative matters.
128 A. S. Farsy, 'Baadhi', 9–14. Interview, Mombasa: 21 December 1974. After Barghash's death, Sh. Ali was released and continued his former activities until his own death six years later. Sh. Ali's conversions appear mostly to have been among his own kinsmen.
129 Interview, Mombasa: Muhammad Rashid Mazrui, 22 February 1975, and information obtained from correspondence with Sh. Muhammad Qasim Mazrui, April 1975.
130 It should be pointed out that the Sultan had to have realized the threat these conversions posed to his claims to spiritual leadership of East Africa's Ibadis. Barghash's involvement with the *mutawwiun* and his attempts at reunifying Zanzibar and Oman under the Imamate – with him as Imam – bear this out. Frere to Granville, 7 May 1873, *CRME*, no. 52.
131 A. E. M. Anderson-Moreshead, *The History of the Universities Mission to Central Africa, 1859–1890* (London, 1897), 90.
132 Frere to Granville, 7 May 1873, *CRME*, no. 52. Interview, Mombasa: 5 March 1975.
133 Churchill to FO, 10 October 1870, FO 2/1325/77. The reason for the ban is not clear. However, some might have been using the *khutba* to spread *tariqa* propaganda or others, like the Mazrui, may have preached against the sultans.
134 A. S. Farsy, 'Baadhi', 6–7.
135 Interview, Mombasa: 3 March 1975.
136 A. S. Farsy, 'Baadhi', 6–9.
137 Interview, Mombasa: 3 March 1975.
138 Interview, Mombasa: 5 March 1975.
139 Sir Charles Eliot, *The East African Protectorate*, quoted in KNA DC/MSA/3/1, 60.
140 Judge Peter Grain's 'Report on the Judiciary', 20 September 1907, FO 367/59/42197.
141 Burton, *Zanzibar*, I, 304–6.
142 E. Reute, *Memoirs*, 216–17.
143 *Ibid.*, 97–8.

144 H. Wehr, *A Dictionary of Modern Written Arabic*, 3rd ed., edited by J. Milton Cowan, (Ithaca, 1971), 727. *Falak*'s Greek pedigree, in fact, was adduced by Yahya A. Omar in conversation at Mombasa, 7 March 1975. Fakhry (*Philosophy*, 19–20) indicates that astronomy entered into Arab/Islamic philosophical thought through the intensive translation efforts which began in the reign of Caliph al-Mansur.

145 This is a term used by Burton in *Zanzibar*, I, 422. It is doubtful that Oman 'teemed' with *falakis*. Burton also applies the term 'sorcerers' to the *falakis*, but the actual Arabic for a sorcerer is *sahhar* or *sahir*. Undoubtedly, this interpretation of *falakis* as sorcerers reflects what was coastal, rather than strictly Arabic, usage in the 1850s.

146 Interviews, Mombasa: Yahya Ali Omar, 7 March 1975; Lamu: Sayyid Bahasani, 1 May 1975. Again, *tibb/tabib* as used here reflects what was/is coastal East African usage, not the strict Arabic application.

147 Ingrams, *Zanzibar*, 435–6; R. Skene, 'Arab and Swahili Dances and Ceremonies', *JRAI*, 47 (1917), 420–34; Kirkman, 'The Zanzibar Diary of John Studdy Leigh', *IJAHS*, 13 (1980), 291–2.

148 KNA DC/MSA/3/1, 227; and L. Harries, *Swahili Poetry* (London, 1962), 225.

149 Such, at least, was suggested in interviews with Y. A. Omar at Mombasa, 13 January 1975.

150 One Abdallah Ridhwani was sent to study *falak*, according to Muhammad Ahmad Matano in an interview, Mombasa: 28 February 1975. A celebrated Siyu *shaykh*, Sh. Abdu'r-Rahman b Ahmad as-Saqqaf (Mwinyi Abudi), also is said to have learned *falak* from Omanis while he was incarcerated at Ft Jesus for rebelling against Sayyid Majid.

151 Interviews, Mombasa: M. A. Matano, 27 February and 13 March 1975.

152 *Ibid.*

153 Interviews, Mombasa: Y. A. Omar, 13 January 1975.

154 Interview, Mombasa: Y. A. Omar, 21 January 1975.

155 Interviews, Mombasa: Abdallah Salih Farsy, 24 and 26 February 1975.

156 Interview, Mombasa: Y. A. Omar, 24 December 1974.

157 Interviews, Mombasa: A. S. Farsy, 7 February 1975; Y. A. Omar, 28 December 1975.

158 Interview, Mombasa: Al-Amin Muhsin Maamiry, 20 January 1975.

159 Examples of all these situations can be found in Farsy, 'Baadhi', 49–50, 72.

160 El-Zein, 'Sacred Meadows', 62–4.

161 *Ibid.*, 68.

162 Burton, *Zanzibar*, I, 263–4.

163 *Ibid.*

164 MacDonald to FO, 21 November 1887, FO 84/1853/180 and 186.

165 MacDonald to Salisbury, 3 March 1888, FO 84/1906/26.

166 *Ibid.*

167 Coupland, *Exploitation*, 175–88.

168 Kirk to Derby, 12 November 1875, FO 84/1417/159.

169 Kirk to Derby, 15 December 1875, FO 84/1417/197.

170 Kirk to Derby, 25 December 1875, FO 84/1417/198. Apparently the religious disputes which Sh. Abdu'l-Aziz b. Abdu'l-Ghany had with Barghash led to Sh. Abdu'l-Aziz's ('a former Kathi of Zanzibar') decision to return to Mogadishu, according to a letter from Sultan Ahmad Yusuf and Sh. Abdu'l-Aziz, dated 16 November 1875, enclosure 202 of Kirk to Derby, cited above.

171 Kirk to Derby, 11 November 1875, 84/1417/158.

7 NEW SECULARISM AND BUREAUCRATIC CENTRALIZATION

1 Mannheim was concerned with the problem of 'false consciousness' when he wrote that, 'antiquated and inapplicable norms, modes of thought, and theories are likely to degenerate into ideologies whose function is to conceal the actual meaning of conduct rather than reveal it'. Quoted from *Ideology and Utopia*, 175f in W. M. Watt, *Islam and the Integration of Society* (Evanston, 1961), 254–5.

2 Owen, *Narrative*, 341.

3 S. B. Miles, *The Countries and Tribes of the Persian Gulf* (London, 1966), 355–74; Salil ibn Razik, *History of the Imams and Sayyids of Oman* (New York, 1871), 380.

4 Miles, *Countries*, 266 and *passim*; Salil ibn Razik, *History*, 384. See the presentation in Nicholls, *The Swahili Coast* (New York, 1971), 101–8.

5 Miles, *Countries*, 304 and *passim*; Salil ibn Razik, *History*, 380. It was rather common among nineteenth-century European writers to confuse Ibadi fundamentalism with Wahhabi fundamentalism.

6 Owen, *Narrative*, 340.

7 Ingrams, *Zanzibar*, 174.

8 F. J. Berg, 'Mombasa under the Busaidi Sultanate', Ph.D. thesis, University of Wisconsin, 1971, p. 338.

9 Owen to Palmerston, 8 April 1834, FO 54/1.

10 Burton, *Zanzibar*, I, 261–2, 405–6.

11 *Ibid.*, 4–6.

12 E. Roberts to J. Forsyth, 23 October 1835; R. Waters' journal entries for 18 March 1837 and 18 October 1842 in Bennett and Brooks, *New England Merchants*, 164, 194, 223, 253.

13 Waters' journal entries for 16 September 1837 and 21 October 1842 in *ibid.*, 204 and 253.

14 Report of Badger's interview with Barghash, 14 January 1873, Frere to Granville, 26-3-73, *CRME*, no. 36, enclosure 1.

15 Zahir b. Saᶜid, *Tanzihu'l-Absari Wa'l-Afkari fi Rihlatu'l-Sultani'l-Zanjibar*, edited by L. Subunjie (London, 1879), 83, 85–9.

16 Burton, *Zanzibar*, I, 259–60.

17 Reute, *Memoirs*, 137; M. Loarer, 'Ile de Zanzibar', 292; Capt. Thomas Boteler, *Narrative of Voyage of Discovery to Africa and Arabia*, I, 167–8.

18 Coupland, *Exploitation*, 243–4; 'The Book of Zenj', 391.

19 Reute, *Memoirs*, 137.

20 Hemedi b. Abdallah, *Utenzi wa Vita vya Wadachi*, 23.

21 *Ibid.*, 23 and 27.

22 Reported in the *Gazette for Zanzibar and East Africa*, 11 April 1894, p. 2.

23 *Ibid.*

24 Interview, Mombasa: Abdallah Salih Farsy, 17 February 1975. Of course, Barghash was not cultured in a truly Arab sense, but in what *waungwana* perceived to be Arab.

25 Interview, Mombasa: Y. A. Omar, 13 January 1975.

26 Wehr, *Dictionary*, 601; J. deV. Allen, 'Swahili Culture Reconsidered', 121.

27 Robert N. Lyne, *Zanzibar in Contemporary Times* (London, 1905), 221.

28 Pearce, *Zanzibar*, 236.

29 Interview, Mombasa: 13 January 1975.

30 Allen, 'Swahili Culture Reconsidered', 121; see also by the same author, *Lamu Town, A Guide* (Nairobi, n.d.), 1–3.

31 Allen, 'Swahili Culture Reconsidered', 114–15.

32 Interview, Lamu: 21 June 1975.; J. deV. Allen, *Lamu* (Nairobi n.d.), 7–8.

33 Interview, Lamu: 21 June 1975.

34 Pearce, *Zanzibar*, 228.

35 Interview, Lamu: 21 June 1975.

36 Pearce, *Zanzibar*, 230.

37 See the example of Sh. Muhammad b. Khalfan al-Filany in Farsy, 'Baadhi', 38; Pearce, *Zanzibar*, 230; Interview, Lamu: 18 May 1975.

38 Burton, *Zanzibar*, I, 421 and 423.

39 Burton, *First Footsteps in East Africa*, 71; also, see B. G. Martin, 'Arab Migrations', 383.

40 Interview, Lamu: 9 June 1975.

41 Guillain, *Documents*, II, 115; Burton, *Zanzibar*, I, 405.

42 Martin, 'Arab Migrations', 379–80.

43 L. Harries, 'The Arabs and Swahili Culture', *Africa*, XXXIV, 3 (1964), 228–9; also *Swahili Poetry*, 27.

44 Harries, *Swahili Poetry*, 27.

45 Harries, 'The Arabs', 229.

46 Farsy, 'Baadhi', 21–2.

47 *Ibid.*, 21–2; Harries, *Swahili Poetry*, 86. The *Duraru'l-Bahiyya* is described by Sh. A. S. Farsy as a 'small book' of instruction on elementary obligations of the Islamic faith (personal communication from Sh. Abdallah). Sayyid Mansab's obvious concern over the Swahili disregard of Islamic practices is apparent in his choice of works to be translated.

48 Harries, *Swahili Poetry*, 22. I take 'lost at sea' to mean, as in the following story of Sharif Muhammad Hasan, that somebody was bribed by reactionary *ʿulamaʾ* to 'lose' the manuscript.

49 Harries, *Swahili Poetry*, 21.

50 *Ibid.*, 128.

51 Interview, Mombasa: 27 February 1975.

52 See Al-Amin b. Ali Mazrui, *Uwongozi* (Mombasa, n.d.).

53 Ingrams, *Zanzibar*, 433.

54 Interview, Mombasa: 27 February 1975.

55 Badger's interview, 21 January 1873, in Frere to Granville, *CRME*, no. 36, enclosure 18.

56 Badger's interviews, 21 and 29 January 1873, Frere to Granville, *CRME*, no. 36, enclosures 10 and 18.

57 Coupland, *Exploitation*, 227 and 246–7; Kirk to Derby, 20 April 1876, and Kirk to Wylde, 6 May 1876, FO 84/1453; also, Hardinge to Kirk, 30 January 1880, in Kirk to Salisbury, 6 March 1880, FO 84/1474, enclosure.

58 Reute, *Memoirs*, 252.

59 Kirk to Derby, 24 August 1877, Kirk Papers, *Via*, 167, quoted in Coupland, *Exploitation*, 238.

60 *Ibid.*

61 Ylvisaker, 'Political and Economic Relationship', 157–8.

62 In Vuga, this was the *Diwan Ruga*, whereas in Lamu this was the *Wazee wa Mui*. Zanzibar had its *Mwinyi Mkuu*. The exact situation at Mombasa, as it was under the Mazrui, is not clear, but it does appear that the Mazrui, who are remembered as especially just men and *qadis* in local traditions, did settle inter-clan disputes with the advice of the *wazee, walimu*, their own *qadis*, and the al-Malindi *shehe*.

63 Interview, Mombasa: Abdallah S. Farsy, 7 February 1975. According to Sh. Abdallah, some *qadis* even kept stocks or 'jails' in their own houses. See also Burton, *Zanzibar*, I, 263–4, where he says that *qadis* punished by 'more or less severe' imprisonment.

64 Burton, *Zanzibar*, I, 263–4. H. Greffulhe, 'Voyage de Lamoo à Zanzibar', *Bulletin de la Société de Géographie et d'Études Coloniale de Marseille*, II (1878), 211.

65 Burton, *Zanzibar*, I, 89.

66 Guillain, *Documents*, II, 237.

67 Burton, *Zanzibar*, I, 264 and 353; Guillain, *Documents*, II, 26–7, 51, and 237.

68 Burton, *Zanzibar*, I, 372 and 404, where he refers to the opposition of the Ghafiri to the Busaidi and whom he mentions as inclined to 'Wahhabism'. These early Ibadi reformers are described by Salil ibn Razik (*History*, 244) as *ʿulamaʾ* who stood for the unity of God and the doctrine of predestination and who opposed Islamic 'polytheism' (250). Coupland (*Exploitation*, 91) also mentions that Barghash annulled judicial decisions made by Majid and his *qadis* wherever they were at odds with strict Ibadi doctrine.

69 Palgrave's description, found in Salil ibn Razik, *History*, 247, note 2.

70 Wendell Phillips, *Oman, A History* (London, 1967), 139–42.

71 Churchill to FO, 10 October 1870, FO 2/1325/77.

72 Kirk to Wedderburn, 1 January 1872, FO 2/1357/8.

73 More will be said about Barghash's press and his connections with fundamentalist

Ibadism in Chapter 10. In addition, Barghash remained under the influence of an 'aristocratic council' of three *mutawwiun*, Sh. Muhammad Sulaiman Mandhry, Sh. Hamud b. Hamid al-Fuᶜahi, and S. Hamud b. Hamid al-Busaidi; see Kirk to FO, 5 June 1873, FO 84/1374/49.

74 M. Wilson, *Religion and the Transformation of Society* (London, 1971), 16.
75 Lyne, *Zanzibar*, 239.
76 Interview, Lamu: Sayyid Bahasani, 14 March 1975.
77 Portal to Salisbury, 10 September 1892, FO 84/2233/208.
78 MacDonald to F.O., 21 November 1887; FO 84/1853/180.
79 Van den Berg, *Le Hadramout*, 33.
80 P. Lienhardt, 'The Mosque College of Lamu and its Social Background', *TNR*, (1958), 239–40.
81 Martin, 'Arab Migrations', 378–9.
82 In the seventeenth and eighteenth centuries, Pate was trading heavily with the Comoro Islands principally for cowry shells.
83 Martin, 'Arab Migrations', 382.
84 *Ibid.*, 383. Interview, Mombasa: 18 February 1975.
85 Interview, Mombasa: 18 February 1975. Msa Fumo, in turn, warred with Ali b. Umar al-Massila of Anjouan, who, with French assistance, ousted Msa Fumo.
86 Interview, Lamu: 23 April 1975.
87 Interviews, Lamu: 18 May, 23 April, and 9 June 1975.
88 Martin, 'Arab Migrations', 384.
89 Interview, Lamu: 18 May 1975.
90 Interview, Lamu: 23 April 1975; Mombasa: 7 February 1975.
91 Martin, 'Arab Migrations', 384 and 386.
92 Farsy, 'Baadhi', 53 and 68–9.
93 Interviews, Lamu: 1 May and 9 June 1975.
94 Martin, 'Arab Migrations', 378.
95 R. B. Serjeant, 'Saiyids', 26.
96 Farsy ('Baadhi', 54) mentions, especially, one S. Abdu'l-Hasan b. Ahmad Jamal al-Layl (1801–83), who was instructed by a Maghribi of unknown name and by various ᶜ*ulama*ᵓ from the Hijaz. After performing the *hajj*, he held *darasas* at Tsujuni.
97 El-Zein, 'Sacred Meadows', 28.
98 *Ibid.*; Interview, Lamu: 1 May 1975.
99 Interviews, Lamu: 15 April and 1 May 1975.
100 Ibuni Saleh, *Comorians*, 9.
101 Farsy, 'Baadhi', 5–6, 26–7.
102 I. M. Lewis, 'Sufism in Somaliland: A Study in Tribal Islam – I', *BSOAS*, XVII, 3, 592–4; Lewis, 'Conformity and Contrast in Somali Islam' in *Islam in Tropical Africa*, edited by I. M. Lewis, (London, 1966), 263–4.
103 Interviews, Mombasa: Sayyid Athman b. Abdu'r-Rahman Saqqaf, 23 January and 3 February 1975.
104 Interview, Mombasa: M. A. Matano, 27 February 1975; A. S. Farsy, 'Baadhi', 16–17.
105 Farsy, 'Baadhi', 17–19. Interviews, Mombasa: S. Athman b. Abdu'r-Rahman Saqqaf, 23 January and 3 February 1975; Yahya Ali Omar, 26 December 1974.
106 Farsy, 'Baadhi', 1.
107 *Ibid.*, 2.
108 *Ibid.*, 14–15.
109 The rejection of Sh. Abdu'l-Aziz at Mombasa is a classic example of several aspects of town Islam. First of all, according to informants, poor people generally have little influence, as previously discussed; hence, Sh. Abdu'l-Aziz encountered 'sarcasm' and apathy when he tried to lecture in the Mlango wa Papa mosque. Secondly, Sh. Ali b. Abdallah's greater influence locally, which eventually ensured his ideological victory of the interloper, follows the pattern where 'foreign' ᶜ*ulama*ᵓ had great difficulty in gaining

recognition as equals to locally born *ʿulamaʾ*. Finally, the principal ideological weapon used by Sh. Ali against Sh. Abdu'l-Aziz was that his knowledge and *dhikr* came from Barawa, rather than from the Hijaz, where Sh. Ali had most of his training. The success of this last tactic indicates that already by the 1840s, a literary education from Arabia was considered more prestigious to some forms of local training. Interviews, Mombasa: 23 and 26 December 1974; 5 March 1975.

110 The reasons for this can only be guessed. By the 1840s and 1850s, Zanzibar, unlike Mombasa, was becoming quite cosmopolitan. Obviously, local Islam already had to have been under considerable ideological stress since the local *waungwana* certainly were suffering from loss of social status to the Omanis. In this situation, then, the esoteric, yet adaptive character of a *sufi tariqa* would have been (and was) an ideal institution both for escape from status deprivation and a ready sort of organizational vehicle for the defence of local, tradition-based perceptions, usages, and practices. See Farsy, 'Baadhi', 15.

111 Interview, Mombasa: 5 March 1975. It is said that Sh. Abdu'l-Aziz was one of those responsible for the conversion of Sh. Ali b. Khamis al-Barwani, as discussed above. Sh. Abdu'l-Aziz was a great debater both with Ibadi *ʿulamaʾ* and with European missionaries, which perhaps, along with his Qadiriyya beliefs, exposed him to the wrath of Barghash.

112 Interview, Mombasa: 5 March 1975.

113 Euan-Smith to Salisbury, 24 December 1888, FO 84/1911/385. According to this communication, the executions were ordered by Khalifa with the advice of 'the Kazi' who most likely was Abdu'l-Aziz, – the *ʿalim* closest to Khalifa at that time and his constant companion.

114 Euan-Smith to Salisbury, 16 January 1890, FO 84/2059/16; and 18 March 1890, FO 84/2060/116.

115 Euan-Smith to Salisbury, 11 February 1890, FO 84/2059/59.

116 Farsy, 'Baadhi', 14.

117 Rodd to Rosebery, 25 March 1885, FO 107/3/82.

8 A NEW LITERACY

1 Monica Wilson, *Religion and the Transformation of Society* (London, 1971), 16.

2 Such literature, in fact, was introduced to the coast in the nineteenth century, according to Becker. In listing titles of 'religious' texts commonly found in the libraries of coastal *ʿulamaʾ* during the early years of colonial rule, he found a numerous literature on *fiqh*, much to the detriment, interestingly enough, of materials on the Quranic sciences. The fact that the titles he discovered were to be found *commonly* in centres of learning scattered all along the Indian Ocean periphery led him to conclude that, by then at least, one could, 'almost speak of an Indian Ocean literature'. C. H. Becker 'Materials', 22. Among the texts of *fiqh* which Becker encountered most frequently were Muhyi ad-Din Nawawi's *Minhaj at Talibin*; and Shams ad-Din Abdallah Ahmad ar-Ramli's *Nihajat al-Muhtaj*, both of which, incidentally, are listed by Van den Berg as having been popular in the Dutch East Indies during the 1880s; q.v. L. W. C. Van den Berg's translation of the *Minhaj at-Talibin* (Batavia, 1882), vii–viii. See also the various texts mentioned in Farsy, 'Baadhi', *passim*.

3 Wilson, *Religion*, 12–13. It should be said, however, that Wilson's ideas need further analysis. Irreligion or non-commitment equally could result from new work routines and modes of production.

4 *Ibid.*, 5, 47, and 50.

5 Interviews, Lamu: 1 and 18 May 1975.

6 Such, for example, is one of the examples cited by Lienhardt for the success of Habib Salih Jamal al-Layl at Lamu; see Lienhardt, 'The Mosque College at Lamu', 241.

7 Interview, Mombasa: Mwinyi Faki Sulaiman, 26 March 1975. See also H. Greffulhe, 'Voyage de Lamoo', 213.

8 Interviews, Mombasa: Y. A. Omar, 21 and 23 December 1974.

9 Interviews, Mombasa: 29 February and 13 March 1975.

10 Interviews, Mombasa: 28 December 1974. See also similar discussions which Lienhardt overheard at Kilwa in his 'A Controversy over Islamic Custom at Kilwa Kivinje, Tanzania', in I. M. Lewis (ed.), *Islam in Tropical Africa* (London, 1966), 370, *passim*, esp. 375.

11 The reasons for this are unknown. One might be that they filled an ideological gap created by the abandonment of old ideology and values in the face of externally induced changes. A more interesting reason, however, is suggested by Wilson's discussion of the effects of economic growth and change on people's religious views. It will be remembered that she suggests that in such a situation people abandon old deities and turn to a belief in a higher, more potent God. Yet, she claims, as God becomes more approachable, people fear less what formerly was thought too dangerous to seek out. This attempt to get closer to God, be it through religious studies or *dhikr* exercises, could account for the *tariqas*' popularity since, among other things, they promoted means of getting nearer to God often through the Prophet's intercession. See Wilson, *Religion*, 47–8.

12 Y. A. Omar (16 December 1974) claimed, in fact, that it was S. Ahmad b. Sumayt and the Jamal al-Layl who introduced and promoted the Alawiyya in East Africa. Sh Abdallah Bakathir who, though not a *sharif*, also followed its doctrines and studied under various Alawi ⁿulama³ in the Hadhramawt was the originator of the Ramadhan *darasas*, for which the Gofu Mosque became famous, and the equally famous Ukutani *madrasas* associated with the Msikiti Gofu. Habib Salih, likewise founded the Riyadha *madrasa* at Lamu. Both of these men will be discussed below.

13 Van den Berg, *Le Hadramout*, 84–5.

14 Lienhardt, 'The Mosque College', 236; also, Farsy, 'Baadhi', 25 and 55–7, where he tells of S. Ahmad b. Sumayt's ties with the *shurafa³* of the Hadhramawt.

15 Lienhardt, 'The Mosque College', 236, and J. S. Trimingham, *Islam in East Africa* (Oxford, 1964), 102 According to Yahya Ali Omar, no *dhikrs* at all were performed – interview, Mombasa; 26 December 1974.

16 Lienhardt, 'The Mosque College', 237; and R. B. Serjeant, 'The Saiyids', 26. Y. A. Omar claimed, in fact, that much Alawi study time was devoted to works by Ghazzali, such as the *Kutu'l-Kulub*, and *Ihyaa Alumi ad-Din, Bidaya'tu'l-Hadiya, Arba'ini'l-Asl*, as well as other works on *tasawwuf* by other scholars. Interview, Mombasa: 26 December 1974.

17 Interview, Mombasa: Y. A. Omar, 26 December 1974.

18 R. B. Serjeant, 'The Saiyids', 20.

19 As pointed out above, the revolution in Islamic learning on the coast came with the increase in literacy. Religious literature, in the form of shorter poetry and epic works (*tenzi*) of a didactic nature, came with the great *sharif* families who translated Arabic classics into Swahili, apparently for instructional purposes. The northern coastal origins of this new literature are indicated by the facts that Pate and Lamu had become the homes of the Jamal al-Layl and the Abu Bakr bin Salim by the nineteenth century and, as Trimingham notes, the Ki-Amu dialect in which this *tenzi* literature usually appears. See J. Trimingham, *Islam in East Africa* (Oxford, 1964), 77–8.

20 It appears to have been the great number of ⁿulama³ and *shurafa³* under whom S. Ahmad bin Sumayt and Sh. Abdallah Bakathir al-Kindi studied which contributed to their fame in East Africa, rather than the actual material they covered. According to Farsy ('Baadhi', 30), Sh. Abdallah Bakathir obtained *ijaza* from certain Hadrami ⁿulama³, 'just to benefit from their *baraka*'. Furthermore, it is clear that what Sh. Abdallah read under these ⁿulama³ did not amount to much since he completed several of these studies in only a few days.

21 Farsy, 'Baadhi', 44–5.

22 Again, the case of Abdallah Bakathir comes to mind. See Farsy, 'Baadhi', 23 and 25.

23 *Ibid.*, 50 and 72.

24 Interviews, Mombasa: A. S. Farsy, 7, 24 and 26 February 1975.

25 Interview, Mombasa: A. S. Farsy, 7 February 1975.

26 Interview, Mombasa: A. S. Farsy, 7 February 1975. The Shatiri, for example, rejected Muhyi ad-Din al-Qahtani because he was a 'foreigner' from Barawa and chose S. Ahmad b. Salim Abu Bakr bin Salim as their *qadi* since he was a relative by marriage.
27 Interview, Lamu: Harith Swaleh al-Maawi, 19 April 1975.
28 Interviews, Mombasa: 17, 24, and 27 March 1975. To prevent Sulaiman b. Ali from getting the position, an examination was required of all applicants. *Liwali* Ali b. Salim al-Busaidi guessed right when he thought the proud Mazrui *'ulama'* would not submit to a Government-sponsored test of their knowledge; therefore, Sulaiman b. Ali Mazrui was eliminated and Mwinyi Abudi eventually got the appointment.
29 Interviews, Mombasa: A. S. Farsy, 7 and 19 February 1975.
30 Reute, *Memoirs*, 230–1.
31 Churchill to FO, 7 and 8 October, and 5 December 1870. FO 84/1325/75.
32 Reute, *Memoirs*, 231.
33 Kirk to FO, 4 and 7 March 1870, FO 84/1325/29 and 7/49, and Churchill to FO, 8 August 1870, FO 84/1325/57/188.
34 Farsy, 'Baadhi', 34–44, 58–67.
35 *Ibid.*, 49–50.
36 *Ibid.*, 69–72.
37 *Ibid.*, 50.
38 *Ibid.*, 74.
39 *Ibid.*, 55–7.
40 *Ibid.*, 24.
41 *Ibid.*, 57–8. B. G. Martin, *Muslim Brotherhoods in Nineteenth Century Africa* (London, 1976), 175 and 176, quoting Ahmad bin Sumayt, *Al-Ibtihaj fi Bayan Istilah al-Minhaj*, 28. Also, interview, Mombasa: A. S. Farsy, 18 February 1975.
42 Interview, Mombasa: A. S. Farsy, 3 March 1975.
43 'Report on the Judiciary', by Judge P. Grain, 20 September 1907; FO 367/59/42197.
44 Cracknall to Kimberley, 24 March 1894, FO 107/18/55; and Hardinge to Kimberley, 7 January 1895, FO 107/34/4.
45 Hardinge to Kimberley, 8 April 1895, FO 107/35/66; Hardinge to Salisbury, 25 September 1895, FO 107/34/184.
46 Interview, Mombasa: 17 February 1975. According to this same informant, however, this cost S. Ahmad some of his popularity. The British Consul, E. Clarke, opposed bin Sumayt's decision and pressured S. Ali b. Hamud and S. Ahmad to free some of those imprisoned by this decision. Those freed jeered the famous *shaykh* and, in open defiance, held *dhikrs* before his very house on several Fridays.
47 Interview, Mombasa: 18 February 1975.
48 A. S. Farsy, 'Baadhi', 26 and 49–50.
49 *Ibid.*, 71.
50 *Ibid.*, 36–8. Interview, Mombasa: A. S. Farsy, 12 May 1975.
51 Interview, Mombasa: M. A. Matano, 27 February 1975.
52 Farsy, 'Baadhi', 19.
53 *Ibid.*, 6; interview, Mombasa: A. S. Farsy, 17 February 1975.
54 See Martin, *Muslim Brotherhoods*, 164–9.
55 This refers to the Barmakid *wazirs* of the early Abbasid Caliphs. Since they were Shiites, in referring to them here Sh. Muhyi ad-Din was conjuring a name which was sure to prove anathema to most Sunnis.
56 A. S. Farsy, 'Baadhi', 4.
57 Coughing here probably refers to the hyperventilation employed by some in more extreme *dhikr* exercises.
58 According to Sh. Abdallah Farsy (interview, 17 February 1975), Sh. Husain was a Baluchi from Mombasa who actually first introduced the Qadiriyya to Zanzibar.
59 Farsy, 'Baadhi', 14–15.

60 Interviews, Mombasa: 23 December 1974, and 28 February 1975. Interestingly enough, *tariqas* and *dhikrs* usually were associated with the poor and illiterate. This indicates, once again, the class nature of learning on the coast.

61 H. M. Smith, *Frank, Bishop of Zanzibar* (London, 1926), 105. Also, F. Albrand, 'Extrait d'un Mémoire sur Zanzibar et sur Quiloa', *Bulletin de la Société de Géographie*, X (1838), 72–74.

62 El-Zein, 'Sacred Meadows', 116–21.

63 Interview, Mombasa: M. A. Matano, 20 March 1975.

64 See the précis of the Mombasa High Court of the East African Protectorate Civil Appeal 12 of 1913, *Thelatha Taifa vs. the Waqf* Commissioner and the Land Officer, KNA DC MSA/3/1, 88–109, where the Three Tribes tried, unsuccessfully, to introduce such evidence into court. Similarly, this happened in case 60 of 1913, *Jibana tribe* vs. *Abdu-Rasul Alidina Visram*. KNA DC/MSA/3/1, 110–26.

9 THE EARLY COLONIAL ERA 1885–1914

1 R. Coupland, *Exploitation*, 395–405.

2 *Ibid.*, 407–79.

3 See Euan-Smith to Salisbury correspondence, especially FO 84/1907/93, 125 and 150, and F.O. 84/1908/224 for events associated specifically with these concessions.

4 Coupland, *Exploitation*, 402–18, 469n., 482. Naturally, some resistance ensued. In the German sphere there was the famous Abushiri revolt which resulted in the Anglo-German blockade of the coast. At Mombasa, too, the IBEA Company experienced some tense moments when rioting broke out against a company caravan in October. See Euan-Smith to Salisbury, 22 October 1888, FO 84/1920/312; MacKenzie to Euan-Smith, 12 October 1888, FO 84/1910/312 encl.; and Euan-Smith to Salisbury, 14 November 1888, FO 84/1910/328 and 330 for these affairs.

5 J. E. Flint, 'Zanzibar, 1890–1950', in *History of East Africa*, II, edited by E. Chilver, V. Harlow, and A. Smith (London, 1965), 641.

6 A. I. Salim, *Swahili-Speaking Peoples*, 73.

7 Portal to Salisbury, 23 October 1891, FO 84/2149/277 and enclosure. Also, see Flint, 'Zanzibar' in Chilver *et al.*, 642.

8 L. W. Hollingsworth, *Zanzibar under the Foreign Office, 1890–1913* (London, 1952), 191, where the author reflects the prevailing attitude that 'it was certainly not possible to obtain either an adequate or trustworthy staff from the local population'.

9 Portal to Salisbury, 23 August 1891, FO 84/2149/223 and 224; 25 August 1891, FO 84/2149/228; 9 September 1891, FO 84/2149/245; and 29 September 1891, FO 84/2149/254. Also, Flint, 'Zanzibar' in Chilver *et al.*, 642–3.

10 Rodd to Foreign Consuls, 11 January 1893, FO 107/2; and Flint, 'Zanzibar' in Chilver *et al.* 643–5.

11 See especially, Rodd to Rosebery, 17 March 1893, FO 107/3/9; Hardinge to Kimberley, 30 June 1894, FO 107/21/48. Also, G. Hamilton, *Princes of Zinj* (London, 1957), 232–3.

12 Hardinge to Kimberley, 25 June 1895, FO 107/36/112.

13 Cave to Salisbury, 26 August 1896, FO 107/54/243.

14 Cave to Salisbury, 29 August 1896, FO 107/54/244; Hardinge to Bertie, 5 September 1896, FO 107/54; Cave to Salisbury, 10 October 1896, FO 107/55/277.

15 G. Hamilton, *Princes*, 246; F. B. Pearce, *Zanzibar, The Island Metropolis of East Africa* (London, 1920), 273. Also see *The Gazette for Zanzibar and East Africa*, 9 September 1896 for accounts of Hamud's accession.

16 Pearce, *Zanzibar*, 273.

17 D. A. Low, 'British East Africa: The Establishment of British Rule, 1895–1912' in *History of East Africa*, II, edited by Chilver, Harlow, and Smith, 6.

18 A. H. Hardinge, *Report, 1897*, 26; Hardinge, *Report, 1898*, 226. Also, Salim, *Swahili-Speaking Peoples*, 77; Flint, 'Zanzibar' in Chilver *et al.*, 652.

19 This followed moves taken as a result of the total cession of the coastal strip to the Foreign Office by S. Hamud b. Muhammad in return for guarantees that his son, S. Ali b. Hamud, would succeed him. Eliot to Landsdowne, 5 June 1901, FO 2/457/56:

20 Flint, 'Zanzibar' in Chilver *et al.* 653.

21 See Smith to Salisbury, 9 September 1891, FO 84/248/248; Portal to Salisbury, 28 November 1891, FO 84/2150/293.

22 Portal to Salisbury, 28 November 1891, FO 84/2150/293.

23 Portal to Salisbury, 22 August 1892, FO 84/2232/183.

24 Portal to Rosebery, 12 October 1892, FO 84/2233/233; Portal to Salisbury, 3 December 1892, FO 84/2234/261.

25 FO 107/3/73.

26 Hardinge to Kimberley, 25 June 1895, FO 107/36/112. Actually, a third cut ensued in January 1896. Taking advantage of the British men-of-war sent to quell a fight brewing between Government police and Ali b. Said's personal bodyguards, Hardinge got the Sultan to 'volunteer' another reduction 'as a sign of good faith'. See Hardinge to Salisbury, 14 January 1896, FO 107/49/7.

27 Cave to Salisbury, 11 October 1896, FO 107/55/282.

28 Hardinge to Kimberley, 7 January 1895, FO 107/34/4.

29 Eliot to Landsdowne, 5 June 1901, FO 2/457/56.

30 Cave and Ali b. Hamud to Landsdowne, 18 February 1905, FO 2/923, memo enclosed.

31 Interview, Mombasa: 3 March 1975.

32 S. Khalifa to Euan-Smith, 19 December 1888, FO 84/1911/385 enclosure. This incident itself was quite interesting both because of the unusual behaviour of Khalifa which preceded it, as much as for the incident itself. Previously, it had been the custom for Sultans, possibly out of deference for European opinion, to imprison most felons. Quranic executions and mutilations had become extremely rare. Once the Germans forced Khalifa to cede Tanganyika and the elusive nature of British 'friendship' and 'protection' became apparent, Khalifa suffered a series of physical breakdowns. Along with Peera Dewji, Abdu'l-Aziz, and Bakashmar, he retired to his *shambas* and remained incommunicado to all Europeans for weeks at a time. Once he did emerge, however, with the encouragement of Abdu'l-Aziz, he briefly tried to restore complete Quranic law to the land. Obviously recognizing the virulent effects of European influences which previous Sultans had allowed to seep into coastal Islamic society, Abdu'l-Aziz and Khalifa attempted, too late, to banish all European influences from Zanzibar. The fact that so many Arab clans rallied to the British side and openly opposed Khalifa and Abdu'l-Aziz, however, doomed these measures and reflect just how much Western ways and habits already had taken hold. For a complete report on these events, see Euan-Smith to Salisbury, 24 December 1888, FO 84/1911/385 and enclosures.

33 Euan-Smith to Salisbury, 24 December 1888, FO 84/1911/385.

34 Euan-Smith to Salisbury, 16 January 1890, FO 84/2059/16.

35 Euan-Smith to Salisbury, 11 February 1890, FO 84/2059/54.

36 Euan-Smith to Salisbury, 18 March 1890, FO 84/2060/116.

37 E. Reute, *Memoirs*, 293.

38 *Ibid.*, 293–4; Euan-Smith to Salisbury, 24 December 1888, FO 84/1911/385.

39 Reute, *Memoirs*, 293–4.

40 Euan-Smith to Salisbury, 24 December 1888, FO 84/1911/385; Euan-Smith to Salisbury, 27 February 1889, FO 84/1977/104.

41 Interview, Mombasa: 3 March 1975.

42 Churchill to Stanley, 19 August 1868, FO 84/1292/30.

43 Kirk to Rigby, reported in C. E. B. Russell, *General Rigby, Zanzibar and the Slave Trade* (London, 1935), 306.

44 Badger's interviews with Barghash, 15–17 January 1873, Sir B. Frere to Granville, 26 March 1873, *CRME*, no. 36, enclosures 2 and 4.

45 Interview, Mombasa: A. S. Farsy, 12 May 1975; Euan-Smith to Salisbury, 25 April 1888, FO 84/1906/71; Euan-Smith to Salisbury, 3 December 1888, FO 84/1911/357.

46 See Euan-Smith to Salisbury, 1 February 1889, FO 84/1976/49; Euan-Smith to Salisbury, 7 February 1889, FO 84/1976/63; Portal to Salisbury, 28 July 1889, FO 84/1979/284.
47 Portal to Salisbury, 28 July 1889, FO 84/1979/284.
48 Portal to Salisbury, 19 August 1889, FO 84/1980/311.
49 *The Gazette for Zanzibar and East Africa*, 9 September 1896.
50 Interview, Mombasa: Sh. Hyder Kindy, 31 January 1975.
51 Salim, *Swahili-Speaking Peoples*, 63. Also see Salim, 'Sir Ali b. Salim' in K. King and A. I. Salim (eds.), *Kenya Historical Biographies* (Nairobi, 1971), 115–17.
52 A. Hardinge, *Report on the East Africa Protectorate, 1898*, 27.
53 W. H. Ingrams, *Zanzibar, Its History and its Peoples* London, 1931), 252.
54 Hardinge, *Report, 1898*, 26; Salim, 'Sir Ali b. Salim', 117.
55 Salim, 'Sir Ali b. Salim', 41.
56 Salim, *Swahili-Speaking Peoples*, 90–1; J. Middleton, 'Kenya: Administration and Changes in African Life' in Chilver, Harlow, and Smith, *History of East Africa*, II, 365–8; B. A. Ogot, 'Kenya under the British, 1895 to 1963' in B. A. Ogot (ed.), *Zamani* (Nairobi, 1974), 262–3.
57 Salim, *Swahili-Speaking Peoples*, 43–4.
58 Ingrams, *Zanzibar*, 252.
59 Quoted in Sir John Gray, *The British at Mombasa*, 116–17.
60 *The Gazette for Zanzibar and East Africa*, 2 September 1896, p. 6. Interestingly enough, both defended their actions as being 'customary' in Mombasa. Crawford's decision, as can be imagined, 'apparently produced a considerable effect upon the audience'.
61 Hardinge, *Report, 1898*, 37.
62 Anderson to Rodd, 15 February 1893, FO 107/1; J. N. D. Anderson, *Islamic Law in Africa* (London, 1970), 81–2.
63 Anderson, *Law*, 82.
64 Hardinge to Salisbury, 24 March 1896, FO 107/50/91.
65 Anderson, *Law*, 82–3; Hardinge, *Report, 1898*, 34–5.
66 Hardinge, *Report, 1898*, 35–6.
67 Hardinge to Salisbury, 24 October 1898, FO 107/97/333; Hollingsworth, *Zanzibar*, 163.
68 Hardinge to Salisbury, 24 October 1898, FO 107/97/333.
69 Cave to Landsdowne, 6 September 1905, FO 2/124/102.
70 Interviews, Mombasa: 7 and 18 February 1975.
71 Judge Peter Grain, 'Report on the Judiciary', 20 April 1907, FO 367/59/42197; Hollingsworth, *Zanzibar*, 204–5; Flint, 'Zanzibar' in Chilver *et al.*, 654.
72 Cave to Grey, 21 April 1908, FO 367/93/18421.
73 Hardinge to Salisbury, 21 March 1899, FO 2/190/99; Salim, *Swahili-Speaking Peoples*, 86.
74 FO 2/924/116 enclosure. Here it should be pointed out that two of the four commissioners – Salim b. Khalfan and Ali b. Salim – were *liwalis* and not *qadis* and were of the notorious Salim b. Khalfan branch of the al-Busaidi. Furthermore, Muhammad Qasim was another 'Arab' aristocrat and the three of them hardly represented the majority of the *waungwana* of the coast.
75 Anderson, *Law*, 94–5.
76 *Ibid.*, 95.
77 Cave to Landsdowne, 7 August 1905, FO 2/924/86.
78 Cave to Landsdowne, 6 October 1905, FO 2/924/116 and enclosure; Cave to Grey, 5 May 1908, FO 367/103/18437, enclosure.
79 See Chapter 7. Also, interview, Mombasa: Sh. al-Amin b. Muhsin Maamiry, 20 January 1975.
80 Interviews, Lamu Sayyid Bahasani, 14 April 1975; Harith Swaleh Maawi, 19 April 1975
81 The remaining 46.22 per cent were tried by European officials. Compiled from data in KNA DC/LAM/1/9.
82 Salim, *Swahili-Speaking Peoples*, 91.
83 Salim, 'Sir Ali b. Salim', 118–19.

84 KNA DC/MSA/3/3, 4–5.
85 Interviews, Mombasa; S. Ahmad b. Abdu'r-Rahman as-Saqqaf, 23 January and 3 February 1975; Y. A. Omar, 23, 24, and 28 December 1974.
86 Cave to Clarke, 21 June 1907, FO 367/56/25205.
87 E.g., see Churchill, 'Handing over Report of 1924', p. 2 in KNA DC/LAM/2/1.
88 Kirk to FO, 8 August 1878, FO 84/1325/57/188.
89 Reute, *Memoirs*, 230–1.
90 Churchill to F.O., 7 October 1870, FO 84/1325/75/277.
91 Hardinge to Kimberley, 8 April 1895, FO 107/35/66.
92 Farsy, 'Baadhi ya Wanavyuoni', 69. Also, interview, Mombasa: A. S. Farsy, 18 February 1975.
93 Salaries reported for 1907 and 1908 in FO 367/52/21438, and FO 367/104/23872, respectively.
94 Farsy, 'Baadhi', 18; interview, Mombasa: A. S. Farsy, 18 March 1975.
95 F. Cooper, *Plantation Slavery on the East Coast of Africa* (New Haven, 1977), 136.
96 *Ibid.*, 123.
97 *Ibid.*, 61 and 131.
98 Cooper's analysis in *ibid.*, 136–49.
99 Interview, Mombasa: Y. A. Omar, 13 January 1975.
100 J. deV. Allen, *Lamu* 2–3.
101 One manifestation of this was the excessively long *ngomas*, taken as a sign of prosperity, reported by P. C. Reddie for Lamu District in 1910. KNA DC/LAM/177, p. 6.
102 Quoted in Russell, *General Rigby*, 332.
103 Hardinge, *Report, 1898*, 14.
104 Sir F. Jackson, *Early Days in East Africa* (London, 1930), 353–4.
105 Hardinge to Salisbury, 10 January 1896, FO 107/49/6.
106 F. B. Pearce, *Zanzibar, The Island Metropolis of East Africa* (London, 1920), 218–19.
107 Hollingsworth, *Zanzibar*, 197. When Cave suggested the creation of an agricultural bank to alleviate the problem of credit, Clarke chose to ignore it. It was the latter's opinion that additional borrowed income simply would launch *shamba* owners into another cycle of 'new extravagances'.
108 Salim, *Swahili-Speaking Peoples*, 121.
109 Clive, 'Short History', 23.
110 Salim, *Swahili-Speaking Peoples*, 119–20.
111 Account in *ibid.*, 130–2. The 5,000 acres went to the Maawi who, unlike other clans, had taken the precaution of allowing their claim to be surveyed, precisely delineated, and, thus, given a legal status, Interview, Lamu: Abdu'l-Malik b. Abdu'r-Rahman Maawi 19 May 1975.
112 Salim, *Swahili-Speaking Peoples*, 121–3.
113 *Ibid.*, 112.
114 KNA DC/LAM/1/5, 'Annual Report for 1912–13', 2, 5–7.
115 *Ibid.*, 2. Siyu alone was reported to have lost 500–600 labourers.
116 Annual Provincial Report for 1917, KNA. DC/LAM/1/9.
117 Report of P. C. Reddie, KNA DC/LAM/1/7, 8–9.
118 KNA DC/LAM/3/2, 71.
119 Taken from the report of P. C. Reddie in KNA DC/LAM/1/7, 8–9, and KNA DC/LAM/3/2, 70–1.
120 A. H. Hardinge, *Report on the East African Protectorate, 1899, Parliamentary Papers*, vol. LXIII (London, 1899), 7.
121 J. W. Milligan and H. F. Ward, *Handbook of British East Africa* (Nairobi, 1912), 141 and 142–3.
122 P. C. Reddie, KNA DC/LAM/1/7, 6.
123 Milligan and Ward, *Handbook*, 141.
124 KNA Coast Province, 1/38.

125 Margaret Strobel mentions another particularly violent episode which took place in the 1920s. Rumours about 'blood drinkers' (Christians?) among Kikuyu and Luo residents at Mombasa offended Muslim feelings and produced an attack on Kikuyu and Luo quarters. See M. Strobel, *Muslim Women in Mombasa, 1895–1975* (New Haven, 1979).

126 Krapf, *Travels and Missionary Labours*, 130–1. That this 'Arab chief' in fact was an *'alim* seems clear from his being capable of expounding in learned fashion upon 'some of the fables of Mohammedan cosmography and geography'.

127 A. E. M. Anderson-Moreshead, *The History of the Universities Mission to Central SAfrica, 1852–1896* (London, 1897), 90.

128 *Ibid.*, 88; Pearce, *Zanzibar*, 209.

129 Interview, Mombasa: Charo Shambe, 11 January, 1975.

130 Al-Amin b. Ali Mazrui, 'Prosody', (unpublished MS), 3.

131 *Ibid.*

132 Interview, Mombasa: A. S. Farsy, 24 and 26 February 1975; Fr Godfrey Dale, *The Peoples of Zanzibar* (London, 1920), 48–52.

133 See Al-Amin b. Ali Mazrui, *Dini ya Islamu* (Mombasa, 1939), 1.

134 *Ibid.;* H. Smith, *Frank, Bishop of Zanzibar* (London, 1926), 106.

135 Al-Amin b. Ali Mazrui, *Dini*, 1; Smith, *Frank*, 106.

136 Interview, Mombasa: Y. A. Omar, 10 March 1975; also, G. Hamilton, *Princes of Zinj*, 255–6.

137 Ingrams, *Zanzibar*, 206. Also, interview, Lamu: Omari Bwana Bwana Abdi, 21 June 1975.

138 Ibuni Saleh, *Comorians*, 15.

139 *Ibid.*, 12–13.

140 Interview, Lamu: A. M. Jahadhmy, 29 April 1975; Harith Swaleh Maawi, 15 April 1975; Abdallah Khatib, 16 April 1975. Also, see el-Zein, 'The Sacred Meadows', 64–8, 95–6, 120–1.

141 See T. O. Ranger, *Dance and Society in Eastern Africa* (London, 1975). Interview, Mombasa: 10 March 1975.

142 Ingrams, *Zanzibar*, 221–2.

143 Annual Report for 1912, KNA DC/LAM/1/5, 2; Pearce, *Zanzibar*, 219–20. Naturally, such things as military defeats, a declining economy, and loss of cultural status do not themselves explain an 'erosion of morality'. If anything North African cities such as Cairo, when faced with a similar situation, continued to enjoy astonishingly low crime rates. The critical point being made here is that, on top of military setbacks, etc., a feeling of helplessness, cultural ineffectuality, and malaise followed such developments and created a cultural void. This cultural void directly explains this declining morality and the search for cultural alternatives in Western culture. In addition, many of these youths came from lower class families which, to begin with, had little stake in the social and cultural status quo of coastal towns.

144 Ingrams, *Zanzibar*, 223.

145 Pearce, *Zanzibar*, 220.

10 CURRENTS OF POPULARISM AND EDDIES OF REFORM

1 Kirk to Derby, 20 April 1876, and Kirk to Wylde, FO 84/1453; Coupland, *Exploitation*, 227; interview, Mombasa: A. S. Farsy, 24 and 26 February 1975.

2 KNA DC/LAM/1/5, 3.

3 Judge's report for 1907, FO 367/95/8177.

4 Town magistrate's report on Lamu, 21 May 1912, KNA DC/LAM/1/5, 3.

5 *Ibid.*

6 Burton, *Zanzibar*, 1, 421 and 423. See also, R. F. Burton, *First Footsteps in East Africa*, 2nd ed. (London, 1966), 71, where he makes similar observations about *'ulama'* in Zeila.

7 Burton, *Zanzibar*, I, 421–2.

8 In the 1850s Burton noted that Swahilis' 'African languor on doctrinal points prevents their becoming fanatics or proselytizers.' See Burton, *Zanzibar*, I, 417; also, C. H. Becker, 'Materials', 16.

9 Burton, *First Footsteps*, 57–8.

10 El-Zein, 'Sacred Meadows', 102. The single exception where Hadramis managed to establish themselves as large landowners was at Malindi. There, two figures, Islam b. Ali al-Kathiri and Ali b. Salim Bashrahil, arrived from Lamu originally as merchants but acquired sufficient capital to buy up extensive holdings in land. See Cooper, *Plantation Slavery*, 92–3. Apparently, a similar situation evolved among Hadrami settlers in Indonesia. Van den Berg, *Le Hadramout, passim*, but especially p. 114.

11 El-Zein, 'Sacred Meadows', 104.

12 *Ibid.*, 97; J. Bujra, 'Conflict', 79–80.

13 El-Zein, 'Sacred Meadows', 93–5; J. N. D. Anderson, *Islamic Law in Africa*, (London, 1970), 94.

14 Flint, 'Zanzibar' in Chilver *et al.*, 648–50; Pearce, *Zanzibar*, 303.

15 C. C. Wrigley, 'Kenya: The Patterns of Economic Life, 1902–45', *History of East Africa*, vol. II, edited by Chilver Harlow, and Smith, 223–4; W. O. Henderson, 'German East Africa, 1884–1918' in Chilver *et al.*, 149, 152.

16 Henderson, 'German East Africa' in Chilver *et al.*, 149–52; Pearce, *Zanzibar*, 242.

17 Henderson, 'German East Africa' in Chilver *et al.*, 150 and 152.

18 J. Bujra, 'Conflict', 60–2.

19 Interview, Lamu: Salim Heri and Amina bti. Salim, 17 May 1975.

20 El-Zein, 'Sacred Meadows', 120–1.

21 Al-Amin b. Ali Mazrui, 'Jee, Ni Kweli Dini Ndiyo Iwa-rudishayo Watu Ngumu?' *Uwongozi* (Mombasa, 1952), 48.

22 Burton, *Zanzibar*, I, 263.

23 Russell, *General Rigby*, 93 and 330.

24 H. M. Stanley, *Through the Dark Continent*, vol. I (New York, 1879), 50; R. F. Burton, *The Lakes Region of Central Africa* (New York, 1860), 42.

25 Interview, Mombasa: M. A. Matano, 27 February 1975.

26 Interview, Mombasa: M. A. Matano, 20 March 1975.

27 El-Zein, 'Sacred Meadows', 44; Becker, 'Materials', 25; interview, Mombasa: Yahya Ali Omar, 6 January 1975.

28 El-Zein, 'Sacred Meadows' 46–7; Becker, 'Materials', 26–8.

29 J. E. E. Craster, *Pemba, The Spice Island of Zanzibar* (London, 1913), 308–9, describes these exercises by saying that they lasted, 'until the monotonous rhythms of the drums and music and the monotonous movement of the dance produce some sort of hypnotic seizure, and the performers one after another fall to the ground insensible. And when this happens the audience think that the devil [i.e. spirit or God] has come and entered into the performers'. The amenability of these exercises to traditional *ngoma* or *tari* dances is quite apparent and accounts for the success of the *tariqas*. Craster mentions further on (p. 311), for instance, that the most popular dance of the above sort was called 'Thikiri' (i.e. *dhikr*) at which women 'sang' and men 'barked' (i.e. performed breathing exercises common to many *dhikrs*?).

30 A. Nimtz, 'Muslim Sufi Order', 57 and 60.

31 El-Zein, 'Sacred Meadows', 118.

32 Becker, 'Materials', 26; A. S. Farsy, 'Baadhi', 51.

33 H. M. Smith, *Frank Bishop of Zanzibar* (London, 1926), 100. According to this author, the missionary, Frank Weston, also mentioned this 'danger' in *The East and the West* (Zanzibar, 1908). Similar apprehensions were expressed by Becker throughout 'Materials' over Islamic practices in East Africa.

34 Nimtz, 'Muslim Sufi Order', 238–9.

35 Interview, Mombasa: Y. A. Omar, 13 January 1975.

36 P. Lienhardt, 'The Mosque College of Lamu and Its Social Background', *TNR* (1958), 138–9, mentions *kiumbizi* dances associated with the spirit cults of ex-slaves and the *Mawlidi* processions of the Riyadha mosque at Lamu.

37 See Nimtz, 'Muslim Sufi Orders', 446–8; also in *Hidayatu' l-Atfaki* (unpublished, n.d.), al-Amin b. Ali Mazrui seems to have been so involved with this local controversy that he was required to ask, 'What did the Prophet look like, s.a.w.? What was his colour?' To which he replied, 'The whiteness of his complexion was suffused with redness and his face shown with the brilliance of the moon' (p. 15).

38 Becker, 'Materials', 16 and 25.

39 Nimtz, 'Muslim Sufi Orders', 394–7.

40 *Ibid.*, 399.

41 *Ibid.*, 400–2 and 411–13.

42 El-Zein, 'Sacred Meadows', 132–3; Lienhardt, 'Mosque College of Lamu', 230–1; interview, Lamu: Sayyid Bahasani, 18 May 1975.

43 Interview, Lamu: Sayyid Bahasani, 18 May 1975. Teaching *tafsir* (exegesis) to the 'half educated' was most touchy since the *waungwana* elite felt that it would be too easy for 'mistakes' to be made in transmitting such knowledge. Actually, of course, what was feared was a further erosion of the increasingly moribund traditional religious ideology and views.

44 Which, according to Serjeant, *The Saiyids*, 26, included a programme of opening *madrasas* and educating people in the tenets of Islam, as well as solidarity and fraternity among followers of the order.

45 El-Zein, 'Sacred Meadows', 136; Farsy 'Baadhi', 21.

46 El-Zein, 'Sacred Meadows', 146. For the relations between S. Salih and Sh. Abdallah, see Farsy 'Baadhi', 23. See also, A. Garabedian, 'Mohammedanism in Capetown', *The Moslem World*, V (1915), 30–2, for indirect references concerning Sh. Abdallah's visits representing 'the high Bishop of Mecca and Zanzibar' in the context of Cape Islam.

47 El-Zein, 'Sacred Meadows', 161.

48 'Pate Chronicle' in Freeman-Grenville, *Select Documents*, 292; Farsy, 'Baadhi', 19; interview, Mombasa: S. Athman b. Abdu'r-Rahman Saqqaf, 3 February, 1975.

49 Farsy, 'Baadhi', 18–19; interview, Mombasa: S. Athman b. Abdu'r-Rahman Saqqaf, 8 February 1975.

50 Interview, Mombasa: Y. A. Omar, 21 December 1974.

51 See Farsy, 'Baadhi', 19.

52 Interviews, Mombasa: S. Athman b. Abdu'r-Rahman Saqqaf, 3 February 1975; Y. A. Omar, 23 December 1974.

53 Interview, Mombasa: S. Athman b. Abdu'r-Rahman Saqqaf, 3 February 1975.

54 Interviews, Mombasa: Y. A. Omar, 23 and 26 December 1974.

55 See the example of Turkey as analysed in N. Berkes, *The Development of Secularism in Turkey* (Montreal, 1964).

56 Serjeant, *Saiyids*, 20–1.

57 Interviews, Mombasa: Abdallah Salih Farsy, 7 February and 3 March 1975.

58 W. M. Watt, *Islamic Philosophy and Theology* (Edinburgh, 1962), 161–2.

59 See Malcolm Kerr, *Islamic Reform* (Berkeley, 1966), 55–6; also see Mohammed el-Awa, 'The Place of Custom (*'Urf*) in Islamic Legal Theory', *The Islamic Quarterly*, XVII, 3 (1975), 178–9, where this is discussed further.

60 Kerr, *Islamic Reform*, 56.

61 Watt, *Islamic Philosophy*, 162.

62 *Ibid.*, 165.

63 See J. J. Saunders, *A History of Medieval Islam* (London, 1965), 61–3, and Watt, *Islamic Philosophy*, 3, 7, and 12, for an explanation of the original decisions of some devout Muslims to 'go out' (*kharaja*) from the rest of the community to retain their spiritual purity.

64 See Pessah Shinar, 'Ibadiyya and Orthodox Reformism in Modern Algeria', *Scripta Hierosolymitana*, IX edited by Uriel Heyd (Jerusalem, 1961), 105–6; T. Lewicki, 'Al-

Ibadiyya' in the *Encyclopedia of Islam* (2nd. edn), vol. III, 648–60; and Salil ibn Razik, *Imams and Seyyids*, 244, note 1.

65 D. C. Holsinger, 'Migration, Commerce and Community: The Mizabis in Eighteenth- and Nineteenth-Century Algeria', *JAH*, 21 (1980), 61–74.

66 Salil ibn Razik, *Imams and Seyyids*, 248 and 251.

67 Ravinder Kumar, 'British Attitudes towards the Ibadiyya Revivalist Movement in East Arabia', *International Studies*, III (1962), 444.

68 Miles, *Persian Gulf*, 348–9.

69 W. Phillips, *Oman, A History* (London, 1967), 139–41; Kumar, 'Ibadiyya', 450; Shinar, 'Ibadiyya', 113–14.

70 Phillips, *Oman*, 141–2; Kumar, 'Ibadiyya', 450. In several dispatches made during 1895, Hardinge described, for example, the complicity of S. Hamid b. Thuwain with the *mutawwiun* in trying to seize power from Faisal in Oman. Hardinge to Kimberley, 7 January 1895, FO 107/34/4; Hardinge to Kimberley, 8 April 1895, FO 107/35/66; Hardinge to Salisbury, 28 December 1895, FO 107/39/295.

71 Shinar, 'Ibadiyya', 107–8.

72 Kumar, 'Ibadiyya', 450.

73 Zygmunt Smogorzewski, 'Essai de bio-bibliographie Ibadite-Wahabite: Avant-propos', *Rocznik Orjentalistyczny*, vol. V (1927), 45.

74 Burton, *Zanzibar*, I, 404.

75 Kirk to Wedderburn, 1 January 1872, FO 2/1357/8; Frere to Granville, 7 July 1873, *CRME*, no. 52.

76 Frere to Granville, 7 May 1873, *CRME*, no. 52; also, Coupland, *Exploitation*, 89–90.

77 Shinar, 'Ibadiyya', 113.

78 *Ibid.*, 113.

79 Several likely explanations can be given for this. For example, he obviously was concerned about Ibadi conversions to Sunni Islam and sought to counter this. Secondly, he probably was dismayed about growing Big Power interference in East Africa and Oman. And, finally, after his brief exile to India, he may even have anticipated, vaguely, the need for some sort of ideological/propagandist defence of Islam in the face of overwhelming intellectual and technological advances of the West.

80 Interview, Mombasa: A. S. Farsy, 7 February 1975. Also, see Smogorzewski, 'Essai', 48. J. Schacht, 'Notes on Islam in East Africa', *Studia Islamica*, 23 (1965), 120–1. Apparently, these Pan-Ibadi efforts did have an impact since one case is mentioned in Becker, 'Materials', p. 4, of a former *liwali* of Dar es Salam, Sulaiman b. Nasir Busaidi, who 'renewed' Zanzibari ties with the Mzab through a visit he had made 'some years ago'.

81 Interview, Mombasa: A. S. Farsy, 18 February 1975.

82 Interview, Mombasa: A. S. Farsy, 12 May 1975.

83 Van den Berg, *Le Hadramout*, 174, note 1. The implication, of course, is that East African Shafiis, because of their close ties, may have been reading many of these same journals and newspapers. This can be verified for the 1910s and 1920s, as will be seen below.

84 A. S. Farsy, 'Baadhi', 57; B. G. Martin, *Muslim Brotherhoods in Nineteenth Century Africa* (Cambridge, 1976), 5 and 176.

85 Farsy 'Baadhi', 37.

86 According to Ibuni Saleh (*Short History*, 4), a cousin of Sayyid Mansab, Ali b. Umar, was given a 'French' education in Cairo.

87 Farsy, 'Baadhi', 7–8; interview, Mombasa: A. S. Farsy 1 February 1975.

88 Interview, Mombasa: A. S. Farsy, 3 March 1975.

89 Interviews, Mombasa: A. S. Farsy, 1 March and 12 May 1975.

90 Pearce, *Zanzibar*, 224.

91 Rogers to Sinclaire, 18 May 1904, FO 2/852/16 enclosure; Pearce, *Zanzibar*, 273. For related material, see Eliot to Landsdowne, 29 April 1904, FO 2/8522, and Clarke, 'Minutes', 5 September 1908, and Kirk to Clarke, 11 September 1908, FO 367/100/31160.

92 This led to a crisis between the Sultan and the British establishment over his issuing

several expensive 'Order of the Brilliant Star' medals (total cost: £315) to his distinguished guests without the consent of the Zanzibar Government. See Cave to Grey, 10 March 1908, FO 367/13720, and Cave to Clarke, 15 April 1908, FO 367/100/12532 and 13104.

93 Interviews, Mombasa: A. S. Farsy, 24 and 26 February 1975; 11 March and 12 May 1975. Hamilton, *Princes of Zinj*, 255–6. Also, see Eliot to Landsdowne, 18 February 1904 and 24 April 1904, FO 2/852, and Rogers to Sinclaire, 18 February 1904, FO 2/852, enclosure 1.

Glossary

Adabu   good manners, proper behaviour in any social setting.

Adala   (Ar.) lit. 'integrity'; (Sw.) *adili.*

ᶜAlim/ᶜUlamaᵓ   (Ar.) one learned in the religious sciences, known to have studied under at least one reputed scholar, and possessing *ijaza* (q.v.).

Aman   (Ar.) see *imani* (Sw.)

Bara   (Sw.) mainland areas behind or across from the Swahili town.

Baraka   (Sw.) 'blessing' from God obtained either from 'walking the path of righteousness' or by being descended from the Prophet Muhammad.

Chuo/Vyuo   (Sw.) a Quran school.

Darasa   (Sw.) a class, usually held in a mosque or in a master's home, where the advanced sciences are taught.

Dawa   (Sw.) anything applied by a healer, including charms, talismans, treatment, or herbal medicines.

Dhikr   (Ar.) a spiritual exercise often involving repetition of Quranic passages and accompanied by some form of music or dancing. In Kiswahili, often used loosely for any *sufi* brotherhood.

Dua   (Sw.) prayer.

Falak   (Ar.) astrology; according to Burton, however, in the 1850s *falak* meant sorcery on the coast. A *falaki* was a sorcerer. Only after the 1860s did Swahili usage approach the original Arabic meaning.

Fann/Fanun   (Ar.) branch(es) of the twelve Islamic sciences.

Fatwa   (Ar.) a formal, usually written, legal judgement issued by a mufti.

Fiqh   (Ar.) Islamic law.

Hadith   (Ar.) a tradition attributable to the Prophet or his Companions; (Sw.) a legend or historical tradition handed down from ancestral figures, usually having a moral or didactic purpose and often having religious significance.

Heshima   (Sw.) dignity, social rank.

Honde/Mahonde   (Sw.) a mainland or bush farm, distinct from a coastal or island farm, on which annual cereal and vegetable crops are grown to supplement the typically coastal diet (see *shamba*).

Ijaza   (Ar.) a certificate given a student as evidence that he studied a certain religious tract under the tutelage of a noted authority on the tract.

Ijma   (Ar.) lit. 'consensus', meaning the consensus of a body of religious scholars representing the community either on a specific point of law or on an entire corpus of legal works, pronouncements, texts, or judgements.

Ijtihad   (Ar.) 'independent judgement' allowed a jurisconsult or *qadi* on a point of law. Such 'judgement' allows for the use of deductive and analogical reasoning, as well as the admission of local custom (ᶜ*urf* or *desturi*) in a legal decision. It reflects mere imitation (*taqlid*) of ancestral figures or past legal experts and permits the adaptation of the law to changing social, economic, intellectual, and cultural circumstances.

Ilm(u)   (Ar.) religious knowledge; (Sw.) any sort of knowledge, but especially knowledge of the religious sciences.

Glossary

Imani (Sw.) security obtainable through religious faith and strict adherence to the 'right path'.

Jinn (Ar.) spirits, some of whom are friendly, and others who are harmful to humans.

Jumba (Sw.) a stone mansion, usually two or more stories high.

Jumbe (Sw.) name for the town council at Lamu.

Khatib (Ar.) the person who is chosen to deliver the *khutba*.

Khutba (Ar.) sermon delivered to the faithful at Friday prayers, usually invoking the name of the recognized suzerain.

Kitabu (Sw.) book, but especially a religious (therefore holy) text, for example, the Quran.

Liwali (Sw.) from the Arabic *wali*, an Arab governor of a town.

Ma°alim (Ar.) see °*alim*.

Madrasa (Ar.) a 'university' where advanced Islamic sciences are taught.

Mantik (Ar.) the science of logic.

Mashindano (Sw.) dance and poetry competitions between the quarters (*mitaa*) or moieties (*mikao*) of a town.

Mawlidi (Sw.) from the Arabic *Mawlid*, the Prophet Muhammad's birthday.

Mchawi (Sw.) a sorcerer.

Mganga (Sw.) an African medicine man, a practitioner of curative medicine using traditional African herbs and 'magic'.

Mi°raj (Ar.) the Prophet's ride taken on 27 Rajab to Heaven.

Mmiji/Wamiji (Sw.) a 'citizen' of a coastal town; used especially in Mombasa with the more restricted meaning of an elder.

Mshenzi/Washenzi (Sw.) a 'barbarian' to a townsman, usually a non-Muslim who comes from outside the town or its neighbourhood; someone who is uncouth.

Msikiti (Sw.) a mosque.

Mtaa/Mitaa (Sw.) a residential neighbourhood of a coastal town, lacking walls, and probably originally made up entirely of one clan and its clients and allies.

Mufti (Ar.) a jurisconsult.

Mungwana/Waungwana (Sw.) a free, 'civilized' townsperson of the East African coast, usually from a clan claiming long-standing ties with the town, learned in its language and traditions, allied to other 'known' local clans, and claiming to be one of the town's 'owners of the soil'.

Mwalimu/Walimu (Sw.) a local authority on the town's 'little tradition', a Quran school teacher, and sometimes a medicine man.

Mwanachuoni/Wanavyuoni (Sw.) lit. a 'child of the Quran school', meaning someone having a locally recognized expertise in the Islamic sciences as they were locally known and applied. Sometimes used interchangeably with *mwalimu* (q.v.).

Mzee/Wazee (Sw.) a local elder, a representative either of a particular clan or of the entire town. Such a title is given informally to anyone who possesses some charismatic appeal to his fellow townspeople based on his knowledge of local affairs, traditions, history, and religion.

Nahodha (Sw.) a dhow captain.

Nahw (Ar.) Arabic grammar.

Ngoma (Sw.) a dance done to the accompaniment of drums.

Nisba (Ar.) a name connoting kinship or relationship by marriage to a certain tribe, clan, or house.

Nyika (Sw.) the 'bush' behind or near a coastal town, usually suitable for cereals cultivation and inhabited by the neighbouring non-Muslim peoples.

Nyumba (Sw.) a Swahili house, traditionally rectangular in shape, made of mud or coral lime and rag, and thatched with coconut fronds.

Pepo (Sw.) a spirit.

Qadi (Ar.) an Islamic judge.

Raml (Ar.) geomancy.

Sarf (Ar.) Arabic morphology.

Shamba/Mashamba (Sw.) a coastal or island farm on which products traditionally found in coastal diets, including coconuts and mangoes, are cultivated. Such crops are perennial and the farms can be hereditary by Islamic law.

Sharif/Shurafa' (Ar.) a person said to be descended from the Prophet Muhammad. Often such claims are supported with long genealogies.

Shaykh (namely, Shaikh) (Ar.) similar to the Swahili *mzee* (q.v.), a leader of a tribe or clan.

Shehe (Sw.) a town elder, q.v. *mzee*.

Shirk (Ar.) religious apostasy.

Siku ya mwaka (Sw.) holiday celebrating the first day of the new (solar) year and the start of the planting cycle. Usually also the day for ritual cleansing of evil from the clan and community. In Zanzibar called the *ku(k)oga mwaka*.

Silwa a book, possibly fictitious, in which the history of the town, as well as the respective nobility and pedigree of the town's noble clans are recorded.

Siwa (Sw.) the traditional ivory, wood, or bronze horn blown to celebrate an event important to the community or to its noble clans, such as weddings, circumcisions, funerals, military victories, etc. Their symbolic significance undoubtedly is very ancient and pre- or non-Islamic in origin – like Swahili culture and religion themselves (hence, referred to in the title of this book).

Sunna (Ar.) the 'way' of the Prophet Muhammad; the prescribed actions to be followed by Muslims in any given situation based on a corpus of sayings and actions attributable to the Prophet; the 'right path' to be followed by a believer throughout his/her life.

Tabib (Ar.) a practitioner of Arabic medicine imported to East Africa, as opposed to a *mganga* or *mwalimu* (q.v.), practitioners of 'bush' or local medicine.

Tafsir (Ar.) a translation or exegesis of a religious tract.

Taqlid (Ar.) 'imitation' or past religious experts' judgements, pronouncements, opinions, and recorded thoughts; legal convention in Islam.

Tariqa (Ar.) a *sufi* brotherhood.

Tasawwuf (Ar.) the science based on a body of writings dealing with *sufi* ideals and theory.

Tenzi (Sw.) an epic poem, written in Swahili, which preserves a historical tradition or narrates an event of special historical or religious significance.

Tibb (Ar.) Arabic medicine, practised by a *tabib* (q.v.).

Uganga (Sw.) 'traditional' medicine of African origins.

Umma (Ar.) the 'charismatic community' in Islam. Somewhat like the concept of the Church in Christianity in that its members, through faith and sticking to the way of life expected of them by God, can expect salvation after death. In East Africa, the concept of the charismatic community became associated with the coastal town in which one resided.

Ustaarabu (Sw.) 'civilization' as it came to be perceived by coastal townspeople after the 1870s, and modelled on the modes of dress, behaviour, worship, and economic practices of the Omani aristocracy. Distinct from *uungwana* (q.v.).

Uungwana (Sw.) coastal 'civilization' centred on the traditions, manners, and religious beliefs and practices of a coastal town.

Waqf/Awqaf (Ar.) property endowed for its use or income by a specific charitable institution to which it is 'willed'.

Zunguo (Sw.) the Swahili ceremony of circumscribing the ground on which the community stands by a sacrificial bullock. The origins of the ritual are unknown, but its symbolic significance is clear. The ground so circumscribed is thought to be sacred soil inasmuch as it is thought to be freed of evil (bush) locality spirits and under the protection (*imani*) of God and his laws.

Bibliography

ORAL INFORMANTS

Mombasa
Abdallah Barua Msegeju
Abdallah Salih Farsy
Ali b. Salim Jeneby
Amin b. Muhsin Maamiry
Al-Amin B. Said Mandhry
Athman b. Abdu'r-Rahman Saqqaf
Charo Shambe
Faki b. Sulaiman Mkilindini
Hyder Kindy
Juma Yar Muhammad
Kamal Khan
Muhammad Ahmad Matano ('Mfunzi')
Muhammad Qasim Mazrui
Muhammad Rashid Mandhry
Muhammad Rashid Mazrui
Muhammad Sulaiman Mazrui
Malik b. Said Basheikh
Said b. Ahmad Qumri
Shihabuddin Chiraghdin
Yahya Ali Omar

Lamu
Abdu'l-Malik b. Abdu' r-Rahman Maawi
Abdallah Khatib Bauri
Abdallah Muhammad Bakathir (Kadara)
Abu Bakr Bwana Kanga Bakari
Ahmad Abdallah Yusuf Maddi
Ahmad Muhammad Jahadhmy
Ahmad Muhammad Mahdali
Aisha binti Nasir Bakari
Amina binti Salim
Athman Lalli Omar Khazrajy
(Sayyid) Bahasani
Bibi Zena Bakari
Harith Swaleh Maawi
Muhammad Basalama
Muhammad Bashrahil
Muhammad b. Shaykh Waili
Muhammad Yusuf Maddi

256

(Sayyid) Nana al-Husayni
Salim Heri

Malindi
Ahmed Shaykh Nabahani

ARCHIVES

The British Museum, London:
  Add. MSS. 5414, 34184, 22116
Church Missionary Society Archives:
  CA 5 series
East African Centre for Research in Oral Traditions and African National Languages
  (EACROTANAL), Zanzibar:
  Documents EAC 003–EAC 022
Fort Jesus Museum, Mombasa:
  Al-Amin b. Ali Mazrui, 'History of the Mazrui Dynasty of Mombasa'. Unpublished MS,
  1945.
Kenya National Archives:
  Coast Province files 1, 26, 30, 32, 40, 45, 52, 54
  DC/Lamu files 1 and 3
  DC/Mombasa files 1, 3, and 8
  DC/Kilifi file 1
Public Record Office, London:
  Foreign Office files 2, 54, 84, 107, 367
  Colonial Office file 618
  War Office file 106
University of London, School of Oriental and African Studies (S.O.A.S.) Library:
  MS 47752
Zanzibar National Archives, Zanzibar:
  Secretariat Series 1
  Secretariat Series 2
  Provincial Administration L.8

DISSERTATIONS

Berg, Frederick J. 'Mombasa under the Busaidi Sultanate'. University of Wisconsin Ph.D.,
  1971.
Brown, Walter T. 'A Pre-Colonial History of Bagamoyo: Aspects of the Growth of an East
  African Coastal Town'. Boston University Ph.D., 1971.
Bujra, Janet. 'Conflict and Conflict Resolution in a Bajuni Village'. University of London
  Ph.D., 1968.
Cassanelli, Lee. 'The Benaadir Past: Essays in Southern Somali History'. University of
  Wisconsin Ph.D., 1973.
Dubins, Barbara. 'A Political History of the Comoro Islands, 1795–1886'. Boston University
  Ph.D., 1972.
Green, Arnold H. 'The Tunisian Ulama, 1873–1915: Sociological Structure and Response to
  Ideological Change'. University of California at Los Angeles Ph.D., 1973.
Harvey, Stephen. 'Hunting and Gathering as a Strategic Adaptation: The Case of the Boni of
  Lamu District, Kenya'. Boston University Ph.D., 1978.
Hersi, Ali Abdu'r-Rahman. 'The Arab Factor in Somali History: The Origin and Development
  of Arab Enterprise and Cultural Influences in the Somali Peninsula'. University of
  California at Los Angeles Ph.D., 1977.
Hinnebusch, Thomas J. 'Prefixes, Sound Changes, and Subgrouping in the Coastal Kenyan
  Bantu Languages'. University of California at Los Angeles Ph.D., 1973.

Bibliography

McKay, William F. 'A Precolonial History of the Southern Kenya Coast'. Boston University Ph.D., 1978.

Nimtz, August. 'The Role of the Muslim Sufi Order in Political Change: An Over-View and Micro-Analysis from Tanzania'. Indiana University Ph.D., 1973.

Pouwels, Randall L. 'Islam and Islamic Leadership in the Coastal Communities of Eastern Africa, 1700 to 1914'. University of California at Los Angeles Ph.D., 1979.

Smith, Cynthia B. 'The Giriama Rising, 1914: Focus for Political Development of the Kenya Hinterland, 1850–1963'. University of California at Los Angeles Ph.D., 1973.

Ylvisaker, Marguerite. 'The Political and Economic Relationship of the Lamu Archipelago to the Adjacent Kenya Coast in the Nineteenth Century'. Boston University Ph.D., 1975.

el-Zein, Abdu'l-Hamid. 'The Sacred Meadows: A Structural Analysis of Religious Symbolism in an East African Town'. University of Chicago Ph.D., 1972 (since published under the same title).

PRIMARY SOURCES AND EYEWITNESS ACCOUNTS

Abdallah Ali Nasir. *Al-Inkishafi, The Soul's Awakening.* Ed. and trans. Willian Hichens. Nairobi: OUP, 1972.

Albrand, F. 'Extrait d'un Memoire sur Zanzibar et Quiloa', *Bulletin de la Société de Géographie,* (1838).

Anonymous. 'Account of the Voyage of D. Francisco de Almeida, Viceroy of India, Along the East Coast of Africa' in *Documentos Sobre Os Portugueses em Mozambique e na Africa Central, 1497–1840,* vol. I. Lisbon: 1962.

'Description of the Situation, Customs and Produce of Various Places in Africa' in *Documentos Sobre Os Portugueses em Mozambique e na Africa Central, 1497–1840,* vol. V, 355–71 and 373–81.

'Early History of Zanzibar under Umani Arab Rule'. MS found among the papers of Sh. Burhan M. Mkelle. On deposit at EACROTANAL as document EAC–007.

'History of Mombasa, c. 1824' in G. S. P. Freeman-Grenville, *The East African Coast, Select Documents.* Oxford: OUP, 1962.

'The History of Pate' in G. S. P. Freeman-Grenville, *The East African Coast, Select Documents,* 241–96.

'Kitab al-Zanuj' or 'Il Libro degli Zengi' in E. Cerulli, *Somalia: Scritti Vari, Editi ed Inediti,* vol. 1. Rome: Curia dell' Administrazione Fudiciaria Italiana dell Somalia, 1957.

'Kurratil Ayun fi Nisbatil Bajun' in V. L. Grottanelli, *Pescatori dell' Oceano Indiano.* Rome: Cremonese, 1957.

Al-Bakari al-Lamuy, Shaibu Faraji b. Hamed. 'Khabari Lamu', *Bantu Studies,* 12 (1938), 3–33.

Becker, Carl. 'Materialen zur Kenntnis der Islam in Deutsch-Ostafrika', *Der Islam,* 2 (1911), 1–48. Ed. and trans. B. G. Martin, 'Materials for the Understanding of Islam in German East Africa', *TNR,* 68 (1968), 31–61.

Al-Biruni, Abu'l-Rayhan. *Kitab al-Jamahir fi Ma'rifat al-Jawahir.* Ed. S. Krenkow. Hyderabad, 1355/1936–7.

'The Book of Zenj' or the 'Kitab al-Zanuj' in Cerulli, *Somalia.*

Boteler, Thomas, *Narrative of a Voyage of Discovery to Africa and Arabia Performed in H.M.'s Ships Leven and Barracouta from 1821 to 1826 under the Command of Captain F.W. Owen R.N.* 2 vols. London: Richard Bentley, 1835.

Bouvat, L. 'L'Islam dans l'Afrique Negre. La Civilisaticn Souahilie', *Revue de Monde Musulman,* 2 (1907), 10–27.

al-Buhry, Hemedi b. Abdallah. *Utenzi wa Vita vya Wadachi Kutamalaki Mrima, 1307 A.H.* Trans. J. W. T. Allen. Dar es Salaam: EALB, 1971.

Buckeridge, Nicholas T. *Journal and Letterbook of Nicholas Buckeridge, 1651–4.* Ed. J. R. Jenson. Minneapolis: University of Minnesota Press, 1973.

Burton, Richard F. *First Footsteps in East Africa*. Ed. G. Waterfield. New York: Routledge and Kegan Paul, 1966.

'The Lake Region of Central Equatorial Africa', *Journal of the Royal Geographic Society*, 29 (1859), 1–454.

Zanzibar: City, Island, and Coast. 2 vols. London: Tinsley Brothers, 1872.

Cashmore, T. H. R. 'Sheikh Mbarak bin Rashid bin Salim el-Mazrui' in N. R. Bennett (ed.), *Leadership in Eastern Africa, Six Political Biographies*. Boston: Boston University Press, 1966.

Cerulli, Enrico. *Somalia: Scritti Vari, Editi ed Inediti*. 2 vols. Rome: A Cura dell' Administrazione Fudiciaria Italiana dell Somalia, 1957.

Clive, J. 'A Short History of Lamu'. KNA DC/LAM/3/1, 2–39.

Dickson, T. Ainsworth. 'Report, 1897–1921'. KNA DC/LAM/3/1, pp. 141–7.

Dundas, F. G. 'Exploration of the Rivers Tana and Juba', *The Scottish Geographical Magazine*, 9 (1893), 113–26.

Eliot, Sir Charles. *The East African Protectorate*. London: Edward Arnold, 1905.

Elliot, F. 'Jubaland and Its Inhabitants', *Geographical Journal*, 41 (1913), 554–61.

Elliott, J. A. G. 'A Visit to the Bajun Islands', *Journal of the African Society*, 25 (1925–6), 10–22, 147–63, 245–63, 338–58.

Farsy, Abdallah Salih. 'Baadhi ya Wanavyuoni wa Kishafii wa Mashariki ya Africa'. Mombasa: unpublished MS, 1972.

'Sayyid Said'. Zanzibar: unpublished, 1942.

'Terehe ya Imam Shafii na Wanavyuoni Wakubwa wa Mashariki ya Afrika'. Zanzibar: unpublished, 1942.

Farsy, S. Salih. *Swahili Sayings from Zanzibar*, vol. 1. Dar es Salaam: *EALB*, 1966.

Fitzgerald, W. W. A. *Travels in the Coastlands of British East Africa and the Islands of Zanzibar and Pemba*. London: Arnold, 1898.

Freeman-Grenville, G. S. P., and Martin, B. G. 'A Preliminary Handlist of the Arabic Inscription of the East African Coast', *JRAS*, (1973), 98–122.

The Gazette for Zanzibar and East Africa, all volumes.

Greffulhe, H. 'Voyage de Lamoo à Zanzibar', *Bulletin de la Société de Géographie et d'Études Coloniale de Marseille*, 2 (1878), 209–17 and 327–60.

Guillain, Charles. *Documents sur l'Histoire, le Géographie et le Commerce de l'Afrique Orientale* 3 vols and album. Paris: Libraire de la Société de Geographie, 1856.

Hardinge, Arthur H. *Report on the East African Protectorate, 1898*. London: Parliamentary Papers, vol. LX.

Report on the East African Protectorate, 1899. London: Parliamentary Papers, vol. LXIII.

Haywood, C. W. 'The Bajun Islands and Birikau', *Geographical Journal*, 85 (1933), 59–64.

Hasani b. Ismail, *Swifa ya Nguvumali, The Medicine Man*. Ed. and trans. Peter Lienhardt. Oxford: OUP, 1968.

Hichens, William (ed.). *Diwani ya Muyaka bin Haji al-Ghassaniy*. Johannesburg: Univ. of Witwatersrand Press, 1940.

Hinawy, Mbarak Ali, *Al-Akida and Fort Jesus, Mombasa: The Life History of Muhammad bin Abdallah bin Mbarak Bakhashweini*. London: Macmillan, 1950.

Hollis, Sir A. Claude. 'Notes on the History of Vumba, East Africa', *JRAI*, 30 (1900), 275–97.

Ibuni Saleh, *A Short History of the Comorians in Zanzibar*. Zanzibar: unpublished, 1936.

Ingrams, W. H. *Zanzibar, Its History and Its Peoples*. London: Wotherby, 1931.

Isaac, F. W. 'History of the Lamu District'. Unpublished, n.d.

'Summarized History'. KNA DC/LAM/3/1, 114–27.

Isaacs, Nathaniel. *Travels and Adventures in East Africa*. 2 vols. London: 1836.

Jackson, Sir Frederick. *Early Days in East Africa*. London: Arnold, 1930.

Kindy, Hyder. *Life and Politics in Mombasa*. Nairobi: EALB, 1972.

Krapf, J. Ludwig. *A Dictionary of the Suaheli Language*. 2nd edn New York: Negro Universities Press, 1969.

Travels, Researches and Missionary Labours during an Eighteen Years Residence in Eastern Africa. London: Trubner, 1860.

Bibliography

'Kurratil Ayun fi Nisbatil Bajun', in V. L. Grottanelli, *Pescatori dell'Oceano Indiano* (q.v.)

Lambert, H. E. *Chi-Jomvu and Ki-Ngare.* Kampala: East African Swahili Committee, 1958.

 Ki-Vumba, A Dialect of the Southern Kenya Coast. Kampala: East African Swahili Committee, 1957.

Le Roy, R. P. A. 'Au Zanguebar Anglais', *Les Missions Catholiques*, 22 (1890).

Loarer, M. 'Ile de Zanzibar', *Revue de l'Orient, de Algerie et des Colonies*, 9 (1851), 290–9.

Lyne, R. N. *Zanzibar in Contemporary Times.* London: Hurst and Blackett, 1905.

Mazrui, al-Amin b. Ali *Dini ya Islamu.* Mombasa: East African Muslim Welfare Society, 1939.

 Faida ya Zaka katika Kuwatengeza Islamu na Kukuza Dini. Mombasa: East African Muslim Welfare Society, 1956.

 'Hidayatu'l-Atfak'. Unpublished MS.

 'Prosody'. Unpublished MS in the possession of Sh. Yahya Ali Omar.

 Uwongozi. Mombasa: East African Muslim Welfare Society, 1955.

Midani b. Mwidad. 'The Founding of Rabai', *Swahili*, new series vol. 1, part 2 (1961), 140–150.

Milligan, J. W., and Ward, H. F. *Handbook of British East Africa.* Nairobi: Caxton, 1912.

Mkelle, Shaykh Burhan Muhammad. 'History of Grand Comoro'. MS on deposit at EACROTANAL, Zanzibar, as document EAC–003.

Omari b. Stamboul. 'An Early History of Mombasa and Tanga', *TNR*, no. 31, 32–6.

Owen, Wilfred F. W. *Narrative of Voyages to Explore the Shores of Africa, Arabia and Madagascar Performed in H.M. Ships Leven and Barracouta under the Direction of W. F.W. Owen, R.N., by Command of the Lords Commissioners of the Admiralty.* 2 vols. London: 1833.

Pearce, F. B. *Zanzibar, The Island Metropolis of East Africa*, 2nd edn London: Cass, 1967.

Pickering, Charles. *The Races of Man and their Geographical Distribution.* London: Bohn, 1851.

Pruen, S. T. *The Arab and the African.* London: Seeley, 1891.

Rabaud, A. 'Zanzibar, La Côte Orientale d'Afrique et l'Afrique Equatoriale', *Bulletin de Geographie d'Aix-Marseilles*, 3 (1879), 158–77.

Reute, Emily. *Memoires of an Arabian Princess.* New York: D. Appleton, 1888.

Revoil, M. G. 'Voyage chez les Bénédirs, les Somalis et les Bayouns en 1882 et 1883', *Le Tour du Monde*, 49 (1885), 1–80; 50 (1885), 129–208.

Rolleston, H. O. 'The Watumbatu of Zanzibar', *TNR*, 8 (1939).

Saadi, Kadhi Amur Omar. 'Mafia – History and Traditions', *TNR*, 12 (1941), 23–7.

Sacleux, Charles. *Dictionnaire Swahili-Francais.* Paris: Institut d'Ethnologie, 1939.

Samson, M., and Darroch, R. G. 'Some Notes on the Early History of the Tribes Living on the Lower Tana Collected by Mikael Samson and Others', *Journal of the East African Natural History Society*, 17 (1943–4), 244–54.

 'A History of the Pokomo by Mikael Samson', *Journal of the East African Natural History Society*, 17 (1943–4), 370–94.

Stanley, Henry M. *Through the Dark Continent.* 2 vols. New York: Harpers & Bros., 1879.

Stigand, C. H. *The Land of Zinj.* London: Constable, 1913.

Strong, S. A. (ed.). 'History of Kilwa', *JRAS*, 54 (1895), 385–430.

Talbot-Smith, L. 'Historical Record of Tanaland'. KNA DC/LAM/3/1, 40–112.

 'History of Tanaland', KNA DC/TRD/3/1.

Taylor, Rev. William E. 'African Aphorisms or Saws from Swahililand'. On deposit in the library of the School of Oriental and African Studies, University of London, as SOAS MS 47752.

Van den Berg, L. W. C. *Le Hadramout et les Colonies dans l'Archipel Indien.* Batavia: Imprimerie du Gouvernment, 1886.

 Minhaj at-Talibin. Batavia: Imprimerie du Gouvernment, 1882.

Velten, Carl. *Desturi za Wasuaheli.* Gottingen: Dandenhoed & Ruprecht, 1903.

Werner, Alice. 'The Bantu Coast Tribes of the East African Protectorate', *JRAI*, 45 (1915), 326–54.

 'A Few Notes on the Wasanya', *Man*, 13 (1913), 199–201.

 'Some Notes on the Wapokomo of the Tana Valley', *African Affairs*, 12 (1912–13), 359–84.

'A Swahili History of Pate', *Journal of the African Society*, 14 (1914–15), 148–61, 278–97, 392–413.
Al-Yaqut (ibn Abdallah ar-Rumi). *Mu'jam al-Buldan.* 4 vols. Ed. F. Wustenfeld. Leipzig, 1866.

SECONDARY SOURCES

Books

Allen, James deV. *Lamu.* Nairobi: Kenya National museum, n.d.
 Lamu Town, A Guide. Nairobi: Kenya National Museum, n.d.
Allen, James deV., and Wilson, Thomas (eds.). *From Zinj to Zanzibar, In Honour of James Kirkman. Paideuma 28.* Wiesbaden: Franz Steiner, 1982.
Alpers, Edward A. *The East African Slave Trade.* Nairobi: EAPH, 1967.
 Ivory and Slaves in East Central Africa. Los Angeles and Berkeley: Univ. of California Press, 1974.
Anderson, J. N. D. *Islamic Law in Africa.* London: Cass, 1970.
Anderson-Moreshead, A. E. M. *The History of the Universities Mission to Central Africa.* London: Office of the UMCA, 1897.
Axelson, Eric. *The Portuguese in South-East Africa, 1488–1600.* Johannesburg: Struik, 1973.
Aydarus b. ash-Sharif ᶜAli al-Aydarus al-Nadiri al-ᶜAlawi. *Bughyat al-Amal fi Tarikh as-Sumal.* Mogadishu, 1954.
Baer, Gabriel (ed.). *Asian and African Studies: The ᶜUlamaˀ in Modern History.* Jerusalem: Israel Oriental Society, 1971.
Bennett, Norman R. *A History of the Arab State of Zanzibar.* London: Methuen, 1978.
Bennett, Norman R., and Brooks, George. *New England Merchants in Africa.* Boston: Boston University Press, 1965.
Birmingham, David, and Gray, Richard. *Pre-Colonial African Trade.* London: OUP, 1970.
de Boer, T. J. *The History of Philosophy in Islam.* New York: Dover Press, 1967.
Bohannon, Paul and Curtin, Phillip D. *Africa and Africans.* Garden City: Natural History Press, 1971.
Boxer, C. R., and Azevedo, C. *Fort Jesus and the Portuguese in Mombasa: 1593–1729.* London: Hollis & Carter, 1960.
Bujra, Abdallah. *The Politics of Stratification: A Study of Political Change in a South Arabian Town.* London: OUP, 1971.
Bunger, Robert L. *Islamization among the Upper Polomo.* Syracuse: Syracuse University Press, 1973.
Caplan, Ann P. *Choice and Constraint in a Swahili Community.* London: OUP, 1975.
Chilver, E. M. Harlow, V., and Smith, A. (eds). *History of East Africa,* vol. II. Oxford: OUP, 1965.
Chittick, H. Neville. *Annual Report of the Department of Antiquities.* Dar es Salaam: Dept. of Antiquities, 1964.
 Kilwa, An Islamic Trading City of the East African Coast. 2 vols. Nairobi: British Institute in Eastern Africa, 1974.
 Manda: Excavations at an Island Port on the Coast of Kenya. Nairobi: British Institute in Eastern Africa, 1984.
Chittick, H. Neville, and Rotberg, Robert (eds.). *East Africa and the Orient.* New York: Africana, 1975.
Clark, Catherine and Horton, Mark. *Zanzibar Archaeological Survey, 1984/5.* Zanzibar: Ministry of Information, Culture and Sport, 1984.
Cooper, Frederick. *Plantation Slavery on the East Coast of Africa.* New Haven: Yale University Press, 1977.
Coulson, Noel J. *A History of Islamic Law.* Edinburgh: Edinburgh University Press, 1964.
Coupland, Sir Reginald. *East Africa and Its Invaders.* New York: Russel & Russel, 1965.
 The Exploitation of East Africa, 1856–1890. London: Faber & Faber, 1934.
Craster, J. E. E. *Pemba, The Spice Island of Zanzibar.* London: T. Fisher Unwin, 1913.

Bibliography

Curtin, Phillip D. *et al. African History.* Boston: Little, Brown & Co., 1978.

Dale, Father Godfrey. *The Peoples of Zanzibar.* London: UMCA Press, 1920.

Dalton, George (ed.). *Tribal and Peasant Economies.* Austin: Univ. of Texas Press, 1977.

Datoo, Bashir A. *Port Development in East Africa.* Nairobi: EALB, 1975.

Davidson, Basil. *The African Genius.* Boston: Little, Brown & Co., 1969.

Ehret, Christopher. *Ethiopians and East Africans: The Problem of Contacts.* Nairobi: EAPH, 1974.

    Southern Nilotic History. Evanston: North-western University Press, 1971.

Ehret, Christopher, and Posnansky, Merrick (eds.). *The Archaeological and Linguistic Reconstruction of African History.* Berkeley and Los Angeles: Univ. of California Press, 1982.

Fage, John, and Oliver, Roland (eds.). *The Cambridge History of Africa,* vol. III. Cambridge: CUP, 1977.

Fakhry, Majid. *A History of Islamic Philosophy.* New York: Columbia University Press, 1970.

    Islamic Occasionalism and Its Critique by Averroes and Aquinas. New York, 1969.

Feierman, Stephen. *The Shambaa Kingdom.* Madison: Univ. of Wisconsin Press, 1973.

Ferrand, Gabriel, *Relations du Voyages et Textes Géographiques Arabes, Persans et Turks Relatifs à l'Extreme Orient du VIIIᵉ au XVIIIᵉ Siècles,* 2 vols. Paris, 1914.

Freeman-Grenville, G. S. P. *The East African Coast: Select Documents.* Oxford: OUP, 1962.

    The French at Kilwa Island Oxford: OUP, 1965.

Garlake, Peter S. *Great Zimbabwe.* London: Thames & Hudson, 1973.

    The Early Islamic Architecture of the East African Coast. Nairobi: British Institute of History and Archaeology in Eastern Africa, 1966.

    The Kingdoms of Africa. Oxford: Phaidon, 1978.

Geertz, Clifford. *Islam Observed, Religious Developments in Morocco and Indonesia.* New Haven: Yale Univ. Press, 1968.

Ghaidan, Usam. *Lamu.* Nairobi: EALB, 1975.

Gray, Sir John. *The British in Mombasa, 1824–1826.* New York: MacMillan, 1957.

Greenberg, Joseph. *The Languages of Africa.* Bloomington: Univ. of Indiana Press, 1963.

Grottanelli, Vinigi L. *Pescatori dell'Oceano Indiano.* Rome: Cremonese, 1955.

Grunebaum, Gustav E. von. *Medieval Islam.* Chicago: Univ. of Chicago Press, 1953.

Guthrie, Malcolm. *Comparative Bantu.* 4 vols. Farnborough: Gregg, 1967.

Hamilton, Genessa. *Princes of Zinj.* London: Hutchinson, 1957.

de Heusch, Luc. *Le roi ivre ou l'origin de l'état.* Paris: Editions Gallimard, 1972.

Harries, Lyndon. *Swahili Poetry.* Oxford: OUP, 1962.

Hollingsworth, L. W. *Zanzibar under the Foreign Office, 1913–1940.* London: MacMillan, 1952.

Holt, Peter M. *Egypt and the Fertile Crescent, 1516–1922.* Ithaca: Cornell Univ. Press, 1970.

    (ed.) *Political and Social Change in Modern Egypt.* Oxford: OUP, 1968.

Hopkins, J. F. P. and Levtzion, N. *Corpus of Early Arabic Sources for West African History.* Cambridge: CUP, 1981.

Horton, Mark. *Shanga, 1980: An Interim Report.* Nairobi: National Museums of Kenya, 1980.

Horton Mark, and Clark, Catherine. *Zanzibar Archaeological Survey, 1984/5.* Zanzibar: Ministry of Information, Culture, and Sport, 1984.

Hourani, Albert. *Arabic Thought in the Liberal Age, 1798–1939.* Oxford: OUP, 1970.

Johnson, Frederick. *A Standard Swahili-English Dictionary,* London: OUP, 1939.

Keddie, Nikki R. (ed.). *Scholars, Saints and Sufis.* Berkeley and Los Angeles: Univ. of California Press, 1972.

Kerr, Malcolm. *Islamic Reform.* Berkeley and Los Angeles: Univ. of California Press, 1966.

Kirkman, James. *The Arab City of Gedi: Excavations at the Great Mosque, Architecture and Finds.* London: OUP, 1954.

    Men and Monuments of the East African Coast. London: Lutterworth, 1964.

    Ungwana on the Tana. The Hague: Mouton, 1966.

Knappert, Jan. *Four Centuries of Swahili Verse.* Nairobi: Heinemann, 1979.

    Myths and Legends of the Swahili. Nairobi: Heinemann, 1970.

    Swahili Islamic Poetry. 3 vols. Leiden: Brill, 1971.

Lévi-Strauss, Claude, *The Savage Mind*. Chicago: Univ. of Chicago Press, 1966.

Lewis, Bernard. *The Arabs in History*. New York: Harper & Row, 1966.

Race and Color in Islam. New York: Harper & Row, 1971.

Lewis, I. M. *Islam in Tropical Africa*. Oxford: OUP, 1966.

The Modern History of Somaliland. London: Weidenfeld & Nicholson, 1965.

The Peoples of the Horn of Africa. London: International African Institute, 1955.

Ma'oz, Moshe, *Ottoman Reform in Syria and Palestine*. Oxford: OUP, 1968.

Martin, Bradford G. *Muslim Brotherhoods in Nineteenth Century Africa*. Cambridge: CUP, 1976.

Mathew, Gervase, and Oliver, Roland (eds.). *The History of East Africa*. vol. I. Oxford: OUP, 1963.

Mbarak Ali Hinawy. *Al-Akida, The Life Story of Muhammad b. Abdallah b. Mbarak Bakashweini*. London: MacMillan, 1950.

Miles, S. B. *Countries and Tribes of the Persian Gulf*. London: Cass, 1966.

Miller, Joseph (ed.). *The African Past Speaks*. Folkestone: Dawson, 1980.

Kings and Kinsmen. London: OUP, 1976.

Nicholls, Christine. *The Swahili Coast*. New York: Africana, 1971.

Nurse, Derek, and Spear, Thomas. *The Swahili: Reconstructing the History and Language of an African Society, 800–1500*. Philadelphia: Univ. of Pennsylvania Press, 1984.

Ogot, Bethwell A. (ed.). *Zamani*. Nairobi: EAPH, 1973.

Oliver, Roland, and Mathew, Gervase (eds.). *The History of East Africa*. vol. I. Oxford: OUP, 1963.

Phillips, Wendell. *Oman, A History*. London: Reynal, 1967.

Phillipson, David W. *The Later Prehistory of Eastern and Southern Africa*. London: Heinemann, 1977.

Polk, William R., and Chambers, Richard L. (eds.). *Beginnings of Modernization in the Middle East*. Chicago: Univ. of Chicago Press, 1968.

Prins, A. H. J. *Didemic Lamu*. Groningen: Instituut voor Culturele Anthropologie der Rijksuniversiteit, 1971.

The Northeastern Bantu. London: International African Institute, 1952.

The Swahili-Speaking Peoples of Zanzibar and the East African Coast. London: International African Institute, 1967.

Ranger, Terence O. *Dance and Society in Eastern Africa*. Berkeley and Los Angeles: Univ. of California Press, 1974.

Ranger, Terence O., and Kimambo, Isaria (eds.). *The Historical Study of African Religion*. Berkeley and Los Angeles: Univ. of California Press, 1972.

Reute, R. S. *Said b. Sultan*. London: Alexandre-Ousley, 1927.

Russell, C. E. B. *General Rigby, Zanzibar and the Slave Trade*. London: Allen & Unwin, 1935.

Sacleux, Charles. *Grammaire des Dialectes Swahilis*. Paris: Prouere des P.P. du Saint-Esprit, 1909.

Salil ibn Razik. *History of the Imams and Seyyids of Oman*. Ed. & trans. G. P. Badger. New York: Burt Franklin, 1871.

Salim, A. I. *The Swahili-Speaking Peoples of Kenya's Coast, 1895–1965*. Nairobi: EAPH, 1973.

Sassoon, Hamo. *Kunduchi*. Dar es Salaam: Ministry of Community Development and National Culture, 1966.

The Siwas of Lamu. Nairobi: The Lamu Society, 1975.

Saunders, J. J. *A History of Medieval Islam*. London: Routledge & Kegan Paul, 1965.

Schacht, Joseph. *The Origins of Muhammadan Jurisprudence*. Oxford: OUP, 1950.

Serjeant, R. B. *The Saiyids of Hadramaut*. London: SOAS, 1957.

Sharabi, Hisham. *Arab Intellectuals and the West: The Formative Years, 1875–1914*. Baltimore: Johns Hopkins, 1970.

Smith, H. M. *Frank, Bishop of Zanzibar*. London: Society for Promoting Christian Knowledge, 1926.

Spear, Thomas T. *The Kaya Complex: A History of the Mijikenda People of the Kenya Coast to 1900*. Nairobi: EAPH, 1979.

Bibliography

Strandes, Justus. *The Portuguese Period in East Africa*. Trans. J. Wallwork. Nairobi: EAPH, 1961.

Strobel, Margaret. *Muslim Women in Mombasa, 1890–1975*. New Haven: Yale Univ. Press, 1979.

Tax, Sol. *Horizons of Anthropology*. Chicago: Aldine, 1964.

Trimingham, J. S. *Islam in East Africa*. Oxford: OUP, 1964.

Islam in Ethiopia. Oxford: OUP, 1965.

Turner, Victor W. *The Ritual Process: Structure and Anti-Structure*. Chicago: Aldine, 1969.

Vansina, Jan. *The Children of Woot*. Madison: Univ. of Wisconsin Press, 1978.

Oral Tradition. London: Routledge & Kegan Paul, 1965.

Verin, Paul. *Histoire Ancienne du Nord-Ouest de Madagascar*. Tananarive: Universite de Madagascar, 1972.

Watt, W. Montgomery. *Islam and the Integration of Society*. Evanston: Northwestern Univ. Press, 1961.

Islamic Philosophy and Theology. Edinburgh: Edinburgh University Press, 1962.

Whitely, Wilfred. *Swahili. The Rise of a National Language*. London: Methuen, 1969.

Wilson, Monica. *Religion and the Transformation of Society*. London: CUP, 1971.

Wilson, Thomas H. *The Monumental Architecture and Archaeology North of the Tana River*. Nairobi: Kenya National Museums, 1978.

Wilson, Thomas H., and Allen, James deV. (eds.). *From Zinj to Zanzibar*. Wiesbaden: Franz Steiner, 1982.

Ylvisaker, Marguerite. *Lamu in the Nineteenth Century; Land, Trade and Politics*. Boston: Boston Univ. African Studies Center, 1979.

Zahir, b. Saᶜid. *Tanzihu'l-Absari wa'l-Afkari fi Rihlatu'l-Sultani'l-Zanzibar*. Ed. Louis Subunjie. London: al-Nahlah, 1879.

Articles

Allen, James deV. 'The *Siwas* of Pate and Lamu: Two Antique Side-Blown Horns from the Swahili Coast', *Art and Archaeology Research Papers*, 9 (1976), 38–47.

'Swahili Culture and the Nature of East Coast Settlement', *IJAHS*, 14 (1981), 306–35.

'Swahili Culture Reconsidered: Some Historical Implications of the Material Culture of the Northern Kenya Coast in the Eighteenth and Nineteenth Centuries', *Azania*, 9 (1974), 105–138.

'The Swahili House: Cultural and Ritual Concepts Underlying Its Plan and Structure', *Art and Archaeology Research Papers*, Special Issue (1979), 1–32.

Alpers, Edward A. 'Gujerat and the Trade of East Africa, *c*. 1500–1800', *IJAHS*, IX, 1 (1976).

'The Mutapan and Malawi Political Systems', in T. O. Ranger (ed.), *Aspects of Central African History*. Evanston: Northwestern Univ. Press, 1968.

'Towards a History of the Expansion of Islam in East Africa: The Matrilineal Peoples of the Southern Interior', in T. O. Ranger and I. Kimambo (eds.). *The Historical Study of African Religion* (q.v.). 172–201.

Beach, D. N. 'The Historiography of the People of Zimbabwe in the 1960s', *Rhodesian History*, 4 (1973), 21–30.

Beidelman, T. O. 'Myth, Legend and Oral History', *Anthropos*, 65 (1970), 74–97.

Berg, Frederick J. 'The Swahili Community of Mombasa, 1500–1900', *JAH*, 9 (1968), 35–56.

Bohannon, Laura. 'A Genealogical Charter', *Africa*, 23 (1952), 302–15.

Bohannon, Paul. 'Some Principles of Exchange and Investment among the Tiv', *American Anthropologist*, LVII (1955), 40–70.

Brown, B. 'Muslim Influence in Trade and Politics in the Lake Tanganyika Region', *AHS*, 4 (1971), 617–30.

Brown, W. T. 'The Politics of Business: Relations between Zanzibar and Bagamoyo in the Late Nineteenth Century', *AHS*, 4 (1971), 631–44.

264

Chittick, H. Neville. 'An Archaeological Reconnaissance of the Southern Somali Coast', *Azania*, IV (1969).

'The Coast before the Arrival of the Portuguese', in B. A. Ogot, *Zamani* (q.v.), 98–114.

'Discoveries in the Lamu Archipelago', *Azania*, 2 (1967), 37–68.

'A New Look at the History of Pate', *JAH*, 10 (1969), 375–92.

'The "Shirazi" Colonization of East Africa', *JAH*, 6 (1965), 275–92.

'Unguja Ukuu', *Azania*, 1 (1966), 161–3.

Dickson, T. Ainsworth. 'The Regalia of the Wa-Vumba', *Man*, 20 (1921), 33–6.

Eastman, Carol, and Topan, Farouk. 'The Siu', *Swahili*, 36 (1966), 22–48.

Ehret, Christopher. 'Cattle Keeping and Milking in Eastern and Southern African History: The Linguistic Evidence', *JAH* VIII, 1 (1967), 1–17.

Ehret, Christopher, *et al.* 'Outlining Southern African History; A Re-evaluation, A.D. 100–1500', *Ufahamu*, III, 1 (1972), 9–27.

Esmail, A. 'Towards a History of Islam in East Africa', *Kenya Historical Review*, 3 (1975), 147–58.

Fadiman, Jeffrey A. 'Early History of the Meru of Mt. Kenya', *JAH*, 14 (1973), 9–27.

Fleming, Harold C. 'Baiso and Rendille: Somali Outliers', *Rassegna di Studi Etiopici*, 20 (1964), 83–90.

Freeman-Grenville, G. S. P. 'The Coast, 1498–1840', in R. Oliver and G. Mathew (eds.), *History of East Africa*, vol. I (q.v.), 129–68.

Garabedian, A. 'Mohammedanism in Capetown', *The Moslem World*, V (1915).

Geertz, Clifford. 'Religion as a Cultural System', in M. Banton (ed.), *Anthropological Approaches to the Study of Religion*. London: Tavistock, 1966.

Gray, Sir John. 'A History of Kilwa, Part I', *TNR*, no. 31 (1951), 1–28.

'A History of Kilwa, Part II', *TNR*, no. 32 (1952), 11–37.

'Zanzibar Local Histories, Part 1', *Swahili*, no. 30 (1959), 24–37.

'Zanzibar Local Histories, Part 2', *Swahili*, no. 31 (1960), 111–37.

Grottanelli, Vinigi L. 'A Lost African Metropolis', *Afrikanistiche Studien*, 26 (1955).

Guthrie, Malcolm, 'Some Developments in the Prehistory of the Bantu Languages', *JAH*, 3 (1962), 273–82.

Harries, Lyndon. 'The Arabs and Swahili Culture', *Africa*, 34 (1964), 224–9.

Hinnebusch, Thomas, 'The Shungwaya Hypothesis: A Linguistic Reappraisal', in J. J. Gallagher (ed.) *East African Cultural History*. Syracuse Univ. Press, 1976.

Hollis, Sir A. Claude. 'Notes', in KNA DC/MSA/6/2.

Holsinger, Donald C. 'Migration, Commerce, and Community: The Mizabis in Eighteenth- and Nineteenth-Century Algeria', *JAH*, XXI, no. 1 (1980), 61–74.

Horton, Robin. 'African Traditional Thought and Western Science', *Africa*, 37 (1967), 50–71, 155–87.

'On the Rationality of Conversion', *Africa*, 45 (1975), 219–35, 373–97.

'Stateless Societies in the History of West Africa', in M. Crowder and J. F. A. Ajaye (eds.), *The History of West Africa*, vol. 1, New York: Columbia Univ. Press, 1972.

Hrbek, Ivan. 'Egypt, Nubia and the Eastern Deserts', in R. Oliver (ed.), *The Cambridge History of Africa*, vol. 3. Cambridge: CUP, 1977.

Joussaume, R. 'Les monuments funeraires protohistoriques du Harrar, Ethiopie, 2me mission', *Documents pour Servir à l'Histoire des Civilisations Ethiopiennes*, 6 (1975), 19–34.

'Les monuments megalithiques du Harrar, Ethiopie', *L'Anthropologie*, 75 (1971), 177–99.

Kimambo, I., and Omari, C. K. 'The Development of Religious Thought and Centres among the Pare', in T. O. Ranger and I. Kimambo (eds.), *The Historical Study of African Religion* (q.v.), 111–21.

Kirkman, James. 'The Excavations at Kilepwa, An Introduction to the Mediaeval Archaeology of the Kenya Coast', *Antiquaries Journal*, 32 (1952), 168–84.

'Excavations at Ras Mkumbuu on the Island of Pemba', *TNR*, 53 (1959), 161–78.

'The Great Pillars of Malindi and Mambrui', *Oriental Art*, 4 (1958), 3–15.

'Historical Archaeology in Kenya, 1948–1956', *Antiquaries Journal*, 37 (1957), 16–28.

'Some Conclusions from Archaeological Excavations on the Coast of Kenya, 1948–1966' in H. N. Chittick and R. Rotberg (eds.), *East Africa and the Orient* (q.v.), 226–47.

'The Zanzibar Diary of John Studdy Leigh', *IJAHS*, 13 (1980), 281–312, 492–507.

Knappert, Jan. 'Social and Moral Concepts in Swahili Islamic Literature', *Africa*, 50 (1970), 125–36.

Kumar, Ravinder. 'British Attitudes towards the Ibadiyya Revivalist Movement in East Arabia', *International Studies*, 3 (1962), 443–50.

Lapidus, Ira. 'The Evolution of Muslim Urban Society', *Comparative Studies in Society and Religion*, 15 (1973), 21–50.

'Muslim Cities and Islamic Societies' in I. Lapidus (ed.), *Middle Eastern Cities*. Berkeley and Los Angeles: Univ. of California Press, 1969.

Lary, Peter, and Wright, Marcia. 'Swahili Settlements in Northern Zambia and Malawi', *AHS*, 4 (1971), 547–74.

Lewicki. 'Al-Ibadiyya' in the *Encyclopedia of Islam*, 2nd edn, vol. III, 648–50.

Lewis, D. 'Religion of the Cape Malays' in Ellen Hellman (ed.), *Handbook of Race Relations in South Africa*. Oxford: OUP, 1949.

Lewis, I. M. 'Conformity and Contrast in Somali Islam' in I. M. Lewis (ed.), *Islam in Tropical Africa* (q.v.), 253–67.

'Sufism in Somaliland: A Study in Tribal Islam – I', *BSOAS*, 17 (1957), 581–602.

Lienhardt, Peter. 'The Mosque College of Lamu and Its Social Background', *TNR*, 53 (1959), 228–42.

'A Controversy over Islamic Custom at Kilwa Kivinje, Tanzania', in I. M. Lewis (ed.), *Islam in Tropical Africa* (q.v.), 374–86.

Mainga, Matumba. 'A History of Lozi Religion to the End of the Nineteenth Century', in T. O. Ranger and I. Kimambo (eds.), *The Historical Study of African Religion* (q.v.), 95–108.

Martin, Bradford G. 'Arab Migrations to East Africa in Medieval Times', *IJAHS*, 7 (1974), 367–90.

'Notes on Some Members of the Learned Classes of Zanzibar and East Africa in the Nineteenth Century', *AHS*, 4 (1971), 525–46.

Mathew, Gervase. 'The Coast, *c.* A.D. 100–1498', in R. Oliver and G. Mathew (eds.), *History of East Africa*, vol. I (q.v.), 94–128.

'The Culture of the East African Coast in the 17th and 18th Centuries in the Light of Recent Archaeological Discoveries', *Man*, 56 (1956), 61–76.

Meillassoux, Claude. 'From Reproduction to Production', *Economy and Society*, 1 (1972), 93–105.

Mgomezulu, G. G. Y. 'Recent Archeological Research and Radio-carbon Dates from Eastern Africa', *JAH*, 22 (1981).

Mohammed el-Awa. 'The Place of Custom (*°Urf*) in Islamic Legal Theory', *The Islamic Quarterly*, 17 (1975), 177–82.

Mudenge, S. I. 'The Role of Foreign Trade in the Rozvi Empire: A Reappraisal', *JAH*, 15 (1974), 373–92.

Nimtz, August. 'Islam in Tanzania: An Annotated Bibliography', *TNR*, 72 (1973), 51–74.

Nurse, Derek. 'Bajun Historical Linguistics', *Kenya Past and Present*, 12 (1980).

'History from Linguistics: The Case of the Tana River', *HA*, 10 (1983), 207–38.

'A Hypothesis Concerning the Origin of Swahili', *Azania*, 18 (1983).

'Segeju and Daiso: A Case Study of Evidence from Oral Tradition and Comparative Linguistics', *HA*, 9 (1982), 175–208.

Oliver, Roland. 'The Problem of the Bantu Expansion', *JAH*, VII, 3 (1966), 361–76.

Phillipson, David W. 'Some Iron Age Sites in the Lower Tana Valley', *Azania*, 14 (1979), 155–60.

Pouwels, Randall L. 'The Medieval Foundations of East African Islam', *IJAHS*, XI, no. 2 (1978), 201–27; XI, no. 3 (1978), 393–409.

'Oral Historiography and the Problem of the Shirazi on the East African Coast', *HA*, 11 (1984).

'Sh. Al-Amin b. Ali Mazrui and Islamic Modernism in East Africa', *International Journal of Middle Eastern Studies*, 13 (1981), 329–45.

'Reflexions sur l'histoire medievale de la côte Est-Africaine', *Recherche, Pedagogie et Culture* (August-September, 1984).

'Tenth Century Settlement of the East African Coast: The Case for Qarmatian/Isma'il-Connections', *Azania*, 9 (1974), 65–74.

Prins, A. H. J. 'Sungwaya, die Urheimat de Nordost Bantu', *Anthropos*, 50 (1955), 273–82.

Ranger, T. O. 'Connexions between "Primary" Resistance Movements and Modern Mass Nationalism in East and Central Africa', *JAH*, IX, no. 3 (1968), 437–53; IX, no. 4 (1968), 631–641.

'Towards a Historical Study of Traditional Religion in East and Central Africa'. Paper presented at the East African Academy, Kampala, 1966.

Ravenstein, E. G. 'Somal and Galla Land; Embodying Information Collected by Rev. Thomas Wakefield', *Proceedings of the Royal Geographical Society*, 6 (1884).

Robinson, A. E. 'The Shirazi Colonizations of East Africa', *TNR*, 3 (1937).

Rugoiyo, Elizabeth. 'Some Traditional Histories of Pate, Siu and Shanga', in M. Horton, *Shanga, 1980* (q.v.), Appendix 5.

Saad, Elias. 'Kilwa Dynastic Historiography', *HA*, 6 (1979), 177–209.

Sadler, A. W. 'Islam: The Parish Situation and the Virtuoso Community', *The Muslim World*, 51 (1961), 197–210.

Sahlins, Marshall. 'Culture and Environment: The Study of Cultural Ecology' in Sol Tax (ed.), *Horizons in Anthropology* (q.v.), 132–47.

Salim, A. I. 'Sir Ali b. Salim' in K. King and A. I. Salim (eds.), *Kenya Historical Biographies*. Nairobi: EAPH, 1971.

Sassoon, Homo. 'The Coastal Town of Jumba la Mtwana', *Kenya Past and Present*, 12 (1980).

'Excavations at the Site of Early Mombasa', *Azania*, 15 (1980), 1–42.

'How Old Is Mombasa?' *Kenya Past and Present*, 9 (1978), 33–7.

Schacht, Joseph. 'Notes on Islam in East Africa', *Studia Islamica*, 23 (1965), 91–133.

Schmidt, Peter. 'A New Look at Interpretations of the Early Iron Age in East Africa', *HA*, 2 (1975), 127–36.

Shepperson, G. 'The Jumbe of Kota Kota and Some Aspects of the History of Islam in British Central Africa', in I. M. Lewis (ed.), *Islam in Tropical Africa* (q.v.), 193–207.

Shihabiddin Chiraghdin. 'Maisha ya Shaikh Mbarak bin Rashid al-Mazrui', *JEASC*, New Series, vol. I, part 2, no. 31 (1961), 150–79.

Shinar, Pessah. 'Ibadiyya and Orthodox Reformism in Modern Algeria', *Scripta Hierosolymitana*, IX. Jerusalem: Hebrew University Magnes Press, 1961.

Skene, R. 'Notes on the Arab Clans of East Africa', KNA DC/MSA/3/1.

Smogorzewski, Z. 'Essai de Bio-bibliographie Ibadite-Wahabite. Avant-propos', *Rocznik Orjentalityczny*, vol. V (1927), 45–57.

Soper, R. C. 'A General Review of the Early Iron Age in the Southern Half of Africa' *Azania*, 6 (1971), 5–36.

'Iron Age Sites in North-eastern Tanzania', *Azania*, 2 (1967), 19–36.

'Kwale: An Early Iron Age Site in South-eastern Kenya', *Azania*, 2 (1967), 1–17.

Spear, Thomas T. 'Oral Traditions: Whose History?' *HA*, 8 (1981), 165–81.

'The Shirazi in Swahili Traditions', *HA*, 11 (1984).

'Traditional Myths and Historians' Myths: Variations on the Singwaya Theme of Mijikenda Origins', *History in Africa*, 1 (1974).

'Traditional Myths and Linguistic Analysis: Singwaya Revisited', *HA*, 4 (1977), 229–46.

Tamrat, Tedesse. 'Ethiopia, The Red Sea and the Horn', in R. Oliver and J. Fage (eds.), *The Cambridge History of Africa*, vol. 3. Cambridge' CUP, 1977.

Trimingham, J. S. 'The Arab Geographers and the East African Coast' in H. N. Chittick and R. Rotberg (eds.), *East Africa and the Orient*. New York: Africana, 1975.

Turton, E. R. 'Bantu, Galla and Somali Migrations in the Horn of Africa: A Reassessment of the Juba/Tana Area', *JAH*, 16 (1975), 519–38.

Bibliography

'Kirk and the Egyptian Invasion of East Africa in 1875: A Reassessment', *JAH*, 11 (1970), 355–70.

Wilkinson, J. C. 'Oman and East Africa: New Light on Early Kilwan History from the Omani Sources', *IJAHS*, 14 (1981), 272–305.

Wilson, Monica. 'Changes in Social Structure in Southern Africa: The Relevance of Kinship Studies to the Historian' in Leonard Thompson (ed.), *African Societies in Southern Africa*. New York: Praeger, 1969.

Wilson, Thomas H. 'Takwa: An Ancient Swahili Settlement of the Lamu Archipelago', *Kenya Past and Present*, 10 (1979), 6–16.

Index